Lady Death

'Lyudmila Pavlichenko's skills with a rifle are matched in this magnificent memoir by her abilities as a writer. In clear, lively prose she describes how her pre-war enthusiasm for target shooting enabled her to become one of the Red Army's most feared front-line snipers on the Eastern Front. Arguably the finest account of sniping during World War II.'

Adrian Gilbert
author of *Challenge of Battle*

'Within a year after the launching of Operation Barbarossa, Hitler's invasion of Russia in June 1941, a twenty-four-year-old Kiev female history student enlisted in the Russian Army and became one of the deadliest military snipers of all times, in any army, in any war. *Lady Death* is Lyudmila Pavlichenko's taut and gritty memoirs of the "most dangerous woman in the world", who accumulated more than 500 confirmed or probable kills. Translated from the original Russian and based on her post-war notes and wartime diary, it is undoubtedly literature's most remarkable account of sniper action.'

Charles W. Sasser
former US Army special forces soldier
and author of *One Shot-One Kill*

'Lyudmila Pavlichenko, the highest scoring female sniper to come out of the Red Army, provides an intimate portrayal of the struggles and obstacles Red Army combatants faced and overcame as the war on the Eastern Front unfolded. She not only proved herself on the field of battle, but also was one of the few Soviet citizens allowed to campaign for the war effort abroad and as such offers an additional, unique view of the west through a Soviet veteran's eyes.'

Yan Mann
Military Historian

GREENHILL
SNIPER
LIBRARY

Available:

SNIPERS AT WAR
An Equipment and Operations History
John Walter

EASTERN FRONT SNIPER
The Life of Matthäus Hetzenauer
Roland Kaltenegger

RED ARMY SNIPER
A Memoir of the Eastern Front in World War II
Yevgeni Nikolaev

Forthcoming:

THE SNIPER ENCYCLOPAEDIA
An Illustrated History of World Sniping
John Walter

Lady Death

The Memoirs of Stalin's Sniper

Lyudmila Pavlichenko

Foreword by Martin Pegler
Translated by David Foreman
Edited by Alla Igorevna Begunova

Greenhill Books

Lady Death: The Memoirs of Stalin's Sniper

Greenhill Books

Greenhill Books, c/o Pen & Sword Books Ltd,
47 Church Street, Barnsley, S. Yorkshire, S70 2AS
For more information on our books, please visit
www.greenhillbooks.com, email contact@greenhillbooks.com
or write to us at the above address.

Publishing History
Lady Death: The Memoirs of Stalin's Sniper was first published by
Veche Publishers (Moscow) in 2015 as *I – Sniper: In Battles for Sevastopol and Odessa*

CIP data records for this title are available from the British Library

ISBN 978-1-78438-270-4

Typeset and designed by JCS Publishing Services Ltd
Typeset in 10.5pt Garamond Pro
Printed and bound in England by TJ International Ltd, Padstow, Cornwall

Contents

Illustrations

Foreword by Martin Pegler

Within the field of sniping literature this memoir is completely unique, for it is the first ever written by a female front-line sniper. Lyudmila Mykhailovna Pavlichenko was not just any sniper, however, for she was to become the highest-scoring female sniper, with 309 official kills. Official kills, it should be noted, were those observed by a second party. In common with most snipers, many of Pavlichenko's kills were made during attacks where stopping to take notes of how many enemy soldiers had been dispatched was neither wise nor practical. Her exact total therefore remains unknown, but around 500 would not be improbable.

On another level, this remarkable memoir also sets the record straight about much of the ill-founded criticism and inaccurate writing that has been subsequently aimed at her, particularly suggestions that she was not a sniper at all, but the product of the Red Army propaganda machine. Once geared up to laud the exploits of an individual, the Soviets were indeed formidable creators of myths, but Pavlichenko as well as fellow sniper Vasily Grigoryevich Zaitsev were the genuine article. Indeed, it is ironic that had their unwanted fame not caused them to be plucked from their front-line duties when they were, there is little doubt that both would merely have become names on a war memorial. The lifespan of a Soviet sniper was normally short; at Stalingrad, neophyte snipers had an expected combat life of two weeks. The longer you survived, the better you became and the stronger the chances were that you would live – up to a point. But in warfare, there is a law of diminishing returns where front-line combat is concerned, and eventually battle fatigue, sheer physical exhaustion and the willpower to continue will take their toll and mistakes happen. The life of a sniper was not unlike that of a pilot, for it could be ended by one mistake and there was seldom a second chance.

Not that Pavlichenko had the slightest inkling that she was destined for a future that would earn her the nickname 'Lady Death', win her the highest awards that the Soviet Union could bestow, meet with Stalin and travel to America, Canada and Europe. Like tens of thousands of other young Russians, before the war she appeared destined to work within the Communist Party system; being an intelligent woman she would probably have become a minor official and progressed upwards through the ranks of the Party faithful. Yet her chance introduction to a TOZ-8 .22-calibre target rifle would change the course of her life. Mostly unknown outside Russia, these little single-shot rifles were manufactured in their tens of thousands and used in rifle clubs and for hunting small game. They were cheap, solidly constructed, accurate and the first rifle that most people learned to shoot. That she had a natural aptitude is one of those quirks of nature, when someone has exactly the right combination of hand–eye coordination, muscle steadiness, good eyesight and patience. But there was another, more nebulous quality, which not every good shot possessed and which differentiates the sniper from an ordinary rifleman. Exactly what it is is often argued about; some define it as an inherent hunting instinct, not always present in men and even rarer in women. Others define it as strength of purpose, the possession of willpower far beyond that of the accepted norm. Certainly, Lyudmila's faith in her country, its politics and the justice of the Soviet cause never wavered, and this provided her with extraordinary determination, often in the face of overwhelming odds. In common with the rest of the Soviet army, dying for the motherland was considered a worthwhile sacrifice and perhaps this provided her with a reason to continue after being wounded so often, when others would have fallen by the wayside. Latterly, the need to avenge her husband must also have driven her on. Yet in many respects, Pavlichenko was not the heroic material the propagandists were looking for. True, she was not unattractive, but she had typical sniper's characteristics. She was reticent, bordering on introverted, shy of publicity and wanted solely to do her job, or 'kill fascists', as she bluntly put it. Gregarious snipers must certainly have existed, but they were rare and probably did not survive in their chosen field for long. As interest grew around her role, Pavlichenko stated, 'a sniper should not draw attention to him or herself. The main prerequisite for operating successfully was remaining hidden.' This applied not solely to the battlefield but also to her wariness of publicity. Snipers needed the patience of a cat, innate cunning and an attitude to their profession that might reasonably be described as obsessive. As an example, consider the effort she put into finding and killing the German sniper concealed on the bridge. Hours of careful observation, putting herself in the mental shoes of the German sniper, returning time and again and being prepared to continue to do so with no guaranteed end result in sight. This was not something that the average soldier would have had the perseverance for.

Perhaps this seems at odds with the woman who undertook a world tour and met presidents and politicians, but she had to make the best of the situation into which she had been placed. Nor should it be forgotten that she had been wounded four times, each of which would have had some deleterious effect on her mental and physical state and, worst of all, she had buried her husband of a few weeks,

Lieutenant Alexei Arkadyevich Kitsenko, in Sevastopol only a few months before being taken out of the front lines. Whilst there is now a considerable body of material available to medical science on the long-term effects of combat on male soldiers, almost nothing has been researched about women, because so few have ever served as combat troops. It is therefore impossible to determine what condition she was in when she left Russia. On the one hand she was expected to show the Soviet army in the best possible light to their allies, with no real experience of mass public speaking, facing the press and radio reporters, or even of being out of Russia. As she stated, simply being in Moscow was like a foreign country to her, so the challenges she faced and the pressure she was under in being sent to Europe and the United States must have been immense. She also had to be careful, as she was accompanied by Party officials who noted every word she said. In addition, she despised much of the media she was exposed to. In particular she could not comprehend the lack of understanding of the realities of war when in America, where journalists asked what make-up she wore in the front lines, and discussed in detail the hemlines on her army uniform. She did on occasion snap, once telling the assembled crowds that they had been hiding behind the backs of fighting men for too long. Nor was she happy about being asked to demonstrate her shooting prowess – she disliked doing it in Russia and even more so on her world tour. She would always refuse, and this gave rise to theories that she could not actually shoot a rifle. She was, of course, a gifted shot but not a circus act and did not believe it was her role to do trick shooting, particularly with rifles and scopes she was totally unfamiliar with.

Perhaps it might be useful to make some comment here about the rifles she mentions so frequently, the Mosin Nagant Model 1891/30 with PE scope, (later supplemented by a modified PEM variant) and the SVT-40 semi-automatic. The Mosin was an old-school military rifle, designed in 1891. It had a barrel measuring 73cm, with a box magazine containing five rounds and it weighed 4kg. It chambered a rimmed 7.62 x 54mm cartridge, itself quite an old design – most countries having adopted rimless ammunition by the Second World War. The Mosin sniper variant had a 4x PE scope that was effectively a copy of the German Zeiss. It was accurate to beyond 1,000 metres, but only if weather conditions were perfect and the sniper was extremely competent. It was Pavlichenko's favoured rifle, being very robust, easy to field repair and with good-quality optics. They continued in production until the very early 1940s, when a new model with PU sight was introduced which was a smaller, lighter scope of 3.5x.

In comparison, the SVT-40 semi-automatic was new technology, based on the earlier, flawed SVT-38 rifle. It too was chambered in 7.62 x 54 R mm but its gas-operated action provided rapid-fire capability that was extremely useful in close combat. It too had the new PU sight, which lacked the magnification power of the PE scope. However, because of its complex gas-operated mechanism the SVT did not have the range or accuracy of the Mosin, and 600 metres was regarded as a reasonable maximum for effective sniping. It also suffered from problems with reliability and accuracy. Pavlichenko's rifle was, of course, a presentation weapon but she would probably not have chosen it herself, although she mentions several instances where its firepower proved extremely useful during large-scale attacks. In general, as a sniping weapon the SVT did not live up to expectations, and in 1942 production resumed of the Mosin sniping rifle.

Although her memoir relates some of her more memorable sniping episodes, it was a fact that most of Pavlichenko's shooting during the sieges of Odessa and Sevastopol were at relatively close range. This was in part because the closer the enemy was, the more certain of a kill you could be, but she does comment on a new and gruesome tactic of shooting Germans in the stomach, as much for psychological purposes as anything. This is a measure of how brutal the fighting was on the Eastern Front, and there was no exaggeration on her part when she mentions saving the last round in her pistol for herself. A sniper caught alive was routinely tortured to death. It is also interesting to note, through her memoirs, how the Russian army slowly began to appreciate snipers fully as the war progressed. They changed from being glorified riflemen, expected to advance in an attack with the infantry, to being accepted as the most revered of front-line specialists. Indeed, they were regarded so favourably as to be given a day's rest every week, an unheard-of concession and this in itself is a measure of the importance attached by the army to them. One reason for this is simply their effectiveness. It is not possible to make an accurate calculation of the numbers of Germans killed by Russian snipers during the course of the war. But some idea of the staggering numbers involved can be gleaned from the fact that the 2,000 female snipers who graduated from Russian sniper schools during the war had an officially accepted collective score of 12,000 German kills, and the top ten male Soviet snipers accounted for over 4,300. Multiplied out over the whole Soviet army, the numbers run into the hundreds of thousands. Compared to the figures we are used to seeing for the fighting across Western Europe after 1944, where the highest-scoring British sniper had an official tally of 119, such numbers are virtually impossible to comprehend. So it is unsurprising that the Russian propaganda machine began to look very closely at these new heroes, in particular the women. After all, it was the only country of the Second World War to employ them in front-line combat roles and the public needed a focus to take their thoughts away from the seemingly unstoppable advances of the Axis forces in 1941–3.

Pavlichenko became one of the most highly decorated women to serve in the Red Army, receiving the Order of Lenin twice and being designated a Hero of the Soviet Union. After the war, she stayed in the military, becoming a historian in the Research Institute of the Soviet Navy, leaving in 1953 with the rank of major. Neither has her status diminished as post-war interest in sniping has continued to grow. As her book clearly reveals, the many criticisms aimed at her are utterly without foundation. But, as with so many veterans, her survival came at a price; she was damaged, both physically and mentally. After the war she fought a lifelong battle with alcohol and suffered badly from the effects of her many head wounds, including deafness. She never remarried. She died aged fifty-eight in October 1974 and was buried with full military honours in Novodevichye Cemetery in Moscow, 1,500km and a lifetime away from her beloved Alexei.

Note to this Edition

Many thanks to David Foreman for translating this book, and to John Walter for his advice and input.

In this translation, place names keep the Russian spellings of the original Russian edition. Many of the places now have alternative Ukrainian names.

Within the text of this English edition there are some insertions in square brackets from the original Russian editor, Alla Igorevna Begunova and from the English translator (marked TN). The endnotes are from Begunova too, with some additional notes from John Walter, Martin Pegler and David Foreman.

Russian Editor's Note

Hero of the Soviet Union Lyudmila Mikhailovna Pavlichenko is the most successful woman sniper, having achieved a personal tally of 309 dead enemy troops and officers. She is among the best-known rank-and-file participants of the Second World War, both in our own country and in the world at large. Between 1942 and 1945 over 100,000 leaflets bearing her portrait (and she was a good-looking woman) and the call 'Shoot the enemy and don't miss!' were distributed on the Soviet–German front. After her death in 1974 the name Lyudmila Pavlichenko was given to a ship belonging to the USSR Ministry of Fisheries, to the No. 3 School in the city of Belaya Tserkov [TN: Bila Tserkva in Ukrainian], Kiev Region, which she attended from classes one to seven, and to a street in the centre of Sevastopol.

The complete and authentic autobiography of this heroine reads like an enthralling novel. It contains tragic pages, for, having joined the ranks of the Red Army on 26 June 1941, with the 54th Rifle Regiment, she made the arduous retreat from the western borders as far as Odessa. It contains heroic pages; while defending the city, she wiped out 187 Nazis in two months. The siege of Sevastopol endowed the best sniper of the 25th Chapayev Rifle Division with further glory, as her tally rose to 309 dead enemies. But it also contains lyrical passages. It was in the war that Lyudmila met the love of her life. The courageous junior lieutenant of her own regiment, Alexei Arkadyevich Kitsenko, became her husband.

On Stalin's orders, in August 1942 a Young Communist League youth delegation comprising Nikolai Krasavchenko, Vladimir Pchelintsev and Lyudmila Pavlichenko flew out to the USA to take part in an international student assembly. They were meant to campaign for the speedy opening of a second front in Western Europe.

In defiance of the ban on such activity, Pavlichenko had kept a war diary. She made very brief notes in it from time to time. A sniper could not just pick up a pencil or pen every day. The combat at Sevastopol was particularly fierce and unrelenting. Upon retiring in 1953 with the rank of major in the Soviet coast guard, Lyudmila remembered about her notes from the front. A historian by education, she took a serious approach towards her memoirs and felt that research in libraries and archives was needed before they could be published. She made the first step towards this in 1958, when she was commissioned by the state political publishing house to write a seventy-two-page factual pamphlet entitled *Geroicheskaya byl. Oborona Sevastopolya* (*The Heroic Past: The Defence of Sevastopol*). She also contributed a number of articles to various anthologies and journals. These were not recollections of her service as a sniper but, rather, general narratives of the main events which unfolded both on the front line and in the rear of the Sevastopol defence district between October 1941 and July 1942.

Following these publications Pavlichenko was accepted in 1964 as a member of the USSR Union of Journalists, becoming secretary of the military history section of the Moscow division. Close contact with her pen-wielding colleagues and active participation in the task of educating the next generation in their spirit of patriotic military duty brought her to the conclusion that a book written by a senior sergeant commanding a platoon of 'super-sharpshooters' and giving an authentic account of many details of infantry service could be of interest to the modern reader.

By the end of the 1960s it was not only recollections by major military commanders of the Soviet army's successful operations in 1944 and 1945 that were beginning to come to light; there were also authentic accounts by Red Army officers and political staff about the difficult, even tragic, beginnings of the Great War for the Fatherland. Among such books one might mention the memoirs of Ilya Azarov, *Osazhdennaya Odessa* (*Odessa Under Siege* (Moscow: Voenizdat, 1966)); the collection *U chernomorskikh tverdyn* (*By the Black Sea Fortresses* (Moscow: Voenizdat, 1967)), which includes articles by the former commander of the 25th Chapayev Division, Trofim Kolomiyets, his fellow service-woman Lyudmila Pavlichenko and the former Young Communist League organizer of the 54th Regiment, Yakov Vaskovsky; and the memoirs of a rank-and-file participant in the defence of Odessa, Nikolai Aleshchenko, *Oni zashchishchali Odessu* (*They Defended Odessa* (Moscow: DOSAAF Publishing, 1970)). Upon reading them, Lyudmila set to work herself.

She now wanted to focus on the role of the sniper at the front and to describe in detail everything connected with this military profession: training methods, battlefield tactics and, in particular, the weaponry, of which she had a superb knowledge and was very fond. During the 1940s and 1950s it was not permitted to divulge such information, but the story of the snipers' battle with the enemy would be incomplete without it.

Recalling previous instructions, Pavlichenko diligently gathered material and sought the best literary form for her manuscript. It became clear to her that the gap of twenty years that had elapsed since the end of the Great War for the Fatherland was not conducive to the speedy fulfilment of her plan. Many things were difficult to recall and many records turned out to be lost. Besides that, she had handed over many of her own precious documents and photographs, as well as personal effects, to museums: to the Central Museum of the USSR Armed Forces in Moscow and the State Museum of the Heroic Defence and Liberation of Sevastopol.

Unfortunately, serious chronic illness prevented the war heroine from completing the work and seeing her memoirs of her life as a sniper published. Fragments of this manuscript have been preserved thanks to the efforts of Lubov Davydovna Krashennikova-Pavlichenko, widow of Lyudmila's son, Rostislav Alexeyevich Pavlichenko.

A.I. Begunova
Editor

Hero of the Soviet Union, Senior Lieutenant Lyudmila Pavlichenko, Moscow, 1944 (State Museum of the Heroic Defence and Liberation of Sevastopol).

Factory Walls

The summer of 1932 saw a significant change in the life of our family. We moved from the remote township of Boguslav, in the south of Kiev Region, to the capital of the Ukraine and took up residence in an official apartment granted to my father, Mikhail Ivanovich Belov. As an employee of the NKVD (Narodny Kommisariat Vnutrennykh Del, the People's Commissariat for Internal Affairs), he had been appointed to a position in the central offices of this authority in recognition of his conscientious fulfilment of his duties.

He was a solid, stern kind of man, devoted to the service. In his younger days he had started work as a fitter at a big factory, spent some time at the front during the First World War, joined the Communist Party (then called the Russia Social Democrat Workers' Party (Bolshevik)), taken part in the revolutionary events in Petrograd, then served as a regimental commissar in the 24th Samara-Simbirsk 'Iron' Division, and fought against the White Guard forces of Kolchak in the central Volga region and the southern Urals. He was demobilized from the Red Army in 1923 at the age of twenty-eight. But he retained his attachment to military uniform to the end of his days and we generally saw him in the same attire: a khaki gabardine service jacket with a turn-down collar and the Order of the Red Banner on his breast. His trousers were dark blue, flared at the thigh like riding breeches, and the outfit was finished with calf-leather officers' boots.

Naturally, Dad had the last word in the case of family disputes – if they ever arose. My lovely mother, Elena Trofimovna Belova, a graduate of the girls' grammar school in the city of Vladimir, knew how to mollify Dad's stern nature. She was a fine-looking woman with a willowy figure that seemed to have been finely shaped; she had luxuriant dark brown hair and brown eyes which lit up her face. She had a good knowledge of foreign languages and taught them at school. The pupils loved her. By turning lessons into games, she ensured that they achieved an excellent retention of all European words strange to the Russian ear. Under her tutelage the children not only read the languages superbly but spoke them as well.

She devoted herself just as much to us: my elder sister Valentina and me. Thanks to her, we had soon been introduced to Russian classical literature, for the works of Pushkin, Lermontov, Gogol, Leo Tolstoy, Chekhov, Maxim Gorky and Kuprin were all in our library at home. Reflecting her gentle, dreamy character, my sister proved more receptive to literature and fiction. I was attracted by history or, more precisely, the military annals of our great country.

Before moving to Boguslav we had lived in the city of Belaya Tserkov, Kiev Region, for several years. There I attended School No. 3 and spent my childhood and adolescent years free of cares. There on Station Street we formed a close gang of friends. We played at 'Cossacks and Bandits', splashed around in flat-bottomed boats on the local river Ros in the summer, roamed through the old and very beautiful Alexandria Park, and raided neighbourhood orchards in the autumn. I was the leading spirit of a gang of teenage boys because I was the best shot with a catapult, could run faster than anybody, swam well and was never afraid of getting into a fight, being the first to strike any offender on the cheek with my fist.

These backyard pursuits came to an end when I was barely fifteen years old. The change happened suddenly, over a single day. Looking back, I can compare it with the end of a world, a voluntary blindness, a loss of reason. Such was my first, schoolgirl, love. The memory of it remains with me for the rest of my life in the form of this man's surname – Pavlichenko.[1]

Fortunately, my son Rostislav is not at all like his father. He has a kind, tranquil nature and an appearance characteristic of our family: brown eyes: thick dark hair, tall stature and solid build. He is of Belov stock and is continuing our traditions of service to the homeland. Slava graduated with distinction from Moscow University's law faculty and the KGB Senior College. He bears the title of a Soviet officer with honour. I am proud of him.

At our new home in Kiev we settled in quite quickly and began to get used to the big noisy capital city. We did not see much of Dad; he was kept at work until late. Thus, our heart-to-heart talks with him usually took place in the kitchen after supper. Mother would put the samovar on the table and, over a cup of tea, we were able to discuss any topics with our parents and ask them questions. The main question soon came up.

'What do you plan to do now, my dear children?' asked Dad, sipping the hot tea.

'We don't know yet,' answered Valentina, going first by right of seniority.

'You should think about a job,' he said.

'What kind of job?' asked my sister in surprise.

'A good job, in a good workplace, with a good salary.'

'But, Dad,' I broke in, 'I've only done seven years at school. I want to study further.'

'It's never too late to study, Lyudmila,' said Dad firmly. 'But now is the very time to begin your working life, and with the right information on the application form. Especially since I've already made arrangements and they are prepared to take you.'

'Where's this?' My sister pouted in a show of defiance.

'At the Arsenal factory.'

From the Askold Tomb Park you could see the broad, smooth, watery expanse of the river Dnyepr stretching out on your left and, on your right, the straight and fairly short Arsenal Street [renamed Moscow Street in 1942]. At the start of the street stood a very imposing building. This was the Arsenal workshops, built under Nicholas I. They say the Tsar himself laid the first brick in their foundations. The walls were 2 metres thick, two storeys high, and the bricks were light yellow, which is why the locals began to refer to the building as the 'tile house'.

However, neither the workshops nor the factory adjoining it had anything to do with delicate artefacts from clay. They had been founded on the orders of Empress Catherine the Great and constructed over a lengthy period, from 1784 to 1803. They made cannons, gun carriages, rifles, bayonets, sabres, broadswords and various other pieces of military equipment.

During the Soviet period the works also mastered the production of items necessary for the economy: ploughs, locks, twin-horse carts and equipment for mills and sugar refineries. The Arsenal staff worked with total commitment and in 1923 they received an award from the government of the Ukraine – the Order of the Red Labour Banner.

The factory building appealed to me at first sight. It bore a strong resemblance to a fortress. Rectilinear in shape (168 x 135 metres), with a large internal yard, a tower, rounded outer walls, with the ground layer adorned with a large ornamental wooden facing, this building looked as if it had come from an engraving of an ancient battle. All that was lacking was a moat below the walls, a drawbridge across it, and heavy gates guarded by warriors in shining armour.

After fulfilling some formalities (for instance, signing a state secrets clause) my sister and I were enlisted in the garrison of this 'fortress' – Valentina as a progress-chaser, because she had already turned eighteen and had a school-leaving certificate, and me as an ordinary worker owing to my youth (I was only sixteen) and lack of any professional skills. It took me half a year to adjust to the rhythm of factory life and to make friends with the other workers. I was accepted into the Young Communist League. In May 1934 I transferred to the turners' shop, where I spent about a month training, and then earned the right to work independently, soon acquiring the qualification of turner, sixth grade.

It was an interesting time. The Arsenal was changing before our very eyes. New lathes of Soviet manufacture were being introduced, improved equipment was installed, new production capacities were coming into force and old premises were being renovated. Seeing the efforts being made by the authorities to expand industry, the factory folk responded with extra effort. Incidentally, the prices paid for our wares also rose noticeably, and the lathe-operators in our workshop operated on a piecework basis.

I had no cause to complain. I had a screw-shaping, turning lathe with a DIP300 gearbox made by Moscow's Red Proletariat Factory in 1933. 'DIP' came from the initials of the Russian words 'Dogonim i Peregonim' [TN: 'we will catch up and overtake']. It was designed to process cylindrical, conical and complex surfaces, both external and internal.

I remember much of it as if it was yesterday – stockpiles of shafts for every possible gear. With one stroke of the cutting tool I would shave off between 0.5 and 3mm (or more) of metal. I would choose the cutting speed in accordance with the hardness of the material and the durability of the tool. In general, tools made from high-carbon steel were used, although there were others – with soldered discs of super-hard tungsten and titanium alloys. The sight of dark blue-violet metal shavings curling out from under the blade still strikes me as incredibly beautiful. However hard the metal, it yields to human strength. You merely need to devise a slick enough implement.

While uniting people in work, our factory also presented them with the opportunity of spending their free time in a sensible way. True, the factory club did not stand out for its bright and lavish decor. It was small, even cramped. However, its premises were sufficient for the activities of various circles: a blue-collar workers' theatrical group, an arts studio – which taught drawing, dressmaking and sewing (very useful for women) – and gliding and shooting clubs. The assembly hall was a regular venue for special festive evenings held under the slogan 'Three Generations Together', at which veterans of the Revolution and Civil War and young production workers who had exceeded their quotas by 50 per cent and more were honoured.

At first my friend and I – she talked me into it – opted for the gliding circle. There was a lot in the newspapers about aviation and the feats of pilots and so we enthusiastically attended the theoretical classes and attentively took notes in lectures given by a gallant air force lieutenant on the lifting force of an aeroplane wing. However, my first flight with an instructor decidedly cooled my ardour. When the grassy field of the aerodrome rushed swiftly to meet us and then suddenly receded somewhere below, my head began to spin and I could feel the nausea in my throat. 'In other words, the air is not my element,' I thought to myself. 'I am a profoundly terrestrial being and have to have my feet on solid ground.'

The instructor of the factory shooting circle, Fyodor Kushchenko, worked in our shop and constantly urged young people to come to the shooting range. He himself had recently done emergency service in the Red Army and become keen on shooting. He assured us that there was something entrancing about the flight of a bullet and the way it hit the target.

A likeable and charming lad, Fyodor tried to persuade me to join with similar arguments. However, I remembered my flight in the glider, which had pretty soundly shaken my faith in my own abilities, even though when you are young – there's no point in pretending otherwise – they seem boundless. Apart from that, I regarded Kushchenko's talk as commonplace skirt-chasing. My limited but harsh life experience prompted me always to be on my guard with members of the opposite sex.

One day (it was at a Young Communist League meeting) I got sick of listening to Kushchenko's stories. I answered Fyodor in a sarcastic tone. Those sitting around us appreciated my joke and laughed loudly. Our League organizer was at that moment reading a rather boring report on the work of Ukrainian League members towards early fulfilment of the workshop quarterly plan. He thought the laughter was directed at him and for some reason got very angry. A verbal skirmish arose between him and some of the League members in the hall – in the course of which some colourful epithets and unlikely comparisons were employed. In the end the organizer expelled Kushchenko and me from the room as the instigators of the disturbance.

Stunned by this banishment, Kushchenko and I made our way towards the exit. The working day was over and our steps echoed through the empty corridor. Suddenly Kushchenko said:

'We really need to calm ourselves down.'

'We do,' I agreed.

'So, let's go to the range and have a few shots.'

'Do you think that'll help?'

'Of course. Shooting is a sport for calm people. Although inborn abilities are also required.'

'And what other abilities?' I could not refrain from a vitriolic question.

'The most down-to-earth kind. Such as a good eye or a precise feel for the weapon,' he replied, jangling a bunch of keys he had taken from the pocket of his leather jacket.

The shooting range was located on some reserve factory land adjacent to the main building. No doubt it had once been storage space – a long, low structure with bars on the windows, which were located almost under the roof. From the lofty heights of my present knowledge I can say that the Arsenal range in the mid-1930s met all the necessary standards. There was a room with desks, chairs and a blackboard on the wall for theoretical classes, a small armoury with lockable cupboards for rifles and pistols, a safe for ammunition, and a firing line allowing one to fire from a rest, kneeling, standing or lying (on mats). Twenty-five metres away from it were thick wooden shields on which targets were mounted.

Fyodor opened one of the cabinets and took out a newish rifle, which was not that long, just over a metre (111cm, to be precise), but fitted with a massive birch stock and a thick barrel. This item from the Tula arms factory was well known in the USSR under the brandname TOZ-8. It was manufactured between 1932 and 1946 and, together with the modified TOZ-8M, it seems that about a million of them were made. This reliable, simple, small-bore single-shot rifle with a longitudinally sliding bolt, designed for 5.6 × 16mm rimfire ammunition, rendered valuable service not only to sportsmen, but also to hunters. I write about it with affection, for it was with the TOZ-8 that my enthusiasm for rifle shooting began, my apprenticeship as a sharpshooter.

There are detailed instructions on handling firearms. Of course, Kushchenko could have talked about them first. Instead, he did something different. He simply handed me the rifle and said:

'Get acquainted!'

To be honest, I had thought that firearms were much heavier and more difficult to hold in one's hands. But this rifle weighed less than 3.5kg. Given my experience of sometimes setting up quite cumbersome items for processing on the lathe, it took no effort on my part to lift it. I also found the coldish chilly metal of the barrel and the receiver pleasant. The downward-curved shape of the bolt handle indicated that the designers had considered the convenience of the person in charge of the weapon.

First of all, Fyodor suggested checking the 'rifle's flexibility' to find out if it was suitable for me. In this regard everything turned out fine. The back of the butt fitted firmly into the hollow of my shoulder, with my right hand I could freely grasp the grip of the butt and I placed my index finger – and I have long fingers – on the trigger between the first and second phalanx. It just remained to incline my head to the right, press my cheek to the comb of the butt and focus my open right eye on the sights. The sighting bar was right in the middle of the notch and was visible in its entire magnitude.

'Now you can fire,' said Fyodor.

'What about cartridges?'

'Just a minute.' The instructor took the rifle from me, loaded it and pointed it at a target. There was a loud sound, like a rod striking a metal sheet. I started in surprise. Kushchenko smiled.

'That's from not being used to it. Have a go. You can do it.'

The rifle ended up in my hands again. Painstakingly replicating all the moves involved in positioning it, I took my first shot. The 'Melkashka' (as we called the TOZ-8) did not have a powerful recoil. Besides, on Fyodor's advice, I had pressed it firmly into my shoulder so that I would not feel any unpleasant sensation. Kushchenko allowed me three more shots, and then went to look at the target. He brought the paper sheet inscribed with black circles back to the firing line where I was waiting for him, not without some nervousness. He looked closely at me and said:

'For a beginner that is simply amazing. It's clear you have ability.'

'Surely not inborn?' I felt compelled to joke for some reason.

'It certainly is.' My first coach was serious. I had never seen Fyodor Kushchenko so serious.

Our shooting circle held sessions once a week, on Saturdays. We began by studying the mechanism of a small-bore rifle in detail, stripping and assembling the breechblock, and getting into the habit of caring for the weapon thoroughly: cleaning and oiling it. Classes were held in the room with the blackboard, where the basics of ballistics were taught. I was surprised to learn that a bullet does not fly directly to its target, but, owing to the impact of gravity and wind resistance, describes an arc, as well as revolving as it flies.

We also had lectures on the history of firearms. It began in the fifteenth century with matchlock guns, when technical developments first made it possible to use the projectile properties of gunpowder. Then flintlock weapons came to be widely used, followed by the caplock mechanism. The truly revolutionary change occurred at the end of the nineteenth century, with the advent of rifles with magazines, grooves in the barrel and longitudinally sliding bolts, facilitating rapid loading, a longer range and greater accuracy.

Manual firearms seem to me to represent the most perfect creation of human mind and hand. Their construction always made use of the latest innovations. The technological solutions necessary for their manufacture were quickly refined and put into a production process that output thousands and millions of items. In the case of the most successful models, those worthy of world recognition, engineering genius finds its fulfilment in an ideal and consummate external shape. In their own way, firearms are . . . beautiful. They are pleasant to pick up and convenient to use. They earned the love of the people who took them into wars of unbelievable ferocity. Some of them (the Mosin Three Line rifle, the Shpagin submachine gun, the Degtyarev light machine gun and the Tula-Tokarev pistol) have even become unique symbols of their era.

However, most of all, my friends liked the actual shooting. We practised at the firing range, aiming at targets from a variety of positions – standing, lying, from a rest, kneeling and aiming with the aid of a strap under the left arm. The 'Melkashka' had only an open back sight with a moveable ring and, at the end of the barrel, a cylindrical front sight with an extended base. For all its simplicity of construction, it nevertheless helped us develop basic firing skills: rapid aiming, smooth pressure on the trigger and holding the rifle in the right position, without 'dropping' it to left or right. With muzzle velocity of 320 metres a second, a

TOZ-8 shot attained distances of 120–180 metres, but in a shooting range this was of no significance.

When spring came, we began travelling to a firing range out of town and training to reach the standards of the 'Voroshilov Marksman' badge, second degree. This included not just sharpshooting, but also finding one's bearings in a locality, grenade-throwing and physical training (running, vaulting, push-ups). We fulfilled all these tasks successfully and then took part in the Osoaviakhim city shooting competitions.

I want to point out that our circle was only one of several hundred units within the structure of Osoaviakhim, the Society for Promoting Defence, Aviation and Chemical Construction. This mass-scale, voluntary, public, patriotic military organization was originally set up in our country in 1927 and played a large role in training young men and women for army service. Its ranks numbered about 14 million people, who trained in the primary organizations of this society, acquiring specialized military skills – from those of pilot and parachutist to rifleman, machine-gunner, lorry driver and dog trainer.

I earned an honorary certificate at the Osoaviakhim competitions, which I put in a frame and hung on the wall in the room which Valentina and I shared. Neither my sister nor my parents took my enthusiasm for shooting seriously. In our domestic life they enjoyed joking about my passion for weaponry. I was unable to explain to them what drew me to the shooting range, what was attractive about an object equipped with a metal barrel, a wooden butt, a breech, a trigger and sights, and why it was so interesting to control the flight of a bullet towards its target.

With the authorization of the Young Communist League, at the end of 1935 I went on a two-week course for draftsmen and copyists. I completed it with distinction and began work as a senior draftsman in the mechanical workshop. I enjoyed this work. Of course, it was different from being a turner-lathe operator, but it also demanded concentration and accuracy. The lathes hummed away on the other side of the wall, but in our office we worked in silence, amidst drawing boards and bundles of drafting paper, checking blueprints and preparing them for transfer to the production workers. Relations between team members were friendly. My enthusiasm for shooting was treated with understanding here.

I am very grateful to the Arsenal factory. In the four years I spent within its walls I acquired two specialist qualifications, became used to working in a defence industry enterprise where semi-military discipline operated. I matured, and began to feel like a real person capable of answering for my aims and actions and achieving a set goal. The factory Young Communist League organization also helped me to transition to a new stage in life: in the spring of 1935 I received authorization to attend the workers' preparatory faculty at Kiev State University. Then I worked for a year in the turners' shop and studied in the evenings. After that I passed the exams and, in September 1936, became the holder of a student card in the history faculty of Kiev State University. In this way my childhood dream was fulfilled, even if I was probably the oldest female student on the course.

2

If There is War Tomorrow . . .

On account of my production experience I was chosen as head of my group. Although I was already attending lectures, taking notes, reading the required literature, compiling reports for seminars, writing assignments and preparing for tests and exams, these duties did not strike me as difficult. It soon became clear which were my favourite subjects: basic archaeology and ethnography, history of the USSR, ancient history, Latin, and – given a choice of two foreign languages – English. I recalled Mother's lessons and things went very well. After the standards for the 'Voroshilov Marksman' badge and the GTO (Gotov k Trudu i Oboronye, Prepared for Work and Defence) programme, which I had undertaken at the factory, university physical education classes presented no difficulty either. My student days were a life of fun and freedom, leaving a lot of time for such diversions as visits to the cinema and theatre, variety concerts, art exhibitions and relaxing evenings, complete with dancing.

Apart from that, we were all quite interested in politics and were, for instance, very sympathetic towards the Republicans in Spain, who from 1936 were engaged in armed conflict with local Fascists and monarchists. The Fascists were aided by Italy and Germany and the Republicans by the Soviet Union. The newspapers reported frequently and in detail on events in this far-off southern country. Excellent articles were published in the newspaper *Pravda* by the journalist Mikhail Koltsov. He wrote about the feats of the International Brigades and the aerial skirmishes between the pilots of the German 'Condor' legion and our own volunteer pilots flying Soviet aircraft. There were even tank battles on the flat plains of the Iberian Peninsula, demonstrating the technology of the same three states: Italy, Germany and the USSR.

A wave of indignation was aroused by the barbarous bombing of the small town of Guernica in the Basque Country. There was no military necessity to strike at it. Nevertheless, in April 1937, more than fifty German aeroplanes launched an attack on the settlement, which was in the hands of the Republicans. The raid almost completely obliterated it. Many civilians perished. Later, the outstanding Spanish artist Pablo Picasso, who was shaken by this crime, created a painting under the title *Guernica*; the work is now renowned worldwide. The story of the tragedy of Guernica troubled Russian hearts for a long time. Along with these emotions we had to think about what a new war would be like and when it would arrive on our doorstep.[1]

I was in my second year in the history faculty when I felt an impulse to refresh my skills in marksmanship, since now they might come in handy. Fyodor Kushchenko advised me to attend the two-year course at the Osoaviakhim sniper school which had recently opened in Kiev. Only those who had a 'Voroshilov Marksman' stage two certificate could apply there. Applicants also had to supply a reference from their workplace or educational institute and a short curriculum vitae, both signed off by the personnel department, and a note from a medical commission on their readiness for military service. I presented the required documents and was accepted. It soon became apparent that in this establishment I had every chance of ascending to new levels of manual firearms handling.

Sessions were held twice a week: on Wednesdays from six to eight in the evening and on Saturdays from three in the afternoon till six in the evening. We were issued with authorizations which served as passes to the school's grounds and we were issued with the dark blue tunics we were required to wear. All this was reminiscent of army rules, but we did not complain; on the contrary, we were infused with a serious attitude and an awareness of our responsibility, given the prospect of the lessons ahead.

I will say just a few words about the sniper school programme. It really did train 'super-sharpshooters' for service in the Red Army. Twenty hours were devoted to politics classes, fourteen hours to parade ground drill, 220 hours to firearms training, sixty hours to tactics, thirty hours to military engineering, and twenty hours to hand-to-hand fighting. Tests on the course content took up sixteen hours. Cadets who had passed the final exams with the grade 'excellent' were included in special lists in city and district enlistment offices and periodically called up for refresher courses and shooting competitions at various levels. In general, snipers were not overlooked and they were given consideration, but even so, up until the Great War for the Fatherland, we had few real aces in the country, experts who could hit the target with their first and only shot. Perhaps there were 1,500 or so.

The first session on firearms training showed that the exercises we had practised in our factory circle were only a prelude to marksmanship – very useful but insufficient on their own. I recalled my old friend the 'Melkashka' with gratitude as I took up the Mosin army magazine rifle, model 1891/1930, often referred to as the 'Three Line'. Of course, it was heavier (4kg without the bayonet) and longer (1,232mm) and calibrated for a 7.62 × 54mm R cartridge with an initial bullet velocity of 865 metres per second and a range of 2,000 metres. The grip of the Three Line butt was less comfortable than that of the TOZ-8, the recoil on one's shoulder was stronger, and, on account of greater weight and length, for me, for instance, firing from a standing position was difficult. But that meant absolutely nothing.

We had to know the ordinary Mosin rifle, with which the Red Army rank and file were equipped, like the back of our hand, and therefore a certain amount of time (ten hours) was devoted to studying its mechanism. I gradually got used to the Three Line; in the end, I could strip and assemble it with my eyes closed, even though the bolt alone contained seven separate parts. The rifle's open back sight and a front sight protected by a ring-like hood made it possible to achieve pretty good results when firing.

The sniper's rifle differed from the standard one in only a few details. Firstly, it had an Emelyanov (PE) telescope sight mounted over the barrel – a fairly long metal tube (274mm with a weight of 598g) with two regulating drums. In the second place, this modification meant that the scope prevented the magazine from being charger loaded; the cartridges had to be put there one at a time. Thirdly, the handle of the bolt stem was bent sharply downwards. There were also differences not visible to the eye: the barrels for the sniper rifles were manufactured from the best steel, processed on precision lathes for greater accuracy, while the components were assembled by hand and adjusted in a special way.

At the end of my studies at the sniper school, that is, in 1939, we were introduced to the new models of weapons that were being delivered to the Red Army. They were the Simonov (AVS-36) and Tokarev (SVT-38) self-loading (automatic) rifles. The principle behind their automatic functioning was based on the use of powder gases, which always accompany the bullet as it speeds along the barrel. The rifles had detachable box-type magazines containing ten to fifteen cartridges. The only thing that gave rise to doubt among us and our instructors was the number of components in the AVS and the SVT and also the construction of its mechanism, which was very complex compared to Captain Mosin's model.

I remember the first lecture on the subject known as 'The Essentials of Shooting', to which twenty-five hours were devoted in the programme. We were sitting in class one day when in walked a lean man of average height, aged about forty, with a prominent scar over his left brow. The monitor shouted: 'Stand up! Attention!' The teacher introduced himself: 'Potapov, Alexander Vladimirovich,' and briefly explained what he intended to teach us. Then, falling silent, he surveyed the auditorium with a stern glance and said, 'I have heard that you shoot quite well. But remember: a good marksman is still not a sniper.'

Thus began our association with Potapov, the school's senior instructor. We found out that he had begun his military career in the Imperial Life Guard Chasseur Regiment in St Petersburg, where marksmanship training for the lower ranks was exemplary. For his feats on the German front in 1915 and 1916 he earned two St

George Crosses, third and fourth class, and also the rank of non-commissioned officer. In the Civil War Potapov commanded a company in a Red Army infantry regiment and was seriously wounded during the forced crossing of the Sivash. In 1929 he was seconded from the regiment to teach the Comintern 'Vystrel' tactical rifleman courses directed at improving the Red Army command structure. It was there that the first group in the country to study the sniper's art began to operate. But he did not get to serve in the army as a sniping instructor; an old wound played up and Battalion Commander Potapov was demobilized. In this way, Osoaviakhim acquired a much-needed specialist.

Incidentally, the Kiev sniper school within this large-scale, voluntary, public, patriotic military organization was renowned, like those in Moscow and Leningrad, not only for the quality of its equipment and technical facilities, but also for its superbly trained teaching staff. Alexander Potapov was a big shooting enthusiast and a connoisseur and passionate devotee of weaponry – especially the Mosin Three Line, model 1891/1930. He set out his experience, observations and reflections on the philosophy of sniping in a small pamphlet, *Instructions for Sharpshooters*, which was published in Kiev.

Without question Potapov was a born teacher. He kept a constant watch over the cadets, not only in lectures, but also on the firing range. He believed that theoretical knowledge and firing practice were, of course, absolutely essential, but they were not sufficient to rear a true professional. He or she had to have more than just a good eye (which is granted by nature thanks to the individual peculiarities of the eyeball structure). They needed a special character: calm, balanced, even phlegmatic, and not subject to fits of anger, merriment, despair or – even worse! – hysteria. A sniper is a patient hunter. He takes just a single shot; if he misses, he can pay for it with his life.

Potapov warned us that in a month he would discharge those who – in his view – were incapable of acquiring the cunning art of the sniper. This caused us some distress. But his teaching methods won respect, as always. One might even say that we liked him. Therefore, we tried with all our might. At least I tried. Aside from me, our group included two other representatives of the fairer sex. With us he went out of his way to be polite, but, as girls aged nineteen, twenty and twenty-two, we tended to be frightened rather than cheered by this officer's courtesy. We suspected that we would be the first candidates to be eliminated. Things turned out differently, however.

Those who ended up parting with their dark-blue Osoaviakhim tunics were a number of ill-bred lads, including three who held the certificate for 'First-Class Red Army Marksman'. Potapov explained that he did not attach much significance to male–female distinctions among his pupils and he was sure that women – not all, of course – were better suited to sniper operations. They were hardy and observant, and they were given an enhanced intuition by nature itself. When undergoing military courses, women fulfilled all instructions precisely and had a considered and careful approach to the process of firing, and when it came to inventive disguises, which were so important for a sniper on the battlefield, they had simply no equals.

The praise from the senior instructor could have turned anyone's head. But Alexander Vladimirovich gave us no time to enjoy it. He became stricter and more inclined to find fault with the cadets who remained in the group and he gave more attention to each of us. He discussed refinements we had never even thought about. For example, he made us observe a construction site – a three-storey building was being built on Vladimir Street for the No. 25 School – and then tell him what the workers had managed to do over a two-hour period, how the situation on the site had changed, where the new doors, window apertures, staircases and internal walls had appeared and what position would be most convenient for a shot to neutralize, say, the site foreman, who was running up and down the plank footways from floor to floor.

Slowly but relentlessly Potapov taught us to observe the surrounding world closely, to examine keenly the details of life's rapid pace, as if through telescope sights, to gain a conception of the whole picture from minor details. With this approach, there was always something losing its significance, receding into or merging with the background. Or something would become particularly important. The true essence of every new object was made manifest, as if magnified by a lens.

It sometimes felt as if our 'dear teacher' was picking on me. There were times when, tackling a task which did not lend itself to swift resolution, I would begin to get hot under the collar. I became irritated at having to spend more time and energy on something which seemed at first glance to be completely commonplace. Potapov would halt the training session and calmly, insistently and even boringly, start to analyse everything, to explain, to point out the error, and follow the way I corrected it. I was surprised at the extent to which he fussed around with me. The senior instructor replied: 'From whom much is given, much is demanded.'

As I have no intention of describing here the whole complex of skills and abilities essential for a sniper (for a civilian readership there is absolutely no point), I will just mention that, apart from actual shooting practice, the school put a lot of weight on theory classes. We were introduced to the laws of ballistics: in particular we were given an understanding of the 'mil' in distance estimation, were taught how to calculate the range quickly according to angles, using a special formula, and the reticles of PE telescope sights, binoculars and periscopes.[2] We were taught how far the rapidly rotating bullet would drift laterally during its travel from the muzzle to the target. We also memorized various tables – for instance, the table of excessive deviations from average trajectories when firing the Mosin rifle with cartridges containing bullets ranging from 'light' to 'heavy', and so on and so forth.

Over four months of training our group came together. Spring arrived and we began to travel, not just to the firing range, but also into the countryside, where the indefatigable Potapov arranged additional exercises on methods of camouflage. In some distant clearing the cadets would unfold a tablecloth, placing on it bottles of lemon-flavoured mineral water and lemonade, and setting out all sorts of foodstuffs brought from home. The senior instructor would give a lecture and demonstrate how to camouflage oneself in a natural setting. Sometimes we were actually unable to find him for half an hour or more. In those cases, we would shout, 'We give in,' and our teacher would emerge before us in some unimaginable yellow-green hooded overalls adorned with tatters of cloth, dry twigs and clumps of grass.

Other times, we would generally take a sniper's rifle into the forest and play a game we called 'bottle base'. After the drink bottles were empty from lunch, we would set up one of them on its side in a cleft stick with the bottle's neck towards us at a distance of about 20 or 30 metres from the firing line. With a single shot we had to knock out the bottom of the bottle – that is, the bullet was supposed to enter the bottleneck and, without damaging the sides of the glass vessel, emerge through the bottom of the bottle, which would be smashed in the process.

Potapov would usually knock out the first bottle himself. Then he would hand the rifle to one of his pupils, and the contest for accuracy and skill began. We had some very ambitious kids, generally very young, who would give anything to lead the field and win Potapov's praises. First, we were required to shoot from a kneeling position, that is, planting your right knee on the ground and resting on your heel. Second, we had to support the rifle with a strap which went under the bent elbow of the left arm. In this way the marksman could rest on the left knee and hold the handguard of the gun, having moved his or her hand closer to the muzzle end. All this demanded strength, stability and good balance.

Anyone who missed exited the game, to the jests and laughter of those present. The victorious were rewarded by Potapov; they received a small chocolate bar and a witty comment. For a while I did not have full confidence in my capabilities. Moreover, I do not like showing off or being the centre of attention, for one of the postulates instilled in us by the 'dear teacher' proclaimed: 'Showing yourself is dangerous. The sniper is invulnerable so long as he is unseen.'

The day came when I was the one to whom Potapov handed the rifle. Suppressing my nerves, I took the weapon, forced the butt into the hollow of my shoulder as usual, placed my index finger on the trigger and, pressing my cheek to the comb of the butt, I stared into the eyepiece of the telescope sight with my right eye. The PE sight provided four-fold magnification. But even so, the neck of the bottle faded between the three black lines and looked just like a full-stop in bold type. All that was left was to rely on intuition, on that 'feeling for the target' which a sniper develops during the training process.

Spending too long taking aim is a common beginner's error and I had long rid myself of it. So, everything went off exactly according to instructions, that is, within a time of eight seconds. Hold your breath, take aim and breathe out as you exert smooth pressure on the trigger. The rifle responded with the crack of a shot and kick in the shoulder. The white sides of the bottle were still gleaming in the sun as before, but the base of the bottle was . . . no longer there!

'Well done, Lyudmila,' said the senior instructor. 'Can you repeat it?'

'All right, let's have a go,' I agreed, for I was overcome by the excitement.

Potapov realized this and smiled. 'Keep calm, my long-braided beauty –' that was how the senior instructor sometimes jokingly referred to us girls in his group. 'You have every chance of victory.'

The others quickly set up a new bottle in the fork. Potapov gave me a cartridge with a 'heavy' bullet and, opening the breech, I placed it in the chamber. Of course the mechanism would work without fail. I would press the trigger and, under the pressure of the action spring, the striker would move forwards sharply. Its end point, like the sting of a snake, would penetrate the ignition capsule at the base of the bullet. The powder charge in it would explode and the bullet, fastened in a brass casing by a ring, would finally win its freedom.

The day had turned out fine and sunny and, yielding to my will, the bullets fired superbly. Three 'bottle bases' – that was my final score from the competition in the forest. To the envy of the other cadets, the senior instructor presented me not just with the chocolate bar, but also with a copy of his booklet *Instructions for Sharpshooters*, autographed: 'To Lyudmila Pavlichenko, my able pupil, in fond memory. A. Potapov'. I do not necessarily agree with this phrasing. After all, abilities are from nature, inborn, but when it comes to super-sharpshooting, one should also add firmness of character, industry, diligence, restraint and the persistent desire to learn.

I graduated from the sniper school with respectable results. The certificate of completion, printed on coated paper and adorned with the round seal of a crest, included the names of the subjects and the grades. The black letters formed words that I was very pleased with: Practical shooting – Excellent; Firearms mechanics – Excellent; Tactical training – Excellent; Military engineering training – Good. Our graduation evening was relaxed, noisy and merry. We talked about the future. Many of the lads intended to apply for military colleges. The girls planned to pursue shooting within the Osoaviakhim system, to take part in competitions and compete for the title 'USSR Master of Sport'. However, it was already 1939.

On 1 September Nazi Germany attacked Poland and the Second World War began. The Poles resisted the invaders, but by 8 September the Germans had nearly reached Warsaw. The siege continued for twenty days. Then the government fled to Romania and Poland was completely occupied by the Germans. In April 1940 the Nazis marched into Denmark and Norway. With British and French help, the Norwegians held out for two months, but capitulated in June. Then came the turn of Belgium and France. The German advance began on 20 May and, by the 28th, the greater part of the Belgian army had already laid down their arms. After the encirclement of the Allied British, French and Belgian troops at Dunkirk on 4 June 1940 the British retreated from the European continent to their own island, leaving to the victors all their artillery and tanks, over 60,000 vehicles, and up to half a million tons of military equipment and ammunition, as well as around 40,000 captured soldiers and officers. On 22 July of the same year the heirs of the valiant warriors of Emperor Napoleon Bonaparte surrendered Paris to the Fritzes without a battle! A Blitzkrieg indeed – that is, a 'swift war'.

Observing the rapid downturn in European events, we could not avoid thinking that sooner or later the aggressor would descend on our own, and the world's first, worker and peasant state. Over our traditional evening cup of tea, my father, who had confidential information by virtue of his occupation, talked more and more often about the difficult times ahead. I argued with him, insisting that, in the words of the Civil War song, 'from our native forest to the British sea, our own Red Army is the best there can be', and that it would be a case of us fighting on foreign territory.

As events demonstrated, Father was right and I (along with millions of other Soviet people) was drastically wrong. I can only explain my misplaced confidence as a reflection the state of my own affairs, which were going magnificently. Because I was passing all my university subjects with excellent grades, I was permitted to combine study with work allied to my specialist subject. At the end of 1939 I was appointed to the position of head of the acquisitions section at the state history library. Just as I had before, at the Arsenal factory, I began once again to contribute towards the general family budget and to spend more money on my son, who had turned seven.

I passed my fourth-year exams in the history faculty along with my fellow students in January 1941, with grades ranging from excellent to good. The management of the state history library in Kiev offered me the opportunity of a lengthy – four-month – secondment to the Odessa public library as a senior research assistant to support local research staff. I was familiar with the rich resources of this library, which was one of the oldest in the Ukraine. I imagined that I would easily be able to write my diploma dissertation there on Bogdan Khmelnitsky, the Ukraine's accession to Russia in 1654 and the activities of the Pereyaslav Council. The following year I was due to defend this dissertation at Kiev State University and receive a diploma of higher education.

I prepared for my departure in the most joyful mood. Nevertheless, the conversations with my father had fortunately had an impact on me. Therefore, I put in my suitcase not only my passport, student card and academic record booklet, but also my certificate of graduation from the sniper school, our teacher's pamphlet and a collection of memoirs entitled *Combat in Finland*, which had been published in Moscow at the beginning of 1941.

The train from Kiev to Odessa left in the evening. My whole family came to the station. Father was earnest and taciturn as always. Mother gave me some last words of advice on healthy eating. My sister Valentina and her young man Boris were whispering about something. My son Rostislav did not want to let go of my hand at all and asked me to take him with me, promising to help me in my work. Tears were welling up in his eyes and I tried to comfort him a little and cheer him up. I could not have imagined that I would be separated from him for almost three years!

3

From the Prut to the Dnyestr

There was nothing unusual about the beginning of that Sunday, 22 June 1941, a day now fixed in everyone's memory. Over Odessa a clear sky was gleaming and the hot southern sun was shining. The sea was dead calm; the smooth blue surface stretched to the horizon and it seemed as if, somewhere out there, in the distance, it merged with the equally blue sky.

My friend Sofya Chopak, who worked at the Odessa public library, her elder brother and I spent the early morning at the beach. We had decided to have lunch at a *cheburek* [Caucasian meat pasty] café on Pushkin Street. We planned to spend the evening at the local theatre for a performance of Verdi's opera *La Traviata* and had already bought tickets.

Sitting on the open veranda of the *cheburek* café at midday, awaiting our order, we heard an announcement from a speaker on the street that the deputy chairman of the Council of People's Commissars and the people's commissar for foreign affairs, Comrade Molotov, would be speaking any minute. What he said seemed to us to be completely incredible: that day, at four o'clock in the morning, Germany had perfidiously attacked the Soviet Union.

'Our entire nation must now be united and rally round as never before,' Molotov's firm but agitated voice intoned. 'Each of us must demand from himself and from others the discipline, organization and self-sacrifice worthy of a true Soviet patriot, in order to provide for all the needs of the Red Army, the Navy and the Air Force, in order to ensure victory over the enemy. Victory will be ours!'

The speech lasted only a few minutes and at first it was difficult to make sense of what had happened. We sat at the table as if spellbound and looked at one another in a daze. But soon the waiter brought our *cheburek* order and a bottle of white wine. As if we had returned to the ordinary world from beyond the looking-glass, we plunged into a loud and unrelated conversation.

Meanwhile, Pushkin Street was gradually filling up. People were gathering under the speaker, engaging in a lively exchange of views. A heartfelt unease was driving them out of their homes onto the street. They wanted to see their fellow countrymen, to know how others had taken the dreadful news, to gauge the general mood, to sense the unity which the people's commissar for foreign affairs was calling for. There was no feeling of panic or bewilderment in the crowd. Everyone was confidently saying: we will crush the Nazis!

Nobody in Odessa thought of cancelling planned visits to the cinema, theatre or concert hall, nor their traditional Sunday stroll along Marine Boulevard to the sound of a brass band. On the contrary, auditoriums were packed – at the opera, the Russian drama theatre and the theatre for young people, which were situated not far from one another on Greek Street, and at the city philharmonia. The public were also still keen to get into the circus for an act featuring tamed tigers.

We did not consider cancelling our visit to the opera either, and just after seven o'clock we were sitting in our seats in box 16 of the dress circle, watching the first act of *La Traviata*. The audience were invited to believe that they were located in the luxurious home of the Parisian courtesan, Violetta Valery. The stage sets, the costumes, the voices of the singers, the orchestra's playing, the very decor of the hall with its gilded mouldings, huge crystal chandelier and the ceiling so beautifully painted by a French artist – all these elements were in complete harmony with one another. But something prevented me from enjoying this refined spectacle. It was as if it related to a different life, one which was rapidly receding from us. During the interval after the first act I suggested to my friends that we leave the theatre.

We went down to the sea. On the summer stage of Marine Boulevard the brass band was playing cheerful military marches. The sound of the trumpets and the loud drumbeats resounded over the shoreline. On the smooth surface of the watery expanse of Odessa Bay the outlines of Black Sea Fleet warships could be seen: the old cruiser *Komintern* which had been re-equipped as a mine-layer, the destroyers *Shaumyan*, *Boykiy* and *Bezuprechnyy*, and the gunboats *Krasnaya Abkhaziya*, *Krasnaya Gruzhiya* and *Krasnaya Armeniya*. The steel hulls, the masts and the mighty gun turrets with their long barrels were more in keeping with our mood. After all, war had been declared.

According to mobilization instructions, which were announced the following day, those born between 1905 and 1918 and liable for military service were subject to conscription in the army. Being born in 1916, I fell into this category. Having no doubt that they would take me on the spot and with pleasure, I set off for the military commissariat of the Odessa water-transport district. My meeting with the enlistment office seemed to me to be a very formal one, and I put on my best crêpe-de-chine dress and some beautiful white high-heeled sandals. In my handbag I had my passport, student card and graduation certificate from Kiev's Osoaviakhim sniper school.

There were a lot of people by the doors of the district enlistment office. It took me about two hours to get inside. The room was stuffy and filled with smoke. There were doors slamming every minute. A hoarse military registrar with a face of red and blue blotches was trying to explain something to two lads of rustic appearance who had approached him. He looked at me with a harassed expression and said: 'Medical staff will be enlisted from tomorrow.'

'I'm not a medic,' I replied, but he immediately turned away, indicating that our conversation was over. However, I was not prepared to accept that and placed my sniper's certificate on the desk in front of him. The irritated registrar said that there was no mention in his list of a 'sniper' category. Then he added a sarcastic comment about Osoaviakhim and women who wanted to be soldiers but had no idea how difficult it was. In a word, he forced me to leave his office.

On my return from the enlistment office, I thought over the situation and came to the conclusion that the hitch was my registered residence. My name would be entered in the list of snipers in the enlistment office in the Pechorsk region of Kiev. The previous year I had successfully competed in the city shooting competitions and passed a re-training course. Perhaps they were looking for me in the Ukrainian capital, but here I was on the shores of the Black Sea. I needed to ask the local enlistment office to make a call to Kiev.

The following day I set off again for the military commissariat of the water-transport district. The registrar greeted me much more amiably. Judging by his reaction, he already knew what a sniper was. He leafed through my passport, found the stamp registering my marriage to Pavlichenko, A.B., and asked if my husband had any objection to my volunteering for the Red Army. I had not seen Alexei Pavlichenko for three years and replied that he had no objections. My passport remained with the registrar and they began to compile military documents in an adjacent office.

On the evening of 24 June 1941, having congregated at the station, all the new recruits, some partly in uniform, others still in civilian dress, were packed onto a special military train. The train moved slowly and took a westward line through the steppe close to the Black Sea. Soon the smooth surface of the Dnyestr estuary came into view, gleaming on the right, and then we passed through the stations of Shabo, Kolyesnoye, Sarata, Artsiz and Hlavani. The train sometimes stood for a long time at the stations, and we were given food there. But nobody explained anything or told us about our final destination. They merely said that we were going to the front, and my heart was involuntarily thumping: 'Make it quicker, make it quicker!' The young people in our carriage were getting indignant: 'We won't be there in time! They'll beat the Nazis without us!' That was how poorly we understood the scale of the disaster which had suddenly been unleashed upon our beautiful, thriving country.

The train stopped at some small station at three o'clock in the morning on 26 June. We were ordered to leave the carriages and line up. Shivering slightly from the morning's cold dampness, the new recruits strode out along a dirt road and by seven o'clock we had reached a fairly dense forest. It turned out that we were on Bessarabian soil, among the rear units of the 25th Chapayev Rifle Division.

I received my first military uniform here, becoming a Red Army soldier of the 54th Stepan Razin Rifle Regiment. The items were completely new, which testified to the excellent state of the division's commissariat service and the order in which its stores were kept. They were sewn from khaki cotton material: a forage cap, a tunic with a turn-down collar, trousers flared at the thigh like riding breeches, and kirza artificial leather boots (two sizes bigger than necessary). Also issued were a belt with a brass buckle, a gas mask in a canvas bag, a small sapper's spade in a cover, an aluminium flask (also in a cover), an SSH-40 helmet (quite heavy), a pack and, inside it, various articles such as a towel, a spare undershirt and briefs, a spare pair of foot wrappings and bags for provisions and toiletries and other items. In the rucksack I hid away my staple-fibre dress with its lace collar and my comfortable canvas lace-ups. Goodbye, civilian life!

My first army breakfast seemed very tasty: hot buckwheat porridge and sweet tea with a solid chunk of bread. The meal took place in a setting approximating to battle conditions. We could hear the sound of far-off machine-gun fire and exploding shells echoing from time to time somewhere to the west. We new recruits all jumped at the sound of the explosions, but the seasoned sergeants and sergeant-majors explained that there was no need to be afraid of a flying or exploding shell – it would never do anyone any harm. And so the day passed in conversation. We were given permission to relax but not allowed to leave the forest.

The ceremony of swearing the military oath took place on 28 June. Senior political instructor Yefim Andreyevich Maltsev, military commissar of the 54th Regiment, came to us. He talked about the combat history of the 25th Chapayev Rifle Division (which was commanded in 1919 by the legendary Civil War hero, Vasily Ivanovich Chapayev), about the glorious rifle regiments: the 31st Furmanov-Pugachov, our own 54th Stepan Razin and the 225th Frunze Domashkin Regiments. In 1933 the division had become the first in the Red Army to be awarded the recently established supreme order of the USSR – the Order of Lenin. It was an acknowledgement of its outstanding feats on the Civil War fronts and its glittering achievements in military training during peacetime.

Then came the command: 'Attention!' The banner of the 54th Regiment was brought out before the assembled troops. With emotion in our voices we repeated the words of the 'Red Army Soldier's Oath': 'I, a citizen of the Union of Soviet Socialist Republics, entering the ranks of the Workers' and Peasants' Red Army, solemnly swear to be an honest, brave, disciplined and vigilant soldier, and strictly preserve military and state secrets.' We then put our signatures on sheets bearing the printed text of the oath and, by doing so, were transformed into people whose lives now completely belonged to our homeland. We were divided between the units of the 54th Regiment. I ended up in the 1st Battalion, 2nd Company, 1st Platoon.

The platoon was commanded by Lieutenant Vasily Koftun, who had graduated from the Mogilyov military infantry college the previous year and was younger than me. The first thing he asked was why I had volunteered for the army, for war was not women's business at all. I took out my 'magic wand' – my graduation certificate from the Osoaviakhim sniper school. The lieutenant was extremely sceptical about it and said that he would petition the battalion commander, Captain Sergienko, to transfer me to a medical platoon, because the only work women were capable of at the front was as medical orderlies.

We went to the command post of the 1st Battalion. There, the same conversation was repeated: why, what for, and did I realize how dangerous it was, and so on. In response I talked about my father, who had served for some time in the Samara Division (later the 25th Chapayev Division) during the Civil War and met Chapayev, about my work at the Arsenal factory, which fulfilled orders from the People's Commissariat of Defence, and about the military history of our country, which I had studied in detail in the history faculty of Kiev University.

Ivan Ivanovich Sergienko, a thoughtful, experienced and serious man, heard me out attentively and ordered Kovtun to forget his inept idea of transferring sniper Pavlichenko to the medical section. I was overjoyed: 'Comrade Captain, I am ready to take possession of the weapon that is appropriate for me.'

'But we have no sniper rifles, Lyudmila,' he replied.

'Well, then a standard Three Line.'

'We don't have those either.'

'How am I to fight, then, Comrade Captain?' I asked in bewilderment.

'For you new recruits the main weapon for now will be the spade. You will help the soldiers to dig trenches and communication routes and to restore them after artillery shelling and bombing raids. Apart from that, we will issue you one PGD-33 grenade in case the Nazis break through. Are you familiar with the mechanism of this grenade?'

'Yes, Comrade Captain.'

'Excellent.' He smiled. 'No other action is required of you at the moment.'

I have read many reminiscences of the first days of the Great War for the Fatherland. They were written by generals commanding large military units, by officers in charge of regiments, companies and platoons, and by political staff. Because the battles unfolded along the entire length of our borders, the participants in the engagements drew completely different pictures. There was, for instance, the Brest fortress, whose defenders continued resistance for almost a month. There were also ferocious two-week tussles which ended in near panic withdrawals with the loss of whole corps and divisions, the abandonment of military machinery, and the encirclement and surrender of many detachments of Soviet troops. For example, this happened on the north-west, western and south-west fronts. There, in the course of three weeks, the Nazi German invaders advanced distances between 300 and 600km across the territory of the USSR. But our 25th Chapayev Division was located on the southern front, on its extreme left flank, occupying an already prepared line of defence of about 60km along the river Prut. Here the situation developed differently, more favourably for us.

On 22 June 1941 the Romanians, who were allies of Nazi Germany, tried to cross the river and were repulsed. The following week passed with minor skirmishes and artillery duels, during which the Chapayevs continued to hold their positions. There were also attempts to push the military action onto the enemy's side. One battalion of our regiment (based in the town of Kagul) made a landing on Romanian soil and there routed two Fascist companies, taking about seventy soldiers and officers prisoner. Our troops also captured the Romanian city of Kilia-Veke, where eight pieces of ordnance and thirty machine guns fell into Russian hands as trophies. The Romanian units that had crossed the Prut on 23 June were also suitably repulsed and around 500 enemy soldiers surrendered in this engagement. All in all, over a period of eight days, from 22 to 30 June, the enemy lost up to 1,500 men and failed to capture an inch of Soviet land.[1]

Then events took a different turn. During the first days of July our defences on the river Prut were breached much further to the north, in the Iasi-Beltsy and Mogilyov-Podolski sectors. With their great advantage in manpower and technology, the invaders quickly mounted an advance and the southern front began to come apart at the seams. This resulted in the 'Bessarabian loop', from which the 25th, 95th, 51st and 176th Rifle Divisions had to be rescued. Therefore, the middle of June saw an arduous retreat across the Black Sea steppes with persistent rear-guard battles.

On 19 July our valiant regiment was located on the line from Cairaclia to Bulgariyka; on the 21st on the line from Novo-Pavlovsk to Novy Artsiz; on the 22nd on the Artsiz line; on the 23rd on the line from Karolino-Bugaz to the Dnyestr estuary. On the 24th the regiments of the division were to be found on various lines: by the village of Starokazachye, by Height 67, Cherkesy, and by the village of Sofiental.

We conducted the retreat in so-called 'stages'. Some units covered the retreat, others withdrew, and others prepared new firing positions. It worked in this way: the 31st Pugachov and 287th Rifle Regiments defended, the 54th Razin Regiment withdrew and the 225th Domashkin Regiment dug in. Then the military units swapped places: the Domashkins would fight, the Pugachovs withdrew and the Razins dug trenches.

The withdrawal sometimes took place in the daytime, sometimes at night, to avoid strikes by German and Romanian aircraft. We travelled in road vehicles, but there were not many of them in the regiment – just eighteen in all – and, besides, nine of them (1.5-ton GAZ-AA from the Gorky works) belonged to the medical company. There was, however, a large number of two-horse carts (officially 233, but, in the middle of July, approximately a third fewer). We also made forced marches on foot.

The steppe spread out on both sides of the road, like an open book. It lay before us on the warm July nights, quiet and mysterious. But during the day it boomed with cannon volleys, lit up with fires and exuded the smell of burnt gunpowder. The population withdrew from Bessarabia with us.

Agricultural machinery (combine harvesters, tractors, sowing machines and so forth) moved along the roads. There were whole caravans of trucks carrying big wooden boxes; apparently, factory equipment was being evacuated. Collective farmers drove herds of livestock, and lumbering along the roads with them were lines of carts carrying household items. This is to say nothing of the multitude of women with small children, teenagers and old men dejectedly trudging along the dusty roadsides, apprehensively glancing up at the sky and shuddering at the artillery cannonades.

Often there would be a 'Frame' circling over the steppe roads – the twin-engine Focke-Wulf 189, which the Germans called *Fliegende Auge* ('Flying Eye') but was known in Red Army slang as the *Rama* (Frame) on account of its construction: twin-boom, with a separate crew gondola placed centrally. It carried out reconnaissance, directed bombers to the columns retreating towards the river Dnyestr and served as a spotter for long-range artillery fire.[2] The 'Frame' did not fly quickly, but it flew quite high. All attacks on it by our red-starred Yastrebki [TN: 'hawks', commonly applied to fighter pilots] came to nothing – not that there were many such attacks.

The Nazis carried out regular aerial raids. They struck at the roads and the villages adjacent to them. We saw fields of wheat completely incinerated, and residential houses, storage facilities, administrative buildings and production premises destroyed by bombs, and machinery burnt out and abandoned. Sometimes before our very eyes Junkers 87 'Stuka' bombers would suddenly drop out of the clouds, swoop down on the roads, and bomb and machine-gun the civilian population, who had no way of defending themselves. All this resembled not so much a normal war, where armies of equal strength fight each other, but rather the deliberate extermination of our people.

We, their defenders, either hid in the forest or headed east along the same roads. The ordinary people, seeing we were offering them no assistance, bitterly protested: 'To hell with you! Why aren't you fighting the enemy? Why aren't you standing up to them?'

The images of awful destruction and enormous personal grief echoed in our hearts, with a pain that was impossible to ignore. Some became depressed, some lost faith in victory and dreaded the future. But I thought of vengeance, inescapable and irresistible. The intruders from the west who had wickedly violated the peaceful life of my native land would have to pay a severe penalty and I would be able to punish them – as soon as I got my hands on a weapon. But the armament situation was not good. There were shortages not only of shells for regimental and divisional artillery, but even of rifles.

In the memoirs of Vice-Admiral Ilya Azarov, who was a member of the Military Council for the Odessa defence district in the summer of 1941, there is a chapter with the revealing title 'Give us Weapons!' He described how he searched army storerooms for rifles, submachine guns, and standard and light machine guns during the breakneck Nazi assault and was everywhere denied. It was only by chance that he managed to arm one newly formed military unit on the southern front: 'We had fifty learners' rifles . . . all with perforated cartridge chambers. The factory closed up the holes at our request. Most of the rifles could be put into action. We tried them out on the firing range and, to our joy, they turned out to be fit for use.'[3]

A standard Mosin rifle, 1891/1930 model, fell into my hands in the second half of July after our regiment had been subjected to heavy artillery fire on the Novo-Pavlovsk to Novy Artsiz line. It was very frustrating to have to observe the course of battle with just a single grenade in one's hand. But it was a million times more bitter to have to wait until your comrade, standing beside you, was wounded and his weapon passed into your hands. A shell splinter severely injured a regimental colleague who had taken cover in a trench. Drenched in blood, he handed his Three Line to me.

After some preliminary artillery fire, the Romanians prepared to attack and, together with the other soldiers of our 1st Platoon, I placed my rifle on the parapet of the shallow trench, set the back sight on mark 3 (that is, for a distance of 300 metres) and pulled back the bolt. Thrusting the bolt forward ensured that there was a cartridge in the chamber, and a light bullet, known as 'Ball L' or Model 1908, was awaiting its release. On the command of Junior Lieutenant Kovtun we opened fire. The company light machine guns also went into action. The outcome of this minor engagement was decided by our successful counter-attack. Climbing out of our trenches, we drove the Fascists back quite a long way. The battlefield was ours, and the troops of the 54th Rifle Regiment went about gathering up the weapons of the enemy dead. The trophies included 7.9mm-calibre vz. 24 Czech Mauser rifles. Our cartridges did not fit them, so we were also required to take the cartridge bags from the bodies. Of course, this only partially solved our soldiers' weaponry problems.

Seeing me with a Three Line over my shoulder, Junior Lieutenant Kovtun came up to me. I was afraid he would order me to hand it over to one of the soldiers. But after the recent victory against the enemy, the platoon commander was in a good mood.

'So, you went on attack with the others, Private Lyudmila?'

'Exactly so, Comrade Commander!' I reported back.

'And how do you feel about it?'

'Excellent, Comrade Commander!'

'Did you get to fire?' he asked.

'Yes, I used up the whole cartridge clip.'

'Fine. The sergeant major will re-register this rifle in your name. We'll see what kind of sniper you are.'

'I'd rather have a weapon with a telescope sight, Comrade Commander,' I said. 'Then the results will be different.'

'I can't promise that at the moment. But at the first opportunity I'll try to fulfil your request.' The junior lieutenant smiled, and I knew that now I would definitely be part of the sub-unit entrusted to him.

Meanwhile, the retreat continued. The Chapayev troops reached the western bank of the river Dnyestr, crossed it and on 26 July we took up defensive positions on the eastern bank, on a line: Gradenitsa–Mayaki village–Frantzfeld–Karolino-Bugaz. To the north lay the fortifications of the Tiraspol fortified district No. 82.[4] They had been erected long before the war and were not badly equipped, with concrete, reinforced-earth, and stone firing points, dugouts and deep trenches. Located here in caponiers and semi-caponiers were around 100 pieces of ordnance of various calibres and several hundred standard and light machine guns. UR-82 also included underground storage space containing various military equipment.

The Soviet high command counted on halting the wave of the enemy advance here, pulverizing the Romanian and German infantry divisions on the banks of the Dnyestr, and then driving them back to the western frontier. I write in detail about UR-82 because its military stores came in very handy for the 25th and 95th Rifle Divisions. Our 54th Regiment at last received some Maxim medium machine guns, Degtyarev infantry ('DP') light machine guns, Three Line Mosins and SVT-40 autoloaders, and totally replenished its ammunition stocks. And I was finally given a completely new (the factory grease still on it) Mosin sniper rifle with PE (Emelyanov) sight.

However, our generals' plans for a radical turning point in the military situation based on UR-82 were not fulfilled. The Romanians and Germans, with their five-to-one numerical superiority, were bearing down strongly. Fierce battles were fought from 26 July to 8 August on the boundaries of the Tiraspol fortified district. Then the military units of the southern front were forced to withdraw to the outskirts of Odessa. The Soviet defence now lay along the line connecting the population centres: Alexandrovka–Buyalyk–Brinovka–Karpovo–Belyayevka–Ovidiopol–Karolino-Bugaz.

Belyayevka, 8 August 1941 – this was the time and place of my wartime sniper debut, so to speak, in the war. I shall never forget that day. Belyayevka was quite a large old village established by the Zaporozhye Cossacks near Lake Byeloye, about 40km from Odessa. A significant part of the settlement comprised rammed-clay cottages with roofs made of reeds. There were also some stone structures: a church, a single-storey school and several houses which, before the Revolution, had probably belonged to wealthy locals. One of them now housed the rural council offices. After a lengthy engagement, the western part of Belyayevka remained occupied by the troops of the Romanian king, Mihai I. Despite our substantial losses, they did not advance at all. By evening our 1st Battalion had secured a position on the eastern side of the village. Captain Sergienko called me up to the command post and pointed to the far end of Belyayevka. Visible there among the overgrown trees was a large house with a porch which had a ridged roof, well illuminated by the setting sun. Two men came out onto the porch in officers' uniforms and helmets reminiscent of rustic pudding basins. The kingdom of Romania had bought up these steel items for its army from their Dutch suppliers before the war.

'Looks like that's the staff headquarters. Can you reach it?' asked the battalion commander.

'I'll try, Comrade Captain,' I replied.

'Go on, then.' He stepped away from me, ready to observe me in action.

Our stay near UR-82 had been a more or less relaxing week and, after withdrawing to the rear, I had been able to bring my new sniper rifle into battle condition. To accomplish this I had had to strip the rifle completely and do some work on its components. For example, I had removed the wood along the whole length of the handguard groove, so that the woodwork no longer touched the barrel, I had filed down the tip of the gunstock, so that the barrel fitted snugly, bedded the barrel properly in the fore-end, and inserted padding between the receiver and the magazine. To ensure that the various parts of the bolt mechanism worked properly, it was recommended that they were carefully worked over with a small needle file. The trigger mechanism of the rifle needs to be efficient, reliable and stable.

The clear and windless weather which had settled over the steppes of the Dnyestr's east bank was conducive to adjusting rifles, first with open sights and then the telescope. The first stage was undertaken at a distance of 100 metres from a square target measuring 25 × 35cm. For the second stage the rifle was fixed on a stand (or something similar) to ensure its immobility. The objective was to regulate the telescope sights with the aid of the open sights.

The rifle was over my shoulder and from my belt hung three leather pouches containing cartridges sorted by type: the first with 'Ball L' light bullets, M1908; the second with yellow-tipped 'Ball D' heavy bullets, M1930; and the third with special 'B-32' armour-piercing-incendiary bullets, with a black tip in front of a yellow band. I took the rifle in my hands and looked through the eyepiece of the telescope sight. The horizontal line covered the figure of the officer descending the steps, approximately down to his waist. I set myself an equation from the course in practical ballistics which we had done at the school and the solution was: distance to the target – 400 metres. Placing a cartridge with a light bullet in the chamber, I looked around to select a place to shoot from.

The captain and I were in the middle of a peasant hut which had been destroyed by a direct hit from a shell. The roof was smashed in, and stones and charred splinters of beams were spread around everywhere. It did not appear possible to fire from a lying position. I decided to shoot from behind the wall, on my knee, using a strap: to rest on the heel of my right boot, to lean on my left bent knee with my left elbow, and to let the strap under the left elbow carry the weight of the rifle. Not for nothing did Potapov often remind us of the snipers' saying: 'It's the barrel that fires, but the gunstock that hits!' A lot depends on the position which the marksman adopts when holding the rifle.

I hit the first target with the third shot and the second one on my fourth attempt, having loaded the rifle with one of the scarce cartridges containing the 'D'-type heavy bullet. I cannot say I was nervous or hesitant. What hesitation can there be after three weeks of desperate retreat under enemy bombs and shells? Still, something got in the way of my concentration. They say this sometimes happens when a sniper first makes the transition from shooting practice at cardboard targets to firing at live enemy.

'Lucy,' said the battalion commander sympathetically, looking through his binoculars at the enemy officers lying motionless by the porch, 'You need to conserve cartridges. Seven on two Nazis – that's a lot.'

'I'm sorry, Comrade Commander. I'll get it right.'

'Do try. Or else, visible or invisible, they'll be crawling in like cockroaches. Apart from us, there's nobody to stop the invaders.'

In the meantime, the Romanians felt like victors.

On 8 August 1941, the dictator Ion Antonescu declared that, having routed the Russians, on 15 August 1941 his valiant troops would enter Odessa and march in triumph through its streets. There were grounds for such euphoria from success. Having seized Kishinau on 16 July, the allied German–Romanian forces moved quite quickly from the Prut to the Dnyestr and in thirty-three days they had seized a significant amount of Soviet territory, which they called 'Transnistria', as if it had belonged to the Romanian kingdom from ancient times. Now they were preparing to purge it of Russians, Ukrainians, Jews and Gypsies (that is, to exterminate them in concentration camps), to hand over their lands and houses to the officers and soldiers of their own army, to forbid the use of the Russian and Ukrainian languages as 'demeaning the dignity of the great Romanian nation', to remove all monuments, to rename all towns and villages in accordance with their own wishes and, in particular, to call Odessa 'Antonescu'.

The Romanians were keen to enter paradise on the back of someone else's efforts. If it had not been for Hitler's Germany with its mighty industry, superb military technology, well-mobilized and battle-seasoned armed forces as well as Operation Barbarossa, there would have been no point in King Mihai's subjects dreaming of any 'Transnistria'. In 1940 the Soviet Union took back Bessarabia and northern Bukovina, which had been snatched from Russia by the Romanians during the turbulent days of the Revolution and Civil War. Back then the royal forces had retreated very rapidly before the advancing units of our 5th, 12th and 9th Armies, avoiding military clashes and abandoning their weapons stashes.

Now their triumphal road across the Black Sea steppes had aroused in the troops of this backward, semi-feudal state the illusion of victory over its fearsome northern neighbour. Probably, the royal generals had decided that the Red Army was demoralized and would not offer further resistance. This illusion cost the Romanians dearly near Odessa.

Through the eyepiece of my telescope sight I often saw their swarthy, hooked-nosed, half-Gypsy, half-Oriental features. Antonescu may have maintained that the Romanians were heirs of ancient Rome, but from the fifteenth century the Wallachian kingdom had in fact been under the rule of the Ottoman Empire. If anyone had an influence on the nation's population, it was the Turks, who had maintained garrisons in major cities almost to the 1870s, had their own trade and forced the Romanians to serve in their army. There were still many Gypsy bands roaming freely through the towns and villages of that peasant country.

Clad in uniforms of a sandy grey colour and pudding-basin helmets or cloth kepis with a comical double-peaked crown, at the beginning of August 1941 the Romanians conducted themselves in an extraordinarily confident and carefree manner, displaying contempt for the rules of war. They strode around their lines fully upright, made no attempt to maintain military security in all areas, conducted inadequate reconnaissance and deployed units from the rear (medical battalions, kitchens, tethering posts, strings of carts, workshops, etc.) close to the front line. In a word, they created excellent conditions for sharpshooters. It was not surprising that my sniper's tally grew day by day.

It goes without saying that Antonescu's order to capture Odessa on 15 August 1941 remained unfulfilled, although the 4th Army under General Nikolae Cuperke numbered over 300,000 soldiers and officers and had eighty military aircraft and sixty tanks at its disposal. There were also some detachments of the 72nd Infantry Division there. To counter them our side had thirty-five aircraft, between five and seven tanks in good working order and 50,000–60,000 troops.

4

Frontiers of Fire

Soviet military engineering units, sapper battalions and residents of the city worked supremely hard in preparation for a lengthy siege. The foremost edge of the main defence line (an 80km perimeter and 3.5km deep) ran through the villages closest to Odessa. This line included thirty-two battalion defence districts, company and platoon support points and firing positions for artillery and mortars. By 10 August they had managed to construct 256 reinforced-earth, brick and reinforced-concrete firing points, dug 1,500 earthworks for various purposes, and these were connected by a unified system by trenches and long, winding communication routes. The trenches were full size – that is, over 1.5 metres deep – and had walls reinforced with planks. There were also dugouts covered with three layers of thick logs. The flat expanses of the Black Sea steppes were crisscrossed by anti-tank ditches up to 7 metres wide and 3 metres deep. In front of the battle positions there were minefields and large areas with rows of posts strung with barbed or smooth wire. The second main line of defence was 40km away from the city, the third one 25–30km and the fourth 12–13km away.[1]

We had dreamed of fortifications like these. This dream had sustained us, both at Novo-Pavlovsk and at Novy Artsiz, as well as by the village of Starokazachye, when we were digging trenches at short notice with small sappers' spades, at night by the light of the moon or in daytime, while being shelled by long-range enemy artillery, or when we were crossing the steppe highways with no food or water, burying our fallen comrades in bomb craters, or fighting off Nazis while trying to economize on cartridges. We believed that the chaos and disorder of the first days of war, caused by the sudden and deceitful nature of the enemy's assault, would come to an end. When and where they would cease, we did not know, but we had no doubt that some strongpoint would shortly appear along our difficult route, some inaccessible fortress, which we, having endured our baptism of fire, would defend to the last drop of blood, and the audacious enemy would feel the true force of Russian arms.

A state of siege was declared in Odessa on 8 August. At the time, the military units of our 25th Chapayev Rifle Division, under the command of Colonel A.S.

Zakharenko, were located on the Belyayevka–Mangeim–Brinovka line. We repelled the onslaught of the enemy's superior forces and prevented the Romanians from breaking through to the south. A regrouping of Soviet forces then followed. The 54th Stepan Razin Regiment (commanded by Lieutenant Colonel I.I. Svidnitsky) – though not all of it – joined a combined detachment under Brigade Commander S.F. Monakhov which was assigned to the eastern defence sector, along with the 1st Regiment of the naval infantry and the 26th NKVD Regiment. The 1st Battalion remained in its previous position and was used as a strike force which was transferred from one sector of the front to another, to take care of enemy breakthroughs.

The core of the battalion consisted of our own 2nd Company, under Lieutenant Dmitry Lubivy. Having received the order 'to restore the situation near village X', we would climb into our 1,500kg trucks (though we more often went on foot), arrive at the destination and go in to attack, to drive the enemy from the positions they had recently occupied. As a rule, we normally managed to achieve this.

The company now had excellent armaments. We acquired a lot of weapons in combat: rifles of various models, machine guns (the German MP. 40, more familiar to us under the name 'Schmeisser'), Soviet TT pistols, foreign pistols such as Mausers, Berettas and Steyrs, Nagant revolvers, DP light machine guns, and a large supply of cartridges. We had learned from our bitter experience of border skirmishes and, when the weaponry was insufficient, we created our own company caches. It was onerous to drag all this from place to place, but we did not want to surrender anything to the regimental store, although we were given all sorts of team talks.

The battle-readiness of our unit was largely facilitated by the closeness of its members' ages, upbringing and education. Our ages varied from twenty to twenty-five. We were all Young Communist League members, mainly called up from the heavy industrial sector or, like me, student volunteers from Ukrainian institutes of higher education. Our sense of army fraternity had been shaped in the battles by the river Prut. We learned to trust one another and knew that, for us, the maxim of General Suvorov – 'Perish yourself, but save your comrade!' – was an unshakeable principle.

In the breaks between engagements we read letters from home together and also wrote letters together, even to our fiancés or fiancées. Everyone regarded it as his or her duty to come up with some striking or witty phrase. There were those among us who had a musical ear and a good voice, and we often sang together. The repertoire consisted of songs from the Civil War period, or from popular films: 'The Woman of Warsaw', 'The Gun Carriage' and 'Over There Across the River', as well as 'Merry Wind' from the Vainshtok film *The Children of Captain Grant*, 'Broad is my Native Land' from Alexandrov's *Circus*, 'The Blue Balloon Twists and Turns' from the Kozintsev and Trauberg film *Young Maxim*, and many others.

The songs helped us in combat. There were times during heavy crossfire, when someone would suddenly sing in your ear with a hoarse voice just one line from a favourite song, or call out as he walked past, 'Hold your line, infantry' (from the well-known verse), and instantly your heart would feel more at ease.

Before an attack you never feel particularly well. There is a sort of vacuum in your head; your mood deteriorates. It is an oppressive and unpleasant sensation. In our company we fought against this: we would relate every possible amusing tale, recall successful combat episodes and not allow people to give in to anxiety. Then the voice of Lieutenant Lubivy would ring out: 'Company, forward! For the motherland, for Stalin, hurrah!' Charging together, we would dash into battle and forget about everything else in the world. Hatred of the enemy overcame other human feelings and the Romanians fled before us like hares. That is how exceptional our 2nd Company was!

However boldly we Chapayevs fought, the harsh conditions of the battle for Odessa sometimes got the better of us. The enemy enjoyed superiority in artillery and – most important – had huge military supplies for ordnance and mortars, which the city's defenders lacked. Our gunners could only respond with one salvo to every three fired by the Germans and Romanians. Our company was once smothered by a wave of fire. It happened on the morning of 19 August. A mortar shell hit the trench parapet – not right in front of me, but about 2 metres to the left. The shock wave smashed my beloved rifle to smithereens, threw me backwards into the bottom of the trench and covered me with earth. I came to in hospital; my regimental mates had dug me out and taken me to Odessa along with other wounded and shell-shocked Red Army soldiers of the 1st Battalion.

A wonderful panorama lay before me through the window of my ward, which was on the first floor of the hospital. The branches of apple, pear and peach trees in an abandoned orchard swayed in the the wind from the sea, the yellowing leaves trembled, and the ripe fruit fell onto the ground. Little grey sparrows and black-headed starlings flew from twig to twig. They probably whistled to one another, but I couldn't hear anything. The mute spectacle of autumn asserting itself was soothing for some reason and conducive to reflection. My hearing returned slowly. The pain in my joints and spine tormented me at night.

Lying on sheets crisp with starch in the clean and tidy room and drinking the strong, sweet morning tea, which was served at eight o'clock, invariably with a bun, I recalled the hot steppe booming with explosions. Here, in the absolute silence, it seemed like a distant, strange and even frightening dream which bore no relation to reality. However, my comrades in arms were still there and my place was among them.

Soon a number of letters from those dear to me were passed on to me from the regiment. My lovely mother, Yelena Trofimovna, was concerned for my health and advised me not to drink untreated water from open waterways on the march. My father, Mikhail Ivanovich, recalled the First World War and the Civil War, maintaining that the Belovs were always lucky in battle. My elder sister Valentina described how her work was going at her new place of employment. They were all a long way away from me, in Udmurtia, where the Arsenal factory had been evacuated from Kiev. Pulling myself together, I sat down to write back to them, trying hard to shape the letters with my right hand, which was gradually recovering its former strength and precision. The writing was a bit rough, but at least it was heartfelt:

Valentina Mikhailovna Belova,
Main Post Office, Votkinsk, Poste Restante,
Udmurt Republic,
     Dear Val,
     Yesterday I made it out of the hospital into the city. I received Lena's postcard, which took a month and a half to get from Kiev to Odessa. Lena gave me your address. Why didn't you take her with you? I have already been in the army for a month and ten days. I have succeeded in being nasty to the Romanians and Germans and spent time on the front line. The swine covered me with earth . . . Now I am in hospital. I leave in two days and go back to my unit, where my special role is as a soldier-sniper. Unless I'm killed, I plan to make it to Berlin, give the Germans a thrashing, and return to Kiev. My calculation is simple – 1,000 Germans, and then I can hold my head up with pride. It could be said that I have set my targets and will not retreat any further. In a word, I'm not bored. It's a merry life. If you can be bothered, write to me care of: Chopak, Research Library, 13 Pasteur Street, Odessa. It will be forwarded to me.[2]

On the penultimate day of August 1941, I was released from hospital for the front line with a certificate testifying to my complete recovery from severe shell shock. I decided to visit my friend Sofya Chopak, who was still working at the library. On the way there I was stopped twice by patrols to check my documents. Suspicion was probably aroused by my tunic, which had been cleaned in the hospital laundry and expertly ironed, and had raspberry-coloured parade tabs sewn onto the collar instead of the regulation khaki-coloured field ones. Or maybe it was my appearance. There were, after all, very few women in military service at the time.

In the two months since the start of the war the previously carefree and beautiful city of Odessa and its fun-loving residents had undergone an abrupt change. On some streets barricades of sandbags had been erected and squares had been equipped with anti-aircraft guns. Many shops had closed, while others had their windows crisscrossed with paper tape. Holiday resort staff had disappeared. Parks, boulevards, streets and squares were deserted. Only patrols of the Home Guard with rifles walked along the cobbled roadway. Industrial enterprises, the port, transport and communication facilities and waterworks were under reinforced guard.

The city was concerned about saboteurs – and not without reason. The Nazis had begun to bomb Odessa regularly. Several times somebody had sent them signals from the attics of multi-storey buildings and directed the bombers to their targets. The port especially suffered damage in this way.

In one incident a small aircraft with no identification marks unexpectedly landed at Odessa's civil aerodrome. Our anti-aircraft defences had, as they say, let it slip through. Seventeen Germans with submachine guns leapt out and opened fire. They tried to seize the airport to pave the way for another landing with a large number of troops. The soldiers of the Ilyichchev Destruction Battalion came to their senses fairly quickly. The enemy were surrounded and annihilated. The aeroplane was seized. The Fritzes never succeeded with any further landings.

Sofya talked about this and much else when we met in the rare books and manuscripts storeroom of the research library. The place was really humming. The staff were filling large wooden crates with folios, leather folders containing ancient manuscripts and various valuable curiosities, numbering them and compiling descriptions. After the announcement of a state of siege in the city many cultural institutions, including the research library, began to prepare for evacuation to the Caucasus. Sofya Chopak had still not decided whether she would go too. This meeting of ours might even be our last.

I spent the rest of the day pleasantly in the friendly and hospitable Chopak household, enjoying a modest supper in their apartment in Greek Street. From 25 August the executive committee of the Odessa regional council had made the sale of fresh bread, sugar, grain and fats subject to ration cards. However, the famous market on Privoz Square continued to operate. For now it still sold everything you could want, but the prices had doubled or trebled. It turned out to be a quiet evening.

On 29 August the gunners of the destroyer flotilla leader *Tashkent* had smashed a Romanian battery that had been firing from the Bolshoi Ajalyk estuary. For three days it had targeted the city, the port and its main navigation channel, preventing the ships of the Black Sea Fleet from unloading new drafted battalions, weapons, ammunition, foodstuffs and equipment for the besieged Soviet forces. As well as that, the coastal army repelled yet another Romanian assault, although the Nazis did manage to get closer to Odessa – to the town of Fontanka in the eastern defence sector and the towns of Freidental and Krasny Pereselyenyets in the western sector.

In the early morning I got a lift out of the city on a truck headed for the Kuyalnik and Bolshoi Ajalyk estuaries. The command post of the 1st Battalion was located near a small village. I reported to Captain Sergienko that I had arrived back at my unit to resume service. I concluded my report with the words 'Red Army Private Pavlichenko'. The captain smiled.

'You've made an error, Lyudmila.'

'What error, Comrade Captain?'

'You're not a private now, but a corporal. Congratulations.'

'I serve the Soviet Union!'

I wanted to shout at the top of my voice with joy, 'Hurrah!' But the done thing was to act soberly and with restraint. Still, it was my first army promotion. Having joined the Red Army as a volunteer, I had thought about a military career, but not expected that my enthusiasm and success as a sniper would be appreciated by the leadership within just a month and a half. However, the big losses in our forces were conducive to rapid promotion up the service ladder – for those who remained alive, that is.

The conversation at the command post continued and I learned that while I had been in hospital there had been changes in our 2nd Company. First, the commander of my platoon, Lieutenant Vasily Kovtun, had lost his life and, along with him, about another thirty men. It had happened during the bloody battles on 24, 25 and 26 August near the Kuyalnik estuary. Secondly, the regiment had recently been replenished – with volunteer sailors from Sevastopol. They were desperate to fight the enemy, but had no experience of infantry service. Other volunteers had also joined us – around 100 Odessa residents.

'I'm glad you're back in the regiment,' said Ivan Sergienko. 'I was really hoping it would happen and I've even got some presents for you. The main one is a new Mosin sniper rifle instead of that old broken one.'

'Thank you, Comrade Captain.'

'The second gift is simpler. But I imagine you'll like it too.' The battalion commander handed me a small grey cardboard box like those in which military goods are packed.

I opened it. In it lay two brass triangles, the insignia of my new military rank. They needed to be attached to the empty raspberry-coloured tabs in the top corners of my collar. Where could he have found such tiny metal things out in the steppe which had been peppered by firearms and dug into trenches? The commander had shown concern for me and this warmed my heart. Captain Sergienko was concerned not only about me, but about all the troops of the 1st Battalion. He was a very experienced, proactive and strict officer and a fair-minded man. When Lieutenant Colonel Svidnitsky was wounded and left our 54th Regiment, we all expected that the duties of commander along with the rank of major (which was due to him in terms of service) would go to Sergienko. But the high command decided otherwise and appointed Major N.M. Matusyevich, who had a good few years on the clock and had taken part in the Civil War as a rank-and-file soldier in the 1st Cavalry Army.

At the battalion command post I attached the triangles to my tabs and set off for the firing lines of the 2nd Company as a uniformed corporal. Sergienko saw me off with some parting words to the effect that I should look out for people among the new recruits who were capable of being trained in the sniper's art. Sadly, in the trenches only a few troops from the old contingent called out to me by name. The others observed me with curiosity. The seamen, who had been sailing the watery expanses until now, did not even want to change into khaki uniform or to take off their peakless naval caps, their dark-blue flannel jackets, blue-and-white vests and wide black bell-bottomed trousers. While they were experts on ships, they had never held a rifle in their hands and the word 'sniper' meant nothing to them. Turning mariners into super-sharpshooters in a short period of time was not, to be honest, an easy prospect. We began by persuading them to wear helmets, tunics and boots instead of shoes.

Meanwhile, the high command of the Odessa defence district had set some specific targets for snipers: to occupy the most advantageous positions for observation and firing, to give the enemy no peace, to deprive him of the opportunity to move freely in the lines closest to the front, and to demoralize him. There was nothing new or original in this, but the theatre of military activity itself – flat steppe with the occasional hill, almost treeless, with sparse population centres – presented few opportunities for setting up snipers' hideouts, while camouflage could not have been more difficult.

We had to look for other methods to combat the invader. We decided to set up hideouts further from our front line, to move them forward into no man's land, which was 400–600 metres away and closest to the enemy. We did this after thorough reconnaissance, which we carried out ourselves, closely studying the locality, determining its suitability for targeted shooting and working out how to leave the hideout afterwards and return to our own unit.

I will describe our first such sortie as an example. Everything had been reconnoitred, and at night three of us set off on the mission: one soldier with a Degtyarev infantry pattern light machine gun (DP), a sniper-terminator (that is me) and a sniper-observer (Pyotr Kolokoltsev). We had gas-mask bags filled with cartridges, and grenades hung from our belts. Apart from a rifle, each of us had a TT ('Tula-Tokarev') pistol – my handgun of choice, on account of its powerful cartridge. On setting up the hideout, we realized that not every shot might be the final one for the enemy. The accuracy of our fire would depend on many circumstances which were at times beyond our control.

As a hideout site we chose a thicket of quite tall, dense shrubs. It was in the shape of a diamond with a length of about 150 metres and 12–15 metres wide. One point of the diamond projected into the Romanian defensive line and ended in a shallow gully in the area of the enemy's second echelon. The hideout lay about 600 metres from the 54th Regiment's first line of trenches. It was quite a long distance, of course, but we had arranged with the machine-gunners that they would keep us under observation and, at a signal from us (the raising of a small sapper's spade), they would cover our retreat.

On exiting the dugout after midnight, we took an hour to cover the distance to the hideout. The moon in the cloudless sky illuminated the surroundings, and all the pathways, uneven patches and shell holes showed up clearly. The quiet, warm, gentle Black Sea night embraced the countryside around us. Neither side engaged in the usual unsettling rifle and machine-gun fire. All around it was so nice, so peaceful! Only the likelihood of a meeting with the enemy right in the shrub thicket spoiled our mood. We had to keep a watch as we strode along and had our weapons at the ready. There turned out to be no Romanians in the thicket. Why they had not occupied it and at least stationed an observation post there we could not understand. I attribute this fact to their Gypsy fecklessness. The punctual and calculating Germans had tried and tried to teach their allies about modern warfare, but they had not succeeded.

We devoted the rest of the night to preparing our positions. We dug trenches with small parapets, reinforced them with stones and turf, placed our rifles on them, got everything to fit, and worked out the distances. The machine-gunner set his weapon up.

It grew light. At five o'clock in the morning there was some movement in the enemy lines. The soldiers walked around fully upright, talked loudly and called out to one another. At six o'clock a field kitchen arrived. Things became livelier. Officers appeared and gave loud orders. At some distance away stood what was probably a medical station; the gleaming white smocks of the medics were clearly discernible to us.

All in all, there were a lot of targets. We divided our forces: the left flank would be mine, and Pyotr Kolokoltsev would take the right side. The machine-gunner kept the centre under observation. We waited till ten o'clock in the morning, studying how the enemy behaved when they were some distance away from the front line, and then we opened fire.

The Romanians got a real fright. For several minutes they could not work out where the shots were coming from and rushed around, intensifying the panic with their wild wailing. But we had measured the range and our sights were adjusted. Almost every bullet found its target. In approximately twenty minutes Kolokoltsev and I took seventeen shots each. The result: sixteen kills to me and Pyotr had twelve. The machine-gunner, who was supposed to cover us in the event of direct enemy attack on our hideout, did not fire because there was no need.

Pulling themselves together, the Romanians opened mortar and machine-gun fire on the thicket. However, they could not see us and therefore their shooting was off the mark. We had to get away. We made it back to our own lines safe and sound, wrote a report for the regimental commander and received an official message of gratitude for our bold action.

We thought about it and decided to go again at night to the same place and lie in wait. We proceeded calmly, without getting nervous, but on arrival at the thicket we became very alarmed. On the first day we had taken water with us in bottles but not brought the bottles back with us on our return. Instead of the three bottles of water we had left behind, we discovered six bottles, and all of them had held sweet wine. The bottles forced us to consider seriously: 'Shouldn't we get out of here altogether?' We also found two cartridges and a narrow furrow on the grass from a Schwarzlose machine gun. The trail led in the direction of the enemy. It was clear: the Romanian sentries had been here during the day. They had finally worked out that the thicket was a very vulnerable spot on their front line, but they had left for the night for some reason. They probably did not expect a repeat attack from the same position. We surveyed our sector again, convinced ourselves that everything was in order, and decided . . . to stay.

We opened fire at noon. It was a repeat of the previous day's scene: I had ten kills, including two officers, while Pyotr Kolokoltsev got eight. This time the Romanians quickly recovered their composure and began to fire back at the thicket with two machine guns. The rounds came closer and closer to our trenches. We ceased fire, withdrew, moved inconspicuously to one side and approached the machine-gunners from the flank. From a distance of 100 metres we took five shots with our sniper rifles and wiped out the squad. Pyotr liked the enemy machine guns; they were quite new and all the components shone. In brief, we took one machine gun away with us and buried the breechblock of the other. The regimental scouts later found it from our directions and took it as their own trophy, along with the machine gun. There were ample boxes of cartridges lying around, and the Austrian machine guns went on to serve the Red Army.

It would have been irrational to use this spot as a sniper hideout for a third time. Therefore, we found another one: a white house which was half destroyed and had been abandoned by its residents. It stood in the same neutral zone, about 400 metres from the thicket. Having occupied it, we observed the following scenario from the attic the next day: at 7.30 in the morning the Romanians unleashed a furious mortar attack on the thicket and thrashed it for about thirty minutes without a break. It is no bad thing when the enemy wastes ammunition to no purpose.

For the twenty-six Romanians who would remain forever in the Odessa steppe (while my overall total was approaching sixty-five) I did not feel that I was due any reward. In the first months of the war we did not expect any decorations and thought more about defending our native land against the frenzied invaders. Later, in 1943, after the establishment of the soldier's Order of Glory, it was awarded, third or second class, to those sharpshooters who had wiped out ten or fifty to seventy enemy soldiers and officers. For example, fourteen young women who were graduates of the central women's school for sniper training were given similar double decorations, first and second class. Only Sergeant Major Nina Pavlovna Petrova, though not a graduate of the central women's sniping school, received the Order of Glory in all three classes: third, second and first (the last awarded posthumously). Her tally came to over 120 Nazis.

Within the 54th Stepan Razin Rifle Regiment the most celebrated heroine at the siege of Odessa was not me, but machine-gunner Nina Onilova. An orphan who was brought up in a children's home and worked in an Odessa factory, Nina came to us as a twenty-year-old in the second half of August 1941, along with other volunteering residents of the city – initially as an orderly in a medical company. Soon she requested a transfer to a field unit because she had studied machine-gunning within the Osoaviakhim educational organization. She was registered with our battalion and served in the 1st Company. So it goes without saying that we knew each other.

Not having witnessed her feats myself, I would like to turn to the recollections of those Odessa veterans who saw Nina both on the field of battle and away from it.

'They first began talking about her after the battle by the village of Gildendorf,' writes Vice-Admiral Azarov.

At a critical moment Nina and her number two in the detail, Private Zabrodin, wheeled their machine gun out into an open space and struck at the attacking enemy. Their firing was on the mark. The Fascists went to ground and those who remained alive hastily crawled away to their own side. The attack was repelled.[3]

'When I returned to base, the head of the political section, Senior Battalion Commissar N.A. Berdovsky called in,' recalls Lieutenant-General Trofim Kolomiyets.

With him was a girl of short stature in a Red Army uniform. Catching my inquisitive eye, Berdovsky introduced her: 'Machine-gunner Nina Onilova of the Razin Regiment. During the defence of Odessa she was wounded and evacuated to a hospital in the rear. Now, she says, she's fit and well . . .' So that is what she was like, this Nina Onilova, who was nick-named Chapayev's 'second Anya'[4] and had shot hundreds of Fascists. To look at – just a young girl with a round sun-tanned face, laughing eyes and charming, with a slightly embarrassed smile . . . In the coastal army, there was probably not a single soldier who had not heard of her.[5]

The Young Communist League organizer in our regiment, Yakov Vaskovsky, described the actions of the gallant Nina in greater detail in his own memoirs:

A further enemy attack caught me at the command post of the 1st Battalion. Battalion commander Ivan Sergienko, who was observing the field of battle through a crack in the wall, suddenly shouted menacingly into the telephone receiver: 'Why is the machine gun on the left flank not firing? Check it immediately. Fire it yourselves if necessary!' This was addressed to the company commander, Lieutenant Ivan Grintsov. He ran along a trench on the left flank. The situation was truly dangerous. Apparently noticing that the fire there was not as strong, the attacking Fascists had begun to move towards that side. The machine-gun detail was new, having only just joined the battalion, and the company commander had not had time to get to know the personnel before the battle.

Running up to the machine-gunners, Grintsov saw that the first one was bent over and not moving, while the second was standing around at the back, as if nothing was the matter. 'Still too far away. Let them come a bit closer . . .' said the first machine-gunner in a completely calm tone, without turning around. But there were only some 70 metres to the enemy ranks.

Grintsov could not restrain himself and shouted: 'What are you doing? They'll pepper you with grenades any minute!' He was ready to push the gunner out of the way in order to open fire himself. But at that moment the machine gun started up. The enemy troops were gathered on a narrow sector. The first round mowed down almost half of them. They were so close that they had nowhere to hide The last ones fell about 30 metres from the machine gun. There was a shout of 'Hurrah!' from our trenches. Nobody in the company, it seems, had seen machine-gun fire like that.

'Well done!' Grintsov exclaimed. 'Just look how many Fascists are lying there! A medal's not good enough for you!' The gunner finally turned to the company commander, who beheld before him a young woman, sun-tanned, with a cheerful round face and hair cut short like a boy . . . Soon the entire regiment knew about machine-gunner Onilova, 'Chapayev's Anya number two', and then so did the entire 5th Rifle Division . . .[6]

Nina Onilova received the Order of the Red Banner – quite soon, too, in December 1941, on the front at Sevastopol. According to data from the defence of Odessa, on that occasion some ten soldiers from our glorious and courageous regiment, which had sacrificed itself for the city and borne significant losses in battles with the Fascists, were awarded decorations.

To be honest, not all of us were ecstatic about Nina's tactical innovation. Captain Sergienko was particularly nervous. Onilova occupied a single machine-gun nest, but he was responsible for the entire battalion's front line. Summoning the gunner, the battalion commander praised her for her boldness, but warned her that firing from such short distances during frontal attacks by the enemy was a very big risk. Moreover, a separate group could burst in from the flank and pepper her with grenades. The Maxim fixed machine guns in the regiment were quite old, of pre-revolutionary vintage; their mechanism frequently failed when under a heavy load, and, if that happened, nothing would save Nina and the other troops with her. She was not starring in the film *Chapayev*, in which the Whites never made it to the Red lines. This was real war and situations on the battlefield could develop in different ways.

As a result, Onilova was not often permitted to employ her innovative method and was forced to observe service instructions to the letter. However, it no longer mattered. The widely distributed newspaper of the 25th Division, *The Red Army Soldier*, and then other military publications, printed enthralling tales about the deeds of this courageous girl, and political staff concerned with propaganda within the army made great capital out of the image of this remarkable machine-gunner who was inspired to great feats by the romantic heroes of the Civil War.

But nobody saw anything romantic in the sniper's art at that time. In the first place, the word 'sniper' was alien and incomprehensible. Secondly, the operations of a machine-gunner and a machine gun were full of action and looked much more interesting than firing from a hideout. A round of fire crackled and a swathe of the enemy instantly dropped to the ground. The way a sharpshooter could take out an officer in an advancing line, thereby choking the attack, could not be so picturesquely presented. Thirdly, there were the snipers themselves. What sort of people were they? Taciturn, unsociable, even morose. They were incapable of describing in detail precisely how they hunted the enemy (not that they were allowed to do this, incidentally, having signed the official secrets clause).

At the beginning of September 1941 (3 to 5 September, I believe) we found out that, while remaining in the eastern sector of the Odessa defensive district, our regiment would be temporarily joining a newly formed rifle division, initially known as the 1st Odessan and then given the number 421. Our old acquaintances ended up with us: the 1st Regiment of the naval infantry under the command of Colonel Y.I. Osipov, now the 1330th, and the 26th Regiment of the NKVD, now the 1331st and strengthened by troops from the former fortified district No. 82 as well as an artillery regiment, a sapper battalion, a machine-gun battalion and some other units. The position of divisional commander was occupied by G.M. Kochenov. Staff headquarters were in the Kuyalnik hospital and its advance command post was located in the village of Ternovka. The division was faced with the task of maintaining a front 17km in length and resisting two fully manned Romanian infantry divisions. We beat back their attacks all day on 6 September and on the 7th we went on the offensive ourselves. The Romanians retreated between 0.5 and 2km to the north on the various sectors of the front, leaving on the field approximately 700 dead and seriously wounded troops and officers. About 200 of them ended up as our prisoners, and ordnance, mortars, machine and submachine guns and a lot of ammunition were seized.

The following day, 8 September, the Romanians fell upon the 3rd Battalion of our regiment, which was taking up positions on the isthmus between the Khajibeisk and Kuyalnik estuaries. We hurried to the aid of our regimental mates and, with our combined forces, drove back the enemy attack. Fierce fighting with strong artillery shelling continued on 9, 10 and 11 September. It was then that the former border guards, the courageous and disciplined troops who had now become the 1331st Rifle Regiment, broke through ahead. They established themselves firmly on the line between Bolgarka village, Avgustovka village and the northern bounds of the village of Protopopovka.

In clashes like this, when huge masses of forces were fighting on a flat plain, what was the sniper to do? The answer was simple – to occupy previously set up fortifications (there were some in this area) with other troops and to carry out targeted fire from their trenches. All the more so since the enemy were advancing regardless of any losses.

At this point I witnessed a scene that was almost fanciful in the context of the Second World War. The Romanians had mounted a 'psychological' attack. First, as was usually the case, the artillery boomed away for about twenty minutes. The Soviet soldiers and officers waited it out in well-equipped deep dugouts and trenches. No great damage was inflicted on the 54th Regiment. Then silence descended. The troops returned to their positions and began to look into the distance. There, something unusual was happening.

The sounds of stirring music reached our ears. We saw that the infantry in their pudding-basin helmets were not spreading out across the steppe, but, on the contrary, sticking together in close, dense columns, standing shoulder to shoulder and marching as if on parade, raising their feet high to the rhythmic beat of the drums. Somewhere in the second or third column a banner was billowing over the soldiers' heads. Keeping their distance and shouldering their unsheathed sabres, the officers were striding along in the gaps between the columns. On the left flank was a priest in full parade garb. His gold-embroidered gown, glinting in the rays of the bright autumn sun, looked strange against the background of the monolithic military formation. Three church banners followed him, carried by Romanian soldiers. The priest, it subsequently turned out, was Ukrainian.

It was not without some amazement that I viewed the attacking force through binoculars. They were approaching closer and closer. Soon it became evident that the soldiers were drunk. They were not maintaining their formation so strictly and their marching was not all that precise. But would it be possible to force sober men to walk out onto an absolutely flat, easily targeted plain, even if they were convinced of their racial superiority over those they intended to exterminate? They had probably been endowed with confidence in victory by one other circumstance: their large numerical superiority. Marching against our 1st Battalion, in which no more than 400 were left, to the sound of loud music from a military band, was an infantry regiment of peacetime proportions – 2,000 bayonets.

Inexorably, the distance was growing shorter. The Romanians approached to within 700 metres and our mortar battery launched a first strike against them. Fountains of earth soared up to the sky amidst the sandy grey columns. Their formation broke down for a while. But, leaving their dead behind them, those still alive closed ranks and continued the advance. At the officers' command, they upped their pace and took their rifles in their hands. The blades of the bayonets gleamed like lightning against the dusty expanses of the steppe.

I waited patiently until the first enemy column drew level with a fence at the edge of a maize field. I drew a preliminary firing diagram and marked out the distances along it. The fence was 600 metres away from my trench, some wolfberry thickets were 500 metres, and a lone tree with a broken crown was 400 metres away. The soldiers of King Mihai I were now unknowingly moving into the field of direct fire.

A direct sniper's shot is an entirely amazing thing! For this shot, the trajectory of the bullet did not rise above the target for the entire distance of the shot. For instance, as in the given situation, by using a setting of 6 and aiming at the heels of the marching enemy soldiers, it was possible to fire several shots without resetting the telescope sight. The enemy would be hit first in the leg, then, on coming closer, in the stomach, and, closer still, at 300 metres, in the chest, and finally in the head. Then, as they approached still closer to the sniper, the order would be reversed – chest, stomach, leg.

I had developed a favourite method of shooting by then: hitting the enemy between the eyes or in the temple. But as I looked at the infantry armada marching to the beat of the drum, I thought that this time a shot to the head alone would be an impermissible luxury. The main thing now was to fire and fire and fire, just to stop the psychological attack of drunk soldiers, who had no idea what they were doing, to prevent the Romanians from reaching our trenches. After all, with their five-fold numerical advantage, they would simply trample our valiant battalion into the ground and wipe out all my comrades in arms.

They didn't make it . . .

The sun was setting, illuminating the muted feather grass of the steppe with weak, slanting rays. Moving back, the Romanians carried away their wounded, but the dead (up to 300 of them, it seemed) remained behind. Stepping over the bodies of the fallen enemy with Lieutenant Voronin, who had replaced our now wounded former company commander, Lieutenant Lubivy, I sought out 'my own' kills and put them down in my sniper's notebook. As well as me, our machine-gunners and other riflemen of the second company had also fired with great success. Everyone had the same rifle cartridges, calibre 7.62mm. I regarded as my own those who had bullet holes in their head, neck or the left side of their chest. There were nineteen of them, including seven officers and one non-commissioned officer.

'Were you specifically aiming at the officers?' asked the lieutenant.

'Yes. That's what the instructions prescribe.'

'An excellent result, Lyudmila.'

'I serve the Soviet Union.'

'They decided on a psychological attack,' said Voronin pensively. 'Did they not feel anything for their men?'

'They simply regard us as weaklings.'

'Two attacks in an hour. And now they've rolled back a kilometre. Neither sight nor sound of them.'

'It's the volatile Romanian nature,' I joked. 'Attack in a bunch with a lot of noise and clamour and, if victory doesn't come, run away as fast as your legs will carry you.'

Lieutenant Andrei Alexandrovich Voronin had graduated from the Kirov Leningrad Red Banner Infantry College in 1939, served before the war in the Volga military district and had recently ended up in Odessa with the drafted reinforcements, but he had no front-line experience. He was very interested in sniper operations and asked about various details. It was the lieutenant's intention to reward me for accurate shooting with an out-of-turn promotion in military rank, and he did this. I became a junior sergeant and was full of respect for the young officer. He came from a dyed-in-the-wool Leningrad family. His father, a history scholar, worked at the Hermitage and wanted his son to follow him, but Andrei had dreamed of a military career from childhood. Nevertheless, he had a good knowledge of history and we sometimes talked about the deeds of our bellicose forebears.

I strove to live up to the new order from the company commander as well as I could. He sent me on a mission to wipe out the enemy machine gun which was directing truly accurate and lethal fire from the direction of Gildendorf village,[7] making it impossible for our troops to raise their heads.

During the last ten days of September the Soviet high command was preparing to inflict a blow on the enemy in the eastern sector, using the forces of the 421st and 157th Rifle Divisions. The latter arrived in Odessa from Novosibirsk on 17 September, a force of over 12,000 troops and artillery consisting of twenty-four 76mm-calibre field guns, thirty-six 152mm-calibre howitzers plus a triple supply of ammunition.[8] This was of huge assistance, because the regiments of the 421st

Division had almost no cannons (three ordnance for a kilometre-long front line versus eighteen on the Romanian side). According to the plan, the advance was to be supported by our air force, the 37th and 38th Coastal Batteries, and also the ships of the Black Sea Fleet with their cannons. The villages of Gildendorf, Bolgarka, Alexandrovka and the Voroshilov collective farm lay in the sector of the main thrust. It was up to our two battalions of the 54th Regiment, along with the five battalions of the 157th Rifle Division, to take Gildendorf by storm.

The troops of our regiment had earlier driven the enemy out of the cemetery situated about 200 metres from the southern tip of the village. There were trees growing in the cemetery: five tall maples with spreading crowns and thick ash-grey trunks which had managed somehow to survive the bombing raids and artillery attacks. The difficulties involved in camouflage on the steppe receded here. From the book *Combat in Finland* I knew that in the Karelian forests the Finnish snipers, the so-called 'cuckoos', engaged in targeted shooting at our forces while hidden in the branches of the trees – pines, firs and spruces. Why couldn't I make use of this experience?

The lieutenant approved my plan. All evening I embroidered my new camouflage jacket with its green hood and brown pattern. The sergeant major had given me some shreds of camouflage netting and somebody's old tunic, which I cut up into ribbons and short strips. Shaggy ribbon came in handy for covering the rifle barrel. I distributed the rest of it, along with maple leaves, twigs and clumps of grass, so that it lost its former clear outline and began to resemble the garb of a wood sprite or a marsh devil.

One and a half hours before first light I set off for the cemetery. The residents of the village of Gildendorf, settlers from Germany, were not altogether poor people. With German thoroughness they had established not only the village but also – not far away from it – the churchyard with its straight paths and graves with stone monuments and fretted grilles. Trees shaded the eternal resting place of Gildendorf's first burgomaster, the worthy Wilhelm Schmidt, who had died in 1899 according to the inscription on the marble monument. Planting my legs on the black slab, I began to clamber up the trunk of a mighty maple which leaned over the tomb.

My equipment comprised only the most essential things: a Mosin sniper rifle with PE sight, a belt with two ammunition pouches full of cartridges with 'L'-type light bullets and black-tipped 'B-30' armour-piercing bullets (because I was intending not just to shoot the machine-gunners but to put their fiendish machine out of commission), a flask in a cloth cover, and a Finnish-type army knife. I did not take binoculars, nor a steel helmet, because my hearing had deteriorated following the shell shock and the helmet made it difficult for me to detect faint sounds.

Just before sunrise a gust of wind blew. The maple leaves began to rustle, but the thick branches spreading out from the tree's massive trunk did not even sway.

Setting my feet on them, I set up my rifle conveniently on another branch at roughly the same level as my shoulders and looked through the eyepiece of the telescope sight at the village. Its one street, lined with single-storey stone houses, a mill, a church and a school, now lay plainly visible before me. In an orchard surrounding a large dilapidated house I saw an MG. 34 all-purpose German machine gun on a tripod and boxes of cartridge belts next to it. The machine gun had telescope sights. So that was the secret of its devastating impact! Well, you noxious Fascist dogs, I'll teach you . . .

At seven o'clock in the morning the guard changed. However, the soldiers with rifles did not interest me. I was waiting for the machine-gunners. They appeared later – three Romanians in sandy grey jackets and kepis with their funny crowns stretched to form a double peak, front and back. First they busied themselves with the machine gun, then they sat under the trees and began to treat themselves to the large, golden-yellow pears, masses of which were lying around under the trees in the orchard.

I planned to take three shots, no more. And one of them would be at the breech of the machine gun. Inserting a cartridge with a light bullet into the barrel bore, I closed the bolt and pressed my face close to the telescope sight. The target, the head of the tall soldier sitting near the MG. 34 tripod, was situated between the two black lines and only seconds remained before the shot was taken. But suddenly there was some sort of commotion in the orchard. The machine-gunners leapt up, lined up, and froze at 'attention'. A minute later some officers in peaked caps came up to them. One of them looked most interesting: a cigar in his mouth, a gold strip along the edge of his cap, a braided loop hanging from his right shoulder, a brown leather satchel at his side and a long whip in his hand. All in all, he had a haughty and authoritative air.

I knew the distance: about 200 metres. The wind had died down. The air temperature was approaching 25 degrees. I took as my target not the soldier, but the man with the braided loop, held my breath, counted out to myself, 'Twenty-two – twenty-two,' and smoothly pressed the trigger.

The Romanians heard the shot. How could one not have heard it in the heavy morning silence? Still, it probably did not immediately cross their minds that a sniper was operating. The adjutant (for the braided loops are part of their uniform) did not even cry out as he keeled over. They began to fuss around him – quite pointlessly, as the bullet had hit him between the eyes. I managed to reload the rifle twice and both machine-gunners also ended up on the ground. The armour-piercing bullet from the fourth shot struck the breech of the MG. 34 and put it out of commission.

The enemy had recovered their senses by now and were pounding the cemetery with mortars and rifle fire. Bullets and mortar splinters whistled around me. I clung to the thick trunk of the maple, but soon realized that it offered poor protection. A clump of five trees was not the equivalent of an age-old Karelian forest in which it was difficult to pick out anything among the shapes of the giant pines. Pieces of hot metal were flying like a lethal swarm, knocking down leaves and breaking the thin twigs. My heart grew cold from a fearful feeling of danger, but there was no confusion. It is the new recruit who believes, 'This cannot happen to me.' A soldier who has been under fire thinks instead, 'This could happen to me, so I need to be more careful.' Anyone who has witnessed the death of his or her comrades a number of times is aware, 'This ought to happen to me. But it will not happen if only I can get out of here.'

I had to jump straight away – even just to the ground, about 3 metres below. So as not to break the expensive optics, I hung the rifle on a branch which was sticking out much lower down and then I plunged down, almost as if I had been hit. I fell awkwardly, striking a gravestone with my right hip, and could not get up because of the severe pain. Voronin sent in some soldiers, and they helped me to get back on my feet and took me to a dugout.

The advance began at nine o'clock of the morning on 21 September 1941, preceded by a lengthy artillery barrage. It seemed as if the earth was shaking from the salvoes of Soviet ordnance and mortars. My regimental mates were preparing for an attack on Gildendorf and I was lying in a dugout, suffering the pain in my right hip and reflecting on the fact that what was written in *Combat in Finland* was of course true, but nevertheless, in applying other people's experience, you need to use your own head and analyse local conditions. The raid on the cemetery and the sharpshooting from the tree now struck me as downright hazardous. But, as the proverb says, all's well that ends well!

Sometime towards eleven o'clock the enemy were driven out of Gildendorf and even out of the Ilyichevka state farm. In a disorderly fashion the Romanians were withdrawing their forces to the north, abandoning dead and wounded, arms and ammunition on the battlefield. Our troops began to survey the newly seized positions and found in the village orchard a shattered German machine gun and, next to it, two soldiers and an officer with bullets through their heads. This was my contribution to the overall victory, and Lieutenant Voronin acknowledged that I had done much to assist the 2nd Company.

He ordered medical orderly Yelena Paliy, a student in her second year at the Odessa medical institute, who had joined the Red Army as a volunteer in August, to handle my treatment, which the disciplined Lena carried out with great diligence: she gave me tablets for pain relief, placed cold compresses on my liver and put me on a special diet of buckwheat porridge boiled without fats. But what helped me more than the porridge were the care and attention which my regimental mates lavished upon me as a reward for taking out that enemy machine gun. They brought me treats: juicy golden pears from the orchard, toilet soap and flacons of eau de cologne from a cart captured from the Romanians.

The company commander also visited me. He told me that the haughty man with the braided loops whom I had shot had turned out to be the adjutant of the dictator Antonescu himself, Major Gheorghiu Karaga. Important staff papers, letters, photographs and a diary were found on his body. The major had written of the grave state of the Romanian army, which had met fierce Russian resistance near Odessa. The diary was transferred to the staff headquarters of the coastal army, and from there to Moscow. Fragments of it were published by the newspaper *Pravda* in October 1941.

A memento of the episode with the five maples in the cemetery at Gildendorf remained with me in the form of a silver cigarette case with beautiful chasing and engraving on the lid, which carried a picture of a beautiful woman in a luxurious hat with ribbons and feathers. It had been found on the dead Romanian major and Andrei Voronin gave it to me as a trophy when he visited me. I pressed on the button, the cigar case opened, and we beheld the long thin brown cigarettes packed densely inside. I offered them to the lieutenant. He declined, saying. 'I don't smoke. Have you been smoking long, Lyudmila?'

'No. I learned at the front. Sometimes it helps to relieve the nervous tension.'

'Does that happen often?' asked the company commander.

'Usually after an operation, when the enemy has been annihilated. When waiting in a hideout I don't feel any emotions. I simply wait and think about making sure the rifle doesn't miss.'

'You think about your weapon?' asked the lieutenant in surprise.

'Of course. For a sniper her weapon is almost sacred.'

Our conversation was interrupted by the appearance of Lena Paliy. She brought in three mugs of hot tea, generously sweetened with honey (a gift from local residents to the valiant troops of the Red Army), and we indulged in memories of life before the war. Andrei proved an interesting conversationalist and gave us a vivid account of the Hermitage. He loved this museum and knew its collections, especially the collection of Scythian gold, which his father devoted himself to studying. I, in turn, described how, following my first year at university, I had gone on archaeological practical work at excavations near the town of Chernigov. There I had seen a spherical-conical iron helmet from the tenth century, numerous arrow- and spear-heads and fragments of chainmail uncovered.

I regret that I am unable to draw a more detailed portrait of the commander of the 2nd Company, Andrei Voronin. Our acquaintance did not continue long. He was a colourful representative of that generation of young people who grew up in the post-revolutionary years, studied at Soviet institutes of higher learning and then went through the crucible of the Great War for the Fatherland. True patriots, they were noble, bold and staunch people who unthinkingly gave their lives for its freedom and independence. Andrei acted in the same way. He held the position of company commander for barely more than a month. He lost his life in the battles around the village of Tatarka while rousing his troops for a counter-attack. An enemy bullet pierced his heart and we buried him in the village cemetery under a red star made of plywood.

After the victory gained on 21 and 22 September over units of the Romanian 4th Army in the sector of the Odessa defence district, the Soviet high command planned to inflict an equally powerful blow on the enemy in the western and southern sectors. We received the order to transfer our base to the Dalnik village–Tatarka–Bogarskie Khutora line, and, in this way, we were finally reunited with two other battalions of the 54th Rifle Regiment, taking our place in reserves of the 25th Chapayev Division. Our path lay through Odessa and we rejoiced at the prospect of seeing the splendid Black Sea city which we were defending.

The overall picture was no cause for joy. First we went through Peresyp. There, only the electricity station was operating and the factories stood with their workshops smashed and their chimneys fallen. The town itself had suffered severely from bombing raids and artillery attacks. We walked along the roadway; the footpaths were occupied by women and children. They held in their hands kettles, jugs and buckets and gave us water to drink, treated us to cigarettes (I recall the brands, Kiev and Litka), and they called to us with welcoming, tender and encouraging words. Only later did we realize that they had shared with us their meagre water ration, which was a total of one bucket of water per person per day.

At the new base we were given a week to relax and I was called over by Captain Sergienko. He said that he had sorted through the reports of the company commanders and checked the documents, and it turned out that my sniper's tally was over 100 dead Fascists. I confirmed this information. The battalion commander teased me a little for my excessive modesty, suggesting that it was up to me to remind him of such an achievement. I thought to myself, 'And what would that have proved? Dozens of times reckless heroes have before my very eyes thrown themselves with grenades at Romanian tanks, fired away down to their last cartridge in the trenches and beaten back the swarming enemy with bayonets and rifle butts in hand-to-hand combat. When has anyone from the high command voiced appreciation of their feats? But they are not bitter in the slightest, for it is not for medals and decorations that we are standing here on the bare steppe under hellish fire.' Sergienko had perhaps somehow guessed my train of thought. He smiled, said that he would soon put everything right, and I would have a trip to the divisional staff headquarters in the village of Dalnik. I did not particularly believe him and answered, 'Yes, Comrade Captain!' and forgot about our conversation.

I had to go, all the same. At that time, I knew nothing about the new commander of our division, Major-General Ivan Yefimovich Petrov; I had no particular regrets about that. Between a divisional commander and the commander of a detachment in an infantry regiment, which was what I had become thanks to Lieutenant Voronin, there was an enormous gulf. Would generals be bothered with junior sergeants?

Petrov's adjutant invited me to enter. Inside the room I saw before me a man of about forty-five, taller than average height, lean, red tinges in his hair, with a brush of coarse hair on his upper lip and a face that was commanding, intelligent and decisive. He wore pince-nez and his tunic was decked with cavalry shoulder straps, because he had until recently been in command of the 1st Cavalry Division, which was then fighting near Odessa. From first glance he appeared to me to be a natural-born military man, an officer from a family of officers. Only later did I discover that he had the most proletarian roots. His father was a cobbler in the town of Trubchevsk but had managed to give his son an education. First he graduated from grammar school and then the Karachev teaching seminary, and from there, in January 1917, he ended up in the Cadet College of St Alexei in Moscow.

The general looked at me calmly, almost with apathy. 'Comrade Junior Sergeant,' he said in a low, hoarse voice, 'in recognition of your services at the front the high command is awarding you a sniper rifle inscribed with your own name. Strike the Fascists without mercy.'

The divisional commander's adjutant handed me a newish SVT-40 rifle with a PU telescope sight, which was shorter and lighter than the PE sight. Beautifully engraved on the metal tube was: '100. For the first hundred, to Jun. Sgt. Pavlichenko, L.M. from the commander of the 25th Div., Maj.-Gen. Petrov, I.Y.'

'I serve the Soviet Union!' I solemnly responded and then brushed my lips against the jet-black barrel, after which I stood it by my side.

The general looked surprised at my action. However, it was not just a weapon, but an award, a sacred object, given to me to fight a sacred war and to wreak vengeance on a treacherous enemy. Petrov stepped forward; I met his attentive and interested glance.

'Have you been in the army long, Lyudmila Mikhailovna?' he asked.

'No, Comrade Major-General. I joined as a volunteer at the end of June.'

'And what were you before that?'

'I was studying at Kiev University. History faculty, fourth year.'

'You handle a rifle superbly,' Petrov remarked.

'I graduated with distinction from the Osoaviakhim sniper school in Kiev,' I reported clearly.

'Are you Ukrainian?' He asked this in a strange, disgruntled tone.

'No, Comrade Major-General!' I replied quickly, for these questions of nationality always irritated me. 'I'm Russian. My maiden name is Belova. I am Pavlichenko only by marriage.'

'Simply amazing, Lyudmila.' Petrov strode around the room. 'I once knew a Belov, Mikhail Ivanovich, but it was during the Civil War. He was a commissar in a regiment back in the days of Chapayev. A man of extraordinary courage. It was along with him that I received the Order of the Red Banner for the attack on Ufa and Belebei. We smashed the Whiteys to smithereens!'

'That's my father, Comrade Major-General.'

'A remarkable encounter!' said the divisional commander and turned to me with a jovial smile. 'So family traditions are alive and well. I think you resemble your father not only in character, but also in your looks.'

'That's what everyone says, Comrade Major-General.'

Of course, as a divisional commander, he had many urgent things to do, but he considered it necessary to treat the daughter of an old comrade in arms to a cup of tea and to ask about our family, my father's life in peacetime and my service in the 54th Regiment. I responded briefly and clearly, as appropriate for a soldier.

'They don't try to upset you?' asked Petrov, in concluding the conversation.

'No, Ivan Yefimovich. They are kind to me and offer help if needed. Particularly since I love military service.'

'Well done, girl!' The general shook my hand firmly on parting.

I went back to the 1st Battalion's lines as if I was floating on air and immediately informed Captain Sergienko of the high command's gift, boasted about the rifle with the inscription of commemoration, but said nothing about the private conversation with Petrov. It seemed to me that my personal acquaintance with the divisional commander was no great matter. Better to remain a sniper than to be known among one's regiment as the girl enjoying the protection of the high command. However, the major-general did not forget our meeting. Three days later an order came through from the divisional headquarters awarding me the next military rank of sergeant.

5

The Battle at Tatarka

There was a feeling, and all the signs were there, that something serious was being prepared. The battle ranks of our 25th Division began to consolidate. Reinforcements arrived from the draft companies transported by sea from Novorossiysk. The 8km-long defence line beside us was occupied by units of the valiant 157th Division, with which we had cooperated in the recent battles for Gildendorf, the Ilyichevka state farm and the villages of Fontanka, Alexandrovka and Bolgarka. Two new artillery regiments arrived with howitzers and cannon. We also saw some tanks: thirty-five military vehicles, including not only the Odessan NE (*Na ispug*, or 'Frightener') vehicles adapted from tractors, but also the standard BT-7 and T-26 army models. Along with our tank crews, our horsemen – the 2nd Cavalry Division – were also preparing for the advance, as used to be the case in pre-war manoeuvres. Finally, we heard that a new and, for the time being, secret weapon had appeared in the lines – BM-13 rocket installations mounted on the chassis of ZIS-6 trucks and brought to Odessa from Novorossiysk at the end of September. They could fire sixteen projectiles weighing 42.5kg in eight to ten seconds. The rockets contained a liquid explosive, so that where they landed everything would burn: earth, stones and metal.

On the morning of 2 October 1941, our military machine went into action. In the southern and western sectors a guards mortar battalion under the command of Captain Nebozhenko and the rocket installations, which had become known in the army as 'Katyushas', struck at the enemy front line.[1]

For the first minute, it seemed as if a storm was approaching, although the sky remained clear and cloudless. A sound reminiscent of distant thunder claps swiftly grew into a deafening roar. The surrounding countryside was illuminated by bright flashes, and puffs of smoke rose over the trees. With a hissing and grinding noise the fiery arrows flew one after another in the enemy's direction. We saw huge yellow blazes of flame envelop the Romanian positions to the west of the village of Tatarka and, further to the south-west, near Bolgarskiye Khutora.

By ten o'clock in the morning the fires had died down. The Chapayev forces went into attack. To our left the 2nd Cavalry Division was advancing. In support of the advance, the Soviet coastal batteries, two armoured trains and a howitzer regiment with 152mm-calibre ordnance maintained a continuous stream of fire. Tanks moved into the gap. They flattened the trenches of the two enemy machine-gun battalions, scattered their troops and sped on to the village of Leninstal. Here the defensive line was maintained by the Border Division of the Kingdom of Romania, seasoned elite forces. But after the Katyusha onslaught they rolled back.

Stumbling as we went, we made our way across the black earth which had been baked by the hellish fire. Only an hour earlier it had been the fortified positions of a Romanian machine-gun battalion. There were dugouts, winding communication passages and firing points. In the fields around grew tall grass, hazel bushes and wild apple trees. All these had been turned to ash. We saw a good few bodies charred almost to the bone, and a strange, sweetish aroma was already mingling with a strong smell of burning. Protruding from the demolished enemy lines here and there were the barrels of defunct machine guns: German MG. 34s, obsolete Austrian Schwarzloses, and new Czech ZB 53s.

War means death, pain and suffering for millions of people. But if the enemy treacherously violates the borders of your native land, you must prepare for a harsh rebuff. You must undergo the transition from peaceful residents of thriving towns and villages to warriors who know no fear or doubt, who are capable of self-denial and the burdens of a lengthy struggle. War highlights the true essence of every person. Cowards and scoundrels commit their foulest deeds and good, courageous, honourable people perform their greatest feats.

Following me in their waterproof capes and helmets were the soldiers of my detachment – ten in all. After Major-General Petrov had presented me with the inscribed rifle, our regimental commander, N.M. Matusyevich, requested that I quickly implement an accelerated programme to train a group of riflemen capable of hitting the enemy without fail. In response to my claim that it was impossible to do this in three or four days, Major Matusyevich generously gave me a week, allowed me to choose the most capable soldiers from the entire regiment and issued 500 cartridges with light bullets for practice in target shooting.

I had to remember how the sessions at our sniper school in Kiev were conducted. I tried to look at the new group through the eyes of my dear teacher. We did not need those who were too self-confident or too temperamental and impatient by nature. It was not at all difficult to test their eye: here's the rifle, here are five cartridges, and there's the target. Have a go!

However, it would not be fair to omit one particular feature of my experience of being in charge. The future riflemen (from other companies) did not at first know that Sergeant Pavlichenko was a woman, and they reacted to my first appearance in front of the squad in a way that was, to be blunt, unorthodox. Quite sharply, but without resorting to unprintable abuse, I took them in hand and subsequently employed very stern methods with the lazy, the slovenly and the not so bright. I had army discipline and order on my side. I soon convinced my subordinates that folk proverbs such as 'A chicken's not a game bird and a woman's not a man', 'The woman's path – from the door to the hearth', 'Long of hair, but short of brain', and other aspersions would have no currency here. I shot better than all of them, I knew a lot about the war, and they had to submit to me unquestioningly.

It goes without saying that the group included soldiers who varied in their ability to take instruction but were able to pick up the basic skills; the rest I sent back to their detachments. Among those who had the potential to become real snipers I would single out two men: Fyodor Sedykh, a young hunter from Siberia, and the Kazakh Azat Bazarbayev, who was, strange though it may seem, a resident of the city of Saratov. They were both naturally endowed with an excellent eye and they had a suitable disposition – very calm. Unfortunately, Bazarbayev lost his life early on, being caught in a mortar attack. Fyodor Sedykh fought with me at Sevastopol.

Making our way through the burnt fields, we looked gloomily around us. The losses and destruction suffered by the Romanians gave us no joy. There is nothing pleasant in such a horrifying triumph of death over life, even if it is the death of a reviled enemy. 'Look and forget,' I thought, stepping over the collapsed trenches and avoiding the smouldering fragments of dugouts and gun placements and the blackened remains of human beings.

After a while a new battle was bound to commence on the area disfigured by the salvoes from the guard battalion of mortar bombers. It was at this point that Major-General Petrov, now commander of the coastal army, deliberately halted our forces' advance. The enemy had withdrawn only 1.5km or so and retained a huge numerical advantage: against the four Soviet divisions the Romanians had eighteen.

On the large-scale map (3 versts per dyuym, or 0.9km/cm) which Captain Sergienko showed me, Height 76.5 was marked as the command post of the enemy machine-gun battalion and was referred to as the Kabachenko homestead. The foe had now abandoned this place. The village of Tatarka,[2] located approximately 0.5km away from it, remained a strategically important point. It lay on a road leading from the town of Ovidiopolye to Odessa, a broad, well-built highway with a hard surface. Not far away there were railway tracks. Our 54th Regiment faced the task of defending the village. First, though, we had to set up advance posts and observation points. The battalion commander had chosen the Kabachenko homestead to be one of them. Three shaded squares on the map indicated the dwelling places. Visible through binoculars were a single-storey building under a red tiled roof, a fence, a large orchard and a gentle slope rising from the house to the south-west. By securing it, one could keep a watch on the road and carry out targeted fire in the event of an enemy advance. Sergienko gave orders for us to be issued with 200 cartridges each. Then he asked me to hold out there as long as possible. Tatarka was considered a close satellite of Odessa (the distance to the city was over 10km) and we would have to fight desperately for it.

I raised my hand to my helmet: 'Yes, Comrade Captain!'

On approaching the homestead, we saw an almost completely burnt-out truck and an overturned motorbike and sidecar. The bodies of soldiers in their pudding-basin helmets were also strewn around here, and along the sides of the narrow dirt road which had been destroyed by shells. The track led directly to some gates, which were wide open. By the gates themselves there stood a 2-tonne Malaxa armoured transport (a Romanian assembled version of the elegant French Renault UE) with a torn left caterpillar track. Attached to it as a trailer was a wagon with caterpillar tracks, and it contained sacks, barrels, crates and a big canvas bundle. Like the village buildings, the armoured transport had hardly suffered at all from the shelling, except that its crew were missing. Both semi-circular armoured turrets were open and the petrol engine was still warm.

We approached the house and knocked on the door. For a long time they would not open to us. Then, when I called out that the Red Army were here, the doors finally opened. The woman of the house appeared, aged about fifty and wrapped up to her eyes in a grey headscarf. I explained who we were. She was surprised to see soldiers under the command of a woman, but after that, conversation became somewhat easier. I listened to her bitter complaints about the occupation forces, who had been behaving disgracefully in the village for two weeks, and her reproaches against the military units of the Red Army which had withdrawn too quickly from there in September, leaving the local population at the mercy of the Fascists.

She was right, this woman. Standing before her, I accepted responsibility for the people's commissar of foreign affairs, Comrade Molotov, who had unexpectedly signed the non-aggression treaty with Germany, for the way the Nazis had insolently broken it, for the high command of the Red Army, who had failed to rout the aggressor's forces in battles on the borders, and for those soldiers and officers of ours who had been absent during the sudden attacks by enemy tank divisions and aerial bombing strikes. But the war was not over, I told her. The war was just beginning. We had been holding the line at Odessa for over two months and thousands of the invaders had already found eternal rest on the Black Sea steppes. Not far from her village we snipers of the 54th Stepan Razin Rifle Regiment would set up an ambush and bury another two or three hundred of King Mihail's wild warriors.

'My name is Serafima Nikanorovna.' The woman opened the door wide before me. 'Come in. You are welcome to what we have.'

Thus began my acquaintance with an ordinary peasant family, the Kabachenkos, consisting of husband, wife and three children: two sons a year apart and an elder daughter. They were neither rich nor poor and they cultivated an orchard, a vegetable garden and a field on which they grew wheat and kept domestic animals and fowl. They had not evacuated at the outbreak of hostilities because they were concerned for their farm, as the land needed constant care and attention. For this they had paid dearly. The Romanians turned the house upside-down from the attic to the cellar, looking for gold and other valuables – a Singer sewing machine or a bicycle. They also rounded up all the chickens, stuck the pigs and drove the cow and calf away to who knew where. Probably the soldiers in the royal army had never been fed so well.

They also committed another criminal act which Serafima Nikanorovna told me about with tears in her eyes. Cruel abuse by the victors against the wives, sisters and daughters of the vanquished goes back to the traditions of the primeval tribes of many years ago. Women were then considered one of the legitimate spoils of war and their fate was not an enviable one. I had read descriptions of these atrocities in historical chronicles, but did not think that 'civilized Europe' would also bring this barbarous custom to our land. The eyes of Maria, the seventeen-year-old daughter of the house, had a martyred look as if sprinkled with ashes; they looked at me with hope. What words she was expecting from me, I do not know. I decided to tell her about the recent battle.

Beyond the gates of the house lay a field which had been incinerated by the rocket shells of the Katyushas. Black dust remained from the rabid Romanians in their pudding-basin helmets. They had been consumed by fire like torches and fallen to the earth, a stream of ash. Nobody would bury them, for that was not necessary, and nobody would remember their faces and names. Their vile seed had become mingled with the dust, vanishing into the hard earth, and would never give rise to posterity. This was the way Fascists ought to die, leaving no trace of their being on our beautiful planet.

'Are you a good shot?' Maria suddenly asked sadly.

'Yes. I've got a rifle with special gunsights.'

'Kill them. However many you see, kill them all.'

'I promise I will.'

'Our Lord Jesus Christ knows all.' The girl devoutly crossed herself and looked at the icon hanging in the corner. 'I will say lots of prayers, and He will forgive you.'

In our Communist family we had grown up as atheists, of course, and the speech about the forgiveness which God would grant me for my accurate shots at the enemy, according to Maria Kabachenko's prayers, meant absolutely nothing to me. But in later years, in peacetime, when I heard snipers referred to as supposedly cold-blooded front-line killers hunting poor defenceless Fritzes, I recalled the appeal of that unfortunate girl: 'Kill them!' Perhaps the quiet voice of Maria and a thousand victims of this war like her would echo once again and be heard not as an explanation for our actions but as an indisputable command.

Back in those days we swore to fulfil it as a sacred duty. And fulfil it we did, not sparing our own lives.

Being in very sombre spirits, I left the house and went into the yard to check how my troops were preparing for the enemy attack. Two soldiers were fiddling around with the Malaxa armoured transport. They were trying to start it, but the engine remained silent. Corporal Sedykh reported that some valuable things had been found in the caterpillar trailer. Apart from two barrels of petrol and a crate full of some spare parts, they had discovered a canvas bundle containing a brand-new MG. 34 German machine gun still in its factory grease. Attached to it were two spare barrels, an asbestos glove designed for changing the barrels during battle, a tripod and boxes containing cartridge belts. It was simply extraordinary!

We had all long learned how to make use of trophy weapons. The machine gun significantly strengthened the firepower of the detachment entrusted to me, and Sedykh and I began to speculate as to where the best position for it would be. Fyodor suggested digging out a deep trench on the slope of the nearby rise, from which a good view of the valley and the road would open up. I agreed with his proposal.

Apart from the machine gun, the petrol and the spare parts, the trailer contained three sacks of grain, flour and sugar. The soldiers looked at me questioningly. They were useful foodstuffs, it would appear, but what use could we make of them with no utensils? I decided to hand the find over to the woman of the house. At first Serafima Nikanorovna did not believe we could be so generous, but in return I asked her to cook the soldiers a hot dinner.

Fyodor and I made our way across the slope, which was overgrown with young trees. There really was an excellent view of the whole valley and the road bisecting it. On the left side of the road lay a small wood and, on the right, a few hills. Beyond the hills the roofs of the houses in the village of Tatarka were visible here and there.

Stepping carefully across the withered autumn grass, we approached the first trench. The soldiers had chosen the right place for it. Behind them was a hillock overgrown with wild roses. The sun illuminated it from the side, so that a thick shadow lay on the ground. It camouflaged both the trench and the soldiers sitting in it. The trench was already 1 metre deep, but I ordered them to dig further, down to 1.5 metres, and then to reinforce the parapet with stones, so that we would be able to fire both standing and prone. Leading away from it was a shallower trench designed to allow the riflemen to move (crawling along the ground) to a different position. It was not going to be possible to set up a real battle line here with a large number of firing points and communication passages; we did not know how much time we had at our disposal and we were hurrying to make at least something resembling infantry fortifications.

After posting sentries we returned to the house in the afternoon at the invitation of the hostess. She had cooked dinner and set the table with what could be called a festive touch: a bottle of cloudy rustic homebrew, plates and cut-glass goblets, and some hors d'oeuvres consisting of sauerkraut and mildly salted gherkins. Not just the food but the way it was served up and the presence of the whole Kabachenko family warmed the hearts of the front-line troops. During combat and marches we had often pined for the comforts of home.

The Romanians did not attack and the day concluded quietly, peacefully and quite splendidly.

For the following two days at the homestead we kept the road in our sights and inflicted some losses on the enemy: we stopped two army trucks by hitting their wheels with armour-piercing bullets and, with our trophy machine gun, we drove the infantrymen who jumped out of them into the woods. Then, with our sniper rifles we brought down three motorcycles with sidecars. Eventually, some Romanian tanks of Czech LT vz. 35 design appeared on the road. Not all of them, it seems, had been burnt up by the defenders of Odessa, who had deftly showered these war machines with Molotov cocktails. The tanks opened fire with their cannon on the slope of the rise where our trenches were located. They were not on target, though, as the snipers were well camouflaged. But it is impossible to fight against tanks without grenades and those Molotov cocktails. They went past us and, further on, right by the village of Tatarka, our regimental artillery dealt with them.

Fierce military action unfolded near the village a little later: on 9, 10, 11, 12 and 13 October 1941. Success favoured now one side, now the other. The Romanians would manage to put pressure on us, and then the valiant Soviet troops would once again charge forward and drive the enemy soldiers out of the rustic cottages at the edge of the village. One who took part in these engagements was our ever-watchful Young Communist League organizer, Yasha Vaskovsky, who wrote about it in his memoirs:

On 9 October the 1st Battalion of the Razin Division drove the enemy out of the outlying village of Tatarka. The foe offered resistance, but hand-to-hand combat resolved the issue in our favour. The remnants of the units expelled from Tatarka began to withdraw towards Bolgarskiye Khutora; however, we had already cut off their path and sixty enemy troops put their hands up. Then, between Tatarka and the Sukhy estuary, the 33rd Romanian Infantry Regiment ended up being encircled on the same day. For two hours the fierce clashes continued, with attacks and counter-attacks. The enemy left 1,300 men on the battlefield, dead and wounded, while 200 surrendered. We seized the regimental standard, operational documents and seal, and a lot of armaments. It might also be added that the success of my regimental comrades in this sector was largely determined by the operations of the guards mortar battalion under Captain Nebozhenko. The Romanians could not withstand the rocket bombardment and withdrew.[3]

A very serious situation developed between 10 and 13 October in the southern sector of the Odessa defence district. The 10th Romanian Division began to advance in full complement on Tatarka and tried to break through against the forces of our 25th Chapayev Rifle Division and the 2nd Cavalry Division. Following an intensive artillery attack, three enemy battalions managed to capture the advance trench line, got through to our rear, and ended up by the embankment of the Odessa–Ovidiopolye railway line. More substantial enemy forces could have moved into the breach at any moment. The 1st Battalion of the 54th Regiment, a battalion of the 3rd Regiment of the naval infantry, the 80th Separate Reconnaissance Battalion under the command of Captain Antipin, and a motorized rifle company on armoured vehicles – we all received the order to move immediately out of reserve to the site of the engagement. the fire of three batteries was also concentrated on the enemy, from the 1st, 239th and 411th and also the No. 22, 'For the Motherland!', armoured train.

The trenches were defended and the Soviet infantry began to occupy their former firing positions. For a while there was silence. But the Romanians were preparing to attack and soon began a mortar bombardment. At first the bombs fell behind the forward line, then in front of it, and then the odd salvo hit it, raising clouds of dust and smoke. With a waterproof cape I tried to cover the gift from Divisional Commander Petrov – the SVT-40 sniper rifle. I had taken it on the assault because we anticipated a frontal attack on our battalion. In such a case the 'Sveta' – as the self-loading Tokarev rifle was called in the army – offered a clear advantage thanks to its rapid fire and ten-cartridge box magazine, which could be simply and quickly replaced during battle.

We had weapons like that in our battalion, but not in great quantity – although, according to the 1940 official schedule, it was already supposed to be replacing the Mosin rifles. In fact, we had 984 SVT-40s and 1,301 Three Lines. There were different views about the 'Sveta'. Some liked its automatic features, based on the action of the propellant gases which always accompany the bullet as it flies along the barrel. They entered a gas port situated over the barrel and pushed against a cylinder with a long rod. The rod was joined with a tappet, the other end of which rested against the bolt. But someone rightly criticized the excessive complexity of this device and the difficulties of looking after it in field conditions. Perhaps somewhere in the northern regions or at sea a self-loading rifle would be a top performer. But on the Black Sea steppe, in trenches dug out of dry, soft, crumbling earth, the risk of dirt in the mechanism – which consisted of 143 small, fine, and very fine components – was quite large.

The rifle would begin to 'snap' (for instance, it would not reload or it would barely expel the used cartridges) if the pressure of the powder gases changed. It also depended, incidentally, on the weather, on the air temperature. In that case the marksman had to regulate the aperture in the gas port manually, to make it bigger or smaller. Apart from that, the 'Sveta' also misbehaved when covered with thick grease or if dust got into its mechanism. Among the deficiencies of the SVT-40 I would also mention its bright muzzle flash upon firing (on account of a barrel that was 100mm shorter than the Three Line) and its loud sound, which immediately gave away one's location. It was superbly suited to clashes with the enemy in the field, when artillery, machine guns and mortars were operating. However, to put it bluntly, it increased the danger of a marksman being detected by the enemy in a single-person hideout, in a forest, for example. Among the sniper fraternity, though, the 'Sveta' had its admirers.

In the summer of 1942 Senior Lieutenant Vladimir Pchelintsev, who was fighting on the Leningrad front, gave me his pamphlet *How I Became a Sniper*, which was published in a limited edition in Moscow and distributed on the front as an instructional and publicity manual. It contains a photograph in which Pchelintsev is demonstrating the SVT-40 mechanism to new recruits. He writes:

> I am indebted to my weapon for my initial success. A rifle is a soldier's best friend. Treat it with care and attention, and it will never let you down. Protecting your rifle, keeping it clean, eliminating the slightest faults, greasing it moderately, regulating all its parts and adjusting it properly – that is the attitude a sniper should have towards his weapon. At the same time it does no harm to be aware that, for all their standardized parameters, there are in principle no identical rifles. As the saying goes, each one has its own character. This character may manifest itself in the tautness of the various springs, the ease with which the bolt slides, the weight of the touch required on the trigger, the state of the bore, its degree of wear and tear, etc. On a number of occasions I have returned from the 'hunt', hungry and shivering with cold and the first thing I have done is to set about cleaning the weapon, putting it in order. For a sniper this is law.

This is all correct – 'protecting your rifle, keeping it clean, eliminating the slightest faults.' I tried to use a waterproof cape to protect the 'Sveta' from the dust which descended like a cloud on my trench, but, apparently I was not quick enough. There was no response when I pressed the trigger. I had to eliminate this fault. I bent over the rifle, but my helmet got in the way. Cursing the devil, I took off my steel helmet and put it down on the bottom of the trench, then grasped the bolt handle. The mechanism seemed to start to yield.

At this point a new salvo of mortars descended; splinters whistled past in various directions. One of them struck my face, on the left, under the hairline. The blood flowed copiously down my forehead, closed my left eye, got onto my lips, and I felt its salty taste. I managed to take a first-aid bag out of my tunic pocket and somehow wind a bandage round my head. The blood flow eased, and then the pain started up; the wound burnt, stung, and it seemed as if it was tugging at the skin all over my head.

Everything around me began to sink into a fog. I pressed my faulty rifle to my breast and leant my back against the trench wall. Splinters of mortars and enemy bullets were whistling over it. Somewhere to the side, one of the company's fixed machine guns had started rattling, and our battery of 45mm cannon entered the fray with a loud '*V-vakh!*' Judging by the sounds, the Romanians had gone on the attack. But I could not contribute to repelling them. Some strange, oppressive thoughts haunted my brain, 'Must wait . . . Must wait . . . Must wait . . .'

'Comrade Sergeant, are you still alive?' the voice of medical orderly Lena Paliy called out.

'Still alive, but wounded in the head.'

'Oh my God, I'll come and help right now.'

Seeing my face and tunic covered with blood and my bandaged head, Captain Sergienko ordered Lena to take me to the divisional medical battalion, since the doctors there were better. Besides, the 47th Medical Battalion , which was attached to the 25th Division, was situated only 5km from the lines of the 54th Regiment. My inscribed rifle, which, as before, I did not let out of my hands, suddenly did me a good turn. At the triage station of the medical battalion Lena Paliy pointed to the inscription on the metal tube of the sights and declared that Sergeant Lyudmila Pavlichenko of the 2nd Company, 1st Battalion, 54th Regiment, was personally acquainted with Major-General Petrov, commander of the coastal army. Without asking a single question, the military doctor handed her a red chit indicating authorization for an urgent operation.

6

Across the Sea

The medics handed me the mortar splinter. It looked like a blackened flat piece of metal, slightly longer than a matchstick, with sharp, jagged edges. Had its trajectory been lower, I do not know what would have happened to me. I would probably be lying with a hole in my head in the damp earth of a cemetery near the village of Tatarka, like 150 of my regimental comrades in arms, along with our courageous company commander, Lieutenant Voronin, and Private Bazarbayev from my platoon, an excellent shot and a good man. We buried them late in the evening of 11 October, when the battle had died down and the Romanians had withdrawn to their earlier positions.

I have little recollection of how the operation went. But my appearance after it was far from military: half my hair had been shorn, my skin had been daubed with brilliant green antiseptic and, after the splinter had been extricated, the wound had been stitched and my head bandaged. When the morphine stopped working, the pain came on again. I felt it in my temples, in the back of my head, and in the place where the splinter had been removed, and I began to suffer from extreme dizziness. The surgeon said that there could be no question of an immediate return to the regiment. I would have to spend ten to twelve days with the medical battalion.

However, I fell into the category of 'walking' patients. Within a day, on 15 October, I was allowed to go out for a stroll. I thrust my arms into my overcoat sleeves, stuck a peaked cap on my bandaged head and set off to view the surroundings and breathe some fresh air.

On 14 October the sun had still been shining brightly in the blue sky and warming the steppe expanses around Odessa with its rays. But on the 15th the warm, crystal-clear Black Sea autumn suddenly came to an end. The horizon was enveloped by low, leaden-coloured clouds and a cold northerly wind began to blow. Soon the first drops of rain fell on the borders and paths of the homely gardens which surrounded the rural school. The 47th Medical Battalion was comfortably set up in its building, which was a stroke of luck. Army medical units were more often situated in fields or forests in large canvas tents. Here the wounded were triaged, operated on, and brought back to health. The severely wounded with amputations, burns and broken bones were dispatched deep into the rear in ambulances. As they left the school I would observe the stretchers bearing them being loaded onto a couple of 1.5-tonne vehicles with red crosses on the sides. They took the road for Odessa, where seagoing transport ships awaited them in the port.

The war had still not reached the rural school, but distant cannon fire roaring away somewhere in the west and south-west reminded us of it. To judge from the mighty racket, the firing came from our own coastal batteries and long-range ordnance on the ships of the Black Sea Fleet. Sometimes the chorus was joined by cannon of smaller calibre – from two armoured trains which bombarded the Fascist lines after approaching to within close range of them.

The fallen leaves rustled under my feet. The bushes of wild rose and dogwood had completely lost their foliage of late, and the thin black twigs now stretched up forlornly to the sky. The juniper was like a green wall, afraid of neither the wind nor the rain. In the borders where gladioli, tulips and roses grew, the soil was dark brown. In spite of the bombing raids and artillery shelling someone was looking after the garden and had dug it over a day or two ago. The determination and industry of people who refused to accept the chaos of wartime commanded respect. I picked up a curled, dry crimson-yellow leaf and tried to straighten it with my fingers. The leaf would not yield. Its life was over.

A khaki-coloured general's car entered the garden through the open gates and drove towards the school. It was the kind of vehicle in which Major-General Petrov usually rode. I went up to the drive and stood at attention, raising my hand to my cap. The Gorky-manufactured GAZ-M1, known colloquially as 'Emka', stopped almost beside me. It was indeed the commander of the coastal army, Ivan Petrov, who stepped out of it, and turned to me.

'Lyudmila, what are you doing here?'

'I'm under treatment, Comrade Major-General.'

'A head wound?' He walked up to me.

'Yes, Comrade Major-General.'

'Was it long ago?'

'No, it was on 13 October, with the 1st Battalion by the village of Tatarka. We were beating off an attack by the Romanian infantry, and a mortar splinter . . .'

'Why don't you wear a helmet, girl?' the major-general asked sternly.

'It was an accident, Ivan Yefimovich.'

'Are you being treated well?' Petrov inquired.

'Excellently!' I responded.

'Well, get ready to move now, Lyuda. We're off to Sevastopol. By sea.'

'But what about our dear city of Odessa, Ivan Yefimovich?' I could not refrain from expressing my grief. 'Surely we're not going to surrender it to the Fascists to be plundered and defiled? They'll raze it to the ground.'

'That's the order from the supreme command, Lyudmila.' In an apparent attempt to comfort me, Petrov brushed my shoulder with his hand in a fatherly way. 'You realize that it's the duty of a soldier always to carry out orders to the letter . . . My orders to you are not to mope, have faith in victory, and fight bravely. By the way, how many enemy have you got in your tally now?'

'A hundred and eighty-seven.'

'You are simply a champion!' the major-general exclaimed in sincere admiration. 'You're shooting well.'

'Well, they attack in dense ranks, the idiots,' I said, thinking that Petrov was expecting an explanation for the situation. 'It's even difficult to miss them.'

Since being appointed to the lofty post of commander-in-chief of the coastal army, Ivan Yefimovich had not changed at all. He remained the same modest, calm and reserved man and thought not so much about the power over people this position imbued him with as about his responsibility for them. He was bearing an onerous task at that time: evacuating all military units from Odessa to Sevastopol by sea. It had to be arranged in a very short time-frame and kept secret from the enemy, preventing them from pursuing our departing regiments. He spent whole days in a car travelling up and down the lines of the Odessa defence district, checking how preparations for the operation were going in the different army units. His face was now weary and grey from road dust, but he took my words as a joke and he liked it. The general's eyes flashed with a mischievous sparkle. He laughed.

'Well, Lyuda, with soldiers like you there is nothing to fear,' said Petrov. 'We'll cross the sea and defend the Crimea. Everything will be fine, you'll see.'

With hurried footsteps Petrov headed for the school, and I remained in the garden, reflecting on the news I had just heard. To be honest, I could not get my head around it. We, the defenders of Odessa, had held our firing lines and never considered retreat. We remained confident that the supreme command in Moscow would not issue such an order but, just as before, send the city reinforcements, weapons, ammunition, equipment and provisions. Since August 1941 embattled Odessa had found itself in the enemy rear and been an example of staunch, heroic resistance to the German and Romanian invaders in that difficult period when German divisions were speeding towards the capital of our homeland.

'At that time we were still unaware that very soon, within eight days, we would receive the decision of the supreme command requiring us to abandon Odessa and evacuate the army to the Crimea, which the Fascist hordes were already threatening to seize, having reached the approaches to Perekop,' Major-General F.N. Voronin, a member of the coastal army's military council, recalled later.

Perhaps because the tense struggle with the enemy at the Odessa base had to some extent shielded us from events on other fronts, this decision was staggeringly unexpected for us. He [i.e. Petrov] had to resolve the question of organizing the withdrawal of forces from battle and the evacuation of the army. By that time the personnel of the staff operational section had made the suggestion: could the forces not be removed from the defence lines straight away rather than in gradual stages, as had been assumed until now? Petrov approved this idea. I supported him in this. Staff headquarters was ordered to rework the evacuation plan. The military council of the Odessa defence district affirmed the new plan based on all forces withdrawing from Odessa simultaneously. In terms of actual military formations it amounted to around 50,000 troops. They were all faced with loading onto transports along with their weapons and departing Odessa in one night – 16 October.[1]

This plan was brilliantly implemented and in the history of the Great War for the Fatherland it stands as a logistical operation of unique complexity.

After sunset on 15 October 1941, the regiments and batteries of three rifle divisions – the 25th, 95th and 421st – and one cavalry division began to leave their firing lines, form into columns in total silence, and depart through the city for the port. So that they would not get lost in the dark and take a wrong turning at street corners or intersections, directions were scrawled there with powdered lime and chalk. The rear-guard battalions remained in their trenches for another two hours, maintaining diversionary fire at the enemy from machine guns and mortars, and then withdrew themselves. Their place on the front line was taken by teams of scouts and by local partisans, who carried on as if the infantry were still there: they lit campfires, fired from time to time and moved around the communication passages. The Romanians and Germans made no attempt to attack and cross the front line.

The 47th Medical Battalion was loaded onto road transport and took its place within its own Chapayev Division, following immediately behind the sapper battalion. The road was considerably damaged, which made it impossible to travel at high speed. Nevertheless, we drove through the outskirts of Odessa in an hour. In the city itself the traffic was even slower. The streets were jammed with abandoned army trucks and lines of carts carrying a variety of military equipment. A particularly large bottleneck developed by the main gates of the port – the customhouse gates, which gave onto Customhouse Square.

The troops and officers of the 54th Regiment had last passed along the streets of Odessa at the end of September. I saw that the situation was significantly worse now. The autumn twilight enshrouded the streets, squares, parks and boulevards of the city, but the destruction caused by enemy aircraft still stood out – especially in the city centre. Many buildings were without roofs, or second and third storeys. With black holes in place of windows they looked out sadly at their defenders, who were now leaving them.

The route of the 25th Division lay through the main streets of the central port district, from Transfiguration Square – via Greek Square and then a turn into Polsky Spusk – to Customhouse Square. When our column halted yet one more time at an intersection blocked by some artillery wagon, I saw, on the left side of the street, the two-storeyed building of the district enlistment office, or rather, what was left of it after a bomb had dropped on it. Not that long ago, I had gone there to join the Red Army as a volunteer and the weary military registrar had explained to me that the army was no place for women. In a safe there had been my passport with the registration stamp of my marriage to A.B. Pavlichenko. Then he disappeared in the fiery crucible of war and I was able to forget about my stupid youthful escapade. No safe, no passport. Only soot-blackened walls, only collapsed beams, only the twisted remains of the iron staircase which I had once ascended to the office where my fate was decided.

While our ambulance stood at the crossroads, I contemplated the ruins of the enlistment office. Without doubt the war had had a sort of magical impact on my life. I had been intending to be a school history teacher or a research assistant in a library or archive. Instead I had become a front-line sniper, a skilful hunter of people dressed in Romanian and German uniforms. Why had those people come here, onto my land? Why had they forced me to give up my peacetime profession?

In the late October evening the Odessa seaport, the biggest on the coast, with its 5km of well-built, modern quays, thriving port economy and cargo turnover of, apparently, over 10 million tonnes a year, recalled the biblical city of Babylon as it endured its last hours before its great catastrophe. Thousands and thousands of people in military uniform were crowding its territory. There were army trucks, tractor units pulling heavy howitzers, tanks, armoured vehicles, mobile kitchens, horse-drawn carts and saddle horses belonging to the troops and officers of the 2nd Cavalry Division.

At first glance it appeared that chaos reigned, but the personnel of the Odessa naval base displayed the highest degree of organization as the forces were being loaded. The army columns pouring into the port area proceeded quickly via routes which had been worked out earlier: onto the quays, to the ships of the Black Sea steamer service and the Black Sea Fleet, which had been designated to transport specific military units.

For instance, we Chapayevs squeezed through the customhouse gates and headed for the Platonov and New Piers in the New Harbour. At the quays were the cargo motor vessels *Zhan Zhores*,[2] *Kursk* and *Ukraina*. The boarding began. Along gangways lowered from the ships 1,000 soldiers climbed onto their decks every 45 minutes – 2,000 every hour and a half. Machine guns and small regimental mortars of 50mm calibre went up the same gangways. Cannons and anti-aircraft guns on wooden pallets awaited their turn on the pier. They could only be taken on board by the loading derricks of the motor vessels, which were working nonstop.

Until now I had never made a trip by sea or been on a ship. I wanted to have a good look at everything, but the embarkation, which was taking place at a truly furious tempo, got in the way. The *Zhan Zhores*, on which our medical battalion was loaded along with the headquarter staff of the 25th Division and some of its other units (including the 69th Artillery Regiment, the 99th Howitzers and the 193rd Anti-Aircraft Battery), loomed before me like a long, tall, black wall rising sheer over the quay. Above it hung a white superstructure with lifeboats and a thick funnel, on which was painted a red strip bearing a yellow hammer and sickle. On the bridge stood the captain – a big broad-shouldered man in a black maritime peaked cap with a golden crest above the peak. He directed all the wounded into the crew mess room. At his command the road vehicles and howitzers were lowered into the No. 1 and No. 2 holds at the bow end of the ship. He left four anti-aircraft cannons on the upper deck, supposing with good reason that they would come in handy in fighting off German air attacks during the crossing from Odessa to Sevastopol.

In the crew mess room I manged to get a place by a big porthole, from which almost the entire New Harbour was visible. The turmoil on the pier was gradually coming to an end. The forces were crossing from the shore onto the ships. The three motor vessels, *Zhan Zhores*, *Kursk* and *Ukraina*, each with a cargo capacity of 5,000 or 6,000 tonnes, were accommodating personnel and machinery on their decks and in their holds according to the plan.

At approximately ten o'clock in the evening of 15 October 1941, the tugs began to lead our cargo vessel away from the wharf. Then the ship's diesel engines started up. The *Zhan Zhores* shuddered and began to move out into the open sea. It was surrounded by impenetrable gloom. The port of Odessa was drifting into the distance, a scarlet and yellow dot. The huge portside warehouses were on fire. There was evidently nobody to extinguish them and no reason to. We were abandoning the city to the foe, but we had no doubt that we would return.

After breakfast the next morning I went up to the top deck. There was a light wind blowing and the rocking was almost imperceptible. The sun peered out from behind the clouds and its rays began to glide along the small waves, giving rise to bright white flashes. The infinite ocean plain spread out on both sides of the *Zhan Zhores*. The Odessa shore had disappeared like a mirage in the desert.

Leaning my shoulder against the metal wall of part of the ship's superstructure I protected myself against the wind with the flap of my overcoat, pulled the silver cigarette case out of my pocket, clicked the lighter and inhaled the slightly bitter smoke. The trophy cigarette case was all that remained as a memento of Lieutenant Andrei Voronin. Those unforgettable battles were over – at Bleyayevka, at Gildendorf and at Tatarka. Each of them had contributed a grain of army experience, taught me something – soldier's ingenuity, patience and tenacity, one might say. But not only that. I had gained an understanding of what human beings were like in war. My reflections were interrupted by a menacing shout from above.

'Comrade! It is only permitted to smoke onboard in designated areas!'

'Can you tell me where?' I asked, raising my head.

Leaning on the bars of the captain's bridge and looking down at me was the navigating officer – the third mate, a man of about thirty in a naval leather jacket and a black forage cap. His face was at first very stern. He was probably intending to dish out a good telling off to an idle landlubber, i.e. me, but the sailor had not expected that someone in a soldier's overcoat and forage cap, with a bandaged head, might be a woman. First, he fell silent in embarrassment, then he smiled and, in a completely different, more polite, tone said: 'There's a place on the quarterdeck, at the stern.'

'No, I'm not going there.' I took a last drag and threw the unfinished cigarette overboard.

'Are you from the hospital?' The sailor continued to examine me.

'Yes, from the medical battalion.'

'And where were you wounded?'

'In the battle at Tatarka.'

'Carrying out the wounded under fire?' he inquired, probably having no idea that women in the army could take part in military engagements on the same level as men.

'Sort of.' I shrugged my shoulders, having no intention of telling him about my service as a sniper.

'Do you want to look at our convoy through binoculars?' The navigator clearly wanted to continue the acquaintance. 'Climb up the gangplank. From here you can see almost all the ships.'

The sailor first kindly explained to me how to use binoculars. Prismatic field binoculars with six-fold magnification are an essential item in a sniper's equipment but I listened attentively to his explanation and asked a few questions. In fact, a medical orderly could not have been so familiar with the mechanism of such things.

Finally, the binoculars ended up in my hands and I looked through the eyepieces. The double-masted bulk of the cruiser *Krasnaya Ukraina*, which was painted a grey-blue colour, had rapidly drawn near. It had ordnance on its prow, quite a high superstructure, three funnels, and eight broadside cannon of large calibre. A powerful and beautiful ship, the real pride of the Black Sea Fleet. Nobody knew then that it would not have much longer to operate.

Krasnaya Ukraina and the cruiser *Krasniy Kavkaz* were sailing ahead of us, clearly delineated against the background of the blue sky. Cruisers could work up a speed of 30 knots, but on the morning of 16 October they were moving at a third of that speed, adjusting to the pace of the other ships in the convoy. The destroyers *Bodry* and *Smyshlyony*, three minesweepers, two gunboats and one patrol boat protected the large transports like our *Zhan Zhores*, and also *Ukraina, Kursk, Kalinin, Kotovskoi* and *Vasily Chapayev*.

While I was viewing the ships through the binoculars, the navigator was briefly describing them, their displacements, power units and dimensions. He spoke about his beloved *Zhan Zhores* with special fascination. I learned a lot of interesting things; for instance, that the motor vessel was built in Leningrad, at the northern shipbuilding dock in 1931, as one of four similar ships, and then made a voyage around Europe, because it was attached to the Black Sea Company. In 1934 the *Zhan Zhores* had brought the celebrated writer Maxim Gorky and his family from Genoa to the Soviet Union. Then it went to New York and carried various cargoes to Italy, France and Batumi in the Caucasus. This highly informative chat on the bridge concluded with an invitation to a cup of tea in the mess and getting to know each other. The sailor's name was Konstantin Podyma and he was born in the city of Novorossiysk.

Except that we did not have time for tea.

Around eleven o'clock in the morning, while the convoy was passing by the Tendra Spit, it was attacked by a group of enemy bombers. However, our ships were covered by several pairs of I-153, I-16 and Yak-1 fighters. They boldly rushed out to meet the German twin-engine Junkers 88s and the single-engine Junkers 87 dive-bombers, or 'Trundlers', as we called them on account of their clumsy-looking fixed undercarriage. There began a real aerial cavalcade of flying and roaring aircraft, accompanied by the crackle of machine-gun rounds, anti-aircraft salvoes, and bombs exploding as the Fritzes dropped them into the sea. At risk of being hit by their own fire, our Yastrebki prevented them from carrying out precision bombing and also joined battle with German Messerschmitt-109 fighters, which were defending the heavy, sluggish bombers.

One fragment of this battle was played out right beside our ship. A Junkers 87 shot down by an accurate round of fire from a red-starred Yastreb, began to smoke, went into a steep dive and splashed flat into the water about 10 metres away from our ship. However, it did not immediately sink into the watery depths. I thought I saw the face of the pilot, distorted by a grimace of horror. The wave that arose from the aircraft's landing rocked the *Zhan Zhores* strongly on the right, but the ship, which was more than 100 metres long, quickly corrected itself. The crew greeted the victory of the Soviet pilot with a loud and harmonious shout of 'Hurrah!'

While I was observing the manoeuvres of a dozen yellow-nosed 'Trundlers' with black crosses on their wings and fuselages swooping down on the ships and flying at 200–300 metres above them, I remembered my rifle in its case in the *Zhan Zhores'* crew mess hall. It had been my cherished desire ever since our sad retreat along the roads of Bessarabia – when, before our eyes, the Fascists shot peaceful civilians with impunity – to shoot down one of these vultures with my rifle. However, at that time I did not have even an ordinary Mosin rifle.

Firing at moving targets is the hardest part of front-line service for snipers. The difficulty lies not only in making ballistic calculations quickly and precisely, but one also needs to have good skills in working with a mobile rifle. The weapon should be pointed not at the target, but in front of it, calculating the time and distance to the point where both moving objects – the bullet and the target – will meet. This method is termed 'deflection shooting', and we had studied it at sniper school. Potapov told us that at the end of 1915 his regiment had shot down a low-flying German Fokker with a rifle.

It is essential to know the speed at which the target is moving. Judging from everything around us, I estimated that the Junkers 87 dive-bombers were swooping down to drop their bombs at a speed of at least 400km per hour. But the *Zhan Zhores* was not standing still. It was travelling quite quickly and manoeuvring as well to dodge the Fascist attacks. Four anti-aircraft cannons on the ship's deck maintained almost continuous fire and the Fritzes frequently turned away from their target. I could only admire the bold actions of the vessel's crew.

The aerial attack did not bring the Germans success. They were not able to sink a single ship, and our red-starred Yastrebki shot down more than fifteen bombers. The ship's anti-aircraft cannons put a further three Fascists into the water. But our own pilots also perished in this battle. The sailors managed to save three wounded flyers from aeroplanes that had been brought down.

In the afternoon another group of enemy aircraft appeared in the sky over the convoy: about forty Junkers 87 and Junkers 88 bombers. Up to meet them went our fighters, which were based at aerodromes in the Crimea and on Tendra Spit – fifty-six war planes in all. Once again we witnessed the dramatic sight of an aerial battle, in the course of which the enemy once again failed to achieve their goals. Only later in the evening did the Germans manage to wipe out the old transport *Bolshevik*, which was at the tail of the convoy. A torpedo hit it and the ship sank. But the entire crew of the motor vessel, which had succeeded in lowering its lifeboats, were picked up by Soviet minesweepers and torpedo boats.[3]

The convoy arrived at Sevastopol on 17 October 1941, at seven o'clock in the evening and moored in Strelets Bay. Unloading began. Having been relieved from his watch, Konstantin Podyma came out to escort me and saw to his amazement that, apart from my kitbag, I was carrying over my shoulder a long object in a cover.

The gallant sailor immediately offered his assistance. I replied that I could not hand over my personal weapon to anyone.

'Surely you don't carry a weapon, Lyuda?' he asked incredulously.

'A sniper rifle,' I confessed.

'So you're not a medic; you're a rifleman? I would never have thought . . .'

'Why, Kostya?'

'There's no place for women in war,' he said with conviction.

I had neither the time nor the desire to argue with the navigator. During the dreadful war, in which our people were fighting for their very survival, everyone who was confident in military knowledge and skills, regardless of his or her sex or national affiliation, had to join the ranks and make whatever contribution they were capable of to wipe out the German Fascist invaders. Only then would we be able to defeat the enemy.

7

Legendary Sevastopol

The weary warriors of the coastal army were greeted by the sight of a magnificent white city as yet unscarred by battle. Here it was unusually calm and peaceful: no artillery attacks or front lines with constant combat. Only now and then did Nazi aircraft appear but they had not inflicted on Sevastopol the heavy damage seen at Odessa. In the rays of the warm Crimean sun its shady streets, parks slightly touched by autumnal colour and public gardens with luxuriant flowerbeds gladdened the eye with their festive and completely pre-war appearance and the brightness of their colours.

The city was spread out over the shores of several bays, and the entrance to the main one was protected by the two ancient forts, the Konstantin and the Mikhail. Their great white stone walls with embrasures were reflected in the waters of the harbour. On the top of Central Hill shone the blue dome of the Cathedral of St Vladimir, the burial vault of four admirals, heroes of the city's first siege. Amidst the winding lanes of History Boulevard stood monuments to the fallen warriors of the Fourth Bastion, the Yazenov Redoubt and the Kostomarov Battery, as well as the multi-figured bronze memorial to General Totleben and his brave sappers who successfully waged a subterranean struggle against the British, French and Italian forces who besieged Sevastopol in 1854.

I had never been here before. After the bustle, variety and many features of Odessa, whose population numbered over 600,000, Sevastopol seemed small and provincial. In Odessa the rhythm of life was set by a large commercial seaport which hosted dozens of ships from different countries of the world. Foreign passenger liners, cargo ships or tankers could not even approach this, the main naval base of the Black Sea Fleet. Only the narrow grey hulks of Soviet destroyers, minesweepers and patrol boats occupied the quays of South Bay or awaited repairs by the piers of the Sergo Ordzhonikidze naval works.

In some unfathomable way the heroic past still suffused the character of modern Sevastopol, its residents, their habits and customs. That appealed to me. The city presented itself not as a jaunty mariner disembarked from the deck of an ocean-going merchantman, as in Odessa, but as a stern warrior gripping his weapon and gazing into the distance. On the southern borders of our homeland he stood as a permanent sentry, responsible for the peace and security of his native land.

The people of Sevastopol greeted the defenders of Odessa hospitably. There were many wounded on the ships of our convoy (up to 3,000). They were immediately put in hospitals, which were located in various districts: in Holland Bay, in Strelets Bay, in Balaklava and in the city hospitals. A place was found for me and other patients of the 47th Medical Battalion in a small infirmary in Strelets Bay. My regimental mates who needed rest rather than treatment were taken to Historic Boulevard, in the centre of the city. The main forces of the coastal army were located in Korabelnaya Storona, the major part in the grounds of the anti-aircraft gunnery college.

Personnel were dispatched to public baths, had their linen and uniforms changed, and were fed in the canteen; 500g of bread were distributed per person. This period of rest was most appreciated by those who had left the battlefield just two days earlier. The Chapayevs hoped they would be allowed to rest for a week at least. Their wishes were not answered; by 21 October our division had already been loaded onto a train at the railway station and dispatched to the north of the Crimean Peninsula to stop the German advance on the Ishun lines.

I remained in Sevastopol as my head wound had not healed. It was rebandaged every two days and the medics promised to take the stitches out soon. In spite of this, I got permission to go out on half-hour walks down to the sea. Then, when the stitches were removed and I was transferred to a battalion of recuperating patients based at the Black Sea Fleet crew premises, I was able to request leave to go into the city.

The leave pass was given to me by Major N.A. Khubezhev, a jovial and talkative man. When I introduced myself, he took an interest in my award – the inscribed sniper rife – and offered me a transfer from the 25th, which was now located heaven-knew-where, to the naval infantry, promising me the rank of principal sergeant major and assuring me that the Black Sea sailor's pea jacket with brass buttons would suit me incomparably better than my khaki-coloured infantry tunic. He extolled his friends among the leadership – Captain Lvovsky in the 16th Naval Infantry Battalion, Senior Lieutenant Unchur in the 17th, Captain Yegorov in the 18th and Captain Chernousov in the 19th Battalion. However, the naval infantry did not seem to me to be any better than the ordinary terrestrial infantry. I had become strongly attached to the Stepan Razin Rifle Regiment, having been through the epic saga of Odessa with them. In war anything can happen. A regiment is not a needle in a haystack; it was bound to turn up somewhere, along with the whole coastal army, which, having retreated from the Ishun lines under pressure from the

Fritzes, was now breaking through to the main naval base of the Black Sea Fleet along dirt roads through the southern Crimean range.

Having got out of the barracks and into the city, I strolled around on my own and took pleasure in its peaceful appearance. The trams were running around the city ring, and the shops, cafeterias, public baths, hairdressers and various services – metalwork, tailoring, shoe repairs – were open. True, Sevastopol, which had had a population of over 100,000 before the war, now looked empty. Many of its residents, especially those with children, had been evacuated to the Caucasus and to Krasnodar Territory. However, in the evenings, after the working day was over, the people of Sevastopol would dress up and go out to stroll along the Marine or Historic Boulevards, visit the Lunacharsky city theatre, where plays were still staged as before, or the three cinemas, which showed the best pre-war Soviet films: *Chapayev*, *The Tractor Drivers*, *In the Enemy Rear*, *Minin and Pozharsky*, *The Little Humpbacked Horse* and others.

First, I visited the cultural venues that were still open: the superb Black Sea Fleet museum, situated in an ancient building with cannons by the entrance, and the panorama of Historic Boulevard, *The Storming of Sevastopol, 6 June 1855*, a work by the artist Frantz Rubaud, which is remarkable for its realistic depiction and the force of its impact on viewers. I did not want to leave, so strong was the attraction of this work of art. It seemed as though time had gone backwards and you were really standing among the defenders of the Malakhov Heights. This brought to mind the thought that we now had to repeat the feat of our forebears and defend the city to the last drop of blood.

Sevastopol, which was founded by an edict of Empress Catherine the Great, also had a more ancient history. I took a tram out to Balaklava, a fishing settlement 12km from the city, to view the ruins of the Genoese fortress of Chimbalo and I also visited Tauric Chersonesus, established as far back as the fifth century BC, where I saw the remains of the ancient Greek city, including the foundations of buildings, the basilica, an ancient theatre, fortress towers and walls forming a special area like a barbican for fighting enemy infantry which had broken through to the fortifications.

I could do this because I had money of my own from four months of my soldier's pay. A serviceman in his first year of service got 10 rubles 50 kopecks a month, a corporal sniper – 30 rubles, and a sergeant sniper and section commander – 35 rubles. I spent about 20 rubles on Vesna (Spring) brand chocolates. To my surprise, they were being sold at the Sevastopol army store at the pre-war price.

In the meantime, events in the Crimea were unfolding. On 26 October 1941 the German 11th Army under the command of Colonel General Erich von Manstein, had made it onto the peninsula. Four days later, on Thursday, 30 October, military action commenced on the more distant approaches to the main naval base of the Black Sea Fleet. The quadruple ordnance battery of the 54th Coastal Defences opened fire on a column of German armoured transports, troop-carriers, motorcycles and Stu.G.III self-propelled guns moving along the road towards the village of Nikolayevka.[1] The column was halted by some accurate firing. This day is regarded as the start of the siege of Sevastopol.

An order of 30 October 1941 from the head of the city garrison, Rear-Admiral G.V. Zhukov, was read out to us during drill on the parade ground at the fleet crew premises. It began:

> 1) The enemy has broken through the front line; his advance mechanized units have entered the Yevpatoria-Saki District, threatening Sevastopol . . . 3) Units of the Sevastopol garrison operating in conjunction with ships and coastal artillery must not allow the enemy into the main naval base and must annihilate him on the approaches to Sevastopol . . .

The order mentioned the dispositions of our military units along the forward line from the village of Kamara to the estuary of the river Kach. On land the defence was up to the sixteen batteries of naval infantry, the militia and other detachments located in the city at that moment. The order did not affect me, as I was registered, as before, in the 1st Battalion of the 54th Rifle Regiment, but nobody knew where it was located. Major Khubezhev did not give me leave on that day and again offered a transfer to the naval infantry. Along with the other recuperating troops, I busied myself with tidying the grounds.

I did not have time to regret this. In the afternoon, following dinner, two young assistants from the naval library turned up. They were on their usual weekly round of fleet units, collecting books they had issued to soldiers earlier and offering new ones. In an instant a crowd gathered around them. The troops were exchanging books, chatting with the girls about what they had read, and putting in requests. I borrowed a tattered booklet in a soft cover with a coloured drawing depicting the 4th Bastion in 1854: a big cannon on a gun carriage with small wheels, some soldiers and an officer next to it. Above the picture was the name of the author, Leo Tolstoy, and the title, *Sevastopol Sketches*. There were books by other writers, too: Chernyshevsky, Chekhov, Alexei Tolstoy, Sholokhov, Maxim Gorky – but Leo Tolstoy enjoyed much greater demand.

It was a long time since my hands had held a book – the student's faithful companion. I had had to forget about them since I donned a uniform and became a Red Army soldier in the 25th Chapayev Division. Books had been left behind, in my pre-war life, and now they reminded me of peace, stability and modern comforts. Not without some excitement, I opened the cover. I had read *Sevastopol Sketches*, of course, but a very long time ago, probably as a child. One of the library girls began to talk to me about the work. She warmly recommended it, saying it was interesting and quite relevant to the current scene. I agreed with her: not even 100 years had passed and new conquerors were now approaching the legendary city with the same intentions.

Reading helped to pass the time. As a participant in the first defence of the city, young artillery lieutenant Count Tolstoy knew what he was talking about when he described military action. In my younger years, I had probably failed to appreciate how accurate the great writer was in his psychological detail. But now, as I recalled the battle for Odessa, I was amazed at the perceptiveness with which he conveyed the feelings of a man who is sensing mortal danger in combat for the first time:

> The long whistle of a cannon ball or shell while you are climbing the hill will have an unpleasant impact. You will suddenly realize, and in quite a different way from before, the significance of those shots which you heard in the city. Some quietly joyous recollection will suddenly flash up in your imagination, your own person will begin to occupy you more than your observations; your attention to everything around will diminish and a sort of unpleasant feeling of indecisiveness suddenly overpower you. Despite this ignoble voice, which has suddenly spoken up within you at the sight of danger, and, especially if you have looked at the soldier who trots past you with a laugh, waving his arms and sliding down the hill across the liquid mud, you force yourself to silence this voice, unwittingly thrust out your chest and raise your head higher.

Tolstoy drew vivid portraits of his comrades in arms, the soldiers and officers of the Russian imperial army who were fighting back then on the bastions. It is as if he brought these heroes closer to us by making their thoughts, dreams and actions comprehensible. I do not think that anyone before him spoke so convincingly of the sources of the Russian warrior spirit.

> It is even highly possible that, out of vanity or simply for pleasure, a naval officer will want to do a bit of firing in your presence, 'to order the gunner and crew to the cannon'. And in a lively and cheerful fashion, about fourteen sailors, some thrusting their pipes into their pockets, others chewing the last fragments of a crust, their metal-capped boots rapping the platform, will go up to the cannon and load it. Take a look at the faces, the bearing, the movements of these men; in every wrinkle of each sun-tanned broad-cheeked face, in every muscle, in the breadth of these shoulders, in the girth of the legs shod in enormous boots, in every movement – calm, firm, unhurried – you can see those principal traits that make up the strength of the Russian, simplicity and stubbornness; but here on every face it seems to you that, apart from those hallmarks, the danger, malice and

suffering of war have also laid down traces of an awareness of their own dignity and of lofty thought and feeling.[2]

I was also drawn to Tolstoy's description of Sevastopol's scenery and weather, and the local placenames: Severnaya Storona, Korobelnaya Storona, Malakhov Kurgan, Sapun-Gora, Mekenzievy Gory, Sukharnaya Balka, Martynov Ovrag, Rechka Chornaya, Pavlovsky Mysuk and Kulikovo Polye. Until now I had operated on flat steppe landscapes where visibility was generally excellent and the distances to the target were easily determined. Target shooting in the hills was a completely different matter.

On the morning of 4 November 1941, Major Khubezhev gave me some good news. The commander of the coastal army, General Petrov, had arrived in Sevastopol yesterday along with his headquarters staff and was lodged at the coastal defence command post at the Chersonese barracks. I decided to obtain a meeting with him, but it was not easy for a sergeant to approach a general. I was helped by the fact that his adjutant recognized me.

Petrov looked to me the same as ever: spruce and energetic. The white dust of the Crimean roads had settled on his jacket with its general's stars on the tabs. A brown cavalry harness with a belt and two shoulder straps firmly gripped his lean figure, and the holster of the Korovin pistol which was issued to senior commanders had been noticeably moved to his right-hand side. As usual, Petrov held a riding crop in his hands, even though it was in a vehicle that he toured the firing lines, acquainting himself with the military units that occupied them and viewing the sites and the military engineering works. The commander stopped as he got out of a Gorky-produced GAZ-M1 car. I strode towards him, stood at attention and announced myself: 'Sergeant Pavlichenko, Comrade Major-General. Permission to speak.'

'Greetings, Lyudmila.' He smiled. 'How are you feeling?'

'Excellent, Comrade Major-General.'

'So, are we going to beat the Nazis in Sevastopol?'

'Absolutely, Comrade Major-General.'

'I have to inform you that you are now a senior sergeant and will command a sniper platoon.' Petrov removed his pince-nez and wiped it with a snow-white handkerchief. 'When the reinforcement drafting takes place, select some suitable personnel and teach them the skills of sharpshooting.'

'Yes, Major-General!' I responded cheerfully and, lowering my voice, asked with concern, 'But where is my regiment, Ivan Yefimovich?'

'I think the Razins are on the road between Yalta and Gurzuf. They'll be in Sevastopol in five days. Will you wait for them?'

'Yes, Comrade Major-General. Since my earliest days of service my heart has been with the 1st Battalion of Captain Sergienko and my beloved 2nd Company.'

'I admire your dedication to the army.' Petrov smiled again.

In accordance with orders from the commander of the coastal army, all the necessary documents were prepared for me at the staff headquarters and I was issued an authorization for the regiment and the quartermaster. I had to acquire various components of the winter uniform – for example, a cap with earflaps, a padded jacket and warm underwear. It was with special pleasure that I attached to the tabs of my tunic the three dark ruby triangles denoting my new military rank of senior sergeant. Apart from that I was entitled to a leather belt with a shoulder strap, a single-pin brass buckle and a holster with ramrod to accommodate a pistol.

I never subsequently parted with this firearm, the Tula-Tokarev given to me in Sevastopol. I had it with me in sniper's hideouts, on leave in the city and, of course, on parade, and, following evacuation, it accompanied me to Novorossiysk and then to Moscow. The TT became my talisman. While hunting for Fritzes in the Crimean forest I relied, in the event of failure, not so much on the grenade which always hung from my belt, but on my 'Totosha' [TN: a pet-name for Anton] (as we called the Tokarev pistol in the army). Neither the Russians nor the Germans took snipers prisoners, but shot them directly on the spot. For women there was another variation – death preceded by gang rape.[3] Therefore, the grenade was for rolling under the enemy's feet, seven bullets from the TT were for anyone who came too close, and the eighth was for yourself.

I do not deny that a pistol weighing 825g without its eight-cartridge magazine is somewhat heavy for a woman's hand. Some even reproached the Russian engineer Tokarev because his weapon was too similar to the invention of the 'pistol king', John Moses Browning, especially the Belgian-produced 1903 model. But is it for those of us concerned with practical shooting to listen to theoreticians' disputes remote from real life? The most important thing was that the TT met all the demands of the front line: a powerful 7.62mm-calibre cartridge which could penetrate a brick wall 100mm thick, a sturdy barrel, a reliable trigger mechanism and a conveniently shaped butt.[4]

My regimental comrades approached Sevastopol on 9 November 1941, and, together with the entire 25th Rifle Division, occupied positions along a 12km line in the third defence sector, i.e. on the Mekenzi hills, between the Belbek and Chornaya rivers, approximately 20 to 25km from the city. Here, forested heights alternated with fairly deep ravines, known locally as 'balkas'. For instance, Tyomnaya Balka, situated close to Kamyshly gully, or Martynov Balka, next to Martynov gully. Also located there were several Tartar villages: Kamyshly, Belbek, Biyuk-Otarka, Zalitskoi, Duvankoi and also the Mekenzi hills railway junction. At a height of over 300 metres above sea level lay the village of Mekenzia, sometimes designated on maps as 'No. 2 Forest Cordon'. At the end of the eighteenth century the village actually belonged to a rear-admiral of the Russian imperial navy, Thomas MacKenzie, who was a Scottish highlander by origin.

By now, the firing lines for the defenders of Sevastopol had already been prepared: the trenches, communication passages, dugouts, artillery and machine-gun emplacements and reinforced-earth firing points. The soldiers and officers of the 54th Rifle Regiment, the 287th Rifle Regiment, and the 3rd Regiment and 7th Brigade of the marine infantry, which were now becoming part of our division, had received an order to make a stand 1 to 2km to the west of Mekenzia village, which had earlier been captured by the Germans.

Arriving at the regiment's positions, I hoped to see all my fellow servicemen in good health, since I had no knowledge of the way the battles had gone in the north of the peninsula at the end of October. But at the command post I was greeted not by Major Matusyevich, who was known to all of us from the defence of Odessa, but by Major Vasily Ivanovich Petrash, who had been transferred to us from the 31st Regiment, where he had previously commanded a battalion. To my question about Matusyevich, Petrash replied that he was wounded but would probably soon return to the regiment. I then went to the command post of the 1st Battalion. Here, instead of Captain Sergienko, I beheld a lieutenant who was not known to me – a tall, slim man of about thirty-five, who had clearly come out of the reserves. On introducing myself I handed him my documents. He glanced through them cursorily, then gave me a stern look of dissatisfaction.

'You wish to become a platoon commander, Senior Sergeant? Are you really up to it?'

'That's not for me to decide, Comrade Lieutenant, but senior command.'

'Which senior command do you mean? I, for instance, am opposed to women occupying field positions in the army. You're a sniper, so fire away at the Nazis by all means. But orders will be issued by those who are supposed to issue them.' And he casually tossed my documents onto the desk.

'Who is supposed to, Comrade Lieutenant?' I was not going to give in.

'Men, of course . . .'

However, Lieutenant Grigory Fyodorovich Dromin was forced to change his views. It was plainly explained to him that the decision about my appointment had been taken not by the commander of the 25th Division, Major-General Kolomiyets, but by the commander-in-chief of the coastal army, Major-General Petrov. Naturally, as a result of this, my relations with the present commander of the 1st Battalion did not improve. True, Dromin left me in peace, but at the same time he had no intention of praising me or reprimanding me, and even less of rewarding me.

From the command post of the 1st Battalion a winding forest trail led to the lines of the 2nd Company. The army sappers had constructed good, deep, dugouts in the Mekenzi hills. On entering one of them, I came across Corporal Fyodor Sedykh. That was a joy and a half. We embraced and kissed three times on the cheek according to Russian custom. My old battle comrade did not look well; he was much thinner, his features were sunken, and he had a light wound on his left hand. We immediately heated some water in a mess tin for tea, got some sugar and plain biscuits, and sat down to talk.

Fyodor painted some gloomy pictures. The Nazis had come into contact with our units on 24 October on the Red Army lines near Ishun. Our troops had stoutly beaten them back and launched counter-attacks, but gradually the enemy's superiority in artillery and aviation began to tell. As well as that, the firing lines were badly prepared; the Soviet forces were deployed almost in open steppe. Captain Sergienko, for instance, was seriously wounded in the leg, the bone was shattered from a direct mortar hit on the battalion command post, which occupied a simple trench; he was dispatched deep into the rear. Almost half the 2nd Company had fallen victim to enemy artillery. The sniper's platoon was not even worth mentioning. The regiment had 600–700 men left from a peacetime contingent of just over 3,000 soldiers and officers.

'To the left of the 95th Division the Razin Regiment of the 25th Division was advancing,' L.N. Bacharov, one of the participants in this combat operation, later recalled.

The Razins began well. They were well coordinated and, shouting 'Hurrah!', took on the Nazis with bayonets. The 2nd Company was sent into attack by the secretary of the regimental Party bureau, Semyashkin. Over 100 Nazis were killed by the 3rd company. Its commander, Senior Lieutenant Yeryomenko, was wounded but continued to direct the engagement . . . The coastal division fought in the Crimea with the same selfless valour as at Odessa, where they had been only eight days earlier. However, there was a feeling that our initial success would not be sustainable; the infantry were very poorly supported by artillery, few batteries had been moved up, and shells were in short supply. The attack was preceded by a burst of fire only fifteen minutes long. None of our air force was in the skies. Everything pointed to the haste and lack of preparation with which the advance had been launched . . . At midday on 26 October the German forces moved forward, supported by a large number of aircraft and tanks. In the days that followed the enemy increased their forces and followed up on their success.[5]

Fyodor and I shared pleasant memories of Captain Sergienko. While he had been in charge of the 1st Battalion, life went well for everyone. Why this was, we did not even bother to think. An experienced and able officer, attentive to the needs of his subordinates, but demanding at the same time, he enjoyed boundless respect from his troops. The regimental commanders, Lieutenant Colonel Svidnitsky and later Major Matusyevich, also paid heed to his advice.

For me Captain Sergienko was like a guardian angel, especially, what is more, regarding personal matters. I am not giving away any secrets if I say that serving as a woman in the army has its particular challenges. One's behaviour in male company must be even-handed, strict and beyond reproach; no flirting with anyone, ever! But life takes its own course and there were times when difficulties arose. They were not created at all by rank-and-file soldiers, but rather by my 'comrade officers', using both their status as commanders and the clause in the military code that a commanding officer's order must be fulfilled and one must answer for failure to do so in accordance with wartime laws. We called this 'taking a fancy to'. That is why I preferred to spend more time on the front line, albeit under enemy fire. Here the chances of catching the eye of some amorous possessor of three or four little cubes or bars on his collar tabs (that is, from the middle and senior officer corps) remained minimal. If something like this happened, Battalion Commander Sergienko would ask the aspirant directly: 'What do you want from her?' For some reason nobody had the courage to answer him honestly. With this, the soliciting, awkward conversations and indecent proposals generally concluded. Unfortunately, I know nothing of the further fortunes of this brave and noble man.

While our 54th Regiment was being kept in divisional reserve, Corporal Sedykh and I tackled various organizational matters. We had to receive reinforcements, take possession of and examine the new rifles (Three Lines with PE sights) and study the defence sector that had been entrusted to the 2nd Company. It was becoming obvious that the trenches were not deep, no more than 50cm, and there were no communication passages at all in some places. The soldiers would have to do something about this and what they needed were not sniper rifles but small sapper's spades. We had the honour of seeing the commander of our division, Major-General Kolomiyets, on the morning of 10 November. He came to reconnoitre the locations, went around the lines and sternly pointed out the poorly constructed earthen fortifications.

According to the establishment laid down by the People's Commissariat of Defence on 5 April 1941, a rifle platoon was composed of quite a large group – fifty-one troops. It was commanded by a lieutenant armed with a pistol; he had a deputy with the rank of senior sergeant, who had a PPD-40 submachine gun and a dispatch rider (for communication with superiors) with a Mosin rifle. The platoon consisted of four rifle sections, which were headed by sergeants (all armed with SVT-40s).

Attached to the platoon was a mortar section (four men along with a sergeant plus a 50mm mortar). I am recounting this in such detail in order to highlight that I had nothing like this at my disposal. Companies and battalions were now often commanded by lieutenants, and this had come to be the case back in Odessa, where the average officer corps in Red Army detachments was usually put out of commission after two or three weeks of combat. It is even strange to recall the numerical strength of a platoon being fifty troops; at various periods in the defence of Sevastopol they comprised roughly between twenty and twenty-five soldiers, but never more than this. The Degtyrev-designed PPD-40 and, later, the Shpagin's PPSh-41 – with drum magazines for the seventy-one pistol-cartridges – were indisputably effective weapons in close combat, but there was a catastrophic shortage of them in rifle units during the first months of the war. It would appear that our two platoons of regimental scouts had only about twenty-five to thirty PPD-40s between them. The 50mm-calibre mortar was referred to generally as the company mortar. According to the records there were twenty-seven of them in the regiment, but that was only according to the records . . .

Over two days, 10–11 November, the regiment received reinforcements. For the most part these were troops from the marine infantry battalions which were hastily formed in Sevastopol at the end of October. Now they had to join ranks with us Razins, who had come through the crucible of war, and quickly accustom themselves to serving on dry land. They were getting ready to fight the Fascist German invaders to the last drop of blood but had a poor idea of what these coming battles would be like.

Those sailors who ended up in my platoon were particularly surprised and our initial acquaintance sometimes resulted in some amusing scenes. Thus, one day four bold young guys in black caps with earflaps, naval pea jackets and trousers 'wide as the Black Sea', as the saying goes, burst into the dugout and declared that they had been assigned to the detachment of Senior Sergeant Pavlichenko. At that moment I was leafing through the book by my great teacher, studying his tips on shooting in hill country. Fyodor Sedykh, who was checking the breeches of new rifles along with three servicemen, offered them a seat. They put their kitbags on the earth floor, sat down unhurriedly on the wall benches and began to look around. They noticed me, glanced at one another and smiled in unison. 'So, you're serving here too, are you, lass?' one of them asked.

'I am,' I replied.

'Great!' He winked at his mates. 'We've ended up in the right place. What a smashing medic! Honestly, a real beauty – can't take your eyes off her. Let's get acquainted. I'm Leonid, and your name is . . .?'

'Lyudmila.'

'Well, Lyuda, don't frown. Be a bit nicer to the sailors. It won't do you any harm.'

'In that case you will have to stand at attention and line up in front of me and announce your presence to the commander, as you are supposed to in accordance with the military code.'

'But where's the commander?'

'I'm the commander.'

'Quit having us on, Lyuda. That's no way to carry on.'

I had to explain sternly to the lads who was in charge here. Completely bewildered, they nevertheless stood in line at attention, introduced themselves as required, and listened to my first instructions as commander. The expression of surprise never left their faces. It was as if the naval infantrymen expected that any minute now this vexatious misunderstanding would be resolved and that those present would be laughing along with them at what was, in their view, a ridiculous situation. For there was no way such a thing could happen in our army: a woman commanding a sniper platoon!

Yet Leonid Burov and his three friends subsequently gave the best possible account of themselves in combat. Of course they were not able to become real sharpshooters in a week of training, but they acquired the initial skills of handling a sniper rifle and shot quite well under my direction (I would calculate the distance to the target and show them how to regulate the drums on the telescope sights) – especially in the event of frontal attacks from the enemy. They were brave men and it is a pity that Burov lost his life so early on.

The village of Mekenzia, or No. 2 Forest Cordon, was situated on the flat summit of a hill rising 310 metres above sea level. It was surrounded by forest with thick undergrowth of the usual Crimean bushes: juniper, hornbeam, garland thorn, dogwood and wild rose. The warden's homestead consisted of several small one-storey structures, with a vegetable garden and orchard adjacent to them. The old manor house, long fallen into ruin, was located not far away from it, but was almost invisible on account of the trees. The village had become a juncture between the positions of our forces and the German ones in the third sector of the Sevastopol defence district. It stood on a strategically important road which led to the valley of Kara-Koba. If they took it, the enemy would be able to get through to the rear of the city's defenders on the easterly side. Besides, by driving our units back some distance from the village, the Germans would force their way through to the Mekenzi hills railway station and from there to the northern shore of the biggest and longest bay, which would have sealed the fate of the city.

In the first days of November 1941 the Nazis seized the village of Mekenzia itself but did not penetrate further for the time being. They were gathering their strength for a new strike. The Soviet senior command considered it essential to drive the enemy out of there, and fierce battles for the village went on for two weeks, almost until the end of November. Here the soldiers and officers of the 54th Stepan Razin Regiment shed blood for Sevastopol for the first time. It was at first light on 12 November. Our battalion was fighting on lines north of the village. The divisional commander, Major-General Kolomiyets, arrived at the command post to observe the battle. After assessing the situation, he set the Razins a combat objective: to attack the Fritzes on 14 November, surround them in the village, and wipe them out after taking control of this point.

'And so to our first serious counter-attack at Sevastopol,' the commander of the glorious Chapayev Division, Trofim Kolomiyets, wrote subsequently.

All the infantry of the third sector opened fire on the enemy forward line and its closest rear units in the district of Cherkez-Kermen [now the village of Krepkoye]. I had moved beforehand to the command post of the 2nd Razin Battalion, which was inflicting the blow and from there I observed the attack. It began successfully. With a speedy assault, the companies reached the first line of German trenches. Over the course of several minutes the enemy was crushed. While the 2nd and 3rd Companies were pursuing the Nazis, who were dashing through the forest, the 1st was cutting off the road leading from Cherkez-Kermen to the village of Mekenzia. The encirclement of the village began.

The Fascists lodged there resisted furiously. The fire was such that our troops had to go to ground. Grossman [chief gunner of the 25th Rifle Division] assisted them with artillery fire. But, while the gunners were crushing the Nazi resistance by the village of Mekenzia, German infantry appeared from the Cherkez-Kermen side. However, the Razins were holding on stoutly and the Fascist attack was choking. Then fresh German units approached from Cherkez-Kermen and everything started again. On our side two reserve platoons were brought into action, but this was plainly not enough. Major Matusyevich decided to withdraw one company from the approaches to the village and counter-attack the enemy reserve with it . . . The battle continued for more than three hours. The Razins were thus unable to complete their objective in full. However, the Germans received such palpable losses that they did not undertake any active moves against our division for another five days.[6]

8

Forest Trails

The village of Mekenzia proved a tough nut to crack. Soviet units undertook a final attack on it on the morning of 22 December. The Razins advanced, along with the 2nd Perekop Regiment of naval infantry. The enemy mounted desperate resistance. The naval infantry managed to seize the road from Mekenzia to the village of Cherkez-Kermen, but got no further. By the middle of the day military action had ceased on both sides. The village remained in the hands of the Fritzes. The Chapayevs secured positions on Heights 319.6, 278.4, and 175.8, located 1 kilometre to the west of this ill-fated village.

Thus ended the first assault on Sevastopol, which had lasted twenty-five days. The invaders enjoyed practically no success. They had managed to push the defenders back 3–4km in the first defence sector to the east of the fishing settlement of Balaklava and 1–2km in the third sector of the Sevastopol defence district by the villages of Duvankoi, Cherkez-Kermen and Mekenzia.

A relatively peaceful period of life ensued on the defence lines. The lines stretched out over 46km of forested Crimean hills and valleys, from the seashore at Balaklava to the shallow and turbulent river Belbek. No man's land was of a similar length and on both sides there were deep trenches, winding communication passages, machine-gun nests and stretches of anti-tank ditches, minefields and fortifications with barbed wire (the barbed wire was often strung straight across the trunks of the trees in the forest). This neutral strip was between 100 and 200 metres wide. There were some crossing points. We snipers and our regimental and divisional scouts were able to cross it completely inconspicuously, especially at night on the Mekenzi hills, along the high ridge of the Kamyshly gully (it stretched for several kilometres, beginning not far from the large village of Duvankoi[1] and inclining to the north-west, towards the village of Mekenzia) and across the slopes of Tyomnaya Balka, which was adjacent to the gully, the floor of which really was covered with reeds [TN: *kamysh* in Russian].

The crossing points were also used by German reconnaissance teams. On occasion a couple of dozen submachine-gunners would break through the forest towards us, armed with MP. 40 submachine guns, better known to us by the popular (if misleading) name 'Schmeisser', although the well-known German engineer Hugo Schmeisser had nothing to do with this weapon and it was originally manufactured by the Erfurter Maschinenfabrik ('Erma'). After stumbling upon our patrols, they would hurriedly pull back. We received no orders to pursue them, but for the sake of training we were able to practise target shooting until the Nazis hid behind trees.

On one occasion smoke from powder was still wreathing the hills, and the echoes of the last shots were resounding around the gullies and general terrain, when a white-haired man in a grey civilian jacket with a knapsack on his shoulders emerged from a thicket by the 2nd Company's trenches.[2] He was very much like a wood sprite with his thin, stooped figure and a shaggy beard, which almost reached his eyes. The soldiers of the sniper platoon almost shot him in surprise. He threw both hands up and frantically shouted: 'Friend!' In his hands he was holding an open Soviet passport and a certificate in the form of brown documents with a purple stamp.

Lowering my rifle, I asked him who he was, what he was doing on the military lines of the 54th Regiment, and how he had managed to get past the enemy lookouts. The old man replied in a way that suggested that this was not difficult at all; the Germans did not venture far into the woods and were afraid to do so, while he, being a local ranger, had skirted round them, using obscure tracks known to him alone. At this point he started weeping. The tears rolled down his white beard and began to fall onto his jacket, which was cinched by a hunter's cartridge belt, albeit an empty one. I have to admit that for the first few minutes I was embarrassed. The incident seemed to me to be very peculiar. But Fyodor Sedykh instantly believed the old man for some reason. He persuaded me to let the ranger through onto our side and listen to his story.

Soon after, over a hot breakfast delivered to the watch trenches by a sergeant major, we discussed the story of the ranger Anastas Vartanov. It was a very tragic one, like many other events in this hellish war. A group of Nazi scouts had turned up at No. 2 Forest Cordon, ahead of their conventional units. For some reason they took a dislike to Vartanov's son, grandson and the ranger's whole family. Without pondering for too long, the Nazis shot them next to the house. Anastas himself had, fortunately or unfortunately, left that morning for the municipal authority offices to register some supplementary expenses and procure oats and hay for winter forage.

According to the ranger, there was now a sort of German staff headquarters in the village of Mekenzia. Under the trees next to his house stood some caterpillar armoured transports with aerials and machine guns on the roofs of the cabs, as well as some tractor-borne cannons, cars and motorbikes with sidecars. Arriving there were not only troops dressed in grey-green uniforms, but also some in short black jackets and berets (in other words, tank crew). The main occupant was a big man of about forty with blue eyes. The ranger had seen him in a parade tunic with braided silver epaulettes and a black and white cross under his uniform collar. He lived in the room of Vartanov junior, who had been shot, and every morning he would dowse himself with cold water at the pump, rub himself with a red towel and vigorously go through some exercises.

'They have everything at their pleasure,' said Anastas, using a spoon to scoop up the dregs of the barley porridge from the bottom of the mess tin. 'But they must be afraid.'

'Of whom?' I asked.

'The Russians,' Vartanov replied. 'I was told you had some sort of rifles with special sights.'

'True.'

'You need to use them. I'll show you the place. The village will be very easy to spot. In fact, it's not far from here. Through the forest, about 5km using a short cut. We can easily get there overnight.'

'Do you want to go with us?'

'Very much. If I'm not there to see it, I've got no reason in the whole wide world for living.'

The old hunter's ambition to punish the enemy for the extermination of his family was one I understood. I found it natural and legitimate. There can be no forgiveness of invaders for their savage deeds, for senseless murder of peaceful residents. The earth should burn under their feet. They needed to be hunted down everywhere and annihilated by every means. Anastas had turned for help to us snipers, and we would fulfil his request, if the information now passed on to us was confirmed at the staff headquarters of the Sevastopol defence district.

The reply came back two days later. Vartanov had told the truth.

The request had not been sent by me, but by the regimental staff deputy head of reconnaissance, Captain Mikhail Bezrodny. He had served in the 54th Regiment, it would appear, from June 1941 and commanded two reconnaissance platoons: one cavalry, the other infantry. Of the cavalry reconnaissance, nothing remained, as the horses had been abandoned in Odessa. The infantry group, now reduced from forty-six troops to twenty-five, was still in existence. Earlier, during the defence of Odessa, I had had occasion to interact with scouts: for example, covering them as they were crossing the front line in search of a prisoner for interrogation. But at that time the battalions of our regiment frequently operated separately, in different sectors of the front, and I had practically no contact with the officers of the regimental general staff. Now that the Razins were all gathered together and in quite cramped positions, meetings with them -- at least with Captain Bezrodny – had become more frequent and very useful.

The captain approved my plan for a raid on the village of Mekenzia on condition that the ranger Anastas Vartanov would act as guide to the group. First, though, it was necessary to find out where the route went, what the situation now was around No. 2 Forest Cordon, and what the group of snipers might run into, if it did go out on the raid. I went with the forester through the forest on the Mekenzi hills to reconnoitre.

I had another goal in doing this. While the Germans were engaged in their first assault, we had to think about repelling their attacks on our fortifications, to operate together with everyone else, as an integrated force. With the stabilization of the front, the time for individual sniper 'hunts' was approaching, but how could I make a start, if I did not know the locality and was not used to shooting in hills covered with dense forest? What was it like, anyway, this forest, which stood like a green wall and rustled in the unruly wind from the sea?

First light was just creeping in. There was a sudden gust of wind. The tops of the trees began to sway and the bare branches knocked together. In the dissolving gloom one could imagine they were reanimated forest beings and that the brief bursts of knocking were their secret language. I listened and raised my head. Leaning over the track was the curiously bent grey-brown trunk of a sycamore. Several large orange leaves, similar to a human palm, were still hanging above on long stalks. Suddenly one of them broke off and, circling in the air, fell onto the path at my feet. Vartanov pointed at it: 'Pick it up. It's a lucky sign.'

The beautiful sycamore leaf did not match a sniper's autumn attire – a dirty-yellow camouflage jacket with brown markings. I put it in my pocket, which already contained an individual toilet pack and a piece of refined lump sugar carefully wrapped in foil, along with a pinch of dry tea. If you chewed the sugar with the tea, it fortified you during the many hours spent in a hideout.

What kind of ambush was awaiting me now, I did not know. I simply followed the forester along a barely detectable hunter's track and kept a close watch on the forest. After the deserted immeasurable Odessa steppes, this seemed to me to be an ideal place for camouflage, but far from ideal for sharpshooting. Where would the bullet fly? A bullet was no hare, able to loop between the tree trunks. How could one correctly calculate the distance to the target when there were gullies rendered invisible by the bushes growing all over them?

'From the bent sycamore to the well is 85 metres,' said the old warden softly. 'Remember that. It'll come in handy, my child.'

Vartanov had almost read my thoughts. Perhaps, in the delicate forest silence of first light, thoughts were shared with extraordinary ease among conversationalists who were close to each other in spirit. A week ago, I would have been unaware of the very existence of Vartanov, born in the Crimea in the previous century into a family of Russified Armenians who had for 100 years faithfully and truly served the Romanov imperial family, which owned vast hunting areas on the peninsula. Vartanov and his close family had spent their whole life at No. 2 Forest Cordon, the village of Mekenzia. There they had a whole property: a house with four rooms, a summer kitchen, a bath house, a woodshed, a barn, a stable, and greenhouses adjacent to a kitchen garden. The ranger toiled from dawn to dusk, because the forest demanded constant care, but he regarded himself as a happy, and lucky, man. His house was an overflowing cup, his eldest son was already helping him, his wife was good-natured and hard-working, and the youngest children were always looked after, clad and shod. It was not to the liking of the Germans, cursed be their name, on that November day.

After the sycamore with the bent trunk the track forked. Had it not been for Vartanov, I would not even have noticed the turning to the right. The thickets of bushes up to 2 metres high spread out wide at this point and concealed the undergrowth like a thick veil. The old hunter pointed to this plant, which he termed 'garland thorn' or 'Christ thorn'. According to legend, Jesus Christ's crown of thorns was woven from it. It grew principally in the Mediterranean and North Africa, but it had also taken root in the Crimea.

By November the leaves of the garland thorn are dropping and its main weapon – the thorns – emerges in its full beauty. A great multitude of zigzagging shoots, both long and short, spread out in different directions from a greyish trunk, and the thorns protrude from them. Some are straight like needles, while others are bent and sharp like fishhooks.

I turned awkwardly, and just such a malevolent barb instantly seized the sleeve of my camouflage jacket! The point went quite deep into the fabric. You had to break the whole twig, whereupon the dry snap in the morning silence resounded like a signal of alarm. A flock of tomtits took off from a nearby acacia. Vartanov turned to me: 'Careful, Comrade Commander!'

Soon we spotted the old water system – a rusty pipe about 20cm in diameter. It led to the abandoned well. A crane with its beak raised to the sky pointed to its presence. The wood was becoming thicker, the trees crowding one another by the source of the life-giving liquid. Suddenly a hoarse sigh was heard from that direction. The forester froze like a statue and, being close behind, I bumped into him.

In the well – a black hole in the earth, roughly walled off by large stones and half covered with planks – was a wild boar, a young one with light brown hair and tusks not yet grown. He could not get out of the trap on his own, though he was doing his best. On seeing us, the beast made a desperate dash, but he was unable to climb out. Turning his head, he looked at the ranger with sad, dark brown eyes and grunted pitifully.

'Do you want to finish him off?' asked Vartanov. 'Fresh pork rissoles. What soldier would turn it down?'

'No,' I replied, looking at the youngster with curiosity. 'I like him. He's still little. Let him live.'

The hunter seemed cheered. He selected a long beam close to the well, thrust it under the boar's belly, lifted it up, transferred it onto level ground and set it down. It took a while for the rescued animal to come his senses. Rolling from side to side, the piglet let out a squeal, as if he could not believe his liberation. Then he jumped to his feet, shook himself and, with a snap of fallen twigs, charged at full tilt away from the cursed spot. All that could be seen was his jauntily twisted tail flashing in the bushes. I could not help laughing.

I did not approve of hunting animals and still don't. Forest creatures seem to me to be defenceless and unfortunate in the face of humans armed with rapid-fire rifles. It was different long ago, when a prince went out alone with a spear against a bear. That kind of duel, in my view, was more honourable and fair.

Judging by the map with which Captain Bezrodny had supplied me, no man's land ended beyond the well and thence began the territory seized by the Germans. We sat down to rest. Drinking water from a well where a piglet had just been bathing was not a good idea, but I had a flask full of boiled water. The dry rations issued at the company kitchen consisted of a crust of rye bread and two strips of rosy fatback sprinkled with salt and ground black pepper. We made do with that. Vartanov, who had received the same rations, began to tell me about the Crimean forest.

He adored it and knew it superbly well; this knowledge was inherited, passed down to him from his father. Vartanov said that I had acted correctly in letting the boar go and the forest would reward me for it, for in a forest, as in a temple, one had to observe the age-old customs and never kill gratuitously, for the sake of amusement. I asked the ranger if it was easy to find your way in a wood and not get lost among the trees.

'It's easy,' he answered. 'They're like people. Each one has its character. Trees differ in species, age, flowering season and fruit-bearing. I can see their faces and shapes. They are very different. You can see it too, if you want to . . .'

It was difficult to take these reflections seriously. They were like a fairy tale, a legend, but I did not interrupt Vartanov. I let him talk, let him teach me about the life of the forest. As it was, I understood nothing and viewed the thick trunks of the elms and sycamores around the well with some confusion. The cold overcast morning invested them with a gloomy colour. I did not really believe that I would be able to adjust to life here and read the enigmatic symbols of the forest.

We came upon Mekenzia from the north-west when the sun was rising. To get a better view of the place, you had to climb a tree. I spent quite a long time with binoculars, observing the regular pattern of life in the rear of the 11th Army. German transport and people in mouse-coloured jackets and overcoats were regularly moving along the road between Mekenzia and the village of Zalinkoi. Crimean Tartars with the white bands of the Politsai (the pro-Nazi collaborationist police force) around their arms were in great heart. They were guarding the barrier at the cordon and standing to attention as they greeted the Fritzes.

Around midday, a field kitchen appeared, and the seductive aroma of meat and potato soup reached our nostrils. About fifty soldiers with mess tins gathered at the kitchen. After receiving their portions, they did not immediately disperse, but chatted among themselves, smoked and waited for the coffee. The lower ranks of the German army were only entitled to ersatz rather than real coffee, and its aroma was not especially pleasant.

After dinner the blue-eyed officer with the braided silver epaulettes emerged from the house. I was already conversant with enemy uniforms. This was an artillery major and recipient of the Knight's Cross as well as of the silver *Sturmabzeichen*. The door of the house from which he had appeared was about 100 metres away from my tree and exactly opposite it – that is, on the same side as the German rear lines. I noted this on a piece of paper attached to a flat field bag, a so-called 'firing map'. The major lit up a cigar and, together with an orderly holding a folder in his hands, got into an Opel-Kapitan car. Bouncing over the bumps, the vehicle set off along the road, but to the settlement of Cherkez-Kermen rather than the village of Zalinkoi. There, according to our reconnaissance reports, the staff headquarters of the 11th Army was located, and its commander, Colonel General Erich von Manstein resided there. The major was probably hurrying off for a meeting with his superior.

I did a rough sketch on paper of the ranger's whole homestead: the house represented by a square, the animal yard and barns by a triangle, the road by a thick wavy line, and the barrier on it by two small lines. I estimated the rough distances between them by eye. In the centre of the composition was a very noticeable landmark – a whitish layered rock, covered with pits and cracks. This is how limestone rocks show up on the surface. The phenomenon is frequently found on the slopes and summits of the Crimean hills and mountains, which have what are known as cuesta geological formations.

Wind is an almost constant presence in the hills. I noted that on the trees around the village the slender branches were swaying, the leaves were fluttering strongly, and white dust was swirling in the air above the road. This meant that the wind speed was moderate, 4–6 metres per second. Not for nothing does the sniper's proverb proclaim: 'The rifle fires the bullet, but the wind carries it.' If we were to choose this position, we would have a wind from the side blowing at a 90-degree angle. In such conditions and at a distance of 100 metres from the target, the sniper had a simple calculation: the horizontal lateral correction would be several milliradians. True, there was one further consideration: in locations high above sea level the atmospheric pressure changes (the air becomes thinner). In this case the distance of the bullet's trajectory and flight would increase. However, Potapov had written in his booklet *Instructions for Sharpshooters* that in hills under 500 metres in height – and here the altitude did not exceed 310 metres – one could ignore a longitudinal wind but a lateral wind must be taken into consideration, for it could cause the bullet to drift laterally to a significant extent.

On getting down from the tree I showed my handiwork to Vartanov. He was very surprised. There was no point in explaining everything to the ranger, but he helped to calculate the distances more precisely, marking the distance from the homestead gates to the limestone rock as 43 metres. I asked him about the wind and was told that in November and December strong winds blew here from the north and north-east, bringing rain and cloud.

We decided not to delay preparations for the operation, since the information could become outdated. Following my report, Captain Bezrodny warned me that in a raid on Mekenzia I would not be in a position to control the fire of the entire group, because there were many new recruits in the platoon. They had not yet learned the ballistic tables by heart, had not set eyes on Potapov's remarkable book and did not know all the finer points of firing accurately in the hills. Besides, it would be a sudden and swift attack and every bullet must hit its target; that would guarantee the success of the entire operation.

The composition of the group was immediately determined. It naturally included Fyodor Sedykh, who had recently, at my recommendation, been promoted to junior sergeant. Fyodor was a brave man, tested in many battles, and he even more or less knew his way around the ballistics tables. His physical strength and endurance were beyond reproach. After consulting, we took with us Leonid Burov from among the new recruits. The former naval infantryman had shown great zeal both as a serviceman and as a student. Seemingly, he wanted somehow to erase the impression left by our first meeting. I should point out that he was succeeding in doing this; he had ability as a sharpshooter. The third sniper was Fyodor's fellow Siberian, Ivan Peregudov. He had joined the regiment from the draft back in Odessa.

Captain Bezrodny provided two soldiers from the infantry reconnaissance platoon. They could shoot all kinds of manual weapons, had skills in hand-to-hand combat and had ventured into the enemy rear a number of times. I was not acquainted with them, but the captain assured me that these were his best troops. In regimental reconnaissance the best people are usually too independent, and I asked the captain to explain to them that I would not stand for any nonsense on the raid and they must obey me without question. He did this in his characteristic ironic manner: 'I'm warning you, lads, that Sergeant Lyudmila Pavlichenko is a serious woman and doesn't like tomfoolery. Anything amiss, and you'll end up with a knife in your foot.'

On Bezrodny's orders, the scouts were issued with two newish PPSh-41 submachine guns and a DP light machine gun with three spare drums. I took my honorary 'Sveta' with me and the snipers their Mosin rifles with PE sights. We thought for a long time about how to arm Vartanov. He only knew how to fire the antiquated Berdan II single-shot bolt-action rifle. Naturally we did not have any of these ancient Berdans in our armoury, and so we provided him with an ordinary Three Line. Apart from the weapons, we took with us sapper's spades, Finnish (or combat) knives, flasks of water, dry rations, a supply of 200 cartridges and five grenades each. Hanging on my belt as always was the TT pistol with two magazines – sixteen shots. However, if the pistol needed to be used on such a raid, that would mean that things had taken a bad turn.

But the pistol was not needed. At first light we approached the village and, in accordance with the plan we had worked out, took up positions in the Nazi rear. I was with the old ranger opposite the house, keeping its entrance in our sights. The three snipers were fifteen paces to the left, and the two scouts fifteen paces to the right, their target being the middle of the clearing and the limestone rock where the field kitchen stopped. The wind rose a little later and blew in gusts, strengthening to 8–9 metres a second. We worked out its direction: it was at right angles to our position. I calculated the necessary correction for the dial of the lateral drum on the tube of the telescope sight and showed my troops, so that they could regulate the sights on their rifles too.

The Germans – very disciplined soldiers – had gathered at the right place, at the right time and in the right numbers. The kitchen rolled up at 11.37 in the morning and began dishing out at 11.50.

Observing them through binoculars, I waited until they had crowded more closely around the kitchen. I kept my sight on a lanky junior officer with two crossed stripes on his epaulettes – a candidate for officer rank. He stood out among the others, telling them something in a loud voice, and the ordinary soldiers were listening to him. Finally, the junior officer went up to the cook, who was ladling out the soup. His head with its uniform cloth cap ended up exactly between the three lines in the eyepiece of my sight. The moment had, as it were, arrived.

The commander always shoots first and this serves as a signal for the remainder of the group, who await it impatiently and then quickly proceed to carry out the order given in this unusual way. We unleashed a hail of fire from three points. The bullets flew into the grey-green crowd, began to make mincemeat of them and knocked the enemy to the ground. The Germans did not have their weapons with them and could not immediately respond. In any case, many were already dead within the first few minutes of the attack. Among this number were the junior officer and the cook, who had received a hot gift in the head from my 'Sveta'.

The artillery major leapt out of the house on hearing the shots and shouts. A bullet got him between the eyes. Not for nothing had I devoted so much time to studying this position. The old ranger was also firing, and quite accurately. He felled an orderly. We charged towards the house across the clearing, which was covered with Nazi bodies. I pulled the major's documents out from his tunic pocket, used my Finnish-style knife to cut off one epaulette and the metallic Knight's Cross, and took the Walther officer's pistol from the black leather holster at his waist. Meanwhile the scouts burst into the building, firing their submachine guns. They wanted to grab staff papers.

'*Partisanen!*' came a shout from inside.

The corporal radio operator did not manage to impart any more to his superiors, as he had taken a bullet in the chest. Everything lying in front of him on the desk – maps, orders, reports, codebooks – ended up in the hands of the brave soldiers of the 54th Stepan Razin Rifle Regiment. As they ran back, they also grabbed a tightly packed knapsack hanging on the wall and took an MP. 40 submachine gun from the chest of a sentry lying by the doorway.

The group left the scene of combat as swiftly as it had attacked. We ran through the forest for almost 1.5km. We were heading away to the south-east along a hunter's trail known to Vartanov. He was leading us towards no man's land, but we could not cross it in daytime. The ranger had a distant place in mind: a wooden shack half dug into the earth not far from a spring, surrounded by tall trees, with thick undergrowth of wild rose and prickly juniper. There we collapsed onto the ground from overwhelming fatigue. Vartanov, who had not been into his house but observed our action from the clearing, nobly offered to be sentry. The rest of us lay down on the soft reddish-brown conifer needles under the wild rose and dropped off into the deep sleep of the soldier.

Three hours later it was as if an alarm clock had gone off: I opened my eyes – there was something different about the forest. The wind had died down and it had become much colder. The air temperature had dropped below 5 degrees and a thick milky-coloured cloud was slowly descending down the slopes of the hill. Waiting to be immersed in it, the trees seemed to freeze and stretch upwards. The old ranger had told me the truth: they feared the mist of autumn.

Vartanov together with Fyodor Sedykh were organizing things down by the spring. They had dug a hole and built a small fire. Its smoke mingled with the mist and was therefore not dangerous to the group. Over the fire hung a fair-sized pot, not ours, but found in the area. The water came to the boil. The soldiers laid out their mugs, flasks, thickly cut hunks of bread and cubes of pea puree concentrate, which would be dissolved in the boiling water.

With a smile, Fyodor showed me the German knapsack that the scouts had deftly taken from the wall of the room in the confusion. The booty proved very opportune, as it contained foodstuffs completely unobtainable by the rank-and-file defenders of Sevastopol. I gave permission to use them immediately. They were probably the major's rations: tins of sardines in oil, several bars of chocolate, packets of dry biscuits, a stick of smoked salami wrapped in foil, and a 1.5-litre flask of brandy. The scouts were gleefully rubbing their hands in anticipation of a feast. They realized that the raid on the enemy headquarters had been very successful. In their view I was directly connected with this success, and the soldiers addressed me with respect.

While dinner was being prepared, I occupied myself with my own trophies. First of all I examined the Walther pistol closely. This was the first time that a weapon of this kind had fallen into my hands. From Romanian officers I tended to encounter more often the fairly clumsy Austrian 1912-type Steyr, the light 1934-model Italian Beretta, the powerful 1908-model German Luger Parabellum and the 1895-pattern 'gas seal' Nagant revolvers – Belgian designed, but usually Russian-made – which I did not like because of the time that was wasted reloading their cylinders cartridge by cartridge. The Walther P. 38 was undoubtedly one of the best examples of German military industry dating from the Second World War. It was compact, simple to use and look after, and suitable for the most varied tasks. The pistol stood out for its reliable safety catch. Apart from that, it operated with a soft touch on the trigger. Its trigger mechanism also allowed for single- and double-action cocking. As became clear later, Captain Bezrodny also had a good opinion of the Walther.

I managed to work out a few things in the Nazi officer's documents: for instance, his name, date of birth and the sites of the battles where the major had been involved. His decorated military path had led through Czechoslovakia, France and Poland. One photo showed a beautiful fair-haired woman with her arms around two adolescent boys, looking directly at the camera and smiling. Inscribed neatly in black ink on the back were the words: 'Mein Hertz! Mit Liebe, Anna . . .'. A fairly lengthy letter from her was there too. I could not read it, though I noticed that the major had written a reply to his wife but not had time to send it. 'Yes indeed, my dear Baron Klement-Karl-Ludwig von Steingel, this is no France. The Russians do not surrender their main cities without a fight. So, there was no point in you turning up here with tanks and cannon,' I thought, and put the enemy papers away in my field bag.[3]

Vartanov and Sedykh set up a proper table on the flat rock, opened the tins of sardines, cut up the salami, poured the soup into some aluminium bowls found in the area, and the brandy into soldiers' mugs, having divided it, in fraternal fashion, into seven portions. Leonid Burov cautiously handed me a mug and the soldiers kept quiet in anticipation of a word from me. 'We've done very well, lads! May we always have such luck!' I said.

Brandy burns the throat and warms the insides, other people's food sharpens the taste, and soup from concentrate boiled on the march over an open fire seems most appetizing of all in a circle of people who have just faced mortal danger together. There is in such company an amazing feeling of togetherness, which I value very highly. Not without good reason did our ancestors feast on the battlefield when they had routed the enemy. A large cup of wine or home-brewed beer would be passed around the brotherhood and everyone could moisten his lips with the sweet beverage of victory.

During our quiet conversation about who fired how, who ran where, and what they saw of interest in the brief minutes of the clash, Vartanov remained silent for a whole hour, but then suddenly he raised his voice. The old ranger solemnly requested to be accepted into the ranks of the sniper platoon and to be taught the art of sharpshooting, so he could wipe out the enemy like we had in this area next to his house, next to the graves of those close to him. He said that from now on his heart would be at rest and that, in gratitude, he would teach us bold, successful young soldiers how to live and hunt in the Crimean forest.

I heard roughly the same verdict from Captain Bezrodny when I presented him with a report and our trophies: German staff papers, documents found on the dead officer, and his decorations and major's epaulette. He did not conceal his pleasure at the information we had obtained. Taking advantage of his good mood, I asked about the ranger and recommended that he be accepted for permanent service despite being beyond call-up age. I reinforced my request with a gift – Baron von Steingel's pistol – and this had the desired effect. Putting the weapon away in his desk drawer, the captain promised to discuss this matter with the regimental commander, Major Matusyevich.

In the end, Red Army volunteer Anastas Artashesovich Vartanov was recognized as a soldier of our platoon. Later, in a 54th Regiment order, gratitude to us was voiced for the bravery and ingenuity shown in the raid into the enemy rear. All the snipers, including me, were credited with a personal score of seven dead Nazis – although who could now count those soldiers and junior officers in grey-green uniforms who remained lying next to the field kitchen we had shot up? In my estimate, there were at least sixty men killed or left with wounds either serious (in the stomach) or light.

At the beginning of December 1941, the weather in the Sevastopol defence district was gloomy and foul, with light frosts at night. This did not prevent the defenders of the city from toiling to improve the field fortifications, which had suffered during the first assault. The gun emplacements were repaired and equipped with telephone communication, and the trenches and communication passages were deepened. Even the senior command kept a watch on the works on the front lines of our 25th Chapayev Division. We were often visited by Major-General Petrov, Vice-Admiral Oktyabrsky and members of the military council of the coastal army and the Black Sea Fleet.

'Amidst the thick greenery of the bushes we descend to a communication passage and I led my superiors to the trench of the first line of defence,' Divisional Commander Trofim Kolomiyets recalled later.

The winding route is almost undetectable from above. It is laid under spreading bushes. Only here and there was it necessary to cover it with logs and mask it with stones. Not far away from the trench is a fork. A telephone is placed in a niche. A plaque indicates the way to the nearest medical station . . . Such is the trench. There is no need to stoop – it is excavated to the depth of a man's height. A soldier from the current watch reports that in his observation sector the enemy is quiet. From the trench a passage leading off in the direction of no man's land is carefully camouflaged by branches of evergreen juniper bushes tied to stakes.

'Over there is a double trench,' I explain. 'They extend another 5 or 6 metres out front. Trenches like this reduce losses in artillery attacks. The enemy strikes at the trench line, but our troops are in front of it. And it's more convenient to conduct observations from there.'

. . . In the trench are two soldiers. There is a small awning over them. Grenades and spare machine-gun drums are spread out on a bedding of wood. On a peg driven into the wall hangs a flask of water . . .[4]

Some quite roomy company dugouts had now been excavated 400–500 metres from the front line. There, two or three pot-bellied stoves had been installed as well as some long benches along the walls, which had been reinforced by planks. A kind of club atmosphere developed here. When they were off duty, the soldiers would gather there in the evening. Young Communist League and Party gatherings, political information sessions for personnel, and officers' meetings were held there.

Life on the front was much improved by the commissioning of a bathhouse and laundry service on the north side. The quartermasters found the building and repaired it with the help of the local population. Now, soldiers' visits to the bathhouse from the front line became regular. At the same time, they had their linen changed and the curse of trench life – lice – did not lead to wholesale infestation during the defence of Sevastopol.

The lull in fighting and the transition to a positional war demanded a change of tactics from the snipers. They became more important participants in resisting the Fritzes. Constant observation of no man's land, reconnaissance, hunting for enemy soldiers and officers on their front line – that was what we now faced. For a start, we had to study thoroughly the firing line assigned to our battalion, the 1st, the space in front of it, including no man's land, and those positions which the Nazis from the 132nd Infantry Division of the Wehrmacht had set up for themselves.

We were on the northern slopes of the Kamyshly gully, about 1.5km to the west of Height 278.4. The long gentle slope had a peculiar surface: small dips, rises and limestone rocks. The forest cover was uneven and there were both wide glades and almost impenetrable thickets, as well as piles of fallen trees that had been smashed by shellfire. Growing here were the main Crimean species: sessile oak, smooth elm, maple, forest apple, white acacia, black sambucus (quite a big tree, incidentally, up to 6 metres in height) and wild juniper (both trees and bushes). All this knowledge I gained from Vartanov, who accompanied Fyodor Sedykh, my sniper lookout, and me in journeys along no man's land and some adjacent sectors which had been occupied by the Germans. We were seeking out suitable spots for sniper hideouts of various kinds: open, closed and base hideouts, reserve hideouts, decoy hideouts, hideouts conducive to a swift attack and others set up for a speedy withdrawal.

The deep, reticulated communication passages excavated in the peninsula's stony soil by Soviet sappers and by ordinary infantrymen looked out directly onto no man's land. They helped us to get out onto it without being noticed, even in daytime, although the best time for a sharpshooter is an hour and a half after midnight. We took small sappers' spades with us and sometimes a pick, axe and big knives. To set up a closed position we used folding metal frames, armoured shields and fake tree stumps made from whatever material was at hand, especially sliced-up car tyres stuck to bark. In the fake positions there was space for a 'dummy' – a mannequin in a helmet and overcoat and a mirror thrust into a split wooden peg.

However, there were spots I was particularly fond of. For instance, a deep trench amidst juniper thickets, where the ground, sprinkled with several layers of blue-green conifer needles, was not only soft and warm, but gave off a pleasant scent, which was also intolerable to various kinds of forest parasites. Consequently, there were no mosquitoes, ants, bark-eating beetles, wasps, flies or other sniper's foes that would prevent him or her from concentrating and remaining stationary for hours on end.

Behind a greyish-white limestone slab concealing the position well from the left lay a large sessile oak felled by the wind and half-rotten with age. Ivy had wound itself in a weird fashion around its massive boughs, which were spread out in different directions. The jet-black barrel of a rifle thrust between uneven shoots looked of course to the inexperienced eye like a twig. Between the branches one could set up a rifle very conveniently and it was also possible to lie resting on a tree when the forest ground was damp.

I came to like the garland rose with its repulsive thorns; it was an amazing and wonderful plant. Its thickets – and these fine low trees always grow in groups – created the effect of a lace curtain spread across the bases of the elms, maples and acacias. All easily distinguishable outlines disappeared. Smoke from a shot also quickly dispersed in their midst.

My inscribed SVT-40 was not suitable for hunting in the forest. After thoroughly cleaning it (including sluicing out the barrel with washing soda) and greasing it with rifle oil, I wrapped Major-General Petrov's gift in sacking, then put it in a cover and hung it on the wall in my dugout. The 'Sveta' could have a rest and just be a parade weapon for a while. My working weapon would be an unfailingly reliable Three Line. It fired more quietly, was more accurate, and the PE sight offered four-fold magnification.

With a Mosin rifle over my shoulder, a cartridge pouch hanging from my belt, a TT pistol, a Finnish knife in a metal sheath, a flask, small sapper's spade in a cover and two grenades, Fyodor Sedykh and I would set out after midnight for no man's land and one of our fox holes (as we termed our set-up sniper's positions or hideouts). We found the way by means of gashes on tree trunks or special markings left earlier. Even so, the locality had to be learned by heart like Pushkin's verses at school.

We usually spent several hours in our position, observing the Fritzes' front line through binoculars. Whatever changes occurred there – individual soldiers and officers appearing, earthworks on fortifications or the construction of new machine-gun nests, movements of machinery, sentry changes, the timing of field kitchens, the arrival of orderlies at the staff headquarters dugout, the laying of telephone cables between different sectors, sappers working on new minefields and other similar things – all this we wrote down, marked on maps and reported to our battalion commander, Lieutenant Dromin.

It should be mentioned that at the beginning of December 1941 the Germans conducted themselves in a rather carefree way on the front line. They walked between their positions at full height. They probably thought that the Russians did not have snipers and therefore a no man's land 150–200 metres in width was an impenetrable barrier to accurate bullets. We put an end to this almost immediately, wiping out about twelve men in the course of two days: ten soldiers and two officers. The response was an insane mortar attack. For an hour or two the Nazis fired 5cm le. GrW. 36, the light mortars that they kept in every infantry platoon. From one fox hole we would instantly switch to another one that had been equipped in the depths of the forest, and from there we would observe mortar bombs weighing 910g exploding by our former refuge among the trees, lighting up with little orange puffs and scattering dozens of small splinters all around. I used to refer to such enemy action as a 'concert of German classical music'.

There were times when I would set off on my own into the enemy rear. This could only be done on one, very small, sector of no man's land, where the forest turned into an impenetrable thicket. The old ranger showed me a barely traceable trail there, which was concealed by tall bushes of wild rose and hornbeam. You had to make your way through the undergrowth, alternately crawling, doubled up, or using a knife to slash the hanging branches. The trail brought you out onto a dirt road, which ran within roughly 0.5km of the German front line. It turned out that soldiers of the Wehrmacht's 132nd Infantry Division were very fond of this road. It connected (judging from the documents later found on their dead) the command points of two of its regiments, the 436th and the 438th.

I chose a firing position beyond the bend in the road, the sides of which were covered with wild rose. Under the bushes I made a shallow trench with a parapet of stones and concealed it with turf. The soil here tended to crumble and therefore the work went well and did not take long. As well as that, I used a ploy I had known since my days of study at the Osoaviakhim sniper school: I buried a flask half-full of water, placed one end of a rubber tube in its neck, and held the other end to my ear. In this way the sounds of steps, movement of machinery and earthworks were easily detected. In order to recognize such sounds, or rather traces of sounds, a sharpshooter must 'become all ears' – that is, forget about everything around and concentrate attention to the maximum, which demands a great expenditure of energy. The protective forest required an similar renunciation of one's own existence. You had to dissolve within it, become silent, immobile, as if you were an arboreal being yourself. Vartanov could sense this on his skin, breathe in rhythm with it, understand superbly all its signs and manifestations. For me, a natural-born townie, it was not easy to achieve this state. It took a huge effort of will.

I heard the noise of a motorbike engine through the tube long before the rider himself appeared on the road. I took a cartridge with a yellow-tipped 'D'-type heavy bullet from the inside pocket of my padded jacket and pushed it into the chamber. A soldier in a black leather jacket stopped by a wild rose bush to enjoy its dark red berries. Rosehips are generally better collected in late autumn, dried and consumed as tea. Possibly the Fritz did not know that. He got carried away, gathering the semi-frozen berries in the palms of his hands and trying to sample them.

The shot rang out loud in the silence of the cold, early winter morning, but the road was otherwise empty at that time and there was nothing to threaten me. I quickly pulled his documents out of his pocket and took the field bag bulging with papers, which hung by a long strap from the shoulder of the dead man. I also acquired his MP. 40 submachine gun and two spare ammunition clips for it. Nothing else was found on the motorbike rider other than a packet of cigarettes and a lighter. His vehicle, a light single-cylinder DKW RT125 was standing at the roadside. Enemy machinery had to be put out of commission at all costs. I had to shoot out its motor. I did not dare to shoot at its petrol tank, as a fire would attract enemy attention to the road and I still had to get out of there.

For a lone sniper, hitting the target is only half the job. The second half, no less important, is getting back to your unit safe and sound. In August 1941, I wrote to my sister that I intended to raise my tally to 1,000 Nazis. But before you can wipe out the thousandth cut-throat, you have to survive 999 times after taking an accurate shot at an enemy who wishes to kill you whatever the cost.

Of course, I would like to have followed the rule I laid down for myself: no day without a dead enemy. But, alas, it did not always work out like that. In the first place, the Fritzes became much more careful. They began, like us, to dig themselves deep into the ground. Secondly, the enemy strengthened its observation of no man's land. At night the Nazis often let off flares, and in the daytime they engaged in unsettling machine-gun and mortar fire. German reconnaissance groups started operating on this same territory and, if they discovered our hideouts, they would destroy them or lay mines. One of our sniper pairs was blown up on 11 December by an anti-personnel mine hidden near a fallen oak tree. Thus perished Leonid Burov and another soldier of my platoon who had also joined the 54th Regiment from the naval infantry.

However, for the first half of December 1941, life on the front lines of the Sevastopol defence lines passed in relative calm. In good weather both German aircraft and our own launched raids. Ships of the Black Sea Fleet – the cruisers *Krasnya Krim* and *Krasniy Kavkaz*, the destroyer-leader *Kharkov*, the destroyers *Zhelyeznyakov*, *Sposobny* and *Nezamozhnik* regularly fired into the enemy rear with long-distance ordnance. We rejoiced when their 180 and 102mm shells hissed over our heads. There were occasions when Soviet units up to one or two companies strong conducted reconnaissance by combat on some sectors of the front. The Fritzes did exactly the same. For instance, on 8 December, a strong salvo was heard much further to the west of our battalion's positions, beyond the Kamyshly railway bridge, which had been blown up not so long before. It was the 8th Marine Infantry Brigade with powerful artillery support which first drove the enemy out of the positions they had occupied, but the following day, when the Fritzes brought in their own assault aircraft and tanks, they retreated.

9

The Second Assault

On 16 December we marked a festive occasion. At the command post of the 54th Regiment, which was situated in the Kamyshly gully by the village of the same name, the divisional commander, Major-General Kolomiyets, was to present government awards to ten of my regimental comrades who had distinguished themselves in the defence of Odessa. I had returned from sniper duty in the forest quite late that day and immediately gone to bed. But Lieutenant Dromov ordered me to go to congratulate the recipients on behalf of the 2nd Company. Also in attendance, apart from me, were representatives of our other detachments, probably about forty people in all.

First to speak was Kolomiyets. He said that our great homeland always marked the feats of Red Army soldiers and officers and he called on them to fight as bravely by the walls of Sevastopol as they had at Odessa. The next speaker was regimental commander Major Matusyevich. He assured the general that the Razins would live up to the honour conferred upon them. Third to take the floor was, appropriately, the military commissar for our regiment, Battalion Commissar Maltsev. He talked about the Communist Party and Young Communist League members who were setting an example of courage and staunchness in combat. Then came the presentation of awards. I witnessed in person the official award to the gallant machine-gun company sergeant, Nina Onilova, who received the Order of the Red Banner and, when my turn came, I addressed her with a speech befitting the occasion, albeit a very short one.

It had been a clear, sunny day with a slight frost. The winter daylight was quickly coming to an end. Returning to the 2nd Company lines, I sat down on a fallen tree and lit up my pipe.[1] It had been given to me by Anastas Vartanov after our successful attack on the village of Mekenzia and was the only item of value he had left after the Germans destroyed his house. The old Turkish pipe made from the root of a pear tree, with an amber mouthpiece, had a most unusual appearance. It was also an award, but from an ordinary man.

I easily learned how to use it: to pack it with tobacco correctly, smoke it unhurriedly and maintain a slow glow of dry tobacco fibres in the gleaming polished bowl made of dark brown wood. It was pleasant to feel the warmth of the bowl in your hand. The mouthpiece seemed to moderate the strength of the smoke and prolong the pleasure for the smoker, which was unwittingly conducive to reflection.

Since my officer comrades had been commemorating the battles for Odessa that day, my thoughts also returned to those recent events. We had come through our first lessons in the arduous and dangerous school of war and benefited much from the experience; we had matured, become smarter, hardened our characters, grown accustomed to looking death calmly in the eyes and skilfully deceiving her. Without such habits you are not a real soldier.

Could Nina Onilova and I be measured against each other in terms of enemies annihilated? At the staff headquarters of the 25th Rifle Division she was credited with having sent 500 Fascists to the next world. By the middle of December 1941 I had just over 200. The most important thing was that they were no longer fighting, trampling our land, killing our compatriots. Perhaps the suddenness of their demise drove some sense into other invaders who had come here in the hope of a swift and easy conquest.

'This is the first time I've seen a girl with a pipe,' said a pleasant baritone voice behind me.

I looked around. A junior lieutenant was approaching the fallen tree. I had seen him somewhere before. Not in the 54th Regiment, but quite probably in the 287th or 31st, which were also part of our division and had fought at Odessa. He was a big, statuesque and broad-shouldered man with blue eyes and dark brown hair, about thirty-five years of age. He sat down beside me, took a cigarette case out of his overcoat pocket and opened it. It contained Kazbek brand cigarettes from the officers' rations. The junior lieutenant offered them to me. After hesitating, I took one. He also took one, then clicked his lighter, and we started smoking.

'What do you use in your pipe?' the officer asked.

'Shag tobacco.'

'Isn't it a bit strong?'

'It is, but I've got used to it.'

'It's funny,' he continued. 'Good-looking women don't usually smoke pipes.'

'In other words, I must be ugly and unusual.'

'The fact that you're unusual is well known to the entire 54th Regiment, Lyudmila Mikhailovna,' he said respectfully, looking at me. 'But the question of female looks is quite a complex one. Our ideal is dictated by time, fashion and custom. For example, I consider you good-looking . . .'

In this first conversation of ours he behaved in a restrained, courteous and sensitive way. He introduced himself at once: Kitzenko, Alexei Arkadyevich, from the city of Donyetsk: called up in 1941, he fought in the ranks of the 287th Regiment, had a technical education (as an electrician), had been a sergeant, then a senior sergeant, and recently become an officer, on 30 November of this year, on completion of an accelerated course for the middle-rank officer corps under the coastal army general staff. His reason for making my acquaintance was quite simple. Kitsenko had been appointed commander of our 2nd Company, and now he was going around the battle formations to get to know people and study the fortifications he was tasked with defending.

Alexei Arkadyevich's speech was coherent, grammatically correct and even quite witty. He concluded his narrative with a funny story about the final examinations on his officers' course. While assembling a TT pistol, his friend got so nervous that he lost one of the components. He put the gun together, but it could not be dismantled any more and would not fire. After lengthy consultations, the commission came up with the verdict that he had passed the exam: his knowledge of his weapon was obvious, and the rest was beyond the commission's competence.

In a word, Alexei made a good impression. I hoped that this would not evaporate in the course of further service together. I can add that men like him – big, well-proportioned, blue-eyed and blond-haired – generally appealed to me. Privately I called them 'Vikings', the bold warriors of the far-off northern seas.

How were we to know that on this quiet evening the invaders were completing preparations for a second assault on Sevastopol, moving up the last of 645 pieces of field ordnance and 252 items of anti-tank artillery? As well as that, they had already set out 378 mortar-guns of various calibres behind no man's land, and now had twenty-seven weapons per kilometre of front, while we had only nine. Over 200 bombers and fighters were about to attack the Soviet positions, while we had only ninety aircraft.

Beyond the crests of the Mekenzi hills, covered in bushy forest, three German infantry divisions, the 22nd, 24th and 132nd, were lining up in battle formation. They were preparing to strike at the junction between the third and fourth sectors of the Sevastopol defences, that is, on the narrow stretch from Mekenzia village to Aziz-Oba hill, in order to break through to the north side of the biggest bay in the Black Sea Fleet's principal naval base. If the Nazis reached its shores, then the city, being completely surrounded on the landward side, could not stand. Sea transport – and this remained the only way – of draft reinforcements, military supplies, weapons and provisions would then cease.

The Fritzes unleashed a hail of artillery and mortar fire on the city's defence positions at 6.10 on the morning of 17 December 1941. The earth shook. The crashing, wailing and whistling of shells and mortars were deafening and seemed impossible to bear. Hidden in our deep earth refuges, we waited for the end of the cacophony. The ammunition of the enemy, even one as calculating as the Germans, could not be infinite. The artillery attack continued for about twenty minutes. Then the enemy infantry advanced across the entire front. Twin-engine Junkers and

Heinkels appeared in the sky. They bombed not just the city, but the front line of the Soviet forces.

I wrote about this after the war.

The enemy now counted on inflicting its main blow in a different sector, from the Duvankoi district across the Belbek river valley and the village of Kamyshly to the north-east extremity of Northern Bay. The invaders intended to split the defensive front, to encircle the units of the fourth sector, and come out at Sevastopol. The Nazis switched the main forces of their 11th Army to the district of Aziz-Oba hill, to the north of the Mekenzi hills. As well as that, auxiliary reserves were gathering there to ensure the success of the military action . . . The enemy planned to conclude this operation in four days, by 21 December.

By using the natural features of the locality, Nazi submachine-gunners managed to penetrate through to the rear of our defences on some sectors of the front. They counted on encircling the Soviet units. The Nazi manoeuvre did not come off. Our destruction squads, consisting mainly of Communist Party and Young Communist League members, isolated the enemy movements. The enemy submachine-gunners were surrounded and annihilated.

The first day of the second assault was not a successful one for the Nazis. They lost nine aircraft in aerial battles and from anti-aircraft fire. There were great losses of tanks and manpower, too. The enemy came up against increasing resistance from rifle units and naval infantry detachments, which engaged them in heavy, prolonged fighting.

Of the coastal army units, the soldiers of the artillery regiment, led by Lieutenant Colonel Bogdanov, fought with special distinction. They had earlier battled heroically for Odessa. The Bogdanov gunners always took up positions close to the forward line and there were times when they had to beat off the attacks of the enemy infantry. At critical moments in major advances Bogdanov himself would go out into no man's land and serve as a spotter for his own regiment. Fearlessness and courage were the gunners' main watchwords.

The fighting proceeded not only on land, but also at sea. The sailors of the cruiser *Krasniy Krim* fought courageously during these days under the command of Captain (2nd Class) Zubkov. His crew – gunners, engineers, electricians, torpedo personnel – self-sacrificingly repelled the furious attacks of the Nazi bombers. This floating fortress covered the Soviet ships heading into Sevastopol Bay and trained destructive fire at the enemy infantry and vehicles. The ship's gunners did not know the meaning of the word fatigue. They inflicted lethal blows and shocked the foe with the suddenness of their attacks.

Once in the very heat of battle an enemy shell exploded by the gun of Starshina (Warrant Officer) (2nd Class) Mikhailenko. The commander of the weapon and some of the gun crew were wounded. But the firing continued. The sergeant major was replaced by a sailor. Despite the losses, the ship's artillery operated without a hitch.

Many heroes of the Sevastopol defence were known in the city by name. One popular name was that of minesweeper captain Dmitry Andreyevich Glukhov. His boat was the first to go out to deal with acoustic mines. They were very difficult to counter. These mines were called acoustic precisely because they would explode as a result of insignificant sound oscillations . . . With no fear of danger Glukhov's minesweeper would set about disarming them. This bold-spirited crew needed only a few hours to completely clear the approach routes for ships into the bay.

I recall another feat of this team. A convoy of heavily loaded Soviet transport ships was heading for Sevastopol. Protection was provided by a chain of boats under Glukhov's command. Nazi air reconnaissance discovered the ships and directed their bombers against them. Bombs whistled down, raising huge fountains of water. They tried many times to attack the transport ships, but the fire from our boats drove the planes away. The Soviet transports got to their destination unharmed.

The glorious defenders of Sevastopol were inspired by the initial victories of the Soviet armies near Moscow.

Striving to downplay the significance of our victories and somehow restore the myth of their army's 'invincibility', the Nazi high command set an objective for their forces at Sevastopol: to capture the city, regardless of the losses.

The date laid down by the Nazis for entry into the city was 21 December. They wanted the capture of the city to coincide with the six-month anniversary of war with the Soviet Union. The enemy were advancing. Sevastopol was placed in an extraordinarily difficult situation. The fate of its future defence was being decided. On 20 December a message concerning the seriousness of the situation was sent to the supreme command headquarters. In the reply that followed four hours later the commander of the Black Sea Fleet was ordered to send to Sevastopol part of the naval infantry, some draft reinforcements and shells . . .[2]

Within the military formations of the 25th Chapayev Division, the first day of the assault, 17 December, was particularly difficult for the soldiers and officers of the 287th Rifle Regiment, who were occupying positions by the Yaila-Bash hill and the southern extremity of the Kamyshly gully. Advancing against them was an infantry force of several battalions, supported by ten tanks. Soon there was hand-to-hand combat in the trenches of the 5th Company of this regiment's 2nd Battalion. Junior political instructor Golubnichy distinguished himself here. He bayonetted six Nazis and continued in action, despite being wounded.

However, by the middle of the day the troops of the 287th Regiment were forced to retreat towards the village of Kamyshly. At five o'clock in the evening they were already 800 metres east of the village, while the 9th Company was completely encircled and heroically fighting off the attacks of the Nazi submachine-gunners. By the end of the day the regiment had withdrawn still further – towards the north-east slopes of the Kamyshly gully.

The soldiers of the 2nd, Perekop, Regiment of naval infantry, which was part of our division, also withstood a significant blow. Launching themselves in a bayonet attack, they stemmed the Fritzes' advance, but were gradually forced to withdraw and managed to establish themselves only on the western slopes of Height 264.1. They were assisted in getting away from the enemy by the gunners of the 69th Regiment, who wiped out ten enemy tanks by direct fire from their 76mm-calibre ordnance.

These ferocious clashes occurred approximately 1 kilometre to the left of the 54th Regiment's dispositions. The Razins also engaged in crossfire with the Nazis, but did not experience such desperate enemy pressure. True, a number of times the German infantry ranks ventured into no man's land, which had been cleared of bushes and trees. However, on encountering solid machine-gun and rifle fire, backed up by mortars, they went to ground and then drew back.

For two days the cannons roared on the Mekenzi hills. The Nazis were unable to overrun our front, or to achieve a definitive advantage over the defenders of Sevastopol. The Russians charged in counter-attacks and won back their firing lines that had been occupied by the Germans.

On the morning of 19 December silence reigned along the 1st Battalion's sector. But suddenly the enemy began intensive firing from cannons and large-calibre mortars. This was a normal occurrence, and we hid in our dugouts under three layers of beams. Our military outposts then informed us of the approach of German vehicles. With clanking caterpillar tracks a Stu.G.III self-propelled vehicle with a short, seemingly sawn-off, cannon had crawled into the clearing along with an Sd.Kfz. 250/1 armoured transport, which was maintaining continuous fire from a machine gun situated behind the armoured shield on the cab roof. Following immediately behind these vehicles were about two battalions of riflemen and submachine-gunners. Our anti-tank battery set their sights on the self-propelled vehicle. It was up to the infantry to deal with the caterpillar armoured transport.

According to Battalion Commander Dromin's plan, in the event of a German advance on the positions of the 1st Battalion, the soldiers in the sniper platoon were to stand alongside the machine-gunners and, together, repel the enemy attacks, under directions from the officers. I was allowed to occupy an earlier prepared concealed trench, in order to direct fire at the flank of the advancing force and to neutralize machine-gun nests and mortar crews.

At that moment the machine-gun nest was moving towards me at a speed of around 25km per hour. Low-built and not very big in size, the beige-coloured armoured Sd.Kfz. 250/1, weighing almost 6 tonnes and painted with brown and green patches, was turning on its left track and directing a continuous spray of bullets at the area in front of the 1st Battalion's trenches. Clearly visible on its side was a black and white cross and vehicle number 323, which stood for armoured transporter No. 3, 2nd Platoon, 3rd Company. The distance was growing shorter. The vehicle was approaching a familiar marker, the long trunk of a young elm tree which had been broken off low down. I looked through the eyepiece of the PE telescope sight on my Three Line.

I had a minute to solve the ballistics problem.

First, the armoured transport had quite high sides and, consequently, the heads of the machine-gunners operating their MG. 34 so fearlessly were over 2 metres above ground level. My trench, which was firmly dug into the ground, had a parapet about 20cm high, where the rifle rested. Between the aiming line and the weapon horizon was an angle of 35 degrees – the so-called 'target angle' – and, at that moment, it was positive. Consequently, the sights had to be set at a reduced level.

Second, the armoured transport was moving. This required deflection shooting, that is, the barrel of the weapon had to follow the target and stay ahead of it at a corresponding speed. It was easy to calculate the deflection at a distance of 200 metres. A bullet from a Three Line would reach it in 0.25 seconds. In this time the German vehicle would have travelled 4 metres. Using the concept of milliradians in my calculations, I turned the windage drum on the metal tube of the sight several units, then softly pressed the trigger with my index finger. The butt of the rifle kicked against my shoulder as usual and a momentary flash appeared from the muzzle.

With that the machine-gun fire from the roof of the Sd.KFz. 250/1 ceased. The soldiers fell into the bottom of the armoured transport. Their helmets did not save them. The Russian bullets had flown from below and struck them through their eye slots. The junior officer in charge of the transport's crew acted very stupidly. In his surprise he climbed out of the cab onto the body of the vehicle to see why the machine gun had fallen silent. After all, the enemy were firing only from the front, where the vehicle was protected by armoured sheets about 1.5cm thick. He did not have time to consider the possibility of a sniper; my bullet shot him through the temple.

But those who were watching the attack from the command post of the German reconnaissance battalion guessed, of course. Literally within a minute, salvoes of 8cm-calibre GrW (*Granatwerfer*, mortar) descended on the clump of trees where I was located. I had a deeper, well-equipped, reserve lair adjacent. Rolling over three times on my left side, I almost reached it. However, it was not a mortar but a heavy shell which suddenly rent the air and threw up clumps of earth, twigs, fragments of trees and fallen leaves. It felt as if the burning paw of a huge beast had prodded me in the shoulder, a sharp pain penetrated my right shoulder blade, and then everything went black.

I came to, woken by the cold. My overcoat and camouflage smock had been reduced to rags on my right shoulder and my back. My helmet was lying alongside with its strap torn. The wooden stock of the rifle was broken, the barrel was bent and the telescope sight was completely missing. The worst thing was that the crown of an acacia tree, shattered by the shell, had fallen down and pinned me to the ground, making it impossible for me to get up. The pain was concentrated between my spine and right shoulder blade. But I could not reach the wound and bind it by myself. I could just feel that I was losing blood. The back of my undershirt and tunic were soaked with it.

Twilight was descending. It was very quiet in the forest. The sound of distant cannon fire was echoing somewhere. But here the fighting was probably over. How had it finished? Where were my regimental mates now? How far had the Fritzes managed to get? Would they come looking for me?

In my brain, which was now clouded by pain, major blood loss and intensifying cold, words dissolved into syllables, lost their sense, vanished . . . They were replaced by visions – at first unclear and dim. These were followed by others which had outlines, figures and faces. I was now preparing for death and imagining that I ought to see all those I had lost over months of war. However, it was my mother Yelena Trofimovna, tenderly known in our family as Lenusya, who was addressing me, my good friend and adviser, now living in far-off Udmurtia. The stern face of my father also appeared. 'Belovs simply don't retreat' – his phrase did not so much resound as imprint itself in my brain. And then there was my son Rostislav, my dear beloved Morzhik, who had grown up over the half-year we had been apart, and was now a gawky adolescent rather than a child. He stretched out a hand to me: 'Mum!' The hand was warm. I felt its touch and struggled to open my eyes.

The bare branches of trees crippled by the artillery attack looked black against the grey winter sky. The last ray of the setting sun shone through their sad tangle and fell on the gleaming armour of a Viking. The bright specks sparkled on his helmet with its raised visor. But this was the last manifestation of a clouded consciousness. Leaning over me in actual fact was Junior Lieutenant Alexei Kitsenko, clad in an overcoat, with his helmet tilted slightly towards the back and his submachine gun over his shoulder.

He was saying something, and I caught his words: 'Lucy, don't die! . . . Lucy, I beg you! Lucy, please! . . .'

How the commander of the 2nd Company had managed to find me in this forest, I simply cannot imagine. Some soldiers appeared behind him. They disentangled

1 Sniper Lyudmila Pavlichenko of the 54th Stepan Razin Regiment.

2 Senior Sergeant Lyudmila Pavlichenko, Sevastopol, March 1942, carrying a Mosin Nagant M.1891/30 with PEM scope.

3 A Mosin M.1891/30 sniper rifle with PU sight (courtesy John Walter).

4 An SVT-40 with PU sight (James D. Julia, Inc., auctioneers, Fairfield, Maine, USA).

5 The sniper's diploma awarded to Lyudmila Pavlichenko, 6 April 1942, held in the Central Museum of the Russian Federation Armed Forces.

6 Bombed buildings and transport services, Sevastopol, 1942.

7 A bombed building in Sevastopol, 1942.

8 Junior Lieutenant Alexei Kitsenko and Senior Sergeant Lyudmila Pavlichenko, Sevastopol, January 1942 (from Lyudmila Pavlichenko's personal files).

9 The leaflet *Shoot the Enemy and Don't Miss!* (State Museum of the Heroic Defence and Liberation of Sevastopol).

Доблестный снайпер Людмила Михайловна Павличенко

Верная дочь Ленинско-Сталинского комсомола, она вступила в ряды Красной Армии добровольцем в первые дни великой Отечественной войны.

Огнем своей винтовки Людмила Павличенко уничтожила под Одессой и Севастополем 309 немцев.

«Это самое верное и правильное отношение к немцам. Если их сразу не убьешь, то беды потом не оберешься», — писала она однажды своей матери.

Высокое воинское мастерство и отвага Людмилы Павличенко вдохновляют на подвиги тысячи снайперов Красной Армии — стахановцев фронта.

Воины Красной Армии! Истребляйте врагов так же беспощадно, как истребляет их Людмила Павличенко!

БЕЙ ВРАГА БЕЗ ПРОМАХА!

Когда я проходила по улицам Севастополя, меня всегда останавливали ребятишки и деловито спрашивали:

— Сколько вчера убила?

Я обстоятельно докладывала им о своей работе снайпера. Однажды мне пришлось им честно сказать, что я уже несколько дней не стреляла по врагам.

— Плохо, — в один голос сказали ребятишки.

А один, самый маленький, сурово добавил:

— Очень плохо. Фашистов надо убивать каждый день.

Он верно сказал, этот маленький суровый севастополец. С того памятного дня, когда фашистские разбойники ворвались в мою страну, каждый прожитый мною день был наполнен одной лишь мыслью, одним желанием — убить врага.

Когда я пошла воевать, у меня была только злость на немцев за то, что они нарушили нашу мирную жизнь, за то, что

10 Lyudmila Pavlichenko with an SVT-40 over her shoulder, Sevastopol, probably taken in January/February 1942 (State Museum of the Heroic Defence and Liberation of Sevastopol).

11, 12, 13 In January/
February 1942 several
press photographs were
taken of Pavlichenko with
her presentation SVT-40
(© Histoire & Collection).

Прославленный снайпер, Герой Советского Союза
Людмила Павличенко на огневой позиции.

14 Pavlichenko in the summer of 1942, probably after 16 July when she was promoted to junior lieutenant and received the Order of Lenin (© Histoire & Collection).

15 A press photograph, perhaps also from summer 1942 (© Histoire & Collection).

16 Soldiers and officers of the coastal army with their decorations and medals. In the middle of the first row are Major-General Trofim Kolomiyets, commander of the 25th Chapayev Rifle Division, Senior Sergeant Lyudmila Pavlichenko of the 54th Regiment and Lieutenant-General Ivan Petrov, commander of the coastal army, Sevastopol, April 1942.

17 Junior Lieutenant and sniper platoon commander Lyudmila Pavlichenko with her troops (32nd Guards Parachute Division), Moscow military district, August 1942 (© Histoire & Collection).

18 Pavlichenko in front of a portrait of the Supreme Commander, shortly before her visit to the USA (© Histoire & Collection).

19 Lyudmila Pavlichenko, probably at the time of her trip to the USA (© Histoire & Collection).

20 Another photograph from the same time, with her decorations visible (from left): Badge for Distinguished Sniper, Guards Badge, the Order of Lenin and the medal for Battle Merit (© Histoire & Collection).

21 The Soviet delegation to the 1942 international student assembly: Nikolai Krasavchenko, Vladimir Pchelintsev and Lyudmila Pavlichenko (© Histoire & Collection).

22 The Young Communist League delegation outside the Soviet embassy in Washington, DC (© Histoire & Collection).

23 Pavlichenko with Eleanor Roosevelt and Justice Robert Jackson (© Histoire & Collection).

24 From left to right: Lyudmila Pavlichenko, Donald Brown, owner of a tea factory and activist in the charitable public organization Russian War Relief, and Vladimir Pchelintsev in Baltimore, USA, October 1942 (from Lyudmila Pavlichenko's personal files).

25 Lyudmila Pavlichenko meeting Joseph Davis, former US ambassador to Moscow (© Histoire & Collection).

26 A photograph given by Eleanor Roosevelt to Lyudmila Pavlichenko. The inscription above reads: 'To Senior Lieutenant Liudmila Pavlichenko with warm good wishes from Eleanor Roosevelt' (from Lyudmila Pavlichenko's personal files).

27 A rare informal photograph of Pavlichenko, from the time of her visit to the USA (Library of Congress).

28 Photograph taken during Pavlichenko's address to the international student assembly in September 1942, in the Grand Hall of the American University in Washington, DC (Library of Congress).

29 The Lord Mayor of Birmingham, Walter Lewis, with Pavlichenko and Pchelintsev. The Soviet visitors are examining what appears to be a US M1917 Enfield rifle. These guns, supplied under Lend-Lease, were used in large numbers by the Home Guard. They had broad red strips around the fore-end and the butt to remind firers that they chambered US .30-06 cartridges and not the British .303 (© Histoire & Collection).

30 Pavlichenko and an officer of the British Royal Air Force view Allied aircraft at RAF Heathfield, in Ayre, November 1942 (from Lyudmila Pavlichenko's personal files).

31 Pavlichenko with textile workers in Manchester, November 1942 (© Histoire & Collection).

32 Pavlichenko with Agnia Maiskaya, the wife of the Soviet ambassador to Britain at the reception to celebrate the twenty-fifth anniversary of the October Revolution (© Histoire & Collection).

33 Major Lyudmila Pavlichenko of the Soviet coast guard, 1964. Among her decorations are: Hero of the Soviet Union, and medals for the Defence of Odessa, Defence of Sevastopol and Victory over Germany.

34 Veterans of the second defence of Sevastopol at a jubilee celebration in honour of the city's liberation (May 1964).

the splinters of acacia. Alexei picked me up in his arms and carried me out of the thicket into the trenches. There our medical orderly, Yelena Paliy, cut open my overcoat and tunic and bandaged the wound tightly, to stop the bleeding. Kitsenko asked the regimental commander for his car. In twenty minutes I was driven from the slope of Kamyshly gully to Inkerman, where divisional Medical Battalion 47 was located in tunnels, along with Field Hospitals 316, 76 and 356.

Over the three days of the second assault approximately 3,000 soldiers and officers from the coastal army had ended up there. But this huge underground medical centre was designed to cope with such numbers. There were two superbly equipped operating theatres, bandaging rooms, isolation wards, various clinics (physiotherapy, dentistry, etc.), and wards for treating the sick.

The wounded were quickly triaged in reception, and I ended up in an operating theatre, where operations were being carried out on four tables simultaneously for those wounded in the stomach and chest. I was lucky. The splinter was removed from my back and three stitches put in my wound by the surgeon of our divisional medical battalion, Vladimir Fyodorovich Pishel-Gayek, an excellent doctor and a remarkable man. Because I had had major blood loss and my general state was quite serious, he intended to dispatch me to unoccupied territory. Late in the evening of 19 December, the transport ship *Chekhov* was due to depart from the Kamennaya wharf in Southern Bay, and loaded on it were over 400 seriously wounded soldiers and officers who had been operated on.

If that had happened, Alexei Kitsenko and I would never have seen each other again. It is quite possible that my wartime career would have taken a different turn. But the commander of the 2nd Company waited until the end of the operation, escorted me into the ward and then spoke to the surgeon. He asked him not to evacuate Senior Sergeant Pavlichenko from Sevastopol, promising that the troops not only of the 2nd Company, but of the whole of the 54th Rifle Regiment's 1st Battalion, would donate blood for me – and not just for me. For a start, the junior lieutenant suggested that his very own blood should be taken by the surgeon.

The offer regarding the troops of the company and battalion was hardly credible. Nobody would release soldiers from the front line to the rear while the Nazis were advancing. However, Alexei Kitsenko apparently possessed the gift of persuasion, and Pishel-Gayek believed him. I do not know what special words Alexei came up with during his conversation with the doctor. Perhaps they were prompted by love. The doctor realized this and changed his decision. I stayed in hospital for two and a half weeks, during which the junior lieutenant visited me several times.

Our brief meetings were very cordial. The company commander turned up with various gifts: a trophy bar of Belgian chocolate found in the bag of a dead German officer, or a small flacon of 'Red Moscow' perfume (some shops were still open during the siege), or half a dozen cambric handkerchiefs, edged with lace (a present from the wonderful women of Sevastopol). He talked about life at the front for our own 54th Stepan Razin Rifle Battalion in a detailed and fascinating way.

For example, on 20 December a large group of enemy submachine-gunners under tank cover had broken through to the Soviet rear at the boundary between the 54th Regiment and the 3rd and 2nd, Perekop, Regiments of naval infantry, but they were wiped out with the aid of the naval infantry from the 7th Brigade, which arrived just in time. The Germans did not rest and, on the night of 22 December, a battalion of Fritzes again broke through at the boundary between the Razins and the 3rd Naval Infantry Regiment. The breakthrough was covered with the help of the divisional reserve sent up by Major-General Kolomiyets. This was a company of sailors in peakless caps (although the temperature was sub-zero) from the Perekop Regiment. On top of that, they had brought mattresses with them, but they left those in the trenches and went into the attack. The Germans opened a frenzied burst of fire, but the sailors still kept advancing and they routed the Germans in the end.

Some 300 dead Nazis were left on the field, along with their weapons: eleven medium machine guns, seven light machine guns, two mortars and 300 rifles. The Razins also took part in this glorious action and launched bayonet charges. To back them up, the commander of the coastal army also sent three small tanks. However, they were of no benefit; they got stuck in the forest among the fallen trees and had to be towed out later.

The soldiers and officers of the corps battalion of the 265th Artillery Regiment gave a brilliant account of themselves on 22 December. Left without infantry cover, from a distance of 300–400 metres they fired their cannon and howitzers directly at the mass of Nazis rushing straight at them and held the enemy back.

On 24 December the Nazis renewed their advance on the positions of the 54th Regiment; the situation became very difficult, but our troops held out. At the same time an order came from the army staff headquarters to gather up the weapons left on the battlefield, both our own and the enemy's. In the evening of 29 December two battalions of Germans suddenly attacked our positions north-east of the village of Mekenzia. This assault was also repelled with the aid of regimental artillery.

The plans of the Wehrmacht's 11th Army commander, Colonel General Erich von Manstein, who wanted to greet the new year of 1942 in Sevastopol, were not fulfilled. It was a pity that I did not manage to make my contribution to the deeds of the city's defenders and lay a dozen or two champions of 'European civilization' in Crimean soil for eternity.

I was unable to tell Alexei Kitsenko anything interesting. He knew about my accurate shooting at the armoured transport and the artillery attack that followed, or else he would not have come to look for me in the forest. The weird visions of a seriously wounded sniper would scarcely be of any value to him. I would never have admitted my fantasies to him, and they still amaze me to this day by their coincidence with reality. His words 'Lucy, don't die!' still rang in my ears, and tears welled up in my eyes, although I am a far from sentimental person.

Everything seemed to happen of its own accord. After I was discharged from hospital, Alexei took me back to the 1st Battalion's lines and straight to his commander's dugout. He had decorated it: on a table knocked together from freshly planed planks and covered with a canvas tablecloth he had placed a 45mm shell-case holding a winter bouquet of green juniper shoots and maple twigs with red and yellow leaves which had miraculously been preserved. In the cellar-like premises illuminated by the dim light of a battery-powered lamp they glowed like two torch beams. There was even a dinner service: tin plates with thinly sliced black bread and salami, an open can of meat stew, boiled potatoes in a mess tin, and a flask of vodka.

'Today is a special day, Lucy,' he said very solemnly, and, leaning over towards the vase, he tore off one palm-shaped leaf and handed it to me. 'A small souvenir for you, my one and only. Now I am offering you my hand and my heart.'

I replied by accepting. I will not deny that events were unfolding too quickly, but in wartime there was no point in pondering too long. Today we were alive, but tomorrow . . . What would happen tomorrow, nobody knew. I had one request and at first it surprised Kitsenko. I said that my first husband was also called Alexei. I did not wish to remember this man and I would call the junior lieutenant by something different, 'Lyonya'. He laughed, hugged me and gave his permission: 'Call me what you like, my dear!'

We actually sent in a request to our superiors to formalize out relations in the established way. It was also signed by the battalion commander, Lieutenant Dromin, and the regimental commander, Major Matusyevich. The document was given the regimental stamp of approval and accepted for implementation at the staff headquarters of the 25th Chapayev Division. Our regimental mates made some hints about wedding festivities, but more as a joke than in earnest. The people of Sevastopol had repelled a second assault, but borne heavy losses – 23,000 killed, wounded or missing. In some companies in our regiment there were only sixty or seventy soldiers left. It was tough, for instance, for the 8th Naval Infantry Brigade, which had been fighting not too far from us in the fourth defence sector, by the Aziz-Oba hill and the village of Aranchi. At the beginning of the second assault it comprised about 3,500 men, but by 31 December there were just over 500. It would have been more appropriate to stage a wake than a merry marriage feast.

My husband Alexei Arkadyevich Kitsenko was eleven years older than me. His family life, like mine, had not worked out particularly successfully. At the insistence of his domineering mother he had married early and to a woman she chose for him. Then followed a scandalous divorce, accompanied by various unpleasant details.

Nevertheless, by the age of thirty-six his character, kind and mild by nature, had stood firm and nothing could move the junior lieutenant from his chosen path. As an officer, he enjoyed unquestioned authority with his subordinates. As a husband, he was always concerned for me and protected me from various adversities as far as that that was possible on the front line. With him I felt for the first time the meaning of love, requited and all-consuming love, and I was completely happy during those days.

No doubt a dugout with earth walls and a low ceiling made of three layers of logs bore little resemblance to a cosy family nest, but we lived there as happy as can be, in whatever comfort a front-line officer and his wife could afford. From here I would go off into the forest hunting for enemies and come back knowing that at any time of the night or day there would always be a pot of hot water for me on the pot-belly stove, a mug of sweet tea, a fresh undershirt, a bunk with a flannelette blanket, that the orderly of the 2nd Company's commander would pick up dinner or supper in the kitchen and bring it to us.

The honeymoon had a profoundly positive effect on my shooting. The bullets fired well – only along the set trajectory – and seemed to find the target of their own accord. Sometimes it seemed to me that the enchanted forest approved of our marriage and was helping me, prodding the self-confident Fritzes either into snowy clearings (to check on mine-laying), or onto roads (to connect broken telephone cables), or up into the tallest trees (to be spotters for artillery fire). Love drew me back again from woods that were chilled from the January wind. The enemy often accompanied my crossings of no man's land with his usual 'concert of German classical music' performed by mortar bombs. I would request assistance from our machine-gunners, calling out to them or raising a small sapper's spade above the bushes. They would initiate an exchange of fire and I would get out of the forest alive.

The troops of the sniper platoon had the right attitude towards my personal success: they strove to follow my example, to adopt various camouflage skills more speedily, to improve their mastery of their weapon. A significant part of the initial training of soldiers joining us from draft companies delivered from Novorossiysk was now undertaken by Fyodor Sedykh. He had been promoted to the rank of sergeant for the courage and distinction he had shown during the second assault. He was assisted by Anastas Vartanov, who had long studied the sniper's rifle and inventively employed his hunting skills against the invader. Those beginners who showed an aptitude for sharpshooting were sometimes taken by me into the forest as lookouts for real-life tuition. The finer points are easier to understand if you are operating alongside a master.

I know what the soldiers said about me. First, they considered me somehow enchanted, as if some witch in the village near Odessa which I had saved from the

Romanians had placed on me a magic spell protecting me from death. Second, they maintained that nobody was able to find me in the forest, because there I was followed by the lord of the forest himself – the wood sprite, who had not the slightest fear. It was he who protected me from enemies with his huge, tree-like body and, with his gnarled snags of hands, deflecting onto himself the bullets and shrapnel aimed in my direction. The third legend (and in my view the old ranger had made them all up) related to my abilities. I had, the claim ran, learned from the wood sprite's keen hearing to know what was happening a kilometre around me, to see at night as well as I could in daytime, to move along forest trails with absolute silence and to hide where nobody else could. Hence my strange nickname within the regiment – the 'lynx'.

10

Duel

From the first few days of January 1942 a relative calm descended on the front. Exchanges of artillery fire between Soviet and Nazi German forces continued. Also operating here were, for instance, 305mm-calibre, long-range ordnance from the armour-turreted 30th and 35th Coastal Batteries, the 152mm-calibre howitzers, and the 122mm cannon of the 134th and 265th Artillery Regiments based in our third defence sector, and the shipboard ordnance of cruisers and destroyers which had supplied Sevastopol with reinforcements, ammunition, provisions and machinery. Our air force was active in good weather. They bombed the enemy rear, carried out aerial reconnaissance and acted as spotters for coastal artillery fire, protected the main naval base from Nazi air attacks, and even distributed leaflets over the German and Romanian trenches.

The ground forces would conduct reconnaissance by combat on various sectors in order to study the enemy's front line, fire power and centres of support and resistance. These clashes were not particularly lengthy or fierce, but they gave an idea of what was happening and what things were like behind the Fritzes' lines.

There were some sad stories, too. On Thursday, 8 January 1941, the coastal army's chief-of-staff, Major-General N.I. Krylov, headed out in a car for the third sector, to inspect the dispositions of combat detachments. He was accompanied by the adjutant of the army commander, Senior Lieutenant Kokharov. They visited the staff headquarters of the 79th Brigade and were driving along the dirt road towards us, the 25th Division. Suddenly the general stopped the car. He wanted to take a look from a small rise at a picturesque outcrop in the Kamyshly gully which had been the site of tenacious fighting at the end of December. A minute later a mortar exploded behind him, then a second one to the side, and a third one in front of him. Kokharov was killed instantly. Krylov received three wounds from mine splinters. He was rushed by car to hospital, where he underwent several operations. Fortunately, the major-general survived and returned to duty.

The thing was that the Kamyshly gully, through which a winding stream flowed, covered with reeds and hidden in places by apple orchards, was now in no man's land. Its two slopes, the gentler northern one and the steep forested southern one, formed a deep ravine. The crest of the southern slope rose in places to a height of over 300 metres above sea level. This crest was occupied by the Chapayevs: our 54th Regiment was 2km to the north of Mekenzia village; 1.5km to the north of us was the 2nd Perekop Regiment of naval infantry, and, behind it, the 287th Rifle Regiment (almost by Height 198.4). On the northern slope were units of the Germans' 50th Brandenburg Infantry Division. Using mortars and machine-gun fire from short distances, they could spray the bottom of the gully, its southern slope and our positions on the crest. We naturally responded. In return for their appalling attack on the head of the coastal army's chief-of-staff, the Fritzes received a good few hot 'presents' from us.

The beautiful mountain landscape which had so keenly interested the general also boasted a bridge. It was called the Kamyshly bridge and connected the two high sides of the gully. The bridge had been built during distant Tsarist times, when a railway was laid from Moscow to Sevastopol and goods and passenger trains began to use it. During the siege of the city the bridge was not needed by either the Russians or the Germans, and it was blown up. The grey concrete piles were now topped by a disorderly heap of twisted, broken and smashed metal constructions. The central section of this fairly lengthy bridge had collapsed, and only two or three spans on either side had survived. A magnificent feat of engineering had been turned into ruins, testifying to the merciless and senseless force of war.

From time to time I viewed it through binoculars. It was clear that the demolished bridge constituted an advantageous position from a military viewpoint. It dominated the area. One side – I shall call it the northern side – offered an excellent view of the front-line and rear positions of our forces over a distance of 800–900 metres. From the southern side the German positions could be seen. Among the bridge's iron wreckage above the gully it would be quite possible to find a suitable spot for a sniper hideout. I gave it some thought. My attachment to the Crimean forest stopped me making a speedy decision. I was now used to trees, and the pile of twisted metal had to be studied and its significance considered. Besides, the bridge was in the 79th Brigade's zone of responsibility, about 4km to the north-west of our regiment.

What is interesting about this case is how professionals think and evaluate circumstances in roughly the same way.

On the morning of the same day Fyodor Sedykh and I were busy in our platoon, dealing with supplies of SVT-40 rifles (3,000 of them had been delivered to Sevastopol at the end of December the previous year, and we had been issued eight of them, along with the same number of PU sights with mountings). It was no secret that the Tokarev self-loading rifle had quite a complex construction. Even an incomplete dismantling of it demanded good skills, thoroughness, care and, I would even say, caution.

We designed an activity whereby I would tell the soldiers about the components of the weapon and Sergeant Sedykh would slowly demonstrate how it was stripped. We began, needless to say, by detaching the ten-cartridge box magazine. The next operation was to remove the breech cover. Fyodor released the catch and placed the rifle on a table with the sight upwards. Then, with his left hand, he pushed the cover as far forward as it would go, pressing down with his right thumb on the driving-spring guide rod to disengage the rod from the retaining notch in the cover. Using both hands to press the two parts of the driving spring together then allowed the spring and its rod to be detached without touching the cover, and, raising up the front end of the cover, he separated it from the receiver. The number of dislodged components on the table, large, small and very small, gradually grew – matched by the restlessness of the soldiers. They did not yet know that complete dismantling of the SVT-40 would take no fewer than fourteen operations, the final one being to detach the firing pin from the breechblock. There was a sense that this would not be an easy operation.

I had no wish to be distracted, but an orderly appeared in the dugout and passed on a message from Major Matusyevich that the platoon commander was to report immediately to the regimental command post. Apart from the major, there was one other officer there – a man of average height and sturdy physique, about thirty-eight years old and dressed in a black sailor's uniform with four gold stripes on the sleeves. Matusyevich introduced me to him as Senior Sergeant Lyudmila Mikhailovna Pavlichenko, commander of a platoon in the 1st Battalion's 2nd Company, and him to me: Colonel Alexei Stepanovich Potapov, commander of the 79th Naval Rifle Brigade. The colonel looked at me closely.

'They say you're the best sniper in the Chapayev Division, Lyudmila. I saw your photograph on the divisional board of honour.'

'It was only put up there a short time ago, Comrade Colonel.'

'I've got a serious matter for you. It seems that a top-class German rifleman has appeared on our defence sector. Over the last two days five of our men have been killed, two of them officers, including the commander of the 2nd Battalion. All by shots to the head.'

'Has his hideout been discovered?'

'We reckon that he's firing from the wreckage of the railway bridge.'

'From the bridge!' I could not restrain myself from exclaiming.

'So you know this place?' asked Potapov in surprise.

'I wouldn't say I know it, Comrade Colonel, but I've been thinking about it.'

'And what do you think about it?' Potapov gestured for me to come up to the table where there was a large-scale map showing the local area and the dispositions of military forces from the third defence sector. With a pencil the colonel pointed to the Kamyshly gully and a thin black line crossing the narrowest part of it on the north-west.

'It's a very advantageous position,' I said, 'especially if you can find a place on one of the surviving spans and hide among the metal wreckage. It's possible to hit a target from a distance of 600 to 800 metres. The front line and the closest sections in the rear of the Fritzes' 50th Infantry Division will be plainly visible. From the other side the firing lines of our brigade are probably just as easy to see, so he's been able to fire at his pleasure.'

'Can you put an end to these strikes?'

'Yes,' I said firmly. 'If, of course, the major will release me.'

'No question.' Matusyevich, who had been listening to our conversation, smiled cheerfully. 'We'll do anything the naval infantry wish.'

'Apart from that, I'll need a lookout. The best one would be Sergeant Fyodor Sedykh, my regular experienced partner.'

'Understood and agreed.' Matusyevich nodded. 'Today there will be a regimental order for Senior Sergeant Pavlichenko and Sergeant Sedykh to be placed at the disposal of the commander of the 79th Brigade.'

At supper my husband and I discussed the latest service news as usual. Alexei Kitsenko regarded the appearance of a German sniper as a natural development. At a recent meeting of company and battalion commanders he had attended in the third sector, they had talked of new approaches in Nazi tactics. In the first assault they had hoped to smash the city defences without pausing for breath. They had been repelled in November 1941, but they had not abandoned hope of a speedy victory and had begun to strengthen their assault units and prepare them for a second siege. The failure of the attack mounted in December had noticeably cooled the conquerors' ardour and forced them to examine the situation seriously. 'Sevastopol has turned out to be a first-class fortress,' Erich von Manstein, commander of the German forces on the peninsula, commented in his report to the Führer.

If it was a fortress, then it had to be besieged in the right way. A positional war was the best time for sharpshooters to operate and in January 1942 they appeared on the German side in large numbers. Soviet units had already come up against their operations in other sectors of the front. Some it had been possible to neutralize. Documents from their soldiers testified that the German command had transferred snipers from divisions based in Poland and France to the Crimea. There were also novices who had completed short training courses in the rear of the 11th Army itself.

We did not bother to speculate as to who my opponent was. My husband begged me to be careful and alert. He approved my choice of a lookout. Sergeant Sedykh, in his opinion, was better suited than the other soldiers in my platoon to the role of assistant in this duel, which would be neither straightforward nor easy, nor quick.

We knew of only one possible site for the German's hideout, and that not very precisely. We had no idea yet how many other positions he had prepared earlier.

The following morning Potapov sent a car for us. Loaded with sniper's equipment, our kit bags on our backs, our Mosin rifles on our shoulders, in overcoats and caps with earflaps, we settled down on the back seat of the GAZ-M1 and drove to the dispositions of the 79th Naval Rifle Brigade. After the second assault the Nazis had managed to put pressure on the city's defenders, and the naval infantry now occupied lines on the crest of the south slope of the Kamyshly gully, at Height 195.2, and further on, on the eastern slopes of Height 145.4, north and east of Height 124.0 and, closer to the railway track, the Belbek river and the Tartar village of the same name. The local area had a terrain familiar to us: outcrops, hills, deep gorges with steep slopes, covered with thick bushes and – here and there – forest, and valleys between them with vineyards, orchards and small population centres. The defence sector of the 79th Brigade, which ran through here, was 4km long and 2.5km deep.

The soldiers and officers of this military formation had not been in Sevastopol long. A detachment of ships from the Black Sea Fleet had brought them here from Novorossiysk on 21 December the previous year. The brigade arrived with 4,000 men, fully armed, and was immediately assigned to the most difficult sector of the front – the Mekenzi hills. The naval infantry went into battle straight after disembarking from the ships and, with a bold attack on 22 December, it dislodged the Nazis from the occupied Heights 192.0 and 104.5, which was a major contribution to repelling the second German assault. However, the 79th Brigade had suffered severe losses: by 31 December less than a third of its original force remained.

The brigade was now taking in reinforcements and restoring the defence line destroyed in the fierce fighting. We saw the first continuous deep trench running along the front line. Its three rifle battalions in battle formation had 50mm and 82mm mortars and both medium and light machine guns. There were also shallow trenches, well-equipped firing points and pre-fabricated, permanent, reinforced-concrete emplacements with gun ports. Communication passages up to 2 metres deep stretched for several kilometres.

The command post of the 79th Naval Rifle Brigade was situated quite a long way from the forward defence line, 1km to the south of the 'Mekenzi Hills' No. 1 Forest Cordon, in a small white house by the highway. We went there first and presented ourselves to Colonel Potapov and the brigade's commander, Regimental Commissar Slyesarev. Then, accompanied by two officers from the 3rd Battalion, we set off for Height 124.0, which was the closest to the Kamyshly bridge.

It became clear to me from first glance that it would be impossible to set up a sniper's hideout at the bridge's southern end because it had suffered badly in the explosion. Only one span of the bridge had survived, and even that was not undamaged. The picture was completely different on the enemy side, at the northern end of the bridge. There, three spans had survived. They were quite sturdy, even though they were surrounded by bent metal beams, twisted bars, rails that had risen from their bed, and charred and splintered sleepers. It would be very easy to hide in that chaotic pile of metal and wood. I did not doubt that that was where the Fritz was firing from. But would he return to the position where he had already twice been successful?

With a detailed report I set off to see Potapov and concluded with this question. The colonel listened to me attentively. He pondered for a long time, then asked: 'Would you choose that position yourself?'

'I probably would. It's a very good spot. An absolute sniper's dream.'

'If that is so, how will you get the better of the enemy?'

'The old Russian way: cunning, persistence and patience,' I answered.

Within the 79th Brigade there was a sapper company numbering up to 100 men. The sappers helped Fyodor and me to set up the hideout. At night, among the juniper and hazelnut thickets in no man's land, they quickly and expertly dug a trench to my design which was up to 80cm deep and up to 10 metres long in front of the 3rd Battalion's first line of defence. This trench led into another, large, deep, trench. Over it we set up a folding metal frame and covered it with twigs and snow. The trench was camouflaged in the same way, so that from above it looked like an ordinary ditch. Apart from that, we made a 'decoy', a mannequin on a stick, dressed in an overcoat and helmet, with a rifle tied to his back to make it look more authentic.

For two days I studied the ruined bridge through binoculars. There were only two spots which were ideal for positioning a soldier with a rifle. Fyodor and I observed each of them in turn, with focused attention, in the hours before first light. The pernicious German did not appear. I had become concerned that our forces had already finished him off somewhere in the forest after he had headed there in search of new prey. Sedykh's reply was along the lines that, being extremely calculating people, the Nazis would simply not be able to ignore a bridge with such a remarkable view of the front lines and the closest rear units of the 79th Naval Infantry Brigade. The marksman would appear. The important thing was to detect him in time.

I was dozing as I squatted there with my shoulder against the trench wall. The winter uniform – warm underwear, tunic, pleated, padded, sleeveless vest and pants, overcoat and white camouflage smock – prevented you from freezing, but did not keep you warm very well. Suddenly the sergeant touched my shoulder with his finger and then pointed to the bridge. I quickly took my binoculars out of the case hanging on my chest and raised them to my eyes. The January night was gradually retreating. The outlines of the bridge were becoming visible in the early morning haze. The dark figure of a man picking his way through the twisted beams emerged against the background of the brightening sky and instantly vanished.

Fyodor and I exchanged glances. He gave the thumbs down. I nodded, agreeing with my lookout that the quarry had arrived at the combat zone. Now we had to give him a chance to take a look round, set up his rifle, load it and find some familiar markers in the area where he had earlier managed to make himself at home. The Fritz was hardly likely to discover our hideout. We had toiled hard at it, completely fulfilling all the rules of camouflage taught at the Kiev Osoaviakhim school.

We had coordinated our subsequent plan of action earlier, before going out into the trench. After clambering out further along the trench, the sergeant would end up near our front line, take the decoy and await my signal that I had completed preparations for a shot. The preparations were simple and long familiar. It would be a shot from below, with a correction for the angle of the target's location.

Half an hour went by.

Friday, 23 January 1942, began extremely quietly. On Sevastopol's land defence lines neither side was conducting combat operations. The cannons, mortars and machine guns remained quiet. No bombers, dive-bombers or fighters rose into the sky. The war had, as it were, withdrawn from view. During these minutes and hours – and they were rare now – you imagined that the slaughter was over, that peaceful life was returning, and our skills would no longer be required. Unfortunately, for the time being it was dangerous to believe this.

As I listened to the unusual silence, I put two fingers to my lips and whistled. Sedykh responded with the same short whistle. I did not take my eyes off the bridge and I knew that Fyodor, hiding in the trench, had already dragged the decoy into no man's land. From a distance it looked as if a Soviet sentry had abandoned his trench and was viewing the area in front of him. Would the German fall for an old ploy which had been used back during the First World War?

The shot from the bridge sounded muffled, as if someone had struck a wooden plank with a metal rod. The brief flash glittered precisely where I had anticipated. To be honest, I would also have chosen the German's little den. On the left his position was safely shielded by a metal beam. His rifle lay conveniently on a bent twig, the marksman himself was sitting on the heel of his right leg, his knee resting against a shattered sleeper and his left elbow on his left knee. Finally I've got you, you Nazi bastard – after all this sitting around here in the perishing cold! Through the eyepiece of the telescope sight I could see his head. The Fritz pulled the bolt of his rifle, picked up the spent cartridge, put it in his pocket and looked out of his hiding place. My great teacher had counselled wisely: 'Do not imagine that your shot is the last one, and do not show excessive curiosity!'

Holding my breath, I smoothly pressed the trigger.

From a height of 5 metres the German fell to the bottom of the Kamyshly gully, which was thickly covered by reeds and made a little bit warmer by the water from the stream. His rifle fell down after him. To my surprise, he was operating not with the Zf. Kar. 98k, but with a Mosin-system weapon with PE sight, obviously a trophy. Many of our excellent, fundamentally improved, weapons (which we Red Army Razins could not obtain) ended up in the hands of the invaders during the first months of the war.

Taking his PPSh-41 submachine gun, Fyodor remained in the trench to cover my dash over to the victim, who had been shot between the eyes. After a quarter of an hour spent running and sliding, I made it through the reeds and ended up next to the body. I did not like looking at the faces of dead enemies, even less remembering them.

The minutes were ticking by. I quickly searched the Nazi's corpse, which was clad in a camouflage suit on top of a thermal tunic. There was his soldier's passport, his epaulettes, embroidered with silver lace, the red ribbon of his decoration with its black-and-white braiding in the second button-hole of his tunic and the emblem for his Iron Cross. With my Finnish knife, sharp as a razor, I cut these things off. Captain Bezrodny would be pleased. He valued souvenirs like this and said they superbly complemented his reports of reconnaissance in the field.

Apart from that – let's be frank – a woman can never have too many bandages or too much cotton wool. The Fritz had plenty. There was a large packet in the inside right pocket of his overcoat and a smaller one (containing 5 metres of bandaging) in the right breast pocket of his tunic. There was also a gift for my beloved husband – a flat flask of brandy and a cigarette case with some cigarettes in it. The metal cylinder designed to hold a gas mask contained in fact no such thing. Instead there were his sniper's dry rations, apparently for one day: four packets of plain biscuits, two bars of chocolate in foil and a tin of sardines in oil, with a key to open it soldered onto the lid.

Shouldering the Three Line with telescope sight, which the Nazi no longer needed, I went back to my trench. Fyodor Sedykh was eagerly awaiting me. He helped me to get back over the parapet into the trench and asked with a smile: 'Who have you done in this time, Comrade Senior Sergeant?'

'A big shot. Look at his regalia.' I took the foreign decorations out of my pocket.

'Well, the most important thing', replied Fyodor, 'is that our sailor boys will have a quieter time now.'

'Look, it's silent everywhere. That means he went out on the hunt on his own, had confidence in himself.' I took out the German soldier's notebook and read aloud, 'Helmut Bommel, 121st Infantry Regiment, 50th Brandenburg Infantry Division, Oberfeldwebel. All right, let's get out of here before they come for him.'

Sedykh took both rifles from me – my own and the trophy – and we both quickly crawled along the trench to the front line of the 3rd Battalion of the 79th

Brigade. Soldiers from the military outposts greeted us. The machine-gunner who was entrusted with covering 'guest snipers' in the event of the enemy discovering them also waved to us. We had barely found ourselves between the high earth walls of the communication passage before the mortars started whistling over the Kamyshly bridge and machine guns began rattling. The Germans had realized what had happened and were spraying no man's land with a torrent of fire. Our side responded. The day had begun quietly and peacefully, but war had nevertheless got its own way in the end.

Sitting at his desk, Colonel Potapov spent a long time examining Helmut Bommel's soldier's notebook, the Russian translation attached to it, and the Iron Cross. Fyodor and I stood at attention before him.

'Which of you took out the sniper?' asked Potapov, looking for some reason at Sergeant Sedykh, who was a big strong man with a good-natured face.

'I did, Comrade Colonel.' My reply was loud and clear.

'How did you manage it?'

'The usual way, Comrade Colonel,' I answered.

'I read here', the 79th Brigade commander continued unhurriedly, 'this Bommel was transferred here recently, that he had previously fought in Poland, Belgium and France, and served as a sniper instructor in Berlin. He has a tally of 215 dead soldiers and officers. And how many have you got, Lyudmila Mikhailovna?'

'227.'

'So you were well matched?'

'Yes, Comrade Colonel.'

'He had two decorations. But what about you, Comrade Senior Sergeant, do you have any government awards?'

'No, Comrade Colonel.'

Silence reigned in the room. Potapov was looking at me pensively, as if he was seeing me for the first time. I had always tried to keep quiet during such discussions with superiors. Half a year in the armed forces had brought me to the conclusion that lengthy conversations with the senior command corps yielded nothing of benefit for the junior command. Therefore, I looked not at the colonel but at the coloured sign above his head showing a stern young woman in a red headscarf and the message, 'Hush, the enemy is listening!'

'Get ready, Comrade Sergeants!' Potapov suddenly broke the silence. 'We are off to the staff headquarters of the coastal army. With a report on your achievement.'

Potapov was highly respected by the command of the coastal army. He had begun his military service in the ranks of the 3rd Crimean Rifle Division, then become an officer, completed the Red Banner Vystrel senior rifle and tactical course in 1939, and taught at the Ukrainian Young Communist League naval military college of coastal defence. The Great War for the Fatherland had revealed his talent as a military leader. The 79th Naval Brigade entrusted to him had covered itself with eternal glory in the battles for Sevastopol, and its soldiers and officers had been models of mass heroism. Potapov had a reputation as a stern but fair commander. The colonel regularly recommended his subordinates for awards, believing that those at Sevastopol who had repulsed the 11th Army, which had a two-to-one advantage over the city's defenders, were fully entitled to medals, decorations and preferential promotions.

It goes without saying that Fyodor and I did not hear the exchange between Colonel Potapov and Major-General Petrov. When they had concluded their fairly vigorous conversation, the adjutant of the coastal army's commander invited us into the office. Petrov smiled at me as an old acquaintance, asked about my father and, shaking hands, said with a smile: 'So, you fooled the Fritz, did you, lass?'

'Yes, Comrade Major-General.'

'In other words, you already know all their tricks?'

'There's nothing complicated about them, Ivan Yefimovich.'

'Well done! I am proud of your achievement and congratulate you. It seems I owe you an apology, Lyudmila. But never mind, I'll soon put it right.'

He also shook hands with Sergeant Sedykh and praised him for the courage he had shown in the duel with the German sniper. The commander also voiced the hope that the soldiers of the 54th Stepan Razin Rifle Regiment would not rest on their achievements, but continue to wipe out the enemies of our socialist homeland until complete victory was gained. This positive experience, said the army commander, should be broadcast throughout all units of the Sevastopol defence district and Fyodor and I would be photographed for some combat leaflets, including a detailed account of the clash between the Soviet soldiers and the Nazi killer by the Kamyshly bridge.

At that time we did not attach particular significance to these words. We were very keen to get back to our own regiment after a two-day watch in a cold trench, to lie down in a dugout warmed by a pot-belly stove and drink hot tea with sugar (and we had chocolate as well) with a hunk of rye bread baked in the tunnels of Sevastopol. The senior commanders let us go and were kind enough to take us by car to the command post of our regiment's 1st Battalion. From there Sergeant Sedykh and I stepped out along a forest trail, holding onto the canvas straps of the rifles slung over our shoulders.

However, the next morning, breakfast with my husband was interrupted by the appearance of an unfamiliar senior political instructor. He introduced himself as the editor of the widely distributed coastal army newspaper *For the Motherland*, Nikolai Kurochkin, and said that I must tell him how I had fought the German invaders. According to the instructions of Major-General Petrov, he was required to write an interesting piece about it for the next issue of the newspaper. The more I told him, the better the article would be. Apart from that, a photographer would be arriving to take photos of me to illustrate the piece. Indeed, a chirpy youth (I don't recall his name) with a Leica camera stepped over the threshold of our front-line dwelling and declared straight off that I was very photogenic.

I had a strong urge to evict this impertinent young pair immediately. Let 'Machine-Gun Annie' from the 1st Company be interviewed and photographed; a sniper should not draw attention to him- or herself. The main prerequisite for operating successfully was to remain hidden, while the newspaper *For the Motherland* had a distribution of several thousand copies and I had no idea whose hands they ended up in. Besides, at the orders of the USSR People's Commissariat of Defence, information about the guidelines for teaching marksmanship, the types of sniper rifles, optics, camouflage techniques and methods employed against the enemy was not subject to general release. It was intended *only* for specialists. It is possible that I would have bluntly told the journalists so, but new guests arrived in our dugout: Military Commissar Maltsev of the 54th Regiment, along with Military Commissar Novikov of the 1st Battalion. Lyonya and I had never earned such an honour before and it became clear to me that my successful shot on the Kamyshly bridge had had some special consequences. Whether this was good or bad, time would tell.

On the morning of 24 January 1942, in the presence of two military commissars, I replied briefly to Kurochkin's questions, then posed with my ceremonial SVT-40 rifle for the photographer full-face, in profile, standing, and also lying in the nearest bush with the 'Sveta' by my shoulder, holding it 'machine-gun style', i.e. with my left hand on the butt.

My meetings with representatives of the press continued. I was visited by correspondents of the city newspaper *Mayak Kommuny* (*Beacon of the Commune*), the newspaper of the Black Sea Fleet, *Krasny Chernomorets* (*Red Black Sea Sailor*), and the newspaper of the Crimean Party regional committee, *Krasny Krym* (*Red Crimea*). The war cinecameraman Vladislav Mikosha spent half a day in the lines of our 2nd Company, filming various subjects. He was particularly vexing for me because he was looking, as he put it, for the 'right angle' and eventually forced me to clamber up a tree with my SVT-40 rifle and to pretend that I was aiming at the enemy from there. It was pointless telling him that in Sevastopol I did not shoot from trees and this would mislead the viewers. The camera chap obstinately insisted. In order to get rid of him, I had to climb with my rifle up an old apple tree which was growing next to the big 'club' dugout 50 metres from the forward defence line.

The 'brotherhood of scribblers' became still more perplexing. The correspondents laid it on with a trowel when it came to depicting Helmut Bommel: fat as a toad, lifeless eyes, yellow hair, a heavy jaw. I, of course, had told them nothing of the sort, as I did not remember the appearance of those I shot. They did not exist for me; they were just targets. Some of my regimental mates spoke of cold hatred towards the invaders. But even that I regard as too strong, more suited to propaganda leaflets. Sharpshooters do not think about it. They arrive at their firing position with their heart at rest and the firm, deep, conviction that they are right. Otherwise they risk missing and falling victim in the duel to a cruel and wrathful enemy.

Nor were the writers too scrupulous with the Nazi sniper's tally; they even credited him with 300 dead, and 400, and 500, although for the beginning of 1942 that was an entirely unrealistic figure. It never entered the reporters' heads that Germany's war with the countries of Europe had proceeded quickly, with no positional fighting. It was only in positional fighting that the sniper had the opportunity to increase his tally significantly. In the Soviet Union combat had only been going for half a year and, besides, in the main the Germans had been advancing. A big role here was played by tanks and aircraft. The Fritzes had no particular need of sharpshooters. And we had more to think about than snipers' rifles. It takes long sieges and blockades of cities for snipers to operate really productively, as happened at Odessa, Sevastopol, Leningrad and, later, Stalingrad.

To my surprise, for some reason the duel on the wrecked railway bridge did not inspire the correspondents. Perhaps we should have taken them to the Kamyshly gully, shown them the unusual character of this place and explained that Helmut Bommel was wise to have chosen it, but that, in view of his traditional German self-confidence, he had not anticipated a speedy response. But why waste time on uninformed people who are convinced they are right? They will still write as they like. Take, for instance, the following:

And so, they lay all day and night without stirring. In the morning, when it grew light, Lyuda saw, hiding behind a dummy tree root, a sniper moving forwards in barely noticeable thrusts. Closer and closer he came towards her. She moved to meet him, holding the rifle in front of her, keeping her eyes on the telescope sight. A mere second acquired new, almost endless, dimensions. Suddenly Lyuda caught in her sight the lifeless eyes, yellow hair and heavy jaw. The enemy sniper was looking at her; their eyes met. His tense face was distorted by a grimace; he realized it was a woman! Life was decided in an instant – she cocked the rifle. By a merciful second Lyuda beat the enemy to it. She waited for her chance. The German submachine-gunners were silent. Only then did she begin to crawl towards the sniper. He had frozen where he was, taking aim at her. Lyuda took out the Nazi sniper's notebook and read 'Dunkirk'. Beside it was a figure, and some more figures. Over 400 Frenchmen and Englishmen had met their deaths at his hands.[1]

In the end, after some consideration, I came to the conclusion that the reporters composing this nonsense after talking to me were still, nevertheless, spreading propaganda for the sniper's cause in the Sevastopol defence district. The main principles of a sharpshooter's operations in war were laid out correctly: to camouflage oneself cleverly, to wait patiently till the opponent makes a mistake, and immediately exploit it to shoot accurately at the target. No information about handling a special weapon and the telescope sight, not a word about calculating the trajectory of the bullet in different geographical and weather conditions, about the immutable laws of ballistics and other profound military knowledge which enabled an ordinary person to become a sniper. Anyone interested in our art would learn the details from attending one of the two- or three-week courses for sharpshooters which were already being set up for rank-and-file infantrymen at some divisional headquarters.

Journalistic invention is just one component of propaganda. People need a living hero to make things more convincing. It seemed that I had been chosen for this role in the coastal army's political department headed by Regimental Commissar L.P. Bocharov. That, at least, was how it appeared to me when an order from the regimental staff headquarters came to the dugout occupied by Alexei and me: on 2 February 1942 platoon commander Senior Sergeant Pavlichenko, L.M. was to leave the front line for the city and take part in a conference of women activists in the defence of Sevastopol, which was to be held in Teachers' House. At the conference I was to give an address of up to fifteen minutes devoted to the operations of snipers.

I was perplexed on reading the command. Our forest hideouts had sharpened my vision and hearing but accustomed me to keeping quiet, to observing silence. Nor did dealing with my subordinates in the platoon require oratorical skills. And now I was faced with an address of fifteen minutes. How many words was that? And in front of a large audience, in a noisy hall, under the glare of lights!

My precious husband, an inventive man, strove to calm me down and inspire me. Lyonya said it was high time I visited the rear, the wonderful city of Sevastopol, unwound, showed myself, and took a look at other people. This usually well and truly raised the spirits of front-line soldiers – particularly since there were still three days until the address and that interval was enough to prepare a dozen speeches.

'But what about a parade uniform?' I asked.

'Fiddlesticks! I'll ring the sergeant major now. He can have a look in the regimental stores,' replied the commander of the 2nd Company.

I had not even dreamed of wearing the attire considered appropriate for service women: khaki fabric with a turn-down collar, belt and slit pockets. The most the sergeant major could come up with was a skirt, a new tunic with raspberry-coloured parade tabs and some relatively new boots on which half a tin of black shoe polish had been expended. I had kept two pairs of skin-coloured stockings in my kitbag – an incredible pre-war treasure – and they had finally come in handy.

On the morning of 2 February we travelled to the city in the regimental commander's car – myself plus Senior Sergeant Nina Onilova, machine-gunner of the 1st Company. Nina was surprised to see me in the car. She considered herself an acknowledged heroine, but she had no idea for what feats I was being sent to this conference. However, as she was a straightforward and good-natured woman, within ten minutes she was merrily chatting away to me. This was not the first time that Onilova had taken part in such functions and therefore she talked about it in lively fashion all the way – how to maintain the right bearing on the rostrum, how to read your speech, how to answer questions from conference participants, if any such arose. She would not let me concentrate. It was just like the Civil War song 'Two Maxims': Trat trat trat goes the machine gun . . . I did not regard myself as an orator and had written down the main points of my address, following the advice of my husband. It would be good not to mix anything up, to speak with conviction, and to present our profession, little known to civilians, in the best light.

Quite a lot of people had gathered for the conference. Women had come from various workplaces, schools and hospitals. Among the multi-coloured dresses and blouses the uniform tunics of service-women– radio-operators, medical orderlies, doctors from medical battalions and field hospitals – looked particularly austere. With her Order of the Red Banner on her breast, Nina enjoyed great popularity. Many greeted her, asked about things on the front line and shared jolly repartee. Nobody knew me and I modestly took my seat by the window to read through my notes once again.

The address by Major-General Petrov, commander of the coastal army, gave a survey of the main events on the front. The women greeted it with lengthy applause. They were really fond of Ivan Yefimovich in Sevastopol because of the huge contribution he had made to the defence of the principal naval base. This address was followed by other speeches, some lively and informative, others not very. The women talked about their work and their thoughts and feelings regarding their hometown. To me it all seemed interesting. I had never imagined how one could teach children at a school situated in a bomb shelter, stand for twelve hours at a lathe stamping hand-grenades, spend one's day in a sewing workshop making linen packages for the army and then set off, in the evening, for an underground hospital and care for wounded soldiers.

The women of Sevastopol had replaced the men who had left their factories for the front and were coping with the work every bit as well. How could I forget Anastasia Chaus, a woman of my own age, who worked at the No. 1 special industrial combine? She had been wounded in a bombing raid, lost her left arm, but stayed in the city, went out to work, mastered the skill of stamping and, with one arm, actually doubled her quota.

Life in Sevastopol was difficult. There were ration cards for bread: 800g for skilled workers at defence factories, 600g for state employees and pensioners, and 300g for dependants. Fishermen did much to help out the city residents. They went out to sea under artillery fire, made their way through minefields and caught and delivered to cafeterias and shops thousands of kilograms of fish, mainly anchovy and plaice.

The conference attendees also spoke of difficulties, but somewhat in passing. It was as if they had been left outside the walls of Teachers' House. It was not for that kind of discussion that these women of various ages and professions had assembled; they had something else to convey to one another. Perhaps it was their sacred faith in victory over the Nazis, perhaps their strength of spirit, perhaps their hope for a speedy change in the situation in their beloved city. Sometimes it sounded roughly like this: 'I, a small unit in the rear, am doing all that I know how to do, and I want to do still more. Having given up four sons to the struggle against the enemy, I will not spare myself and I will go to any sector. . .' (Alexandra Sergeyevna Fedorinchik, teacher, No. 14 School).

After such passionate speeches, a dry account of the number of Nazis wiped out would have sounded simply absurd. I put aside my page of earlier prepared headings and began to say what lay in my heart, what moved me to the depths of my soul.

On No-Name Height

The Sevastopol winter tends to be changeable. Two days earlier the sky had been covered with low clouds, snow was falling, the frost crackled, and it was -15°C. Today everything was different: the snow had melted, the sun was beaming and the air temperature was above zero. On the gentle slopes of the Crimean heights the grass was visible again, yellowy brown and withered, while juniper bushes, upward-striving cypresses and low cedars showed bright green against this backdrop.

Through binoculars I viewed the panorama of the Balaklava valley from a position by the gun port of a machine-gun emplacement not far from the village of Verkhny Chorgun.[1] Visible far in the distance was the grey ribbon of the Sevastopol–Yalta highway and, closer to me, the narrow river Chornaya, which weaved its way through the hills, fields with parallel lines of grapevines, and the slopes of the beautiful Gasfort hill covered here and there with oak woods, as well as the white wall around the Italian cemetery, smashed by shells, and the roof of its chapel, reminiscent of a child's toy building block with its low, straight walls.

During the second assault, the front line of the second defence sector had run through here with its trenches, reinforced-earth firing installations, mortar-firing facilities and deep trenches. Enemy attacks were heroically resisted by the troops and officers of the 7th Brigade of naval infantry and the 31st and 514th Rifle Regiments. The hill and the heights alongside changed hands several times. In the end the Germans squeezed our forces out and installed themselves there.

A group of Nazi snipers had occupied the height known on the map as 'No-Name'. From a distance of 500 metres they began to target the dirt road between the villages of Kamara and Shuli, which passed along the rear of the second defence sector and played an important role in supplying our forces with provisions, arms and ammunition.

Their final act of impudence was to kill or heavily wound more than half the personnel of the 45mm-calibre anti-tank gun and the twenty-four horses which were harnessed to this ordnance to haul it along the roads. All attempts to crush the enemy with artillery and mortars came to nothing. The snipers would change their positions on the height and renew their firing.

It was no accident that I had ended up here, far from my own Chapayev Division. After we had carried out several successful expeditions into no man's land and into the enemy rear, the commander of the coastal army came to the view that, since there was a bold and well-trained group of snipers in the 1st Battalion of the 54th Regiment, they could be used not only in the third defence sector, but also in other areas of the Sevastopol front. We began to go 'on tour' along the entire front line of defence, undertaking missions of special complexity. On this occasion we were entrusted with conducting an operation on 'No-Name' Height in the area of the Gasfort hill and the Italian cemetery.

Before we set out there had been a meeting at army staff headquarters between me and the commandant of the regiment's second sector, Colonel Nikolai Filippovich Skutelnik, commander of the 386th Rifle Division, in whose zone of responsibility this sector lay, and the head of the division's general staff, Lieutenant Colonel Dobrov. I then went to the village of Verkhny Chorgun, to view the locality and work out a suitable operational plan for the sniper group to seize the height and wipe out the Nazis.

Gasfort hill (named in honour of Colonel V.G. Gasfort, hero of the first siege of Sevastopol and commander of the Kazan infantry regiment which fought here in 1854–5 against the Anglo-French–Italian–Turkish alliance) was about 15km along the highway from Sevastopol to Yalta and was not in itself very high, just 217.2 metres above sea level. But it was surrounded by lower heights, and hollows between them, alternating with flat fields. Part of Gasfort hill was occupied by the Italian cemetery. The remains of Italian soldiers were reburied there in 1882 by permission of the Russian government: over 2,000 soldiers and officers of the Sardinian corps who had perished in combat or died here from the cholera epidemic.

The rough, broken terrain of this locality raised hopes of a successful attack. However, the exercise required the thorough reconnaissance and study of the enemy's forces and defensive system. I mentioned this to Colonel Skutelnik. He agreed with me and promised that the fighting units of the second sector would render the necessary assistance to the snipers.

I went back to the 2nd Company's dispositions and assembled the section commanders of my platoon in the dugout shared by Alexei and me. We had to think of something. No-Name Height could not be climbed in broad daylight. We would be below, the Germans would be above, and they would easily spot us and then pick us off like hares. Despite the observations which the troops of the 386th Division had conducted, the locations of the snipers' hideouts had not been found. The Fritzes had probably set up a few dozen camouflaged nests there for their sharpshooters.

At that time the commander of the first section was, as before, Sergeant Fyodor Sedykh and, of the second section, Junior Sergeant Vladimir Volchkov, who had been transferred to the platoon from the 3rd Company on the orders of Lieutenant Dromin as a rifleman who had demonstrated excellent form in wiping out the German battalion which had broken through to our rear during the second assault – on 22 December, to be precise. The third section existed for the time being in name only; along with Corporal Anastas Vartanov, it numbered five men, and we were awaiting the arrival of draft reinforcements from Novorossiysk. I gave the old ranger the opportunity to speak first because he was the most junior of us in terms of rank. Anastas expressed his regret that the Balaklava valley was not as familiar to him as No. 2 Cordon on the Mekenzi hills, or else he would have led us there via hunters' trails.

Before us on the table lay a large-scale map of the second defence sector, issued to me at the staff headquarters of the 386th Division, on which I had made additional markings after visiting the village of Verkhny Chorgun. In my briefing I strove to supplement the existing information on No-Name Height. But a lot – distances in particular – remained unknown because I was unable to get near the object of the proposed attack. The area in front of it was exposed to fire.

We spent quite a long time examining this map. I no longer remember which of the sergeants drew attention to the fact that the western slope, thickly covered with juniper, wild dog rose, elderberry and garland rose, was very uneven. By using the bushes for camouflage it would be possible to approach the foot of the height and then, having cut several fronds from these bushes, to carry them higher up and 'plant' them there before concealing ourselves behind the hunks of limestone which protruded above the ground in a number of spots. What would the Fritzes do when they discovered new bushes which had grown up overnight on a bare slope? Of course, they would open fire at them, and we would see how many of them there were and where they were directing their fire from.

'But why cut the bushes on the hill?' asked Fyodor. 'Let's do it beforehand and take them up there. It's safer, and they will look natural.'

I entrusted the preparation of the bushes to Vartanov. He already knew the forest plants of Crimea well and quickly constructed six decoy bushes, comprising branches of juniper up to 40cm long, with dark-green prickly leaves, and round grey-blue berries. Some of these adornments had to be secured with wire. But, on the whole, they looked quite convincing and were securely fastened to sharp stakes, which we would use to 'plant' them on the slope.

There were seven in the group, not counting me. As commander of the company, Alexei Kitsenko did a check on each one of them. He wanted to see us returning victorious – as far as that was possible – rather than perishing in an unequal battle. The experience acquired in previous raids had taught us all to be careful, to help one another out in combat, and to fulfil orders to the letter. My verdicts on the qualities of the combatants usually coincided with the junior lieutenant's opinion. Therefore, we both immediately and unanimously chose Fyodor Sedykh (at which he was very pleased), Vladimir Volchkov (I did not know him so well, but Alexei assured me of the junior sergeant's complete reliability) and Anastas Vartanov (we did not doubt his courage but rather his strength and stamina, as the warden had recently turned fifty). The remaining participants in the raid had served in the sniper platoon for about three months (a pretty good spell, given the extent of the fighting and the losses at Sevastopol) and were good marksmen.

A special word needs to be said about the group's equipment. We turned down overcoats and caps with earflaps in favour of padded jackets and trousers, helmets and forage caps. On top of them we donned autumn camouflage jackets with mustard-coloured hoods and dark-brown patterns on them, and similar trousers, which were quite capacious and tucked into our boots. On our belts we had four leather ammunition pouches, three grenades, a TT pistol in a holster, a Finnish knife in a metal sheath, a small sapper's spade in a cover, a flask of water, also in a cover, and – over our shoulders – a waterproof provisions bag with dry rations for three days (black bread, fatback and a tin of meat stew). Apart from that we took binoculars, torches with batteries and a flare gun. The question of weapons was not discussed at length: four Mosin rifles with PE sights, four SVT-40s with PU sights and 200 cartridges each for them, and three PPSh-41 submachine guns with two spare magazine drums. We decided not to take our favourite Degtyarev light machine gun on this occasion. Instead, we packed a sack with decoy bushes carefully tied with rope.

I do not like to spend a long time saying goodbye. Lengthy farewells make the heart sad, especially in wartime. Lyonya gave me a firm hug in the dugout and kissed me. One step over the threshold, and we were no longer man and wife but regimental comrades. Along with the other soldiers I went out to the battalion command post, where a 1,500kg truck awaited the group, for there was a long way to go – to the other end of the Sevastopol defence district. Then, just a final handshake and voicing of good wishes to the snipers from the company commander, a final glance from him and a final message: 'Safe return!'

The first day was spent on basic survey of the locality. We discovered nothing here to give us comfort. We could not hide in the bushes; they were situated quite a long way from No-Name Height. The Germans controlled the entire area and periodically fired machine guns and mortars along the valley.

Our forces responded, but they had to economize on ammunition. At my request the machine-gunners of the naval infantry's 7th Brigade promised that night, at three o'clock, to direct a volley at the height and to keep it up for about twenty to thirty minutes, in order to cover our progress up the slope. It would have also been nice to request (but from whom?) a dark night, a moderate wind and an air temperature no colder than five degrees above zero.

Night descended, and it really was moonless, windless and warm.

Having begun our ascent at three o'clock in the morning to the crackle of machine-gun rounds resounding from the Soviet lines, we crawled almost to the summit, and the Fritzes failed to notice us. At a distance of 70 metres from their trenches we stuck our decoy bushes in the ground and withdrew about 30 metres back from them, towards the grey-white limestone rocks, which had wild rose growing behind them.

At the first rays of dawn the Nazis opened a furious volley of machine-gun fire at the handiwork of the old ranger Vartanov. They literally shredded them, turned them into fine scraps of wood, bark and leaves. They pitted the ground around them with bullets to a diameter of 2 to 3 metres and did not rest until a cloud of dust had risen up. When silence descended, the Nazis crept out of their trenches and began to view the slope of the height through binoculars. No doubt they wanted to see the bodies of Russian snipers so quickly annihilated.

We easily gauged their firing points while they were shooting. Now all that remained was to aim so that not a single bullet missed its target. The distance did not exceed 100 metres. The target was much higher than the weapon's horizontal plane, and, consequently, the target angle approximated 50 degrees. According to the laws of ballistics, in such conditions the rising arc of the bullet's trajectory begins to straighten out and the earth's gravity moves the bullet less and less in a horizontal direction. Apart from that, in the rarefied mountain air a bullet encounters less wind resistance.

All this is worked out via special tables which my subordinates, who had not graduated from sniper school, could not have known. However, that is why a commander has a head on his or her shoulders. Upon setting out I had ordered them to reduce their gunsights setting, to make a correction of minus half a unit for 7.62 × 54R calibre cartridges with 'L'-type lightweight bullets.

In accordance with our usual practice, I was the first to fire. Another seven shots then thundered away, after which – with an interval of ten seconds while we reloaded our Three Lines – another eight followed. But their sound was largely muffled by a cannonade. The enemy's long-range artillery was operating, directed at the city centre. Our artillery began to respond, in order to quash the enemy batteries. Engines began to hum in the sky, and aircraft appeared with red stars on their wings. They departed in the direction of Alushta. A number of powerful ordnance salvoes came from the sea. The firing came, it seemed, from the destroyer-leader *Kharkov*, which was stationed in South Bay following unloading.

Such a noisy background helped to blot out the true picture of the fighting. The Fritzes were dropping: some into the bottom of their trenches, some onto the parapet, some even rolling down the slope. There were no misses on our part. All fifteen Nazis perished. The enemy outpost ceased to exist.

'Forward, lads!' I shouted, pointing at the summit of No-Name Height.

Panting, we covered the 100 metres of the steep climb and jumped into the enemy trenches. We had gained a superbly equipped position with deep communication passages, reinforced by planks and beams, machine-gun nests and trenches leading to them, and four dugouts excavated 2.5 metres into the ground. There was a lot of weaponry lying around: rifles, including sniper models, submachine guns, grenades on ledges in the trenches, and three MG. 34 machine guns, with loaded ammunition belts in them. The view of the surroundings which opened up from the height was simply breath-taking and it was no wonder that the Fritzes had fought so furiously for it and not wanted to withdraw.

We sent up a red flare to give our forces the signal: No-Name Height has been captured. They responded with a green one: congratulations, well done! Soon there was intense movement along the dirt road from Kamara to Shuli. The general staff of the second sector was carrying out a regrouping of forces and setting about bringing up ammunition and provisions.

We needed to take a look around. Whereas previously snipers executing an unexpected attack on the Germans would hurriedly withdraw, now they were expected to remain in the captured lines until further orders. The position enabled us to defend successfully, but we had to study and understand everything – what were the strong points of the position and what were the weak ones – to measure the length of the communication passages with our own steps, to adapt to alien trenches dug in the hard Crimean ground, to see where the machine guns were pointing, what their firing range was like, etc., etc.

We soon reached the dugouts as well. Here another tussle ensued. At the threshold of the most distant earth refuge a corporal with a Walther pistol charged at us. We had to shoot him. Further on, a junior officer was hiding behind a door and a Finnish knife expertly wielded by Vladimir Volchkov came into play. We found ourselves in a small, but thoroughly well-constructed, underground space similar to an officer's dwelling or staff quarters. On the table stood a fairly large, almost 0.5 metre high, *Tornister Funkgerät* 'b' (backpack radio equipment type 'b' – Torn.Fu.b), a portable radio set with a transceiver and crate for batteries; its rod aerial went through the dugout roof, emerging above the ground surface.

On the table lay ear-phones and a thick exercise book filled with notes. The red letters on the left panel of the transmitter read: *Feind hoert mit*, i.e. 'The enemy is listening in'. In other words, this was not just a sniper position, but rather an observation point for spotters as well as for German reconnaissance.

A radio set in working order was a valuable trophy. But we could not make use of it; in the group there were no radio-operators or personnel even slightly acquainted with means of communication. It only remained to disconnect the radio from the batteries and get it ready for transport. We decided to take it with us when we came back, although its weight was significant – up to 40kg.

We searched the bodies. I ended up with a whole pile of documents in my hands: soldiers' record books, letters and photographs belonging to twelve rank-and-file soldiers, a corporal, a junior officer and one Feldwebel of the 170th Infantry Division. The Feldwebel had a decoration – an Iron Cross, second class – and a coloured ribbon sewn onto the tabs of his tunic. All this would now go to Captain Bezrodny, and then to a translator. The letters would never reach their addressees in German towns and cities.

A victory feast was held by way of breakfast, with German sausages and Russian black bread. Also found were tins of sardines in oil, so beloved of Sergeant Sedykh. A wooden box containing twelve half-litre bottles of rum was finally hauled out of the staff headquarters dugout (the Fritzes had hidden it under a table) and I began to consider how to make use of them. One of them we finished off over breakfast. The rest we decided to pour into aluminium German flasks and take to our regimental mates. Indeed, the taste of the trophy rum was strongly reminiscent of our own rustic moonshine.

After a sleepless night, the snipers needed rest. I posted two sentries and set off for the officers' dugout. Without removing my padded jacket, I lay down on a bench and fell asleep immediately. Closer to evening I was awakened by a sentry who had been keeping watch over the eastern slope of No-Name Height, which faced the enemy front.

'Comrade Senior Sergeant, we've got company!'

A group of German submachine-gunners had appeared in the distance, probably about twenty of them. They were climbing up a narrow path which cut through some hazel thickets. It was evident through binoculars that the soldiers were proceeding calmly, without looking around, smoking cigarettes and talking to one another. They did not have their weapons at the ready and were carrying them over their shoulders. Everything suggested that the enemy had still not guessed that their observation point had been captured. The submachine-gunners had headed out for No-Name Height for inspection purposes rather than for real combat.

We were now faced with shooting down from above over the same distance as before. Like shooting up from below, this is a very complex exercise, involving regulating the telescope sights. When you are shooting down from above, the air density is greater, but the velocity of the bullet increases at the same time. The force of gravity drags it down. The midpoint of the target becomes higher, and substantially so. Therefore, the sights must be lowered (i.e. diminished), or else one needs to select a lower aiming point.

I made the calculations and gave the command to my subordinates. We waited till the submachine-gunners came within 100 metres, then opened fire. The detachment coped with the task no less accurately than when firing up from below. We dispatched all the German submachine-gunners to another world, and very quickly. Thus, eight sharpshooters had wiped out around thirty-five men in one day. Altogether not bad. During the course of the next four days the snipers operated just as skilfully. We managed to beat back the enemy attacks by using the advantages of our position on No-Name Height. On one occasion the Fritzes undertook an artillery attack. We waited it out in the dugouts which had been so soundly constructed by the Führer's valiant soldiers.

How many of them now lay on the slopes of the height with their heads shot through I struggled to work out. Some remained in the dense thickets of juniper and wild rose, others had rolled down into the hollows between the rises, and still others their advancing fellow soldiers had managed to carry away. But there were clearly over 100.

Senior command sent up a company of riflemen to relieve the sniper detachment. The Red Army troops climbed the height under our cover. We handed the site over to them safe and intact and, wishing them success, went back on the same truck to the 25th Division.

Nobody organized a triumphal greeting for us. On the firing lines of the Sevastopol defence district soldiers and officers of Soviet units were performing notable feats every day. Even the most ordinary fulfilment of one's service obligations under regular enemy bombing raids and artillery attacks constituted a feat, as did the work at factories hidden deep in the tunnels of Inkerman.

I wrote a report of the raid on No-Name Height and submitted it to Captain Bezrodny, along with the German documents, the radio set and other objects of interest (a flask of rum, for instance). The quantity of material greatly surprised the general staff deputy head of reconnaissance. We also discussed this episode, and I asked him whether it would be possible to recommend the participants in this raid for government awards, since the snipers had demonstrated exceptional courage, determination and superb discipline. Bezrodny smiled enigmatically. 'Senior command have got it in hand,' he replied.

The captain was not joking. At the beginning of March I was presented with a 'Sniper-Destroyer' diploma from the military council of the coastal army which testified that Sergeant Pavluchenko (they made an error in transcribing my name) had wiped out 257 Fascists. The diploma was signed by the army commander, Major-General Petrov, and also by Battalion Commissar Chukhnov and Brigade Commissar Kuznetsov, both members of the military council. This was the first official acknowledgement of my modest achievements. Apart from that, in April Fyodor Sedykh, Vladimir Volchkov and I received medals 'For Battle Merit'.

I spent a long time discussing our expedition with my husband, but more from the viewpoint of how each of the snipers had performed in it. The military behaviour of my subordinates was beyond reproach and I believed we had fulfilled our orders because we did not lose a single man. For me, as commander, this was the most important indicator of success. It is a very bitter experience to lose one's comrades-at-arms in war, especially if they have been tried and tested in combat. I thought then, and I still do, that war, for all its cruelty, is the best way of finding out what a person is like. Those who stood beside me at Sevastopol were people of the highest quality. Only later did the fate of each of them turn out differently.

12

The Spring of 1942

We nevertheless did receive a reward for the capture of No-Name Height – a leave pass for the city. People recommended that Alexei Kitsenko and I visit the museum which had opened on 23 February in the premises of the picture gallery on Frunze Street. We wandered slowly through the galleries and viewed the exhibits. This was a real journey into history – from the first siege of 1854–5 to the era of the Great October Socialist Revolution and the Civil War, and then the events and heroes of the second siege. Among the photographs and documents I found information about the Chapayev Division, about machine-gunner Nina Onilova, and even about myself. In a separate hall the organizers had displayed the weapons and ammunition manufactured for the coastal army at Sevastopol factories and hung portraits of production shock workers. Also on exhibit were trophies: German weaponry, fragments of aircraft shot down over the city, letters and diaries of the invaders, standards of Fascist regiments captured in combat, Nazi orders for the local population in which the most frequently encountered word was 'firing squad'.

Despite the military action, the residents of Sevastopol constantly undertook operations to restore the shattered economy and the city did not look neglected, dirty or deserted. Shops, polyclinics, public baths, hairdressers and various trade services were open and the trams were working. And now they had opened a new museum which everyone was happy to visit: Sevastopol residents themselves, people recently arrived from unoccupied territory and those on leave from military units.

The attitude to front-line troops was very cordial. A shoe-shiner offered us free service, and women we met in Commune Square by the Udarnik cinema offered to do washing and ironing. Yet the water supply in the city was strictly rationed. We said goodbye to winter without regret. It had been one of combat and anxiety, but it had strengthened the defenders in the belief that they were capable of holding out against the furious onslaught of the Nazis. Some relief was expected with the spring. The forests on the Mekenzi hills would turn green and the foliage would conceal our dugouts, trenches, communication passages and firing points from the enemy, so that there would be fewer losses. The warm south wind would blow from the sea and guard duty at night would not be so cold. Rain would fall, albeit not very plentifully, but there would still be more water in the mountain springs. The sun would peep out more often through the clouds and we would imagine that this was the sun of victory.

On the morning of 3 March 1942 the weather was so fine and warm that it was impossible to stay in the dugout. Alexei and I decided to breakfast in the fresh air – to the chirping of the irrepressible Sevastopol sparrows. With his arm around my shoulders, my husband was sitting beside me on a fallen tree and relating some humorous incident from his childhood. The enemy artillery attack on the lines of the 54th Regiment started suddenly. It came from long-range ordnance. The first shells exploded far in the rear, the second salvo fell short, but the third . . .

'You're not tired, are you?' Kitsenko had just asked me when the third shell exploded behind our backs. Dozens of splinters whistled through the air. My junior lieutenant shielded me from them, but did not escape wounds himself. In the first minute I did not think that it was serious. Alexei clutched his right shoulder and groaned. But then the blood streamed profusely down the sleeve of his tunic, his arm hung limp, and a pallor began to cover his face.

'Lyonya, hold on! Lyonya, I'll bandage you right away!' I tore open a first-aid pack and began hurriedly bandaging his shoulders. The white gauze went on in a first, second, and third layer, but the wounds proved to be deep and the blood seeped through the gauze.

Fyodor Sedykh came to our aid. We laid the commander on a blanket and carried him to the first-aid station at the double. Fortunately the company medical orderly, Yelena Paliy, was on hand, as well as a cart harnessed to a pair of horses. Placing the company commander on the seat, we quickly set off for Inkerman – to the divisional medical battalion and our surgeon Pishel-Gayek. There, Lyonya was placed on the operating table without delay. I stayed to await the outcome.

The hope of a miracle was still alive in my heart. During the hour-and-a-half wait I reflected on many things, recalling my first meeting with him, the forest at sunset, when the junior lieutenant had found me under the shattered tree, his declaration of love, and our happy conjugal life. There was no one closer or dearer to me than Alexei Arkadyevich. He had remained cheerful in difficult circumstances, did not despair at failure, and success did not go to his head. But the main thing was that he was always able to find the right words for the occasion, and I trusted him more than I trusted myself.

Our amazing doctor, Vladimir Fyodorovich Pishel-Gayek, came out of the operating theatre with a gloomy face, squeezed my hand, and said: 'Bear up, Lyudmila. There's not much hope of a recovery. His right arm had to be amputated; it was hanging by a single tendon. What's much worse are the seven splinters in his back. I've taken three out, but the rest . . .'

I do not remember what happened next. I came to on a narrow hospital bed in a room somewhere. A rather young nurse in a white gown and headscarf gave me a glass of some liquid which smelt strongly of valerian, and asked me to drink it all. I did as she requested, still in a strange, twilight state. I automatically placed my hand on the holster containing my TT pistol and realized that it was not there. The girl gave me a frightened look and began to explain: the weapon would be returned to me without fail, but later.

'My pistol! Give it back to me right now!' With a sudden jerk I got up from the bed.

'Lyuda! Lyuda! Stop it!' It turned out that Pishel-Gayek was standing not far away. 'What are you intending to do? Why do you need a pistol?'

'It's my assigned service weapon. It should be in my possession at all times.'

'You need to calm down first.'

'Do you think I want to commit suicide?' I said, no doubt too loudly. 'No, that won't happen. They won't live to see that. The Fritzes will pay dearly for his death. I'll get even with them.'

To cut a long story short, the 'Totosha' was returned to me after some commotion and, tenderly stroking the ribbed handle, I placed the heavy pistol in its holster and buttoned it up. Battalion Commander Dromin gave me permission to remain in the hospital by my seriously wounded husband. At night Alexei alternated between bouts of delirium, losing consciousness and coming to, when he struggled to smile and tried to say something encouraging. By noon on 4 March it was all over. He died in my arms.

The funeral took place the following day at the Fraternal Cemetery. It was attended by all the officers from the 54th Regiment who were not on duty, the regimental commander, Major Matusyevich, Military Commissar Maltsev, many troops from the 2nd Company and by my platoon in its entirety. Matusyevich delivered a brief but powerful and colourful address. Then Junior Lieutenant Kitsenko was bade farewell by his subordinates. The lowering of the coffin into the grave was accompanied by the volleys of a farewell rifle and submachine-gun salute. The officers saluted with shots from their pistols, but I was unable to reach for my TT. Maltsev asked me why I was not saluting. To be honest, our political instructors could sometimes demonstrate astonishing insensitivity, and it was impossible to give them a sincere response. My reply probably sounded insolent: 'I'm not a performer who fires into the air. My salute will be directed at the Nazis. I promise to fell at least 100 of them, if not more.'

Of course, the truth lay elsewhere. I did not want to come to terms with the departure of my beloved husband. He still remained beside me, and I felt his presence. Lyonya's mangled body lay in the earth of Sevastopol, but his kind, sensitive soul was yet to find a resting place. It was not appropriate for me to bid him farewell with shots from a weapon which we both loved to the same degree. For me it had long become a sacred object. The country and the army had given it to me to defend with, to attack with, and to have faith in one's own strength at moments when one is required to make a final choice: either instant death or long-term shame.

My life changed after Alexei Kitsenko's funeral. Returning to our dugout home, I spent three sleepless nights. Then I tried to pick up a sniper rifle and realized that I could not hold it, my hands were trembling so much. I had to go to the medical battalion, to a neuropathologist. He made a diagnosis – post-traumatic neurosis – and proposed that I spend two weeks in hospital, regularly drinking some infusion from valerian root and some medicine which included a bromide solution. In the treatment centre, situated in the tunnels of Inkerman, it was quiet, calm and very boring. I was visited by Fyodor Sedykh, now promoted to the rank of senior sergeant and Vladimir Volchkov, who had become a sergeant. On the ninth day after the death of our company commander we decided to go to the cemetery and visit Alexei.

The cemetery lay in the fourth defence sector. There were three roads leading there from our, third, sector, one of them asphalted. The Germans had bombed it a number of times, but our sappers had restored this important transport highway again and again, since the burial grounds were also the location of the staff headquarters of Colonel Alexander Grigoryevich Kapitokhin, commandant of the fourth sector and, at the same time, commander of the 95th Rifle Division. Army vehicles often went there and it was no effort to find one going your way.

Surrounded by a fairly high wall of Crimean limestone with iron gates and pyramid towers on either side, from a distance the Fraternal Cemetery resembled a fortress. Here thousands of participants in the first siege of the city had found rest, among them thirty generals and admirals. The defenders of Sevastopol were interred there not just during the military action but – in accordance with a decree from the emperor and their own testament – for many years after, up till 1912. This magnificent warriors' memorial was enhanced by a church dedicated to St Nicholas the Wonderworker, which was also pyramid-shaped and had wonderful mosaics inside. The church now stood without its cross and with its roof smashed in. Our troops had earlier maintained an artillery spotter's post there. Learning of this, the Nazis had destroyed the ancient church by a direct hit with a shell.

The interment sites for Soviet soldiers and officers were by the north-east wall of the cemetery, on the other side of a hill. We entered the burial ground through the southern gates and began to climb slowly up along its central path towards the church standing on the hill. Eight days earlier I had had neither the strength nor the time to view the lavish gravestones of white and black marble, granite and diorite on either side of the path. Now we were in no hurry and stopped at the very beginning of the path, by a beautiful fluted white marble column, crowned by the bust of a man clad in an overcoat with his uniform showing underneath. Below the bust a double-headed eagle sculpted in marble held in its claws a round shield bearing the inscription: 'To Khrulev – from Russia'. General Khrulev, hero of the first siege, had personally led the infantry of the Trans-Balkan, Syevsk and Suzdal regiments into attack in the defence of the Malakhov Heights. With their bayonets the soldiers had turned the French and British to flee a number of times.

On this fine March day the marble statue of Khrulev looked down sadly from the top of the column on the visitors to the cemetery. Beyond the memorial lay communal graves interring thousands and thousands of the city's defenders, their names unknown. But the designers of the memorial had addressed them with this inscription: 'Close your ranks, you men of unparalleled courage, and gather fraternally around the hero of the battle of Sevastopol in your family grave!'

We went further along the path. The gravestones here had no doubt been created by the best sculptors, architects and artists. They had used for their handiwork marble, granite, and metal castings with quaint ornamentation. Despite the destructive force of time, the metal preserved the names, ranks, duties, and birth and death dates of the heroes of the first siege.

There was nothing like this yet in place in the area behind the Church of St Nicholas set aside for the victims of the second siege. Carefully arranged mounds of earth surmounted by plywood stars stretched along the grey wall. The grave of Junior Lieutenant Alexei Arkadyevich Kitsenko of the 54th Rifle Regiment nevertheless stood out from the others. The star and the stand under it were thickly daubed with red paint and a more extensive inscription had been recorded: 'Born 08.10.1905, died from wounds 04.03.1942'. Beside it stood a tree stump. We sat down on it and viewed the entire sad row. Here and there the earth had already dried and become crumbly, so that the mounds had lost their shape, but in other places it remained funereally black.

I placed some green juniper fronds on the grave, then took a crust of bread from my canvas gas-mask bag and crumbled it by the stand bearing the star, so that the birds would fly here more frequently. Fyodor pulled out a flask of diluted spirit, poured it into a metal beaker and also placed it by the star. After this we each drank a mouthful of this commonplace front-line beverage and pondered for a long time.

'Rest in peace!' I could have repeated these words, often encountered on the ancient memorials of the Fraternal Cemetery. With the greatest reluctance I bade farewell to my beloved. We had to return to the firing lines and resume our soldier's duties with sangfroid, patience and iron tenacity.

Back at the regiment some mail awaited me. There were letters from my sister Valentina, my mother, father and son. I sat down to reply to their missives:

Dear, beloved Lenusya,

This is the first time in nine months that I have received letters from you (two from Valya, and from you, Morzhik and Dad). Today I am writing to each of you. Lenusya, it is scarcely possibly to convey my relief! It's difficult for you, but, dearest, you are far behind the front lines, that is the main thing.

Lenusya, you cannot imagine what modern war is like. How I have worried about you, my dear! In a day or two I'll send you a document to say that I am in the army, and that should improve things a little for you materially. Now allow me to write about myself. I am a senior sergeant, a sniper, and my tally is 257. The other day I received a certificate from the army's military council and a diploma. My name has been put forward for a military Order of Lenin. That is all. True, I was first on the army honours board. And that, Lenusya, is all – well, specific episodes can wait till the war's over. Now's not the time to indulge in memoirs. All this time – that is, from 6 August up until now – I have been continuously in the front line of fire. I am now a sniping instructor. I am sending you a newspaper cutting and my ration card. In my view, that is enough. Your silly Lyuda is becoming even sillier from joy that you, my dear one, are well behind the front lines.

Lenusya, I don't need anything; we have everything. The people feed us. I have, dear, suffered a great loss; Lyonya was buried on 5 March. He is no longer with me. But never mind, Lenusya, I will fight on by myself. It is difficult to come to terms with it, but I am proud of him. He was a magnificent man; there are few like him. Three times he rescued me, Mum, and rescuing someone in war really does mean rescuing them.

Well, Lenusya, I won't talk, or rather write, about this any more. It's still too painful . . .[1]

The letter from my son was touching. He passed on his news from school. He had got an 'Excellent' for Russian dictation and 'Good' for his mental arithmetic test. But what he liked most of all was the textbook *Our Native Language* and, in it, the story of military leader Alexander Vasilyevich Suvorov.

This is how it has been from ancient times: Russians always defeat the enemies of their fatherland. After rereading Morzhik's short sentences several times, looking at the lined paper filled with his elaborate penmanship, I began to think. I had to tell this ten-year-old boy about the war that was currently in progress on the territory of his own country. This was an unprecedented war, unparalleled in the ruthlessness which had been unleashed to exterminate our people. As long as I did not frighten the little man, or fill him with fear unbecoming to a future soldier.

On the defence lines at Sevastopol there was, as before, relative calm. But the snipers had a full workload, and, by way of giving them recognition for their contribution to the struggle against the invader, the command of the Sevastopol defence district decided to hold a rally where sharpshooters could swap experience. We gathered on Monday, 16 March 1942.

A red calico banner hung over the stage. The big white letters on it read: 'Greetings to our snipers – the Stakhanovites of the front!'[2] Seated at a table on the stage under the banner were the VIPs: the commander of the Black Sea Fleet, Vice-Admiral F.S. Oktyabrsky, the commander of the coastal army, Major-General I.Y. Petrov, Divisional Commander I.I. Azarov, a member of the military council for the fleet, and Brigade Commissar M.G. Kuznetsov, a member of the army military council. They listened to an address on the development of sniping in the Sevastopol defence district by the coastal army's deputy chief-of-staff, Major-General V.F. Vorobyov.

It was an honest speech, which depicted the situation fairly. Vorobyov began in a somewhat poetic fashion. The general said that spring had arrived and the nights, alas, had grown short. This was bad for the defenders of the city, because supplies were delivered principally by sea, on the ships of the Black Sea steamship service and the Black Sea Fleet. They arrived at Sevastopol at night and were unloaded at the wharves of South Bay, undetected by enemy aerial reconnaissance. Now there would be fewer such opportunities and, given the superiority of the Nazi air force, new difficulties could be expected in the delivery of ammunition, weapons, provisions and reinforcements.

The enemy were preparing for a third assault on the main naval base. According to reconnaissance data, the numbers in the German 11th Army had risen and now amounted to approximately 200,000 – twice the number of Soviet troops and officers in positions around the city. The Fritzes were constantly transporting new ordnance and mortars up to their firing lines.

The total number of such weapons could be close to the impressive figure of 2,000. And we had only 600 artillery units in working order. The 8th Air Corps under the command of the well-known ace, General von Richthofen, was being transferred to the Crimea and the Germans would have at their disposal around 700 aircraft against our 90 war machines.

Turning to the audience of about 150 of the best soldiers in the Sevastopol infantry, each with at least forty dead enemy soldiers and officers in their tally, Major-General Vorobyov spoke frankly:

There are more Fritzes now. That means that we have to kill them in greater numbers in order at least to even up the chances of those attacking and those defending. According to our statistics, an ordinary soldier requires eight to ten cartridges to neutralize a single enemy, while a sniper needs only one or two. Dear comrades, bear in mind that there will be less ammunition coming in and therefore it will have to be used more sparingly and expended more effectively. The command of the Sevastopol defence district calls on you not only to operate like Stakhanovites yourselves, like shock workers, in your firing positions, but also to teach other soldiers the art of sharpshooting. Each of you should select a group of ten to fifteen pupils and tutor them for a short period. We, for our part, promise to supply them with rifles and telescope sights.

I was the first to speak on behalf of the snipers at the rally because I had the largest tally of dead Nazis – 257. I said that we had been given the honorary title 'Stakhanovites of the front' and we had to back this up with good results in our shooting and undertake new obligations. Personally, I was pledging myself to raise my tally to 300 Nazis.

Taking second place in this tacit competition was the chief sergeant major of the 7th Naval Infantry Brigade, submachine-gun platoon commander Noi Adamia, with a tally of 165. A Georgian by birth, he had graduated before the war from the Odessa naval college and served in the Black Sea Fleet. In his nervousness Noi spoke not only with a strong Caucasian accent but also very emotionally. He reported to those present that he had already taught the basics of sharpshooting to around eighty soldiers, but intended to continue this work further. In the end he took his tally to 200 Nazis and went missing in action by the Chersonese lighthouse at the beginning of July 1942. He was then posthumously awarded the title Hero of the Soviet Union.

Former border guard Ivan Levkin, a corporal in the 456th NKVD Regiment, which was now part of the 109th Rifle Division, was able to talk about the eighty-eight enemy he had killed. His regimental mate and fellow contributor, Ivan Bogatyr, another corporal, had a score of seventy-five. Ivan particularly distinguished himself later during the last assault on Sevastopol; while wounded, he repelled enemy attacks with a machine gun for five hours on a firing line near the village of Balaklava. For this feat he was awarded the title of Hero of the Soviet Union.

Snipers are untalkative and lone warriors; they do not know how to speak well. The speeches from the other participants in the rally sounded a little monotonous. They mentioned their achievements, undertook greater obligations, talked a bit about their own methods of camouflage in situ, their struggles with German sharpshooters, and the way they looked after their weapons during the conditions of the Crimean winter and spring. The snipers seemed to be afraid of crossing a certain line when it came to addressing their superiors. Major-General Petrov, who was more familiar than Vice-Admiral Oktyabrsky with the situation on the terrestrial defence lines, decided to switch the conversation to other, more specific, topics:

Comrade snipers! As true patriots, you are ready to strike at the invaders all the time and everywhere. But what are your own requests and wishes? How can the command of the Sevastopol defence district help you in the essential work you do for the front? Speak honestly and openly, without being shy. That is why we have convened this rally, to discuss not just successes, but also difficulties.

At this request, which caused a stir in the hall, the snipers went for dinner. The commissariat did not disgrace itself and treated them to a vegetable salad, fish soup from freshly caught mullet, goulash and stewed fruit. Naturally, the menu provided for the classic front-line 'hundred grams' of vodka.

The conversation subsequently became more down to earth. The snipers began to talk about life in the trenches without holding back. For instance, they were upset that camouflage material was not issued in good time, so they had to wear a green suit in October, when a brown one was needed, and that armoured shields which would help them defend their positions often lay unused in army stores . . . It would be good to supply snipers with the simplest ballistic tables, which would not intimidate beginners with their erudite appearance, and to provide those venturing out on a mission with dry rations, including some sour juices which relieved thirst better than plain water . . . Snipers craved for unity of command because in some military units they were at the disposal of anyone who could be bothered. The result was that personnel trained in a complex craft ended up excavating dugouts and trenches, standing on guard, working as drivers and even as cooks, since that was their first recorded military profession . . . There was no point, when on advance, in sending snipers into attack along with regular company troops in formation, for sniper rifles have no bayonets . . . It was better for them to take up some previously selected hidden position and to fire from there at enemy machine-gun nests . . . And how could it not be understood that a sniper needed rest more than an ordinary infantryman? Give him a day's leave once a week and let the good fellow sleep it off somewhere in the rear . . .

Major-General Petrov unhurriedly noted down all the suggestions on a pad. He then delivered a concluding address and answered many questions, saying that fulfilling the various requests and wishes would require different levels of work. It was very easy to issue rations and grant leave, but editing the ballistic tables and printing them anew was a task that would take longer than just a week. Making individual military commanders realize that a sniper was a specialist of a particular type was not something that could be achieved at once. However, an effort would be made. Incidentally, that day's snipers' rally that he had organized was one way of raising the prestige of this military profession in the eyes of the entire coastal army.

Our gathering concluded on a somewhat unusual and even jovial note. A concert for the snipers was put on by the front-line brigade of the USSR touring concert party. It featured classical music performed by stringed instruments, folk music from a bayan duet, popular songs, verse by Soviet poets, humorous tales and, towards the end, conjuror S. Bobrovsky stunned everyone with his magic tricks.

All through March, April and May 1942 our forces and those of the enemy remained on their existing lines and no major changes occurred. Having seen the concern and attention of the Sevastopol defence district command, the snipers operated with considerable enthusiasm. In a column entitled 'On the Approaches to Sevastopol' in the newspaper *Red Black Sea Sailor*, which was regularly delivered to our lines, accounts were published every day of their achievements, along with the number of enemy aircraft shot down by AA gunners and air crew of the 6th Guards Destruction Regiment.

Here are my notes from that period: on 31 March Soviet snipers wiped out thirty-two German soldiers and officers; eighteen on 3 April; twenty-six on 4 April; twenty-five on 6 April; twenty-six on 7 April; sixty-six on 8 April; fifty-six on 9 April; a hundred and eight on 10 April; fifty-three on 11 April; fifty-five on 14 April; fifty on 15 April; eighty-three on 18 April; and sixty-five on 19 April. In total, during the thirty days of April the snipers dispatched 1,492 Nazis to another world, and 1,019 in the first ten days of May.

The people of Sevastopol did not mope and looked to the future with hope. By the time of the May Day celebration the residents had restored order in the city which had been devastated by the six-month siege. At the call of the city defence committee they organized a number of working Saturdays: they cleaned out the yards, burnt the rubbish that had collected on the streets over winter, filled in the shell holes and bomb craters with soil and stones, cleared the piles of wreckage, put planks and plywood sheets over the smashed windows in the ground floors of buildings, painted fences and benches in public gardens and parks, whitewashed tree trunks and mended roads and pavements.

In accordance with the orders of Major-General Petrov, snipers now received a day's leave once a week and I often travelled in to Sevastopol and saw the enthusiasm with which its people were restoring it. In cleanliness and tidiness it had begun to resemble the wonderful pre-war southern city that had stood out from others by virtue of its special 'naval jauntiness'. My favourite place for a stroll was Marine Boulevard. From there a wonderful view opened up of the bay and, further on, of the open sea. The paths on the boulevard had been cleared of the debris of trees smashed by bombs, fresh sand had been spread on them, and flowers planted in the borders – daisies, forget-me-nots and violets – and the wooden benches and gazebos had been repaired. The stone bridge with its mounted dragons looked amazing, as did the celebrated memorial to wrecked ships not far from the concrete pier.

On coming to the city, the front-line troops also had the opportunity to go to the public baths, visit a restaurant, hairdresser's, watchmaker's or photographer's, and to send telegrams to loved ones from the main post office. The cinema was operating, with three sessions during the daytime, showing pre-war Soviet feature films as well as newsreels.

All this was very reassuring. Despite the frequent bombing raids and the shelling (we had got used to that, strangely enough), there was talk within the regiment of Soviet military units shortly moving to Sevastopol from the Kerch peninsula. The coastal army would also strike at the enemy and, in this way, the Fritzes would end up crushed inside a pincer movement, and the siege of the city would be lifted.

It should be mentioned that there were grounds for such suppositions. Back in January 1942 our forces (six rifle divisions, two brigades and two regiments, a total of 42,000 troops) had landed in the east of the Crimean peninsula, pushed the Germans back 100km, liberated Kerch and Feodosia and set up a Crimean front. Ranged against it were units of the German 11th Army (up to 25,000 men).

However, events subsequently unfolded in quite a different way from what the valiant defenders of Sevastopol had expected. In the early morning of 8 May 1942, the Nazis launched an advance on the Kerch peninsula. They did not have a numerical advantage, but they concentrated their forces on one, fairly narrow, section of the front and achieved success. In no small degree this was the fault of the commander of the Crimean front, Lieutenant-General D.T. Kozlov and the general staff representative, Army Commissar (1st Class) L.Z. Mekhlis, who did not anticipate the enemy plans in time, failed to conduct reconnaissance in an appropriate way and then lost operational control of their forces in general. Units of the 51st and 47th Armies began a disorderly retreat to the east, towards the Kerch strait. By the middle of May the Nazis had occupied Kerch, and then the entire Kerch peninsula. Our losses were great: several tens of thousands killed, wounded or taken prisoner. The Germans got their hands on some significant trophies: over 300 tanks, 400 aircraft and almost 3,500 ordnance and mortars.

The routing of the Crimean front made a third assault on Sevastopol inevitable. We soon felt the impact. From 20 May enemy aircraft commenced massive attacks on the main naval base of the Black Sea Fleet. Every day hundreds of Junkers and Messerschmitts rose into the sky. They unleashed thousands of bombs on the city. Planes with black crosses on their wings were constantly in the skies over Sevastopol. One group of bombers gave way to another. The Soviet air force (about 100 warplanes) was unable to resist them. Air crew were operating at the limit of their strength as it was, making six or seven flights a day. Their aerodrome by the Chersonese lighthouse was under attack from long-range German artillery; aircraft there caught fire from the explosions of large-calibre shells and some personnel lost their lives.

The city itself was transformed into a huge blaze, a total sea of fire and smoke. This was intensified by the extremely hot weather – up to 40°C – and the complete lack of water because of pipes destroyed by the Germans. For several days the Nazis bombed all the major buildings which had earlier survived. City blocks – especially those in the centre and adjacent to the shore of the bay – became ruins. Some buildings collapsed; others were badly burnt and stood like huge charred crates without roofs or windows.

Things were hot for us too, in the lines of the third defence sector. The most destructive fire was probably that of heavy mortars, which, according to the latest reconnaissance, the Fritzes stationed along the front at a frequency of twenty pieces per kilometre. Even more artillery ordnance was brought up, at a rate of thirty-seven pieces per kilometre. This powerful, fiery, working-over of our front line continued from 2 to 6 June 1942. However, the 25th Chapayev Division did not suffer great losses in manpower, because its troops and officers hid in deep dugouts and our special refuges which we called fox holes.

At the staff headquarters of the 11th Army they probably supposed that, after such action, the Russians would be, if not wiped out, then at least demoralized and would offer no resistance to the advancing Wehrmacht units. As always, the Fritzes were mistaken.

The third assault on the city began on 7 June, at four o'clock in the morning. The hurricane of artillery fire and massed air attacks continued for around sixty minutes. You might have thought that the environs of Sevastopol had experienced a volcanic eruption. The columns of smoke, the smell of burning, the earth tossed up by the explosions – all this formed a huge black cloud over our positions. The bright summer sun was scarcely visible through it. The enemy's flaming preparations were accompanied by the roar of aircraft engines and the boom of explosions, sounding like some unimaginable, insane cacophony.

Around five o'clock in the morning the German infantry, supported by tanks and mobile ordnance, began to advance on the front line of the city's defenders. It was a long time since I had beheld such a sight – not since the siege of Odessa. The hot June day was only just beginning. A light breeze was blowing away the wreaths of black smoke and the earth and dust were gradually settling. In the silence that followed the hellish racket, tanks with grunting engines were moving forwards in the valley of the river Belbek. They were followed by dense ranks of infantry. Soldiers stripped to the waist were striding along at full height.

There were also groups of riflemen with Mausers and of submachine-gunners armed with MP. 40s. The distance between the Nazis and us Razins, who were occupying the trenches on the orders of our officers, was shrinking; it was now no more than 600 metres.

'Is this a psychological attack?' asked Fyodor Sedykh, who was standing beside me in a sniper trench camouflaged by an oak tree trunk which had broken into several pieces.

'They've become emboldened, the rats,' I said, putting the binoculars to my eyes and viewing the ranks. The magnification showed grey faces distorted by grimaces, and strongly built bodies which were not yet sun-tanned. Well-fed, excellently trained, real 'imperial Germans' who had not been emaciated by the burdens of a long siege had been transferred to Sevastopol from the Donyets Basin, from the ranks of the German 17th Army. We were informed of this by our reconnaissance, which had been crossing the front line to take prisoners for interrogation. Adolf Hitler's crack troops were now before us. They strode on, tripping on the stones, chatting, jostling one another with their shoulders, occasionally tossing their rifles back and forth. I detected something strange in their behaviour and soon realized that the Fritzes were far from sober.

The previous evening, after considering what the layout of our forces should be in the event of an enemy frontal attack in our sector, I had decided that the snipers should take SVT-40s with them to the firing line. Within my platoon there were already twelve of them. I checked them myself and again cleaned my own inscribed self-loading Tokarev rifle. The time had come to hear its loud voice. It would nevertheless be drowned out by the rattle of machine-gun rounds and the salvoes of the mortars and the 45mm- and 76mm-calibre regimental guns.

Our trench was on the right flank, ahead of the main line, next to the machine-gunners. Some of the platoon were on the left flank and several were together with the infantry in a general trench. The snipers' objective was to knock out the officers and junior officers in the columns quickly and then switch their fire to the enemy machine-gun nests and the mortar crews.

The Nazis were marching towards us and we reached for our rifles lying on the parapet. I attached a box magazine to the 'Sveta', removed the leather cover from the eyepiece of the telescope sight and looked through it to determine the distance. I had long been teaching the new recruits the most basic sniper rules and demanded that they know them like their times table: if the broad part of the horizontal crosshairs of the sight covered the figure of the moving target up to the knees, the range was 250 metres; up to the waist meant 400 metres, up to the shoulders equated to 600 metres, and if the complete figure was visible, the distance was 750 metres. Of course, there were other, more precise methods of determining the distance from the marksman to the target on the basis of the PE and PU telescope sights, but that required calculating an equation, and the mathematical skills of many Red Army soldiers were simply not up to it. Never mind, they would cope for today, for the main thing was to listen to the commander.

The platoon was now commanded by Senior Sergeant Fyodor Sedykh and, since the beginning of May 1942, I had been listed as a sniping instructor under the 54th Regiment general staff. The objectives were as before: to train recently arrived Red Army soldiers in sharpshooting, to check on the state of their weapons, to take delivery of new ones and adjust them, to consult with the commanders of detachments on sniping tactics, to convene the snipers every two weeks to pass on experience and undergo instruction, and to organize the sharpshooting sorties in no man's land and the enemy rear, which had gone so well for us while the front was stable. But it looked as if we would have to forget about sorties from this day on. The invaders had begun an assault and, judging by what was now happening in the Belbek river valley, their intentions were serious.

A man striding on the right flank of the German ranks with a pistol in his hands came into my sight range. It was clear that he was an officer, the most suitable target for a front-line sniper. The distance had changed and was now close to 500 metres. Let him come closer. His head was already in the crosspiece of my sight. My right hand was lying freely on the grip of the butt, my index finger on the trigger. Just a slight exertion, a shot resounded, the rifle kicked into my shoulder, and the man with the pistol fell.

As if in response to a signal, our artillery opened fire: the 69th and 99th howitzer artillery regiments and the 905th, 52nd, and 134th Battalions of the howitzer artillery regiments. The gunners immediately knocked out several tanks, and then struck at the infantry ranks. Along with them the large-calibre ordnance from the shore batteries were beginning to overwhelm the enemy. Again black smoke rose into the sky, but this time the artillery attack was mounted by Russians, and nothing remained of the attacking column. The Germans had failed at the first attempt. They had miscalculated in believing that the defenders of Sevastopol would lose heart at the impact of their aircraft and cannon.

Four enemy tanks were burning on the battlefield and the others had crawled away back to their initial positions. The bodies of the half-dressed dead soldiers showed up white against the withered brown grass and those black patches where it had caught fire from the explosions. But the silence did not last long. Some Junkers 87 'Trundlers' appeared. They dropped several dozen bombs on our positions and, diving down, sprayed the Razins with fire from the machine guns in their wings. The soldiers hid in fox holes. About an hour later, after they had restored order among their retreating units and reinforced them with fresh detachments, the command of the 50th and 132nd German divisions again sent their infantry ranks forward across the gentle northern slope of the Kamyshly gully. Fyodor and I returned to the trench and grabbed our self-loading rifles.

I suggested to Fyodor Sedykh that we try a different combat variant: to fire not at the first row, but at the second and, at the same time, to aim for the stomach. A bullet in this part of the body is a lethal wound, but death does not follow at once. After taking several shots, we saw what their effect was. Writhing in pain, the Nazis fell to the ground, screaming and groaning, and begged for help. The soldiers in the first row began to look around, get out of step, and stop. It also caused confusion in the third row. The attack which the Fritzes had begun cheerfully and energetically eventually choked. This was of course facilitated in no small measure by our machine-gunners and mortar crews. They were also engaging in targeted fire. By evening the Nazis had abandoned the battlefield in our sector and we counted up those who still lay there with the aluminium buckles on their belts shot through. There were over twenty of them.

However, the Nazis inflicted their main strike 2km to the left of the 54th Regiment's lines, in the sector of the 79th Naval Brigade and the adjacent 172nd Rifle Division. There, the Soviet forces' situation was becoming much worse. Advancing along the Belbek river valley, one group of German tanks burst through at the junction of these two military formations, while another emerged from the Kamyshly gully and attacked the heights occupied by soldiers of the 79th Brigade. The enemy achieved some success. By the evening of 7 June the Germans had forced a wedge of one or two kilometres into our defences along the line of their main strike.

The following day began with enemy artillery and mortar attacks. Then the Nazi air force delivered their blows. The cannonade did not cease for five hours. After that, at ten o'clock in the morning, the Germans advanced along the entire front of the Sevastopol defence district, but their greatest concentration of forces occurred at the junction of the third and fourth sectors, against the 79th Brigade and the 172nd Division. Only now the Fritzes were advancing not in dense ranks, but split into groups, and with caution, under cover of tanks, self-propelled vehicles and armoured transports.

In the course of these fierce battles our units suffered significant losses. Very few soldiers remained in formation in either the 79th Brigade or the 172nd Division, and they were forced to retreat. The defenders of Sevastopol staunchly performed miracles of heroism, but they suffered from a great shortage of ammunition. On account of German superiority in the air, from the middle of May deliveries by sea from the cities of Novorossiysk, Poti and Tuapse had become problematic. In June ammunition, arms, provisions and reinforcement drafts were basically transported by submarines, which had limited freight capacity to satisfy all the defenders' needs.

From first light on 9 June, tanks and columns of enemy infantry showed up in front of our Chapayev Division along the highway leading towards the Mekenzi hills railway station. A signal under the code name Leo sounded within the artillery units of the third sector, and all the artillery regiments and battalions opened fire on the previously targeted lines. A large proportion of the tanks were destroyed and the infantry turned and fled.

Still, slowly but persistently, like rats, the Fritzes gnawed their way into the Soviet defences. Their goal was to break through onto the northern side of the main bay and thereby strike at the very heart of the heroic city, to capture it.

I met with the lads from our own 1st Battalion for the last time at a Young Communist League meeting. It took place on 16 June 1942, under a cliff in the Martynov gully. The entire Kamyshly gully was already in enemy hands, as were the village of Kamyshly, the Mekenzi hills railway station, Heights 319.6, 278.4 and 175.8, the No. 30 Shore Battery, the villages of Verkhny Chorgun and Nizhny Chorgun, Kamary and some other population centres in the city environs. Fierce battles were raging in the area of the Fraternal Cemetery.

The regimental Young Communist League organizer, Yakov Vaskovsky, briefly outlined the situation on the front lines. He said that over the nine days that had elapsed since the start of the third assault two-thirds of the recorded Young Communist League members in the battalion had lost their lives. There were no reinforcements and the provision of ammunition, foodstuffs and water was getting worse and worse. There was no point in hiding it: the fate of Sevastopol was already decided. But this did not mean that the invaders would be able to march gaily along its streets to the music of a band. The Razins would sacrifice themselves and fulfil their military duty to the end.

We listened to him in silence. There was a deathly weariness on the faces of the young soldiers. Their sweat-stained tunics were scorched by the unbearably hot sun; the bandages on their wounds had turned dark from gunpowder. They had come here with their weapons straight from their firing positions. The organizer turned to me as the only senior sergeant present, expecting a reply to his speech. I did not feel like discussing anything and had only one reply.

'We swear to fight till the last drop of blood!' I said.

'We so swear!' the others repeated, like an echo, after me.

13

A Word from the Army Commander

The enemy's large-calibre artillery strikes against our defences became more and more precise. Of course, this was achieved with German spotters. They were able to direct their ordnance because the Fritzes had occupied some of the heights that dominated the area. I had wiped out about twelve of their men who were hiding in trees, on hills, and in the upper floors of buildings. But now nothing was of any use. The wall of fire directed against the defenders of Sevastopol was too great. It got to the stage where Nazi pilots had begun to pursue individual pedestrians and cars on the streets of the ruined city and on the roads leading to the front line.

The artillery attack on the staff headquarters of our regiment began suddenly. The shells fell in tight clusters and, during the third salvo, one of them hit a dugout occupied by several personnel. There was a lot of smoke, crashing and banging, and whistling shell splinters. Captain Bezrodny was killed on the spot by a head wound. However, I was lucky; a splinter left a deep gash in my right cheek, tore off the lobe of my right ear, and, as well as that, there was damage to my eardrum from the shock wave and general shell shock. I was taken to our divisional 47th Medical Battalion. For the umpteenth time that remarkable doctor, Pishel-Gayek, put stitches in a facial wound for me. The following day an order came to the medical battalion to prepare a group of wounded for evacuation to Novorossiysk, and the surgeon decided that, in my condition, I was up to the journey.

On Friday, 19 June, five submarines from Novorossiysk arrived all together in Sevastopol. They delivered 165 tons of ammunition, 10 tons of aviation fuel and 10 tons of provisions to the besieged city. They did not go back to Novorossiysk empty. They ferried the wounded to hospitals in the rear. At least one of the biggest of them – L-4 (Leninyets-4) – was able, according to the calculations of a special fleet commission, to take up to 100 personnel aboard. Built in 1933 as an underwater mine-layer, it was almost 80 metres in length and 7 metres wide. In 1942 it was commanded by Captain (3rd Class) Polyakov.

It was *L-4* that unloaded in Kamysh Bay, and the soldiers of the Chapayev Division were allotted places on it. Thus, in the late evening of 19 June I found myself on a sloping shore at the edge of the steppe, exposed to all the winds. Protecting itself from the ubiquitous German air force, the submarine lay all day on the bottom of the sea. It had still not surfaced, but many wounded had assembled. The appearance of this craft from the depths of the sea was greeted by cheers of joy. The first thing we all glimpsed in the June twilight was *L-4*'s fairly high conning tower, then the 100mm gun that lay in front of it, and then the entire hull, long and narrow, like a gigantic cigar. The water cascaded off its rounded sides.

Finally the lids of both hatches opened up and the submariners emerged onto the metal deck. The craft was in the middle of the bay and the wounded were to be carried out to it on a motor launch still moored at a wooden wharf. The chief sergeant major, a broad-shouldered man of short stature, took a list out of his pocket and began to read it, with the aid of a torch. The wounded formed a line; there were both some who could move by themselves and others who needed the assistance of the medical orderlies and nurses.

The launch could take about fifteen people. It had to make a number of trips to pick up everyone from the wharf. The water in Kamysh Bay remained calm, and we transferred from the launch to the submarine fairly quickly. The sailors helped us and escorted us to the open hatch beyond the tower. Further on we had to descend by a very narrow flight of stairs to the sixth, catering, sector, where some cork mattresses had been spread out on the floor. You could lie or sit on them, but walking on them was not recommended. I set my kitbag down near a metal partition and looked around. The area had a low ceiling and was poorly illuminated by two lamps.

Beneath us, down below, the diesel engines were quietly humming. At night it remained on the surface and by day it submerged to the maximum depth. *L-4* had been in transit for three days when the Nazis detected our boat. Enemy torpedo boats launched depth charges and planes dropped bombs. Underwater, their explosions were highly audible and sounded like sharp blows on the hull of our warship. It shuddered, the lamps in our section blinked, went out, and then flashed on again. The air temperature rose to 45 degrees and it became very stuffy. When a number of wounded lost consciousness, they were all given oxygen cartridges. These helped them to hold on till the following evening, when the submarine surfaced, the hatches opened and the fresh sea air penetrated the narrow, cavernous corridors and quarters.

At sunset on 22 June 1942, *L-4*, already on the surface, entered Tsemes Bay. The city of Novorossiysk, which was spread out 25km along the shore, received us cordially. The wounded were placed on three 1.5-ton first-aid trucks and taken to hospital. I gazed at the horizon, where the sea was lit up by the rose-coloured light of the setting sun, and thought about what was now happening far away from here on the firing lines of Sevastopol, where my regimental mates, the gallant Chapayevs, had remained. I did not know at the time that this would be my last day of war.

Razed to the ground by the Nazis, the burning city continued military action against the invaders. Hundreds of wounded were evacuated from there to Novorossiysk. These trips were carried out by the destroyer-leader *Tashkent*, the destroyers *Bezuprechny* and *Bditelny*, the patrol boat *Shkval*, the harbour minesweepers *Vzryv* and *Zashchitnik*, and twenty-four submarines. The tales of the soldiers evacuated to the Caucasus left us in no doubt: the Sevastopol defence district would be seized by the enemy very soon. I enquired about the 25th Rifle Division and the 54th Regiment, but nobody could answer my questions. There was just one lieutenant, with his right hand bound in bandages up to the shoulder, who said that he had seen the commander of our division, Major-General Kolomiyets, with soldiers in Inkerman, by the left bank of the Chornaya river, getting ready to repel an enemy attack. I found it hard to believe him. The estuary of the Chornaya river, which flowed into the gulf, had been deep in our rear.

On Saturday fresh newspapers were brought to the hospital wards as usual. On the front page of *Pravda* I read a report from the Soviet Information Bureau:

> By order of the Red Army supreme command dated 3 July, Soviet forces have abandoned the city of Sevastopol. For 250 days the heroic Soviet people had beaten back numerous attacks by the German forces with unparalleled courage and tenacity. Over these last 250 days the enemy had fiercely and continuously attacked the city from both land and sea. Cut off from terrestrial communication with the rear, faced by difficulties in transporting ammunition and provisions, with no aerodromes at their disposal and, consequently, insufficient air cover, Soviet infantrymen, sailors, officers and political instructors performed miracles of military valour and heroism in the cause of defending Sevastopol. In June the Germans threw up to 300,000 of their soldiers, over 400 tanks and up to 900 aircraft against the courageous defenders of Sevastopol. The principle objective of Sevastopol's defenders was reduced to tying down the Nazi German forces as much as possible on the Sevastopol sector of the front and annihilating as much as possible of the enemy manpower and technology.

For those like me, who had been wounded in the course of the third assault and were now completing treatment in Novorossiysk, the words 'forces have abandoned Sevastopol' sounded strange. Apart from three brigades and two regiments of naval infantry, seven rifle divisions had been involved in the defence. If thousands and thousands of soldiers and their officers had left Sevastopol, where had they gone? Where were the divisional staff headquarters, the rear units, the medical battalions, the road transport, the artillery? Where were the operational regiments and battalions? The northern Black Sea area, the Crimean peninsula – it had all been captured by the Germans. It meant our personnel must be here in Novorossiysk, Poti and Tuapse. But no one had seen them.

No official report at the time mentioned that, at the beginning of July 1942, about 80,000 of the city's defenders had remained in the field by the Chersonese lighthouse and become prisoners of the Nazis. This tragedy of the Great War for the Fatherland was hushed up for a long time. As we talked among ourselves, we rank-and-file participants in the defence tried to analyse the reasons for it, to find an explanation (or justification) for the actions of the supreme command, the commander of the Sevastopol defence district, Vice-Admiral Oktyabrsky (he had been flown out of the burning city along with several other generals and senior officers) and the commander of the coastal army, Major-General Petrov (together with members of his staff he had left Sevastopol at night on a submarine and arrived at Novorossiysk on 4 July).

Had there been a plan at the fleet staff headquarters, worked out before these sad events, to evacuate the forces of the Sevastopol defence district from the Crimea to the shores of the Caucasus? Could it have been carried out amidst the total domination of the enemy air force?

I had vivid recollections of the operation to transfer the many-thousand-strong coastal army from Odessa to the Crimea, which was brilliantly carried out in October 1941. But much had changed since then in terms of the balance of forces in the Black Sea area. The Germans had sunk a good number of our ships (a cruiser, four destroyers, four large transport vessels, two submarines). For instance, the cruiser *Chervona Ukraina*, the beauty and pride of the Black Sea Fleet, had sunk after an attack by Nazi bombers in Sevastopol's South Bay on 12 November 1941. The motor vessel *Zhan Zhores*, which I was familiar with, had been blown up by a magnetic mine on 16 January 1942, in the area of Feodosia. The motor vessel *Armeniya*, with over 5,000 wounded and evacuees aboard, was struck by a torpedo dropped by a Heinkel 111 bomber on 7 November 1941, not far from Yalta, breaking up and going to the bottom in a matter of minutes with all her passengers.[1]

True, people had been saying under their breath that in the underground quarters of the 35th Shore Battery, the final refuge for senior officers, they had conducted themselves in different ways prior to departure for unoccupied territory. Vice-Admiral Oktyabrsky felt no pricks of conscience, while Major-General Petrov, on learning the scale of the catastrophe which had overtaken his forces, tried to shoot himself with a pistol. He had been prevented from doing so by a member of the coastal army's military council, Divisional Commissar Chukhnov. I believe this to be true.

After my first meeting with the general in the autumn of 1941 in the village of Dalnik near Odessa, I formed the most favourable impression of him. Petrov seemed to be completely devoid of that arrogance and superciliousness characteristic of some of those in command in the Red Army; he was very democratic and showed his concern for Red Army soldiers not just by what he said, but by what he did. To him we were all like his own children. I remember that in Sevastopol, when he wanted to commend the rank-and-file participants in the defence who had shown widespread heroism in repelling the second German assault, he gave an order for the printing of 10,000 honorary certificates and signed each one personally. They were then presented to soldiers in companies and battalions.

Petrov's character was possibly best understood by the *Red Star* newspaper correspondent and celebrated war writer and poet Konstantin Simonov, who visited the major-general at the command post of the 25th Chapayev Division:

> Petrov was an exceptional man in many respects. He combined enormous military experience and professional knowledge with a high level of general culture, a huge breadth of reading and a devoted love of art, especially painting. Among his close friends were some outstanding painters who were not blessed by official recognition during those years. While treating his own dilettantish efforts at painting with a measure of reserved irony, Petrov nevertheless possessed a distinctive and sure taste.
>
> He was a decisive man by character and in moments of crisis he could be harsh. However, for all his absolute 'militariness', if one can use such an expression, he realized that strict military subordination involved a certain constraint on human dignity, and he did not favour those who were particularly excited by this subordinating aspect of military service. His courage was of the lumbering, unhurried style, the kind that Leo Tolstoy particularly valued in people. And, generally speaking, in Petrov's conduct there was something of the old Caucasian military officer as we imagine him from Russian literature of the nineteenth century.

I never thought that fate would grant me another meeting with the commander, but this meeting would be of special significance. Moreover, it took place completely by chance, in the Novorossiysk commandant's office, where I turned up with a document from the hospital testifying to my recovery.

The general himself hailed me. I turned. At first sight Petrov's appearance distressed me. He was grim-faced and seemed extraordinarily weary, but he shook my hand, smiled and began to ask who was here from the soldiers and officers of the former Chapayev Division. Petrov informed me that the division itself no longer existed. It had perished at Sevastopol, its staff papers were burnt, its seals were buried somewhere on the shore of Kamysh Bay, and its standards had been tossed into the sea. Tears welled up in my eyes at this news. The general looked at me closely: 'Do you remember your regimental companions in arms?'

'How can you not remember them, Ivan Yefimovich?' I replied, wiping away my tears with a handkerchief. 'How many days were we under fire together!'

'Was it a while ago you were wounded?'

'No, in the middle of June. Shell shock, shrapnel in my cheek, and half my ear blown off.'

'What's next?' He looked closely at the scar still noticeable on my cheek.

'Back to the front, Comrade Major-General. Like everyone.'

'Lyudmila, do you have a particular ambition?' the commander suddenly asked, in a completely unmilitary fashion, in a quiet, friendly voice. 'Tell me. Don't be shy.'

'Of course I have.' I sighed. 'Only how can I fulfil it now? The regiment is shattered, the officers are dead, the documents have been burnt . . .'

'So, what ambition is that, Comrade Senior Sergeant?'

'The most ordinary kind. I want to be an officer.'

'You mean, to have the rank of junior lieutenant?' he asked.

'Yes. I think I have earned it.' For some reason I had decided at that moment to be absolutely candid with Petrov. 'I want to continue in the army. I like the military and I can shoot well. Over this last hard year I have learned to command troops, to think about them in combat, to be responsible for them. Apart from that, I have still not got even with the Nazis for the deaths of my army friends, for the deaths of totally innocent peaceful residents. The Nazis must be punished for everything they have committed on our land.'

'That's a great ambition,' said Petrov pensively. 'I like it. But you are mistaken if you think that it can't be fulfilled. In three days I am leaving Novorossiysk for Krasnodar, for the headquarters of the North Caucasian front. Commander-in-Chief Marshal Budyonny has asked me to recommend some Young Communist League heroes from the defence of Sevastopol. You will come with me. The chief-of-staff of the coastal army, Major-General Shishenin, will prepare the necessary papers. He is based here. I have no doubt that the marshal will willingly sign an order to award the rank of junior lieutenant to Senior Sergeant Lyudmila Pavlichenko in recognition of her feats in the defence of the city from the Nazi invaders.'

The following day a Sevastopol Young Communist League group was formed. We received documents and new uniforms and, with the commander, set off by plane for Krasnodar, where we were put up in the hotel of the Krasnodar Territory Party committee. We nervously awaited the meeting with the legendary Civil

War hero, Semyon Mikhailovich Budyonny, speculated on how it would go and wondered what the commander-in-chief would ask us and what we should tell him.

The reception at the headquarters of the North Caucasus front was very cordial and quite informal. Knowing about the glorious feats of the 1st Cavalry Army's commander in the struggle against the Whites, we imagined we would be facing some stern hero from Russian folklore. But we were greeted by a man of about sixty, average height and strong physique, cheerful, affable, with a good-natured smile hiding behind his bushy moustache.

Petrov introduced the young participants in the defence one by one: two machine-gunners, three artillery gunners, one mortar bomber and four infantry, including me. Budyonny questioned each of us briefly, then shook our hands, said some positive words, basically thanked us for the tenacity and courage we had shown in combat, and presented the awards.

The old cavalryman took my hand in a firm grip. He looked at me with a jolly smile and asked: 'What's your combat tally up to now, Senior Sergeant?'

'Three hundred and nine dead Fascists, Comrade Marshal.'

'Well done, Lyudmila! You're a superb shot. You made a considerable contribution to the defence of the city.'

'I serve the Soviet Union,' I answered.

'And, to be sure, the squares of a lieutenant's rank will also look good on such a beautiful woman,' said Budyonny, leaning slightly towards me. 'As will the Order of Lenin.'

'Thank you, Comrade Marshal.'

I was given a little box bound with a velvet ribbon and the booklet that accompanied the Order.

It was difficult to find words to describe the feelings which gripped me at that moment – insane joy, exultation, excitement. The Order of Lenin, established on 6 April 1930, was among the highest awards in the USSR. It was presented for particularly outstanding services and the fact that the senior command had rated my modest achievements in this way aroused within me both pride and embarrassment at the same time. I remembered those who had bravely fought with me on the firing lines of Odessa and Sevastopol, but had not lived to see this glorious day.

My medal, which bore a portrait of Lenin, was made of platinum and was numbered 7606. It was attached on the left side of my tunic with the aid of a pin and a special screw. Only since 1943 has the Order been worn on a pentagonal disc, fastened to a red silk ribbon with two yellow borders.

The leaflet, containing the printed text of Order No. 0137 to the forces of the North Caucasus front, dated 16 July 1942, read:

On behalf of the Presidium of the USSR Supreme Soviet, in recognition of her exemplary fulfilment of combat orders on the battle front against the German invaders and her valour and courage demonstrated therein, Senior Sergeant Pavlichenko, Lyudmila Mikhailovna, sniper of the 54th Rifle Regiment of the 25th Rifle Division, is awarded the Order of Lenin.

Commander of the Forces of the North Caucasus Front, Marshal of the Soviet Union, S. Budyonny, Chief-of-Staff of the North Caucasus Front, Major-General Zakharov. Member of the Military Council of the North Caucasus Front, Admiral Isakov. For the head and military commissar of the personnel department of the North Caucasus Front, signed, Senior Battalion Commissar Kosikov. Issued in four copies.[2]

The order awarding me the rank of junior lieutenant is also dated 16 July 1942, but the formal promotion to officer rank occurred at the army warehouse of material allowances for serving personnel. It gave me no little satisfaction. The tunic was not a cotton soldier's tunic, but made from part-wool gabardine, with raspberry-coloured tabs on the collar, which were delicately trimmed with gold embroidery, a square of red enamel in the middle of the tab and the infantry emblem – two crossed rifles – in the corner. In place of the forage cap scorched by the unbearable Crimean sun I had a peak cap with a raspberry-coloured border and a black varnished peak. The overcoat was of woollen cloth rather than thick unpressed fabric. And the boots, of course, were of real rather than artificial leather. The belt had a shoulder strap and a holster for a pistol with an officer's brass buckle in the shape of a pentagonal star.

The question of my subsequent service arose. I adhered to the old army proverb: 'Don't ask for it and don't turn it down.' It was all the same to me wherever I was sent. As another army saying put it: 'You won't be given less than a platoon and you won't be sent further than the front.' A new German advance was under way and its goal had been determined: Stalingrad. But in the personnel department of the North Caucasus front they took a different view of my career as an officer. I was appointed commander of a sniper platoon in the 32nd Guards Parachute Division. To be frank, I was frightened in no small degree and began to explain that I had been scared of heights since childhood, they made me dizzy, and, on top of that, I did not know how to do a parachute jump.

'Don't you worry, Lyudmila Mikhailovna,' I was told by a foppish young captain sitting behind a desk piled with papers. 'The order for the formation of the 32nd Guards Parachute Division within the airborne forces was received literally only a day or two ago. You won't have to fly anywhere. We haven't enough transport planes. In the current situation the parachute units are merely our elite, or best infantry.'

'With no aircraft?'

'Absolutely.'

'And where is the division located?'

'You will travel to the Moscow military district. There, in August they will begin to form eight new parachute corps, using for the sake of confidentiality the same organizational insignia as before. Do you understand?'

'Yes, Comrade Captain.'

'Call at the next office. You are supposed to receive a guard's badge, as you are now commander of a platoon in a guards' unit, and a sniper's badge, which was established in May of this year as an award for sharpshooters who have especially distinguished themselves.'

An interesting coincidence followed. Major-General Petrov was also about to fly to Moscow to report to Stalin. He told me this at a reception at the staff headquarters of the North Caucasian front, which concluded with minor refreshments for the Young Communist League soldiers who had been presented with orders and medals. It was then that I thanked Ivan Yefimovich for everything he had done for me. A word in the right place at the right time could have significant weight. The major-general just smiled. His grey eyes behind the lenses of his pince-nez did not seem as tired and sad as on the day of our last meeting in Novorossiysk. The pain of loss was gradually easing and becoming less acute. We had to think about fresh battles with the enemy, who was still trampling Russian soil as before. But we did not know if we would again have occasion to fight together. That was probably not important. The saga of Sevastopol bound all who took part in it with certain invisible but indissoluble ties.

14

Moscow Stars

Having lived in Kiev, the Ukrainian capital, for almost ten years, I imagined that Moscow, the capital of the USSR, would be similar. However, Moscow seemed from the first to be completely different: big, majestic, austere. The strength and might of our huge country had found in Moscow its perfect incarnation. The streets and squares in the city centre were amazing in their exceptional dimensions and the same was true of the buildings with their height and their distinctive and impressive architecture.

It was not all that long ago – only half a year – that a great battle had been fought at the walls of Moscow. The Red Army had conducted defensive engagements here from 30 September to 5 December 1941 and went on the offensive through the winter right up to April 1942. The Nazis had planned to take our capital without stopping to draw breath, but failed at the first assault. They then devised an operation under the code name 'Typhoon', whereby they proposed to dismember the Soviet defensive forces with three strikes from their mighty tank groups, encircle them and annihilate them. This plan did not come off either, even though the enemy enjoyed a numerical superiority, with many tanks, ordnance and aircraft. At the cost of immense losses, they managed at the end of November and beginning of December to get through to the Moscow canal in the area of the town of Yakhroma, to cross the river Nara near Naro-Fominsk, and approach Kashira. But then our fighting units delivered a crushing blow against the Fritzes. As early as December they had liberated several population centres: Rogachov, Istra, Solnechnogorsk, Klin, Kalinin and Volokolamsk.

I recall how in Sevastopol we waited impatiently for reports from the Moscow front. The first news of the routing of the Nazi German forces at the walls of the capital aroused tumultuous joy and gave us confidence that the German military machine could be defeated. With the Nazi assault on the main naval base of the Black Sea Fleet, which began in the morning of 17 December, the defenders of the city that repelled the furious attacks reminded themselves of the need to follow the Muscovites' lead. Their example inspired us.

The enemy had now retreated from the walls of the capital, but it was still a front-line environment. I saw anti-aircraft guns in public gardens and at crossroads. There was a barrage balloon team along the road. Pulling on long ropes, the soldiers were restraining a huge balloon which resembled a prehistoric beast. Shop and residential windows were crisscrossed with broad strips of white paper. Some buildings (for example, the Bolshoi Theatre) were covered with camouflaging colours, which distorted their dimensions and enabled them to merge with the city background.

My destination was Maroseika Street and the headquarters of the All-USSR Young Communist League's central committee. In the spacious vestibule some objects stood out as unusual in administrative premises: boxes of sand, spades, picks and tongs for dealing with incendiary bombs. They were used to arm soldiers in the fire-fighting teams who kept watch on the building's roof. The sentries asked to see my documents and I took my Young Communist League card from the breast pocket of my tunic.

The secretariat of the central committee occupied the fourth floor. In the reception area for the first secretary people had already assembled for the talk – the young participants in the defence of Sevastopol like me, who had been decorated and had come to Moscow from Krasnodar at the direction of the general staff of the North Caucasus front. We were received by Nikolai Mikhailov, first secretary of the Young Communist League central committee, a pleasant and very charming man of about thirty-five with brown eyes and dark hair. He congratulated us on our safe arrival in the capital, sat down with us at a long table in his fairly roomy office and began the conversation.

The first secretary conducted proceedings skilfully. The Sevastopol veterans soon felt at ease and began to talk about the recent events in the Crimean peninsula. Mikhailov listened attentively, asked questions, made the occasional joke and told the odd story from his Young Communist League experience. Over all, the meeting proceeded in an unconstrained and friendly atmosphere. Then it was my turn to speak. I did not intend to share my memories of my own achievements, but I did want to pay due tribute to the memory of my regimental comrades who had lost their lives in the struggle against the Nazi German invaders: Lieutenant Andrei Voronin, who led our company into attack at Tatarka; the commander of the 1st Battalion, Captain Ivan Sergienko, who had distinguished himself in the bloody battles at Ishun; Junior Lieutenant Alexei Kitsenko (I called him a sniper); and that valiant senior sergeant from the machine-gun company, Chevalier of the Order of the Red Star Nina Onilova, who had died from wounds on 7 March 1942, in a Sevastopol hospital.

Mikhailov seemed to like my contribution. He was, incidentally, an experienced Party worker and propagandist. Having started work at sixteen as a manual labourer, he was then transferred to Moscow's 'Hammer and Sickle' factory, where he was employed as a roll-bender operator and then joined the Communist Party and began to write articles for the widely distributed factory newspaper. From 1931 he worked as a journalist, first for the newspaper *Komsomolskaya Pravda* and then for *Pravda*. He was nominated as first secretary of the Young Communist League central committee in 1938 and it was said that his promotion was approved by Stalin himself, who placed a high value on his organizational talents and devotion to the cause of constructing socialism in a single, separate, country.

The meeting concluded in quite a conventional way – with the presentation of valuable gifts. But Mikhailov approached me with a request. He said that my speech was grammatically correct and of a good literary standard, I had a loud voice, knew my material superbly (the events of the siege, that is) and therefore he suggested that I go in two days' time to a meeting at the 'Compressor' factory, where I would give the young workers a similarly simple, honest and vivid account of the way events had unfolded at Sevastopol.

'I've never spoken at meetings and I don't know how,' I responded.

'Don't be modest, Lyudmila. I found what you had to say very interesting.'

'Well, that was here, in your office.'

'Never mind, you'll get used to it. You have the makings of an orator. People need to be told about this awful war. Only it has to be told with an optimistic note.'

I would not say that Mikhailov's suggestion was to my liking. However, like many of those who had survived front-line combat, I experienced feelings of guilt about those regimental mates who had perished in the hellish fire. By repeating their names over again, I somehow restored them from oblivion. They were kept alive through our memories.

Within the army things were not going too badly either. On a visit to the city commandant's office, I received coupons for dry rations and accommodation in the hostel of the People's Commissariat of Defence on Stromyn Street. There I was assigned a room of 16 square metres. I then presented myself to the new senior command in the Guards Parachute Division. I was sent to a training centre as a sniper instructor. I had under me a group of thirty soldiers who had been selected from divisional detachments on the basis of their marksmanship results in a learners' squad. I had a month to teach them the basic skills of sharpshooting, run a short course in ballistics and camouflage, and, three times a week, conduct practical exercises at a shooting range on the centre's premises.

Despite all this I was completely alone in the big city of Moscow, with no relatives, friends or acquaintances. There were only meetings with Mikhailov, which occurred fairly regularly. I had to go with him in his chauffeur-driven car to various public functions. Nikolai Alexandrovich was no longer concealing his partiality for me, but I was not altogether happy about that. I was living on the memories of my late husband. In my heart nobody could live up to my dear, unforgettable Lyonya, who was lying in the Fraternal Cemetery in a city now seized by the invader.

Resorting to alternative ways of expressing myself, I explained to Mikhailov that it was not appropriate for a junior lieutenant to respond to courting by a general, that is, by the first secretary of the Young Communist League central committee, and it would be better for us to remain just friends, if indeed he wanted to maintain this friendship. Comrade Stalin's favourite was very surprised at what I said. But, as subsequent events showed, his friendly attitude towards me was to continue and played a decisive role.

In army service matters I also kept to myself, did not flirt with anyone, did not stay behind for the usual officers' parties and hurried back to my room in the hostel. Here I indulged in my sad reflections, read and re-read my favourite novel, *War and Peace*, and wrote letters to Udmurtia. I complained to Mother about my dreadful homesickness and asked her to come to Moscow, even just for a month. I asked my elder sister Valentina about the health of my precious Morzhik and how he was doing at school.

However, Mikhailov soon brought a new element of variety into my life. It was in the first secretary's office and at his initiative that I became acquainted with Boris Andreyevich Lavrenyov, classic Soviet writer and author of novels, novellas, short stories, plays and scripts for films which were shown on our country's screens before the war. Lavrenyov told me that the Red Army central board of political propaganda – or, to be more precise, its press and information department – was required to issue a pamphlet about the sniper Lyudmila Pavlichenko as part of the popular series 'Frontline Library of Red Navy Mariners'. He had undertaken to write this account and he wanted to talk to me about it.

Of course, I knew the name of Boris Lavrenyov, had read his interesting novella *The Forty-First* and had even seen the film based on it, which was shot in 1927 by the director Yakov Protazanov. However, both the characters in this film – the shy factory girl Maryutka, a soldier in a Red Army detachment, and her prisoner, the refined intellectual, book-lover and Tsarist army lieutenant Govorukha-Otrok – as well as the whole conflict between them, seemed to me to be a little contrived. The question of how to deal with an enemy trying to escape would not occupy a real rifleman more than half a minute. It would be resolved simply – by pressing one's index finger on the trigger of one's rifle.

Standing before me now was a man of about fifty, tall, bulky, wearing round iron-framed spectacles and a grey tweed suit. He had a fine head of grey hair. Lavrenyov looked me up and down with a fixed gaze and casually said that he saw in me an exact replica of the heroine from his novella *The Forty-First*, the girl called Maryutka, and therefore he had a good understanding of my character. If I could answer a number of his questions now, the work would be ready in a week and submitted for printing. The pamphlet would come out in November 1942. That way everyone would know about me and that would be very nice.

This was a red rag to a bull. In the first place, I was not a dumb factory girl, but a student at Kiev State University and, as well as that, an officer of the Red Army. Secondly, the situations were very different: that fool of a girl had fallen for her prisoner lieutenant and, judging by the story's text, become his lover, while for me the Fritzes always remained simply targets and aroused no personal feelings. Thirdly, I took no pleasure in my name and life story becoming known to thousands of people I was not acquainted with. Fourth, I had had experience of interacting with writers and journalists and it was negative. The esteemed Boris Andreyevich could go and write about somebody else. There were many heroes today who were boldly and courageously defending the motherland.

The renowned writer did not expect such a rebuff and lost his composure. Perhaps romanticized images from the Civil War had got the better of him and prevented him from viewing reality objectively. In the years 1920–1 Artillery Lieutenant Boris Sergeyev (Lavrenyov was his pseudonym) had switched from the White Volunteer Army to the Red side, fought the Basmachi Muslim rebels in the steppes beyond the Caspian Sea and even commanded an armoured train. Then, along with the writers Konstantin Trenyov and Vsyovolod Ivanov, he had been the founder of a genre of heroic romantic revolutionary drama. But there was little of the revolutionary romantic in the events of our people's resistance to German Fascism with its numerous European allies.

I imagined that my acquaintance with Boris Andreyevich would conclude with this. However, Lavrenyov showed persistence. He complained about my unacceptable behaviour to the Red Army central board of political propaganda. They promised to take measures and they took them: strict orders were issued by the head of the board, Colonel General A.A. Shcherbakov, and Lavrenyov was given the telephone number of the defence commissariat hostel. He telephoned and I agreed to another meeting.

The pamphlet *Lyudmila Pavlichenko* was duly written by B.A. Lavrenyov and came out at the end of 1942, published by the naval publishing house of the USSR People's Navy Commissariat. A little earlier, in August, he had offered the text to the newspaper *Izvestiya*, which published it in issue 209(7895) for 5 September 1942 under the same title. I will quote an excerpt from the beginning of this work:

The morning was warm, a fine July morning. The sky above the old trees on the boulevard on Commune Square shone clear and blue, as in the Crimea. We went down a side path and sat on a bench. She took off her forage cap. The wind rustled her close cropped fluffy hair, which seemed as soft as that of a child. A silken lock of hair fluttered over her clear, prominent maiden's brow. Her delicate, nervous face breathed with an expression of impetuous insatiability, of a profound passion of character. It could be best summed up by Lermontov's lines:

> He knew the power of one idea alone,
> A single, but a burning, passion.

It was a face that bespoke noble human integrity, a character capable only of direct action, unwilling to brook any compromises, to countenance bargains. Her dark brown eyes with their golden spark nestled under her narrow brows. They even seemed gloomy. But after a minute they lit up with a certain *joie de vivre*, with such a child-like transparency, that they illuminated everything around: 'All right, I'll tell you what I remember.'

This was the most truthful part of the account.

For the rest, the writer interwove separate facts from my biography with his own inventions and quotations from the *Great Soviet Encyclopaedia*, retelling the history of the Ukraine. For example, he did not mention when and how I joined the Red Army. On the other hand, the pamphlet contained a colourful description of the bombing of Kiev, which I could not have witnessed because in June 1941 I was in Odessa, and it also related a touching conversation with my mother, who had already set off by train for evacuation in Udmurtia. He devoted a lot of attention to my conflicts with teachers at No. 3 School in Belaya Tserkov (which never occurred) and attributed them to my character's hooligan tendencies. Apart from that, Lavrenyov incorrectly stated my starting dates at the Arsenal factory, Kiev University and the two-year sniper's course, but made up something to the effect that, once graduated, I had put away my diploma and forgotten about it because I disliked the military and had dreamed all my life of studying the history of my native Ukraine.

With a print run of 50,000 copies, this phantasmagoria was quickly distributed throughout the country. Lavrenyov's colleagues, the staff of central and local newspapers and magazines, subsequently used it as a source of reliable information about me when compiling their own articles. I would compare this whole saga to the crooked mirror that smashed to pieces in the Hans Andersen tale *The Snow Queen*, whereupon its fragments, which harmfully distorted reality, ended up in various towns and villages.

However, the Red Army central political authority did not only rely on eminent writers and their exotic fantasies, and sent two rank-and-file propaganda staff to see me as well. They said that, in addition to the pamphlet, it had been decided to issue 100,000 leaflets bearing my portrait and a call to all soldiers of the Red Army: 'Shoot the enemy and don't miss!' They composed the text of the leaflet themselves after a conversation with me of about thirty minutes. It was very simple, but comprehensible and, on the whole, conveyed my thoughts and feelings accurately:

'Death to the German invaders!'
Valiant sniper, Lyudmila Mikhailovna PAVLICHENKO.

A true daughter of the Leninist–Stalinist Young Communist League, she joined the Red Army as a volunteer during the first days of the Great War for the Fatherland.

With her rifle Lyudmila Pavlichenko wiped out 309 Germans at Odessa and Sevastopol. 'This is the right and proper attitude to adopt towards the Germans. If you don't kill them at once, you'll have no end of trouble,' she once wrote to her mother.

Lyudmila Pavlichenko's courage and high level of military expertise are inspiring thousands of Red Army snipers – the Stakhanovites of the front – to further feats. Soldiers of the Red Army! Destroy the enemy as mercilessly as Lyudmila Pavlichenko!

SHOOT THE ENEMY AND DON'T MISS!

When I walked along the streets of Sevastopol, kids would always stop me and ask me earnestly: 'How many did you kill yesterday?'

I would give them a detailed report of my operations as a sniper. One day I had to tell them honestly that I had fired at the enemy for several days.

'That's bad,' said the children in one chorus.

One of them, the smallest, added sternly: 'That's very bad. Nazis should be killed every day.'

He spoke the truth, this serious little citizen of Sevastopol. Since that memorable day when the Nazi thugs burst into my country, every day of my life has been filled with one sole thought, with a single desire – to kill the enemy.

When I first went to war, I felt only anger at the Germans for disrupting my peaceful life, for attacking us. But what I saw later engendered within me such an inextinguishable hatred that it was difficult to express it in any other terms than a bullet through a Nazi's heart.

In one village retaken from the enemy I saw the body of a thirteen-year-old girl. The Nazis had butchered her. That was how they demonstrated their ability to wield a bayonet – the brutes! I saw brains splattered on the wall of a house, and beside it the body of a three-year-old child. Germans had lived in that house. The child had played up and cried, preventing these beasts from getting some rest. They did not even allow the mother to bury her child. The poor woman went out of her mind . . .

Hatred teaches you a lot. It taught me to kill enemies. I am a sniper. At Odessa and Sevastopol I annihilated 309 Fascists with my sniper's rifle. Hatred sharpened my vision and hearing, made me wily and dexterous, hatred taught me to camouflage myself and to deceive the enemy, to anticipate his cunning and his traps. Hatred taught me to pursue enemy snipers patiently for days on end.

It is impossible to quench the thirst for vengeance. As long as there is a single invader on our land, I will think of one thing only: killing the enemy. And I would only talk about one thing to my friends in battle and my fellow-citizens: kill the Nazi!

Junior Lieutenant Sniper Lyudmila Pavlichenko. Published by the Red Army central political authority, 1942.[1]

My life in Moscow continued its usual rounds and on 3 August 1942 I met my mother, Yelena, at the Kazan station. She needed a special pass to come to the capital and I had applied to the divisional command. The pass was issued and I sent it to the village of Vavozh, Udmurt Autonomous Republic. After our long separation Lenusya hugged me on the platform with tears in her eyes and said I had changed a lot and grown up. I had earlier requested a car from the commander and our journey from the station to the hostel on Stromyn Street was exceptionally quick. Lenusya liked my room, even though the toilet and shower were at the end of the corridor. But in the village of Vavozh they lived in a cold dilapidated shack, with a well in the yard and did not even dare to dream of an improvement in their living conditions, while in the hostel the kitchen had taps with hot and cold running water. Mother viewed this achievement of civilization as a great miracle and was genuinely overjoyed.

I know now that on that very day an event occurred which abruptly changed my army career. It was also on 3 August that the US ambassador to the Soviet Union, Averell Harriman, sent the supreme commander-in-chief, Comrade Stalin, a telegram from President Franklin Delano Roosevelt, in which he reported that, from 2 to 5 September, Washington would host an international student assembly, where delegations from the four Allied powers – the United States of America, the Soviet Union, Great Britain and China – were due to play a leading role. The US president expressed his desire for the assembly to be attended by a Soviet student delegation of two to three people, preferably those who had taken part in combat against the German Fascists.

Many different papers demanding an immediate decision ended up on the desk of the man who was chairman of the state defence committee, to which all institutions in the country were now subordinate, supreme commander-in-chief of the USSR armed forces, and people's commissar for defence. Roosevelt's telegram with Russian translation attached awaited its turn. It was only in the evening that Stalin read it again and thought about what the American president was proposing.

The two powers exchanged dispatches quite often. For example, two weeks earlier the Kremlin had received a letter from the Allies refusing to open a second front against German in Western Europe that year. These were extremely unpleasant tidings. In the summer of 1942 the situation on the Red Army fronts was becoming difficult. During the first few days of July Sevastopol fell and the Crimea was completely in German hands. The Nazis were preparing to throw their newly available forces against the Caucasus and seize the oil fields. As well as that, they were planning to occupy the fertile areas of the Don, the Kuban, and the Lower Volga. The German 6th Army was already advancing on Stalingrad under the command of Generaloberst Paulus.

Now the Allies were intending to convene some international student assembly in North America for reasons which were still unclear to our supreme commander-in-chief. Seemingly, they had no other important matters to deal with. What could young people talk about, especially Soviet young people, during such harsh and anxious times? Only the struggle against Fascism, the united efforts of all progressive humanity against the aggressor who had unleashed bloody slaughter in the fields of Europe. In this context, it would be possible – indeed necessary – to raise the question of the second front. If this topic was to be raised at the student assembly, then by all means . . .

Stalin demanded clarification of the programme for the American function. A reply came from Washington: yes, a declaration would be adopted calling upon students, as the most progressive element of young people, to speak out against Fascism. Then followed agreement on conditions for the Soviet delegation's stay in the USA and a discussion of the route for the trip, for it would only be possible to reach North America by plane via a circuitous route, through Iran, Egypt and across the Atlantic Ocean. The staff of the People's Commissariat for Foreign Affairs worked hard on it.

Meanwhile, the Red Army central political authority was hurriedly looking through hundreds of forms from students who had been called up for service. It was considered to be completely impossible to find and call up anyone from distant front-line units in the course of a single week. They decided to confine themselves to the Moscow military district. The first secretary of the Young Communist League central committee, Nikolai Mikhailov, put in a word. He had some candidates. He insisted that not only serving military but also Young Communist League personnel should be able to go to the USA, since at the assembly it would be necessary that they clearly follow the line of the USSR Communist Party.

The membership of the delegation was finally decided: Nikolai Krasavchenko, head of delegation, secretary for propaganda within the Young Communist League's

Moscow city committee, member of the USSR Communist Party, twenty-six years old, active in the partisan movement (he had nearly been captured by the Germans at Smolensk, but managed to cross the front line); Vladimir Pchelintsev, senior lieutenant, Hero of the Soviet Union, member of the Young Communist League, twenty-three years old, formerly a student in his third year at the mining institute in Leningrad, now an instructor at the Central School for Sniper Instructors in the town of Veshnyaki near Moscow; and Lyudmila Pavlichenko, junior lieutenant, Chevalier of the Order of Lenin, member of the Young Communist League, twenty-six years old, formerly a student in her fourth year at Kiev University, now commander of a sniper platoon in the 32nd Guards Parachute Division.

As Mikhailov later informed me, the proposal to include a woman in the delegation aroused the most discussion. At one session of the Young Communist League central committee both opponents of this idea (women are difficult to control) and supporters of it (if they are good-looking, they will present the USSR in the most favourable light) had their say. Nikolai Alexandrovich, who had added my name to the list, vigorously defended his decision. But, of course, it was Joseph Vissarionovich Stalin who had the last word.

Mikhailov went to the Kremlin to report on the situation, with detailed forms, photographs and service particulars of the delegation members. The supreme commander-in-chief unhurriedly leafed through all three files, held mine in his hands and asked the first secretary of the Young Communist League central committee if he was confident of this choice. Mikhailov confirmed that he was, completely confident.

Unaware that anything of the sort was going on, I had just been relieved after a twenty-four-hour shift that day and gone to bed. The shift had been a busy one. Around eleven o'clock in the evening four trucks of ammunition and relatively new weaponry – Degtyarev-Shpagin (DShK) 12.7mm-calibre machine guns – had arrived. The unloading had to be organized, documents made out, and the accompanying crew accommodated in barracks.

I did not hear the knocking on the door straight away. But it was repeated, became louder and more insistent: 'Comrade Junior Lieutenant, you are wanted on the telephone!'

'One minute.'

I did not feel at all like getting up, putting on a tunic, going to the phone at the end of the corridor and talking to somebody while I was half-asleep. But duty was duty, and this was particularly the case in the Moscow garrison; the senior command was just too close.

'Lyudmila, how are you?' Nikolai Mikhailov's bass voice boomed through the receiver. 'Get your act together and come and see me at the central committee headquarters on Maroseika Street.'

'What for, Nikolai Alexandrovich?'

'Duty calls.'

'Can it wait till tomorrow?'

'What are you saying, Junior Lieutenant? It's an order from Comrade Stalin! Every hour counts. Is that clear?'

In the first secretary's office I encountered two young men. One was a big, brown-eyed, dark-haired man in civilian dress and Mikhailov introduced him to me first: Nikolai Krasavchenko, head of the Soviet delegation which was setting off to the international student assembly in Washington. The second man, tall and thin as a beanpole and clad in a military uniform showing the triple squares of a senior lieutenant on raspberry-coloured tabs, was familiar to me. Vladimir Pchelintsev and I had already met in Veshnyaki at the sniper school where I had been on business.

We now exchanged not particularly friendly glances. For the 100 Fritzes he had annihilated on the Leningrad front, Vladimir had become, in February 1942, the first sniper in the USSR to receive the title 'Hero of the Soviet Union'. For 100 Romanians killed around Odessa in the autumn of 1941, I had received an inscribed sniper's SVT-40 rifle. Over twelve months of service he had been promoted three times: to junior lieutenant, lieutenant and senior lieutenant, while his tally now amounted to 154 Fascists. I, who had served since June of the previous year and had 309 dead Nazis in my tally, was able to obtain only the rank of junior lieutenant from the benevolent Ivan Yefimovich Petrov.

Such is the importance of good relations with one's seniors, both in the rear and at the front. I should have thought about this earlier, instead of arguing bluntly with Battalion Commander Dromin, Commander Matusyevich of the 54th Regiment, and Military Commissar Maltsev, instead of challenging Major-General Kolomiyets and other senior comrades by explaining the particulars of sniper operations, defending my subordinates and demanding better supplies of ammunition, weaponry and equipment for my platoon. And, all in all, I should have been born a man instead of a woman. Then the youthful senior lieutenant with the Hero of the Soviet Union gold star on his new and still-unruffled tunic would not be looking at me so haughtily.

Mikhailov's speech made us forget everything else for a moment. It turned out that we three were to be the Soviet delegation setting off to the USA for the international student assembly due to be held from 2 to 5 September in the city of Washington. Thus, in the early morning of 14 August – in two days' time – we would fly out from Vnukovo aerodrome on an Li-2 cargo plane to the United States via Iran and Egypt.

To be honest, for the first few minutes I did not believe my ears and resolved that it was a tasteless joke, for Nikolai Alexandrovich was a jovial man and liked to joke. All around us were war, destruction, death and bloodshed for millions of completely innocent people, and, instead of really helping our state, the British and Americans were devising some strange distractions.

However, subsequent events convinced me that a delegation really had been put together and really would fly across the ocean. From Mikhailov's office we moved fairly quickly to the office of Alexandrov, head of the propaganda section under the Communist Party central committee. He set us a really challenging test on the history of the Party and the Young Communist League and enquired about our biographical details and service in the Red Army, involvement in military engagements and our assessments of the current policy. Judging by his reaction, Comrade Alexandrov was happy with our responses.

The afternoon was also spent productively. We were received by Gheorghy Mikhailovich Dimitrov, general secretary of the executive committee of the Comintern (the Communist International, the international organization uniting workers' and Communist Parties abroad). This eminent Bulgarian revolutionary had been the hero of the Leipzig trial in 1933, where, accused without foundation of the Reichstag fire, he succeeded through his superb command of German in making an indictment of German Nazism. In the Soviet Union Dimitrov was known as a dedicated fighter for the cause of liberating the working class, a man committed to Communist ideals.

Our conversation with Dimitrov went on for over three hours. He spoke about youth organizations in the capitalist countries, class warfare and how we should conduct ourselves at the sessions of the international student assembly. In the evening we were taken to the People's Commissariat of Foreign Affairs. We ended up in its basement, which was like a large department store, but without any customers. In shop windows and under glass counters lay objects of male and female attire which had not been freely on sale in Moscow for a long time.

I was accompanied by a young staff member, and I felt a little uncomfortable at choosing the things I needed in his presence. But he gave very reasonable advice, without the least embarrassment, and soon both of the large suitcases that had been issued to me on the spot were full to the brim. Dresses, blouses, skirts, jackets, underwear, stockings, socks, handkerchiefs, hats, gloves and scarves in various colours and fashions, even footwear – all these were issued, carefully packed and signed for in a lengthy list.

That was not all. Pchelintsev and I were in military service and they decided to equip us appropriately. So we ended up in the experimental sewing workshop of the People's Commissariat of Defence on Frunze Embankment, which was popularly known as the 'general store'. While Pchelintsev's parade uniform was put together within an hour, for me nothing worked out. There were no women's parade tunics in stock and nobody would be able to sew one in twenty-four hours. It was decided to reshape a general's tunic of pure fine wool gabardine, the markings were removed, and they promised to deliver it directly to the Young Communist League central committee headquarters on the morning of the following day. Because there was also a shoemaker's shop on hand, they brought out some boots, which were very beautiful, with high varnished tops in a bottle shape, and fashionable square toes. But the age-old problem of size arose. I had to agree to a size 37 as they did not make anything smaller. Footwear for snipers is a serious matter, given the many kilometres they have to travel. But I had never before worn such light, comfortable boots, so easy on the foot.

It would be misleading if I did not mention the special consultations which the staff of competent authorities held with us. We learned a lot of new things about the present-day policies of the Allied powers, their leaders and the state structure of the USA. We were told what situations could arise, warned about possible provocations (which did indeed take place, organized by those opposed to rapprochement between the peoples of the Soviet Union and the USA), and advised how to behave in such situations. Apart from that, we were given prepared notes for addresses. Some we were advised to memorize, others we were permitted to write down. All this subsequently came in very handy during the course of our visit to the USA, Canada and England.

The question of language was quite a difficult one. Interpreters would be provided to the delegation, nobody doubted that. But it was better to have at least some knowledge of our own, because contact with ordinary people at meetings would be possible – and they were very important. Nikolai Krasavchenko honestly admitted that he did not know any foreign languages. Vladimir Pchelintsev had studied only German at his mining institute. I recalled my lessons at home with Mother and the high standard of foreign-language teaching at university and mentioned that I knew a little English.

Our foreign passports were brought from the People's Commissariat of Foreign Affairs. They looked nice and solid: oblong in shape, hard bound, with a covering of red silk and the crest of the USSR embossed on them. Inside, the text was in both Russian and French, with a small photograph below.

At their own initiative the People's Commissariat staff designated my family status as 'unmarried'. Also appended was a description of distinguishing features. I learned that I was of average height, had brown eyes and a straight nose, and my hair colour was brunette. Other than that, the delegation was provided with foreign currency: $2,000 each. Back then that was quite a decent sum. It was issued in small denominations and the thick pack of greenish American money bearing portraits of their presidents took up a lot of space in a suitcase.

Everything was happening too fast for us to appreciate fully how complex and unusual this mission was. We were not given time for reflection and, severely disconcerted by the kaleidoscope of sudden events and what we had seen and heard in the last few hours, we again ended up late in the evening at the Young Communist League central committee headquarters on Maroseika Street, at the corner of Serov Street, in Nikolai Mikhailov's office on the fourth floor.

He seemed to be the only one who understood what emotions were plaguing us and what thoughts were going through our heads. He said that we were young, but we were not children, that we had war experience, and war was a wise, albeit harsh, instructor. The Americans knew nothing of the present war and we had to convey our knowledge and perception of it in such a way that they realized that it was a life-and-death struggle for the future of all humanity. We would not have to make anything up. The main thing for each of us was to be ourselves. Of course, it was a challenge: to find oneself suddenly in a completely foreign world. But here in Moscow everything possible had been done to prepare the members of the student delegation well for it. We listened to his advice in silence.

We should probably have responded to the first secretary immediately, assured him that we would not let him down, do our best, justify the high level of confidence placed in us. However, the words would not shape themselves into sentences and I looked pensively out of the window at the Moscow summer sky: lofty, clear and glittering with thousands of stars. Down south on the Black Sea the sky at night was darker and the stars were much brighter. How many times had my lonely task begun under those stars! How many times had they illuminated a winding path for me through the enchanted Crimean forest!

'Lyudmila, do you have a question?' Mikhailov's confident voice reverberated.

'No. But I have to tell you: I'm worried that I'll make a lot of mistakes.'

'Nonsense, Comrade Junior Lieutenant!' Nikolai Alexandrovich laughed merrily. 'I have no doubts about your success. Just be yourself.'

Mikhailov invited us to a last supper. He had the right idea: to gather the travellers and their closest relatives around the table in a relaxed, almost domestic, atmosphere. Vladimir Pchelintsev's wife Rita was brought in from Veshnyaki, as was my mother from the hostel on Stromyn Street, and also Krasavchenko's wife, a good-looking young woman named Nadyezhda. Supper was served in his office, simply and modestly. There was vodka and wine. Mikhailov proposed the first toast. Suddenly, on the first secretary's desk, the telephone rang – a special white one with the crest of the USSR printed in the centre of the dial. Nikolai Alexandrovich instantly grabbed the receiver and, in a voice of profound respect, if not fear, responded: 'Mikhailov speaking . . . Yes, I understand . . . We'll come right away.'

Moscow in the first hour after midnight was empty and dark. However, the Borovitsky Gates through which Mikhailov's car travelled into the Kremlin grounds were illuminated from both sides. Standing on guard were submachine-gunners in the uniform of the NKVD internal forces and soldiers with Tokarev self-loading rifles. Our documents were thoroughly checked, but they had a list of the midnight guests and the lieutenant in charge of the watch saluted Mikhailov and gave the order for the car to be let through.

Our steps echoed in the long corridor. One turn, then another, up a staircase and there we were – in the reception area, outside the office door. The secretary of the supreme commander-in-chief, Poskrebyshev, opened it and I beheld the great man himself. He was dressed in a simple tunic with a turn-down collar but no signs of distinction – not as tall as he had appeared to me previously, lean, rather swarthy, with faint pock-marks on his face and holding a telephone receiver in his left hand. What drew one's attention were his dark, tiger-like eyes. One sensed that he possessed enormous inner strength.

We were probably in Stalin's office for about twenty minutes, although we were unaware of the passing of time. Time stood still for us. Mikhailov introduced us one by one, with me last. Joseph Vissarionovich merely said a few sentences about the responsible mission of the Party and government, the Allies, who were unwilling to open a second front, and the American people, who needed to know the truth about our struggle against Nazism.

'Do you have any requests, Comrades?' he asked.

Krasavchenko and Pchelintsev were in a state of profound paralysis and a pause hung over the office. I was not affected the same way. I experienced something different: an unprecedented enthusiasm. I wanted to hear words from the supreme commander-in-chief which were addressed specifically to me.

'Yes, Comrade Stalin, I have a request,' I said softly. 'We really need an English–Russian and Russian–English dictionary, with a grammar textbook as well. Because it's important to know your allies well, just like your enemies!'

'Well said, Comrade Pavlichenko.' The leader of the world proletariat smiled. 'You will receive the books. From me personally.'

15

Mission to Washington

A thick early morning mist was swirling over the Potomac valley. The gentle hills, green meadows, woods, orchards and settlements faded from view in its shroud. The Miami–Washington express train was approaching its destination and had reached speeds of up to 60kph. It sheared through the white cloud that wreathed the land as easily as an incandescent sword.

I woke frequently at the rhythmic swaying and the rapid knocking of the rails, and then went back to sleep again. I was alone in a two-berth compartment and therefore I was able to take off my street clothes and underwear, cover myself with a starched sheet up to my chin and rest in peace.

On the table beside me a small dictionary, three fingers thick, was shuddering from the motion. The supreme commander-in-chief of the USSR armed forces had kept his word. I found it convenient to carry the volume in my pocket. I leafed through it every day, usually towards bedtime, to check my own knowledge and see the neat autograph on one side of the title page: J. Stalin.

In the next compartment were Nikolai Krasavchenko and Vladimir Pchelintsev, my travelling companions on this two-week journey taking in mountains, deserts and the waters of the Atlantic Ocean. To be honest, I was a little weary of their constant presence. They were nice guys, but a sniper is a loner. He or she needs silence, calm, time for reflection, to observe the changes in the surroundings.

The relations which had developed between us were courteous and comradely, with clearly marked bounds as to what was and was not possible. When our 'bi-gender' party was dispatched in Moscow on its journey afar, we were given appropriate instructions. They looked each of us in the eye and laid things down strictly – more so, probably, in the case of the ballroom habitué Pchelintsev and the taciturn Young Communist League leader Krasavchenko than with me, because Mikhailov, the first secretary of the Young Communist League central committee, knew in broad outlines about the death of Alexei Kitsenko and my pledge to wreak vengeance on the enemy for him.

Nikolai held himself somewhat aloof, reminding us that he was the head of delegation. Pchelintsev and I inevitably grew closer and got on well, forgetting about the difference between our sniper tallies and our army ranks. During the prolonged stops – for instance, the three days in Cairo – we walked around the city together and made small purchases. Vladimir in particular could not restrain himself and bought a Swiss watch from an Arab in a shop for $40. It turned out that the various mechanisms in it enabled one not only to keep a count of the days and seconds, but even to record the distance away of a gunshot – an essential for a sharpshooter.

In Cairo we had had to meet the British and American ambassadors. Here for the first time I put on one of the elegant dresses I had picked in the basement store of the Commissariat for Foreign Affairs. I was very fearful that I would not be able to act freely and naturally in it. But it was the high-heeled shoes that gave me much more trouble. Over my year of military service I had become unaccustomed to them. Even without that, my feet were inclined to skid on the parquet in the luxurious palace, which had been polished till it shone. Vladimir had gallantly offered me his arm. The audience went very well. True, the British representative expressed some doubt that we were both front-line soldiers and snipers.

In Miami, where we had flown from Africa, we were delayed for a day. We could hear the ocean booming quite close by and Pchelintsev and I set off for the beach. The golden sand, slow, lazy, leisurely greenish-coloured waves and blinding sun kept us there for three hours. Krasavchenko, who had caught a cold en route, stayed in his hotel room.

The steward's steps could be heard beyond the firmly shut door of the compartment. He was going around the passengers and notifying them that the end of their journey was thirty minutes away. There was a light knock on the door and a soft voice said:

'Washington, Ma'am!'

'Yes, thanks,' I replied in English and began to get dressed.

The express arrived in Washington exactly on time: at 5.45 on 27 August 1942. Our carriage stopped under the canopy of the capital's station. However, it was difficult to get a view of the building because it was still dark. In the meantime, quite a crowd had gathered on the platform. We did not guess that it was on our account and were getting ready to lug our weighty suitcases along the carriage corridor and the platform. We did not know that the news of the arrival of the Soviet student delegation in the USA had been broadcast on 25 August by the Telegraph Agency of the Soviet Union (TASS) and some American newspapers had reprinted it.

Thus, we experienced no problems managing our luggage. On the contrary, we were surrounded by the delighted staff of the Soviet embassy and trade mission, and then by persistent American journalists. In the middle of this noisy crowd we walked from the platform to the square in front of the station, where, amidst much fuss and commotion, we piled into a big limousine and set off – just imagine it! – straight to the White House, the residence of American presidents.

Despite the early hour, we were met at the entrance by Eleanor Roosevelt herself, the president's wife. She congratulated the Russian visitors on their safe arrival and said that we would spend our first days on the territory of the USA under the roof of the White House. That was the decision of her husband, Franklin Delano Roosevelt, the thirty-second president, who was loved by his people and the only man in US history to be elected for a third presidential term.

The First Lady herself conducted us up to the second floor, showed us our rooms, suggested that we rest a little after the trip, and told us that breakfast would be served at 8.30 in the small dining room on the first floor.

I went to the window in my small and simply, but cosily, furnished room. The sun had risen, and its first rays were illuminating the area in front of the White House. It was surrounded by superbly kept gardens in classical French style, with paths sprinkled with yellowish river sand, mown lawns, bright flowerbeds and small clumps of trees here and there. The sound of gushing water came from a fountain in a pool in front of the main entrance. The president's dwelling was reminiscent of the country estate of some gentleman with an income which was regular, but certainly not extraordinary.

At the appointed time we went down to a small dining room and found there not only President Roosevelt's wife, but other people as well. First to be introduced to us was Gertrude Pratt, general secretary of the American committee of the International Student Service, which, it turned out, had organized the international assembly. A striking, slim blonde of about twenty-five, Mrs Pratt vigorously shook everyone's hands, said that she was extremely glad to see the Russian visitors and introduced us to Henry Lush, vice-president of this self-same International Student Service.[1] The conversation was helped along by three young men in American army officer's uniforms who could express themselves quite well in Russian.

Mrs Roosevelt invited us to the table. Smiling, she said that we could begin our acquaintance with the American way of life right there with a traditional American breakfast. It had inherited some things from the no-less-traditional English breakfast, but it had some distinctive features of its own. On the table were not only fried eggs, strips of grilled bacon, sausages (or 'bangers'), and marinated mushrooms, but also small puffy pancakes – among ourselves we called them 'oladi', which are thicker than 'blini' – with maple syrup. The food could be washed down with orange juice, coffee or cold tea.

Food is an excellent ice-breaker among people who do not know one another well. But the breakfast continued, and, as head of the delegation, Nikolai Krasavchenko launched into a boring speech about the agenda for the first session of the international student assembly. The Americans were more interested in accounts of the military action on the territory of the Soviet Union. Vladimir Pchelintsev took pleasure in informing them about the particulars of the sniper's art: rifles with telescope sights, camouflage, observing the enemy. I did not take part in the conversation, but listened attentively, not to him, but to the interpreters. They translated too hurriedly and imprecisely.

Suddenly Eleanor Roosevelt addressed a question to me, and this question was translated into Russian by a young man with lieutenant's epaulettes: 'If you had a good view of the faces of your enemies through telescope sights, but still fired to kill, it would be hard for American woman to understand you, dear Lyudmila.'

The interpreter tried to soften the force of this sentence somehow. It sounded polite, but had a certain unpleasant undertone. The First Lady looked at me intently, without dropping her gaze. Why she had asked this question was not quite clear. Maybe she had decided to subject me to a test. We had already been told about publications in some British and American newspapers which suggested that we were not front-line soldiers or snipers, but merely Communist propagandists specially sent to address the international student assembly. This meant that the president's wife would have to be given a clear and comprehensible answer.

'Mrs Roosevelt, we are glad to visit your beautiful, prosperity country. Many years you do not know the wars. Nobody destroys your towns, villages, plants. Nobody kills your inhabitants, your sisters, brothers, fathers,' I said slowly, and for some reason my words took those present by surprise.

Of course, my speech was not notable for its elegance: there were some mistakes in pronunciation, in the use of tenses, and the sentence construction was too basic. But the Americans got the meaning of it. I explained to those living in a state far from the struggle against Fascism that we had come from a place where bombs were destroying towns and villages, blood was being spilt, where innocent people were being killed, and my native land was undergoing a severe ordeal.

An accurate bullet was no more than a response to a vicious enemy. My husband had lost his life at Sevastopol before my very eyes and, as far as I was concerned, any man I saw through the eyepiece of my telescope sight was the one who killed him.

Strangely enough, Eleanor was embarrassed. She hurriedly looked away and said that she had not wished to offend me; however, she thought this conversation was very important and we would continue it in a more suitable setting, but now, unfortunately, it was time for her to go. The First Lady rose from the table and, hurriedly bidding us goodbye, left the small dining room.

'What did you just say to her?' Nikolai Krasavchenko knitted his brows and, exploiting his status as head of the delegation, looked me very sternly in the eye.

'Nothing in particular.' I brushed him off. 'We can't let the cheeky Yanks get away with things.'

After breakfast Gertrude Pratt arranged a short tour of the White House for us. We visited the ministerial cabinet room, the First Lady's office, and the president's oval office. There, our attention was caught by a photograph of some smiling lads in military uniform. They were Roosevelt's sons: Eliot, a captain in the air force, Franklin, a sub-lieutenant in the navy, and James, who was in the marine corps reserve. Eleanor had borne her husband six children and only one of them had died in infancy.

Our delegation's time was now subject to a strict schedule. Pchelintsev and I hurried back to our rooms and changed into military dress. This was the first time we had had the opportunity to wear it since leaving Moscow. The order was given by the Soviet ambassador to the USA, Maxim Maximovich Litvinov. At ten o'clock in the morning photographers and film cameramen gathered at our embassy. They wanted to catch the heroes of the anti-Fascist struggle in all their military splendour for photographs in tomorrow's newspapers.

We arrived in an embassy car. A crowd of journalists immediately surrounded us. We had trouble getting onto the porch, where we stopped at the request of the press representatives, so that the photographers and cameramen could take a few shots. The cameras were quickly squeezed out by reporters. They thrust microphones in front of us and yelled out their questions. The interpreters were operating flat-out. It gradually became clear that a large proportion of the questions were addressed to me.

After thirty minutes this pandemonium ceased and we entered the embassy building. An elderly, full-figured, round-faced man in pince-nez – Ambassador Litvinov – stepped forward to meet us, and congratulated us on our safe arrival. We had to go out onto the porch once again, this time with him, shaking hands in friendly fashion. The public appearance continued and must have been of maximum benefit to the Soviet Union.

The official banquet at the embassy was formal and quiet. In attendance were staff of the People's Commissariat of Foreign Affairs and their wives. There were toasts in Russian and conversation appropriate to the occasion; in particular, Krasavchenko gave a detailed account of our flight from Moscow to Tehran, Cairo and Miami. Now and then he looked round at me. He was apparently apprehensive that, here too, I would come out with something unforeseen by diplomatic protocol.

His concerns were totally without foundation. Unless provoked, I am a reasonable, calm and quiet person. At six o'clock in the evening there was one more, two-hour, press conference, which was broadcast by radio to the whole of America. Present at it were representatives of fifty-two newspapers and magazines and twelve radio stations. This time everything was organized differently. The floor was first given to the members of the student delegation. In a short speech, the main points of which he had been given in Moscow by Alexandrov, Krasavchenko outlined the situation in our country as a whole: the rear was assisting the front. Pchelintsev talked about the state of the Red Army. It was ready to inflict new strikes on the German armed forces.

I also had in my hands a text agreed upon with the central committee of the Communist Party:

> Dear friends! I am glad to convey greetings from Soviet women and young Soviet people who are fighting in the front ranks against the bloodthirsty Fascists. The Soviet Union is fighting not only for its own freedom, but also for the freedom of all nations and peoples on earth. From the first days of the struggle the Soviet people switched all their potential, all their energy, to defending their country. Soviet women have replaced their husbands, fathers and brothers on the production line.
>
> They have done everything to enable the men to fight. The Soviet people thank you for your help, but the struggle which Russia is leading is demanding more and more resources. We await active assistance, and the opening of the second front. I want to tell you that we will win, that there is no force which could hinder the victorious march of the free peoples of the world. We must unite. As a Russian soldier, I extend my hand to you. Together we must annihilate the Fascist monster!

I then added, off my own bat, in English: 'Fellow soldiers, forward to victory!'

The journalists applauded feebly, but then became animated. Ambassador Litvinov, who conducted the press conference, gave them the opportunity to ask questions. When it was their turn they had to rise from their seat, give their name, state the publication they represented and indicate which member of the student delegation their question was directed to.

At first the journalists' behaviour bewildered us. We expected them to ask questions about our statements, to ascertain and clarify what had been all too briefly expressed in them. But there was nothing of the sort. The Americans simply ignored these fairly official reports and tried to fish for something that had not been voiced. Most of the questions were addressed to me. As I viewed the excited people sitting in the hall and shouting out their questions – sometimes simply stupid questions, in my opinion – I was reminded for some reason of the Romanian and German 'psychological attacks'. In those situations the enemy wanted to frighten, shock and dislodge us from our positions and finally annihilate us. Here one felt roughly the same aspiration: to shock, to force us to say something that went beyond official bounds, to show the speakers up in an unfavourable light, to laugh at them. Here is an excerpt from the verbatim record of the press conference.

QUESTION: Lyudmila, can you take hot baths at the front?

ANSWER: Absolutely, and several times a day. If you are sitting in a trench and there is an artillery attack, it gets hot. Very hot. That's a real bath, only it tends to be a dust bath.

QUESTION: Did you have any protection?

ANSWER: Only my rifle.

QUESTION: Are women able to use lipstick when at war?

ANSWER: Yes, but they don't always have time. You need to be able to reach for a machine gun, or a rifle, or a pistol, or a grenade.

QUESTION: What colour underwear do you prefer, Lyudmila?

ANSWER: In Russia you would get a slap in the face for asking a question like that. That kind of question is usually only asked of a wife or a mistress. You and I do not have that relationship. So, I will be happy to give you a slap. Come a bit closer . . .

QUESTION (from a woman journalist): Is that your parade uniform or your everyday uniform?

ANSWER: We have no time for parades at the moment.

QUESTION (also from a woman): But the uniform makes you look fat. Or don't you mind?

ANSWER: I am proud to wear the uniform of the legendary Red Army. It has been sanctified by the blood of my comrades, who have fallen in in combat with the Fascists. It bears the Order of Lenin, an award for military distinction. I wish you could experience a bombing raid. Honestly, you would immediately forget about the cut of your outfit.

QUESTION: The tobacco company Philip Morris is offering you a contract. They are ready to pay half a million dollars to put your portrait on cigarette packets. Will you agree to it?

REPLY: No. They can go to the devil.

Litvinov was standing beside me. At first I did not know how he would react to such a slanging match. But I could not answer the Americans in any other way, because passion and excitment had got the better of me. At first the ambassador looked at me with surprise, then smiled and began to encourage me: 'Well said, Lyudmila. Serves them right, Washington cockroaches!'

After the press conference the student delegation went back to the White House. Awaiting us there was the president's close adviser and long-time friend, Harry Lloyd Hopkins. On a commission from Roosevelt he had visited the USSR in 1941, when Hitler's Germany had violated the borders of our country, and met with Stalin, who liked him a lot. This sympathy turned out to be mutual. On returning to the USA, Hopkins spoke out in favour of rapprochement with the Soviet Union.

He assured the president that the Russians would be able to withstand a blow of unprecedented force and that they needed help. Now, Hopkins, a thin man with a sickly appearance, questioned us front-line soldiers thoroughly about the fighting at Leningrad, Odessa and Sevastopol. He was genuinely interested in the events of our war and wanted to know all the details. Why did the American press not want to know?

In the middle of our conversation Mrs Roosevelt entered and announced that we were invited to supper at the home of Virginia Haabe, daughter of Joseph Davies, the former US ambassador to the USSR. Hopkins said that he would go with us. There had been some miscommunication with regard to the car. The Cadillac could only accommodate Krasavchenko, Pchelintsev, Hopkins and two interpreters from the Soviet embassy. Then the First Lady suggested that I go with her in a two-seat convertible, which she drove herself.

I was surprised, as I did not expect that this illustrious lady would so soon forget my impertinent reply during that day's breakfast conversation. However, from her full height of 5ft 10in, the president's wife gave me a thoroughly kind look and repeated her invitation.

The small dark-blue car looked elegant. It was capable of a decent speed. And though she was a fifty-eight-year-old woman, Eleanor drove the car like a true speedster. In an instant we broke away from the security patrol accompanying the Cadillac and tore through the Washington streets like a tornado. At corners Mrs Roosevelt would sharply reduce the engine's revs and it roared like a beast. At crossroads with traffic lights she would step heavily on the brakes, and the screaming wheels left black stripes on the asphalt. I had not expected anything like this, and I would alternately grasp the door handle in fright and squeeze myself back into the soft seat beside Eleanor. She gave me knowing looks, but did not reduce her speed. And I did not even ask her to drive more slowly.

We soon found ourselves in a suburb lined with wealthy mansions set in green gardens. When the convertible stopped, I drew breath in relief. Naturally I was unaccustomed to such reckless car trips. We were infantry, and we were more at home walking on the ground on our own two feet.

Virginia Haabe, a nice-looking woman of about thirty, came out onto the steps to meet the First Lady. Virginia had lived in Moscow for several years with her diplomat father and knew Russian quite well. She was a great admirer of Russian classical music, as she immediately informed me. We chatted as we went up to the table with aperitifs in our hands. Bowls filled with various salted nuts and small dry biscuits were set out alongside glasses and bottles containing different kinds of beverages.

How was one to know that they were very strong drink? I had generally supposed that biscuits and nuts could only be accompanied by juice, and when a waiter in a white shirt, black waistcoat and bow-tie pointed to a bottle containing a brown-coloured liquid, I nodded in assent. He filled about a third of a glass for me. I drank it with a single gulp, coughed loudly and clutched my throat. In the glass was real Scottish moonshine, that is, whisky.

'Be careful!' said Mrs Roosevelt sympathetically. She took me by the hand and led me into the dining room.

From all appearances, the supper was attended by people who had long been acquainted with one another and held the same views on life. For them the arrival of a Soviet youth delegation had become an important event which could influence the current policy of the USA. Conversation came easily and was of equal interest to both guests and hosts. But Eleanor sat me down beside her and distracted me from the conversation with various questions.

'Your English is not bad,' she whispered.

'Thank you. But that's just a compliment. Unfortunately I don't speak it well.'

'Where did you learn the language?'

'My first lessons were from my mother, when I was a child.'

'Is she a teacher?'

'Yes.'

I tried to make my replies brief because I wanted to hear what Mr Davis, the former US ambassador in Moscow, was saying just then, as he described the diplomacy of Hitler's Germany in the 1930s.

'And your father?' Eleanor continued the interrogation.

'After the Revolution he served as an officer in the Red Army.'

'Does your love of weapons come from him?'

'Perhaps . . .'

At the instructional sessions before the trip we had been told about Franklin Delano Roosevelt and his wife. Eleanor Roosevelt (1884–1962) came from a rich aristocratic family, had received a wonderful education at home, spent three years in London at the Allenwood finishing school, and then made a trip around Western Europe. In March 1905 Eleanor married her distant relative Franklin, a student in the law faculty of Columbia University. In place of her father, who had died early, she was given away by her uncle, the US president at the time, Theodore Roosevelt.

As First Lady, she sponsored various youth and women's organizations, was constantly engaged in charity work and became a very well-known and respected public activist, journalist and 'minister without portfolio' in the government of Franklin Delano Roosevelt. Since 1921, when her husband had become seriously ill with poliomyelitis and lost some of his mobility, she had run all his election campaigns, touring the country, speaking at gatherings and meeting with constituents. She was known as the 'eyes, ears and legs of the president' because she went where he could not go and influenced his decisions. Eleanor won the love and respect of the people. It was not without good reason that, according to a poll in 1939, the First Lady ranked higher than her husband in popularity. Her record was viewed as 'good' by 67 per cent of Americans, while Franklin received 58 per cent.

Mrs Roosevelt was not noted for her beauty. Her facial features were coarse and not quite symmetrical. But her enormous charm, intelligence and kindness made her irresistible and drew many, many people to her. To tell the truth, at the start of the US trip, I was prejudiced against Eleanor: aristocrat, millionairess, member of the exploiting class, I thought. It never occurred to me that I could be of interest to this remarkable woman.

The morning newspapers, which were delivered to the White House by breakfast time on 28 August, testified to the success of our press conference. Our photos adorned the front pages. The 'free press' of the USA even accorded my modest personage some attention. They gossiped about the cut of my tunic, quoted my replies to questions and considered whether representatives of the weaker sex could really serve in military units. There were some who called me a cold-blooded killer with no pity for unfortunate German soldiers who were merely fulfilling the orders of their senior command.

Pushing away a cup of hot coffee, Eleanor gave me a fresh copy of the bulky *New York Post* and pointed to a long column signed 'Elsa Maxwell'. 'She is an old acquaintance of mine,' said the First Lady. 'She was at your press conference and she liked everything about it. You carried yourself well. Elsa is experienced, observant and a superb master of the pen. In my view, she described you accurately. Or rather, the impression you give.

What Lieutenant Pavlichenko possesses is something more than just beauty. Her imperturbable calm and confidence come from what she has had to endure and experience. She has the face of a Madonna from a Correggio painting and the hands of a child, and her olive-coloured tunic with its red markings has been scorched by the fire of fierce combat. One of those at the press conference, a woman journalist sitting beside me, in a fashionable, elegantly sewn dress, asked Lyudmila with a certain measure of sarcasm: 'I wondered if that was your everyday or your parade uniform?'

Lyudmila looked at my well-dressed neighbour with a certain indifference and said: 'Let me inform you that in Russia there are no parades at the moment. Our thoughts are occupied by other matters.'

The echoes of the women's arguments about clothes also occupied the men, it turned out. They reached the pages of the highly informative business paper *Daily News*. The issue carried a full-length photograph of me and a long caption under it: 'Sniper Lyudmila Pavlichenko: I wear my military uniform with pride! It is sanctified by the blood of my comrades in arms who have fallen on the field of battle. Therefore, I value it more than the most beautiful dress from the best tailor!'

After breakfast Eleanor bade us a cordial farewell. Our time in the White House had come to an end and we set off for the Soviet embassy. Awaiting us there was a new press conference, this one for staff of the international telegraph agencies Reuters and Associated Press.

While packing the voluminous newspapers carrying my picture, which would be needed for my report in Moscow, it occurred to me that the new section of the front to which the Red Army command had assigned me was gradually acquiring clear outlines. It was the battle against journalists. Not that they were such noxious and revolting people, but merely that they had their own idea of what was good or bad, what was interesting and what was boring. They were standing between me and those millions of readers, listeners and viewers in America to whom Comrade Stalin had entrusted me with telling the truth about the war. That meant that one had to be sincere, confident in oneself, extremely collected, jovial and witty. Then they would believe us.

That evening the three of us – Krasavchenko, Pchelintsev and I – went to a performance at the National Theater, the oldest in the USA and situated on Pennsylvania Avenue, not far from the White House. There was a performance of the opera *Madame Butterfly* by the Italian composer, Giacomo Puccini. The auditorium was filled with well-dressed, wealthy members of the public. At first nobody paid attention to us, for we were in civilian dress. But when the lights went on in the interval between the second and third act, the manager went up onto the stage and announced that sitting in the audience were the members of the Soviet student delegation. There was tumultuous applause. We had to go up onto the stage. Vladimir Pchelintsev spoke on behalf of the delegation and his speech lasted no more than five minutes. After that some smartly dressed girls appeared in the auditorium with coloured boxes and began to collect money for the fund to assist the Red Army.

The collection went very well. Many who had given money got up and came over to the stage, tried to shake our hands, and voiced words of support. Similar scenes were repeated a number of times subsequently during our trip through America. All in all, our delegation collected and transferred to the Soviet embassy approximately $800,000, a significant sum. But we often argued among ourselves as to what attitude we should take towards this process. Pchelintsev said there was something humiliating in it – as if our great country and its invincible army were begging loaded Americans to give alms to the poor. As head of the delegation, Krasavchenko never wearied of explaining the facts of the matter to the hot-headed Vladimir: this money would buy foodstuffs and essential items for Soviet people who had been deprived of a roof over their head, lost all their property and ended up being evacuated. That was all correct, but somehow left an unpleasant taste.

Nevertheless, our trip was an official visit and TASS published the following communique about it on 30 August 1942:

The attendance of the Soviet delegates at the
International student congress in Washington.

On arrival in Washington, the Soviet delegates to the international student congress, Comrades Krasavchenko, Pchelintsev and Lyudmila Pavlichenko were invited the same day to the White House, where they spent the night as guests of the US president. On the third day the Soviet delegates spoke on the radio. Their speeches were broadcast by a major Washington station. The Soviet delegates recounted their experiences fighting the Nazis.

The arrival of Pavlichenko, Krasavchenko and Pchelintsev was described in detail in a special radio programme broadcast throughout the USA. The morning papers featured photographs of the Soviet students, a conversation with them and a detailed description of their arrival in Washington.

In conversation with journalists Krasavchenko asked them to pass on to the youth of America and all the entire American nation greetings from the Soviet people who were fighting at the front against the Nazi hordes. Krasavchenko briefly described the many aspects of Soviet young people's participation in the struggle against the aggressor. Lyudmila Pavlichenko conveyed military greetings from Soviet women to American women and described the self-sacrificing toil of Soviet women, who were inspired by hatred of the enemy. Pchelintsev talked about the art of the sniper and said in conclusion: 'We can be victorious and we will be victorious. So said Stalin, and so it will be.'

The Soviet students expressed their gratitude to Mr Roosevelt for the hospitality accorded them in the White House.

On the morning of 2 September we got ready for the first session of the international student assembly. We put on our uniforms, checked that everything was in order, everything in place and, not without some nervousness, speculated on how the session would go and how we would be greeted. 'International assembly!' We repeated the words to one another without realizing that the Americans were past masters at pulling the wool over your eyes. Sitting in the hall were no more than 400 people – such was the total international representation. True, the students had come from fifty-three countries. There were Latin Americans, Africans, Asians and Europeans. It went without saying that there were no delegates from Germany and the states allied with it.

Having looked through the list, experienced Young Communist League functionary Nikolai Krasavchenko said that the aim of the organizers of the international student assembly was clear to him. A solid majority of them were representatives of the USA, Great Britain and Canada. Consequently, they would also influence the voting. Whatever they wanted, they would impose on all the rest by using this voting majority. This meant, Nikolai concluded, that it was necessary to demand that the rules prescribe one vote per delegation rather than one vote for every person in attendance.

Because we arrived in Red Army uniform, we immediately attracted general attention. Correspondents again assailed us at the entrance. Camera bulbs flashed and the questions came thick and fast. After struggling to squeeze our way through to the vestibule, we found Mrs Roosevelt there. She was greeting the delegates. Journalists instantly surrounded the First Lady and asked her to have her photo taken with us.

Eleanor did not object. On her left stood Senior Lieutenant Pchelintsev and I was on her right. She took us both by the hand. In this way the Russian–American military alliance against Fascism was given a vivid and concrete embodiment. The following day the photograph appeared in the newspapers and commentators excelled themselves in suppositions, interpreting it this way and that.

Apart from the introduction of delegations and voting on the agenda, the first day of the assembly was made up of a plenary session and a discussion on the topic 'Universities in Wartime'. One of the addresses came from Nikolai Krasavchenko, who gave a thorough and detailed account of Soviet students in military operations and work in the rear. The evening saw the formal opening of the event, which was attended by numerous honorary guests: representatives of US civic organizations, official persons from the presidential administration, and the president's wife. The reception had still not finished when Mrs Roosevelt came up to us and said that the Soviet delegation was invited to supper at the White House and they would have to leave immediately.

We soon learned the reason for this haste. As if by accident, in the White House we ended up meeting the president of the USA, Franklin Delano Roosevelt. He was in one of the rooms, sitting in a wooden chair with a high back and broad arms, which his own arms were resting on. His legs were covered by a Scottish tartan plaid.

'Frank,' said the First Lady, 'I want to introduce our new Soviet friends to you.'

Without question he was a very exceptional man, possessing a sharp mind and a strong will. That thought immediately went through my head when I encountered his penetrating gaze and pressed his lean, sinewy palm. He listened closely as the interpreter introduced us and repeated the names of the cities from which we had come: 'Moscow . . . Leningrad . . . Odessa and Sevastopol . . . How wonderful! A real brief history of the Germans' current war in Russia!' Like a true gentleman, he spoke with me first, asked what fighting I had been involved in, what I had received my military decorations for, how my regimental comrades had fought. Generally, he was aware of the operations on the various fronts, but he was interested in the details, the impressions of those directly involved.

In nearly three years of war, the Anglo-Americans had not succeeded anywhere in resisting their enemies as long as the Russians had done at Moscow, Leningrad, Odessa and Sevastopol. The president wanted to find out how we managed it. Was it due to Russia's traditionally strong military spirit, the soldiers' military training, the skill of the officers, the strategic talents of the generals, excellent weaponry or the main thing – the unity between the army and the people who were taking up arms against the invaders? Most likely, Roosevelt was already making plans for the future.

Since 7 December 1941, when Germany's ally, Japan, destroyed the US naval fleet in Pearl Harbor, and then quickly pushed the Americans out of South-East Asia, the president had been looking for an answer to the question: who would help America to get back there? The states in the anti-Nazi alliance did not inspire him with particular hope. The might of the British Empire had weakened in the course of military operations. The Nazis had occupied half of France and the other half was under the Vichy regime, which collaborated with Hitler. In China there was civil war. That left Soviet Russia – if, of course, Russia could defeat the Germans at Stalingrad and drive their forces from its territory, if it could restore its industrial potential.

Roosevelt concluded his conversation with me by asking: 'How do you feel in our country?'

'Excellent, Mr President,' I replied.

'Are the Americans cordial towards you?'

'We are greeted everywhere as welcome guests. True, sometimes we are subjected to sudden attacks.'

'Really?' The president was surprised.

'I mean attacks from your reporters,' I said, maintaining the conversation on a serious level. 'They're very persistent people. It's simply impossible to withstand their pressure. You have to bare everything.'

The president smiled. He liked that remark.

I could have gone on joking, but I wanted to ask Roosevelt that most important question – about more active assistance for the Soviet Union, about the opening of a second front in Western Europe which would draw away some of the German divisions now fighting on the banks of the Volga.

Roosevelt seemed to guess what I was thinking. 'Tell the Soviet government and Mr Stalin personally', he said pensively, 'that it's difficult for me at the moment to render more real assistance to your country. We Americans are still not ready for decisive action. We are held back by our British partners. But in their heart and soul the American people are with our Russian allies.'

The proceedings of the international student assembly took their course. There were some interesting addresses, and there were also heated debates, during which the participants almost came to blows. For example, during discussion of the so-called 'Indian Question', a turbaned student from Bombay University yelled at a Briton from Oxford: 'Colonial cur! We'll beat you all sooner or later and win independence!' The Indians and the British were only separated with difficulty and the Bombay delegate ran over to the Russians to complain. We were very sympathetic towards the oppressed people of Asia Minor and South-East Asia, but as for making a scene at an international function – nobody in Moscow had ordered us to do that.

Let me say at the outset that it proved impossible to include a clause about the opening of a second front in Europe in the declaration adopted at the final session of the international student assembly. However, the organizers still came to a compromise with us. The delegates adopted a 'Slavic Memorandum' which harshly condemned German Fascism and called for the union of all peoples in the struggle against it. Many newspapers and radio stations reported the adoption of this memorandum, while TASS gave it the most extensive coverage.

The assembly's participants spent the warm sunny evening of 5 September 1942 on the green next to the White House. The US government had arranged a reception there to mark the completion of this international student congress. It was run by Eleanor Roosevelt. Dozens of young men and women with paper plates, sandwiches and bottles of cooling drinks strolled either alone or in groups along the paths of the amazing classical French gardens and discussed the aims and objectives of the democratic youth movement.

The First Lady paid most attention to our delegation. She already knew five Russian words: *spasibo* (thank you), *khorosho* (good), *da*, *nyet* and *konyechno* (of course). Our chats with her were no longer quite so formal, and we felt more at ease. Eleanor joked, laughed and told us how she had come up with the idea of this function and planned for it. In her vision the assembly was meant to have a profoundly cultural and educational nature and to promote the spread of American values in an international youth context. The appearance of the Russians had changed many things. We spoke about the war with too much passion, too much emotion. We knew a lot about it. Thus, the war, which had previously been distant and incomprehensible to the Americans, suddenly acquired visible features: the sufferings of ordinary people, blood spilt in combat, instant death. Mrs Roosevelt thanked us for this and voiced the hope that other residents of her native land, of the entire continent, would hear what we had to tell.

16

My Darling

The following morning we reported to Litvinov in his office and handed over the texts of the international student assembly declaration and the 'Slavic Memorandum'. The ambassador thanked us for our work and said that we had demonstrated a high level of ideological and political training, a capacity for public speaking and an ability to stand up for Communist ideals in debates with bourgeois opponents. He informed us that our American partners had offered to extend the stay of the student delegation and send us on a tour around US cities to give greater publicity to the activities of the countries in the anti-Hitler coalition. The USSR embassy had accepted this proposal.

We were not overjoyed at this decision. Vladimir Pchelintsev and I dreamed of getting home as soon as we could because fierce combat had begun on the Stalingrad front at the end of July. The Germans were storming towards the Volga. At the beginning of August units of Hitler's 6th Army had drawn near to the outskirts of Stalingrad.

Soviet forces showed determined resistance to the invaders, but, with their numerical superiority, the enemy had closed in on the streets of the city and there were constant skirmishes there. Events were settling into a positional war and consequently it was the best time for snipers to go into action. We had no intention of resting on our laurels: Vladimir had got 154 Fritzes and I had 309, and we both wanted to increase our fighting tally on the firing lines of the city beside the great Russian river.

Litvinov calmly listened to our arguments, reminded us that officers must always carry out the orders of the Red Army's supreme commander-in-chief and suggested that we get ready for the trip to New York on Sunday, 6 September. This was a national holiday in the USA – Labour Day. We would set off in the early morning on the Washington–New York express train and were required to wear our parade uniform.

At the station in New York the delegation was greeted as usual by journalists. But they were not given the chance to indulge fully in their antics and were kept at a distance. We were seated in a car and, under police escort and to the wail of sirens and the racket of motorbike engines, taken to the main entrance of Central Park. There, a big crowd had gathered. Some burly lads in jackets and caps, but with a military bearing, hoisted us onto their shoulders and carried us up to the stage. The city's mayor, Fiorello La Guardia, announced through the microphone that the representatives of the heroic Red Army had arrived and voiced his admiration for the titanic struggle of the Russian people against the German Fascists. The crowd in the park responded to the mayor with an enthusiastic roar. This was followed by a performance from the black singer Paul Robson, who sang in Russian the song by the composer Dunayevsky, 'Broad is my Native Land'.

The meeting concluded with the presentation of a symbolic gift to the Soviet guests – a medallion skilfully carved from sea oak in the shape of a heart, with a silver disc in the middle and the inscription: 'For active participation in the struggle against Fascism'. I was the one who had to accept the gift. After this, a speech in reply had to be made – brief but intelligible. 'Dear friends,' I began, 'sensing his inevitable destruction, the Fascist beast is making desperate attempts to strike a blow at our united nations before we Allies do it to him. It is a matter of life and death for the freedom-loving peoples of every country to harness all our forces to render assistance to the front. More tanks, more planes, more ordnance, you glorious American toilers!'

Amplified by the microphone, my voice soared over the hushed crowd and its echo resounded along the most distant paths of the park. Of course, the residents of New York did not understand what I had said until the interpreter had spoken, but they caught the intonation. I wanted to convey my fervour to the crowd, to arouse compassion for our people, to evoke a response in their hearts. It appeared to come off. The crowd responded first with a restrained roar and then with a storm of applause and shouts of approval.

This was followed by an official dinner hosted by the consul-general of the USSR, Victor Alexeyevich Fedyushin. There was an evening reception in the premises of the association of fur-dealers, where we were given presents: for me – a floor-length raccoon-fur coat, while the lads received luxurious beaver-skin jackets. The fur-dealers assembled a distinguished table of guests; present were many representatives of business circles, civil servants from the city authorities and figures from the world of art and culture.

It was then that I was introduced to one William Patrick Jonson, owner of a metallurgical company and a millionaire.[1] I found nothing out of the ordinary in him. A fairly tall gentleman of about thirty-five, of average build and a pleasant exterior, like everyone else at the reception he lightly brushed my hand with his lips and said a few quite banal words about my looks and my brilliant address at the meeting in Central Park, where, it turned out, he had been present. The only thing out of the ordinary was his insistent invitation to visit his estate on the outskirts of New York, where he had a collection of paintings by Russian avant-garde artists from the beginning of the twentieth century. I had a very vague idea of the avant-garde figures and a good knowledge only of the Peredvizhniki or 'itinerant' artists and particularly appreciated the paintings of the war artist Vasily Vereshchagin.

Individual trips and contacts of this kind were forbidden for us. I had to tell Mr Jonson with a smile that, unfortunately, our tight schedule of appearances would not allow me any opportunity to accept his invitation. I regarded our conversation as over and the meeting as our last. But there was more to come.

Inspired by the resounding success of the meeting in New York, the organizers from the International Student Service, the embassy of the Soviet Union and the administration of the US president planned one further publicity trip – on 10 September, to the large city of Baltimore, on the Atlantic coast. There was an excellent motorway there from Washington with many traffic lanes. We set off in the morning in an embassy car and arrived in the middle of the day. Again we were met by a police escort – the wail of sirens and lines of motor-cyclists in white helmets and black jackets. On the way to meet the mayor we saw people standing at the roadside waving to us in welcome and shouting greetings.

Another meeting in the city square, another speech from me, again the roar of the crowd and banners in Russian and English reading 'Long live the Red Army!', 'Welcome to the fighters against Fascism' and 'We support the opening of a second front'. This was followed by an official reception at the mayoralty involving distinguished Baltimore citizens. And here again William Patrick Jonson – true, in a different suit this time with grey stripes – came up to me and said that he was very glad to see me once more, that in Baltimore he had a cousin who owned a huge department store, which included an outstanding section of ready-made clothing, and would Mrs Pavlichenko not like to visit it, because it had recently taken delivery of the latest fashions from London. When he had finished speaking, a middle-aged woman dripping in diamonds came up to us; this was, of course, Mr Jonson's cousin. She informed me with a smile that the costumes for my figure were simply incredibly nice and suggested that I immediately go for a fitting. Jonson added that he would like to make me a present of any dress that took my fancy.

This was much more serious and the persistent millionaire needed to be given a rebuff, but in a mild, courteous and diplomatic way. I explained that I liked good clothes, but I was under orders from Comrade Stalin. Both local property owners were surprised: what orders could there be for a beautiful young woman if she wished to renew her wardrobe? I asked them if President Roosevelt gave them orders or if they acted only from their own economic compulsion. While the two relatives were collecting their thoughts, Nikolai Krasavchenko appeared beside me;

he had a special knack of doing this at the right moment. I took his arm and quickly walked away to the opposite end of the room.

The following day, 11 September, our delegation returned to Washington. Some pleasant news awaited us at the embassy. The US president and his wife had invited the Soviet students to spend a week at their family estate, Hyde Park, 80km from New York on the Hudson River. Also invited, in addition to the Russians, were other participants in the international student assembly: Richard Miles and Dave Scott from Britain, Johann Walter from Holland and Yoon Wang from China. We would go by train and the First Lady would meet us at the station.

The Roosevelt estate was vast, beautiful, and well-endowed with modern facilities. It would not be possible to cover the whole area in a day. A park with straight paths, flowerbeds, lawns, gazebos and wooden benches merged inconspicuously with thick forest which occupied an area of at least 3km². Not far from the centre of the estate, with its two-storey stone house, lay a large lake. One shore was overgrown with reeds and had quite a wild look, while the other was well tended. There was a bathing shed, and coloured piers stretched into the clean, clear water. Next to them boats moored to posts swayed in the light breeze.

After breakfast I set off for a stroll. My interest was drawn by a strange narrow craft, seemingly covered in leather, with a small seat in the middle and short oars in rowlocks. At one time, back home in Belaya Tserkov, my sister Valentina and I enjoyed taking a flat-bottomed boat called the *Cossack Oak* out on the river Ros. Without pondering for long, I jumped into the American 'Indian' canoe (which was what it was called, it later turned out), pushed off from the jetty and plied the oars.

The boat sped forward as easily as a bird, but it had quite a shallow draught. One sharp turn and I ended up in the cold water, as the canoe had capsized.

My attempt to retrieve my felt hat was not crowned with success. It quickly sank. I was also unable to restore the boat to its former position; my hands slipped on its sheer wet sides, which really were made of leather. All I could do was swim to the shore, towing the boat after me. Standing there were two witnesses to the event: Richard Miles and Dave Scott.

The noble English gentlemen stood there, shifting from one foot to the other, not knowing what to do: whether to rescue the maiden and the boat, which would have meant taking their clothes off and entering the water, or to call the servants for help, which would have required running to the central part of the estate, although that was not far away. They just stood anxiously by the water's edge, loudly discussing the situation. They were soon presented with an unusual sight: an officer of the Red Army emerging from the water in wet clothes which dramatically revealed the shape of her body.

When I saw their serious faces, I could not stop myself laughing. To be honest, it was hilarious to be doing such stupid things in a foreign country. To set off in an unfamiliar watercraft for the other end of the lake, to splash around in the water, diving for my hat, and emerge onto the shore before the eyes of two young idiots, who goggled at me as if they had just seen a Martian invasion.

Still laughing, I made my way to my guest cottage, situated quite a long way from the lake, behind the two-storeyed house. The wet collar of my knitted jacket was clinging to my neck. The flaps of my semi-woollen dress had become heavy and made it difficult to walk. The water sloshed around repulsively in my shoes. But I could not undress right there! And it would be cold with no clothes on.

There was a brisk September wind, not warm at all, and the air temperature was no more than 16 degrees. 'Lyudmila!' The alarmed voice of the First Lady suddenly rang out as she opened a window on the ground floor of the hosts' house. 'What happened?'

'I was swimming in the lake without a bathing costume.'

'But the weather's not at all suitable for bathing. You need to change your clothes quickly. Come over here.'

Mrs Roosevelt met me in the vestibule and took me to her study and bedroom, which was connected to a bathroom and toilet. On the way and still smiling, I jokingly told her about the boat's insidious behaviour, the felt hat sinking like a stone and the sons of Albion who were mortally afraid of the water and had probably not seen women *en déshabillée*.

Eleanor brought a big napped towel and held it out to me. In wet shoes, I was afraid to step on the luxurious Persian carpet on her study floor. 'Undress in the bathroom,' she said. 'I'll be right back.'

The president's wife returned in about fifteen minutes. She was carrying some pyjamas of her own, scissors and a box containing needles and thread. I waited for her, wrapped up in the towel. I left my wet clothes, underclothes, stockings and shoes in the bathroom and stood barefoot on the carpet, highly embarrassed at what had occurred. In the big mirror on the dressing table I saw my own reflection: damp tangled hair, and bare shoulders, arms and legs because the towel, although 1.5 metres wide, did not cover my entire figure.

Eleanor gave me a passing glance, smiled and called the maid. She explained to her what to do with the things in the bathroom: to wash them if they were spattered, then dry, iron and bring them back. The rather stout, black, middle-aged maid wearing a white cap over her wavy black hair and a white apron with a lace border, nodded in agreement while giving me an occasional glance. The president's guests had probably never appeared in front of the servants in such a risqué state of dress. The maid left and Eleanor turned to me: 'You need to change into my pyjamas.'

'But we are not the same height.'

'Never mind! I'll shorten the sleeves and the legs.'

'By yourself?' I was surprised beyond measure.

'Yes, my friend. Or do you think that women from the Roosevelt family are ladies of leisure? I assure you, all American woman really know how to work . . .'

To start with, she laid the pyjamas on the wide bed. Completely new, and made from thick pink satin with violets embroidered on the collar, cuffs and pockets, they were plainly not a cheap garment. But Eleanor enthusiastically snipped along them with the scissors and then took a long tape measure out of the box. After all, prior to cutting, one should take measurements precisely and not just do it by eye.

Deftly employing this tailor's implement, the First Lady swiftly determined the length of my arms, after which she went behind me to measure the width of my shoulders. The towel reached only to my armpits and Mrs Roosevelt caught sight of the long, reddish, forked scar stretching diagonally from my right shoulder blade to my spine. It shocked her; she took a step back and exclaimed: 'Good Lord! What is that, Lyudmila?'

'The result of a piece of metal,' I answered, as at that time I did not know the English words 'scar', 'splinter' and 'shell', and thus resorted to substitutes.

'But how did the metal get in?' Eleanor cautiously touched the scar with her finger.

'In December last year, at Sevastopol.'

'Fighting the Germans?'

'Yes,' I affirmed.

'My poor girl!' Mrs Roosevelt impulsively hugged me and brushed my forehead with her lips. 'What dreadful ordeals you've had to endure.'

The president's wife spoke with genuine compassion, even pain. I believed her, even though our first meeting at breakfast at the White House had not boded well for mutual understanding. Perhaps she now recalled the words of hers that I had found offensive. There had been something she did not like in my behaviour at the time and, being experienced in public debate, she had decided to inflict a light blow with her lance against the armour – as she saw it – of the strange 'Sevastopol Amazon'. But she had received a response that was blunt and to the point. Possibly, after this, Eleanor began to wonder if there was something mysterious in Russian people that was impenetrable to Anglo-Saxons. She wanted to get to the bottom of this mystery.

When Franklin Delano Roosevelt, who was wondering at our absence from the dining room with dinner approaching, arrived in his wheelchair in the half of the house occupied by his wife, he came across us in the bedroom. We were sitting on the wide bed, absorbed in sewing. The task of remodelling the pyjamas was in progress and coming to an end. Bright pieces of cloth lay around us, as well as scissors, cotton threads and needles stuck into shreds of satin. We were having a lively discussion about present-day fashions: the best dress cut for each of us, the most beautiful colours, finishing touches and suitable jewellery accessories. I had already put the pyjama top on; however, on seeing the US president, I leapt to my feet in surprise and, holding the towel around my hips, blurted out: 'I beg your pardon, Mr Roosevelt!'

He burst out laughing. In his view, it was a very amusing scene. Here were two women widely different in age, upbringing, education and social position, not to mention the language barrier, but nothing hindered them from chatting enthusiastically about absolute trivialities. Having discovered a complete coincidence of views on various aspects of life, they were looking at each other in delight and enjoying a frivolous conversation about nothing. It was not providing them with any new information, did not pretend to any serious conclusions and inferences, but nevertheless it was already into its second hour.

In the evening a strong wind blew up on the Hudson, the sky clouded over, and rain started, soon turning into a downpour. The fire was lit in the dining room, which was very timely, because in the spacious room where dinner was served the glass panes in the window frames were shuddering from the stormy gusts. The dismal autumn weather, it seemed, had penetrated the walls of the big stone house and filled it with the damp rising from the Hudson.

Harry Hopkins, the presidential adviser already familiar to us, arrived at Hyde Park for supper. He had brought some papers from Washington and proved pleasant company at the table. Hopkins did not drink alcohol or eat salty, spicy or fried food because of a stomach operation the previous year on account of a cancerous tumour. But this did not have the slightest effect on his mood and he amused the company with witty commentaries on recent events. I noticed that Eleanor was particularly pleased at his arrival. She forewarned the adviser that she wished to discuss a particular problem with him.

The seven days on the Roosevelt estate soon flew by. We returned to Washington and paid another visit to our ambassador, Maxim Litvinov. He conveyed to us the decision taken in Moscow with regard to the further activities of the student delegation. To our great surprise, we learned that the delegation would be split into two. Krasavchenko and Pchelintsev would set off on a tour around the cities in the north-east of the USA: Cleveland, Buffalo, Albany, Pittsburgh, Richmond and others – to meet with students in colleges and universities. I would go to the West and Midwest: Chicago, Minneapolis, Denver, Seattle, San Francisco, Fresno and Los Angeles. The two lads and I bade one another an amicable farewell on 24 September. I knew that during the tour I would often be accompanied by Mrs Roosevelt. The presence of the First Lady determined the level of the meetings with Americans: receptions with the governors of various states or at mayoralties, business lunches, suppers for business circles, press conferences for local newspapers and radio stations.

Gathering speed, the presidential limousine with bullet-proof windows sped along the empty highway, with a security car in front of us and another one behind. The houses and streets of Dearborn, a suburb of Detroit, one of the oldest cities in the American Midwest, faded into the distance. We had only just finished our visit to the headquarters of the Ford Motor Company, the biggest in the USA and famous throughout the world.

It had begun with a visit to the aircraft works, where the twin-engine bombers known to Americans as the 'Tin Goose' were manufactured.[2] We were shown the entire assembly process, from the welding of the frame out of metal tubes and the stamping of the Duralumin wings in a huge mechanical press right through to the main conveyor belt where the war machine acquired its menacing appearance. An explanation was provided by a Mr Lawrence [TN: or Laurence?], the director of the enterprise.

In the factory management building the guests were met by the 'automobile king' himself, the members of his family and staff from the company's top management. Henry Ford, a cheerful, lean old man, was eager to meet me, presented me with a 'Ford Motor Company' gold badge and asked permission to have a photograph taken with me and Eleanor Roosevelt, who had also come on this trip. The reporters immediately rushed forward, clicked their cameras with their bright flashlights, and began to ask questions about the factory, the bombers and American military power.

The representatives of the press were not invited to lunch. A modest repast of sandwiches, doughnuts and Coca-Cola was set out for a small group of us. The founder and owner of the company made a brief patriotic speech, the mayor of Dearborn spoke and then the floor was given to me. The reception lasted exactly thirty minutes. There was no getting away from it: in the empire of Henry Ford, as nowhere else, 'time was money'.

I was very surprised by the behaviour of the workers. They were assembled in some sort of warehouse, probably about 300 of them, no more. They were gloomy, unsmiling and somehow preoccupied men wearing dark-blue company overalls. I was asked to speak briefly and to avoid Communist slogans or invocations. And I did so; I passed on greetings to the proletarians of America from the working people of the Soviet Union who were waiting for help in their struggle against German Fascism. In response there was none of the usual applause, questions or good wishes. As I left, they rose in silence from their seats.

'An enemy of the working people!' I said sarcastically, gloomily looking through the car windows at the trees along the roadside which had been touched by autumnal wilting and were losing their leaves.

'You're wrong, my dear,' replied Eleanor with a smile.

'But how does he treat his workers? They're worse than dumb cattle hassled by guard dogs. Why did they remain silent?'

'They are the working aristocracy. Ford pays well. They have something to lose. Yes, he keeps an eye on them: go to church, don't drink whisky, don't gamble, support your family, don't join a trade union, don't go on strike . . . They were afraid to talk to you. You're from Communist Russia.'

'Fine!' I thumped my knee with my fist. 'Next time I'll have something to tell the Americans!'

The driver and the security agent sitting beside him, separated from the passengers by a glass partition, could not hear our conversation. The gentle hum of the engine was no hindrance to it. The car travelled at the constant speed set down for presidential corteges on intercity routes. From Detroit we travelled to Chicago, a distance of a little over 450km, and the journey took over five and a half hours.

The flat expanses of the state of Michigan spread out on either side of the road. Evidently, Eleanor had specially chosen this route in order to show me the Midwest of her native land with its small, homely cities – Ann Arbor, Albion, Kalamazoo, Benton Harbor. Then the highway turned towards the shores of the huge Lake Michigan, which was like a sea. Here the landscape changed. The mirror surface of the water was occasionally hidden by hills and small woods. Numerous small islands were visible close to the shore. The further south we went, the more we encountered beautiful sand dunes, which were quite high.

The First Lady gave a detailed, witty and entertaining commentary. She loved the USA and had a superb knowledge of it; she had traversed the length and breadth of it while helping her husband in his election campaigns and carrying out various commissions for the president. She wanted me to get to know America better. Of course, the heart of a junior lieutenant belonged wholly and completely to the great country of Russia, she joked, but it was useful for anyone to see other countries and understand the life of other peoples.

Mrs Roosevelt tried hard to speak English slowly and simply, using only the simple present tense. However, given my lack of experience in communicating in a foreign language, even speech composed of short sentences demanded intense concentration and, over the five hours of the trip, pretty well exhausted me. Apart from that, I was not used to travelling by car, even in one as comfortable as the presidential Cadillac.

In fact, I did not get to see the splendid suburbs of Chicago Cicero and Oak Park because I had fallen asleep with my head on the First Lady's shoulder. I was hugely embarrassed when I awoke when the car stopped. Eleanor smiled as if nothing was the matter.

'Please, wake up, my darling. We are in Chicago.'

For the meeting the Chicago authorities had selected Grant Park, a historic area set out in the French style on the shores of Lake Michigan. It was a vast and highly developed space with lawns, flowerbeds, bike tracks, the Buckingham fountain and a statue of Abraham Lincoln, as well as a concert stage. This stage was decked out with the flags of the countries in the anti-Hitler coalition, the USA, Great Britain, the USSR and China, and portraits of their leaders: Roosevelt, Churchill, Stalin and Chiang Kai-shek. News of the meeting and an invitation to attend it had been published in the city newspaper, the *Chicago Tribune*.

Among the honoured guests at the meeting were Eleanor Roosevelt and Fred Myers, director of the charitable community organization Russian War Relief, which was set up in July 1941 by US Communists and liberal sympathizers, mainly drawn from the creative intelligentsia (for instance, actor Charlie Chaplin, film director Orson Welles and artist Rockwell Kent). The meeting was also to be attended by a representative of the US army, Colonel Stephen Douglas, who had come from the Fort Knox military base in the state of Kentucky, adjacent to Illinois. To me fell the honour of representing the Red Army.

As usual, the meeting was opened by the city mayor. After a brief account of the anti-Hitler coalition and the USA's participation in it, he yielded the floor to me. I stepped forward to the microphone. Quite a crowd had assembled before me. I could clearly discern the faces of the people in the front rows – mainly men aged between thirty and forty. They were looking at me quite affably and smiling. I began with a few sentences about the war now raging in far-off Russia, then paused and sharply raised my voice: 'Gentlemen! I am twenty-five years old. At the front I have already wiped out 309 Fascist soldiers and officers. Don't you think, gentlemen, that you have been hiding for too long behind my back?'

Looking round at me in amazement, the interpreter translated the sentences, trying to preserve my intonation. For a few seconds the crowd was silent. Then a real storm broke out over the old park. The people yelled, chanted, something, whistled, stamped their feet, and applauded. Journalists rushed towards the stage. Also heading there, and pushing the reporters out of the way, were those who wanted to make a donation to the fund for assisting the USSR, which the Chicago mayor had requested when he opened the meeting and for which special Russian War Relief collection boxes had been set up in front of the stage. There were also some enthusiasts who wished to give their donation immediately and just to me. Large security guards quickly formed a line in front of the stage and prevented them from causing disorder.

I was still standing by the microphone with my arms lowered and my fingers clasped. The outburst of public emotion seemed too strong and I had not reckoned on anything like this when I composed my speech. It was just that, after the setback at the Ford works, I wanted to think of something that would immediately get through to them, to the fortunate, relaxed and extraordinarily calculating residents of the continent discovered by Columbus.

As I was informed later, an account of the meeting in Chicago and my address there were published on the front pages of many American newspapers. Reuters spread it round the whole world and accompanied it with a positive commentary. They wrote that I had vividly and accurately expressed the essence of the position now taken by the Anglo-Americans with regard to Russia's bloody struggle against the German invaders.

At a reception in the evening, arranged by the Chicago mayor, I was formally presented with a beautifully printed certificate and a golden badge reading 'Honorary Citizen of the USA',[3] an award established in this city. It was a select company in the hall: ladies in evening gowns and gentlemen in dinner jackets. My khaki tunic adorned only with the Order of Lenin, the medal 'For Military Service' and my 'Guard' and 'Sniper' badges in glittering red and white enamel probably looked ostentatiously modest in this setting. But that was the wish of the organizers and I fulfilled it. Many people spoke to me about Soviet–American cooperation in the war and the necessity of opening a second front in Europe. It would be good to back these words up with deeds, I thought. There were many and various pleasant words said about me. I knew how to respond: with a smile, calmly and imperturbably, but without arrogance.

However, it turned out to be difficult to maintain this imperturbability to the end. William Patrick Jonson appeared – suddenly, it could be said – at the end of this smart function. I did not immediately recognize him among the other gentlemen: the same dinner jacket, white shirt, bow-tie, dark hair with a parting, the standard American expression ('Everything's fine with me, I'm happy'), and a genteel smile.

'How did you get in here?' was all I could say in response to his flowery welcome.

'Oh, quite simply, Mrs Pavlichenko,' he replied sadly. 'I followed you in my car from Detroit. Unfortunately, they would not let me in to the Henry Ford headquarters. He has very strict security.'

'Isn't it strict here?'

'Here it's a different matter. There's a metal works in East Chicago. About 30 per cent of its shares belong to me. It wasn't difficult to talk to the manager, and here . . .'

'Listen, William,' I interrupted this strange man, who, judging by everything that was happening, was pursuing me quite deliberately. 'Do you have so much free time?'

'I have no time.' Jonson sighed. 'You see, I'm a widower. My wife, a beautiful young woman, died a year and a half ago from a brain tumour. I read in the paper that your husband also lost his life in combat at Sevastopol.'

'Yes, he did.'

'Therefore, I wish to make you a proposal of marriage.'

'You're out of your mind!' I replied bluntly, although I tried to retain the same affable expression on my face.

'Mrs Pavlichenko, I loved you from the moment I saw you at the meeting in Central Park in New York. You are an extraordinary woman and impossible to resist. My heart tells me that you are my only choice.'

'This is not the place for conversations like this.'

'Of course, it's not.' The metallurgical company owner looked happy. 'Tell me where we can meet.'

The reception was coming to a close, and the guests had begun to leave the hall. They were bidding farewell, exchanging some courtesies, and few paid attention to my conversation with William Jonson. Only Eleanor kept her eyes on me. She instantly guessed that I needed help. Looking over the crowd, the First Lady decisively made her way towards us. The millionaire was not pleased at the arrival of the president's wife. He immediately stepped back, bowed and left, without looking back.

Somewhat unnerved, I explained to Mrs Roosevelt what had happened. She promised to make enquiries about Jonson. Other than that, she hastened to introduce me to Colonel Stephen Douglas from the Fort Knox military base and to the chairman of the Chicago Sharpshooters' Association, a Mr MacCormick. They invited me to meet with members of the association at their shooting club the following day. I agreed.

Over the course of our Young Communist League youth delegation's stay in the United States some local journalists had attempted a number of times to verify their hypothesis that the insidious Bolsheviks had sent over not snipers but specially trained propagandists and agitators who had never been at the front. With this in mind, they imposed on the delegates' visits to military units and officers' clubs which kept manual firearms, as well as their visit to a firing range, which involved some target shooting. Therefore I was not in the slightest surprised when I saw an eager young man with a notepad at the Chicago Shooting Association premises and two solidly built gentlemen with cameras.

On the other hand, for me personally it was interesting to view American snipers' weapons, and I was given such an opportunity. First I picked up a Garand M1 self-loading rifle and then a manually operated Springfield M1903. Both were equipped with Weaver telescope sights. As usual I ran my fingers along the breech, barrel and muzzle, and examined the trigger mechanism and the magazine. The Garand was very reminiscent of the SVT-40, operated by diverting propellant gas through a special port in the bore to unlock the breech. The Springfield, with its sliding bolt, was like the Mosin Three Line. Apart from that, the non-automatic safety catch made it similar to the German army Mauser Zf. Kar. 98k, which I also knew well.

The Americans kept a constant watch on what I was doing. The image of a beauty who had just seen a rifle for the first time apparently fell away immediately and they began to smile. With the aid of an interpreter, I explained to the Allies how their weapons resembled or differed from Soviet models. In essence I had to give a short lecture – as if they were new soldiers in my platoon who had arrived at Sevastopol from unoccupied territory. The members of the shooting association listened to me very attentively, and the reporter with the pad quickly lost interest in the meeting because no unmasking or other sensational event occurred.

From the armoury we next set off for the firing range. I will not deny that I was nervous. I had not held a sniper rifle in my hands for a month and a half, whereas a true professional ought to practise at least twice a week. Nor did I have too much faith in the American weapons. But they turned out to be of quite good quality and the firing range was superbly equipped. I enjoyed the target shooting as usual and almost all my bullets hit the bull's eye.

From the firing range the marksmen proceeded in a harmonious, merry band to a hall where refreshments were served for them. On the table were strong alcoholic beverages like gin, whisky and brandy. The association was mainly made up of former soldiers and officers of the US army, many of whom had taken part in the First World War and actually served as snipers. But they did not drink much. A single measure amounted to 40ml. I agreed to drink two toasts with them: to military cooperation and to the opening of a second front. After this, relations became more open and direct. The veterans eagerly shared their memories and I heard some interesting stories about their weapons, camouflage methods, duels with the enemy, and so on.

At the end of the visit a pleasant surprise awaited me. To the sound of loud applause, the chairman of the Chicago association, Mr McCormick, presented me with a gift – a Colt M1911A1 in a mahogany box, which contained various accessories plus two magazines with cartridges. On the lid was a silver disc with an inscription to mark the occasion. Without holding back, I immediately picked up the weapon. The powerful .45-calibre pistol really appealed to me. The inventor of this item was that world-renowned arms engineer of genius, John Moses Browning. The Colt firm had simply concluded a contract with him. The pistol had been adopted by the US army in 1911. It was purchased for Russia by way of Britain during the First World War (and also by a number of other European countries), but I had never seen a Colt in the hands of our own military servicemen.[4]

On returning to the hotel, I dismantled the gift into its component parts in order to become better acquainted with its mechanism. I was distracted from this by Eleanor. The pistol had to be reassembled and put away in its box. In the meantime the First Lady ordered dinner by room service because, like my appearance at the local Grant Park, restaurant visits usually turned into a marathon of autograph signing, which really irritated me.

The dinner was delivered, and Mrs Roosevelt and I sat at the table. She looked at me with a smile. 'I have good news for you, my dear.'

'What is it?'

'William Patrick Jonson really does own a metallurgical company. He really did become a widower a month and a half ago [TN: sic.]. A severe illness suddenly took away his charming young wife.'

'Why is that good for me?'

'You could consider his proposal.'

'Are you serious, Eleanor?'

'Why not, my dear?' The First Lady reached for the salad dish. 'You would be marrying a gentleman of means who is madly in love with you and would guarantee you a happy life to the end of your days. You would remain in our country and we would be able to meet. I am appreciative of this unlikely chance presented to us by the whims of fate.'

'I don't like Mr Jonson.'

'Good Lord!' exclaimed the president's wife. 'You have only seen him three times. You could be mistaken. He is a very nice, pleasant, well-bred man.'

'No, I'm not mistaken!' I got up from the table, took a fresh copy of the city newspaper *Chicago Tribune* and handed it to Eleanor. 'Look at this! "Mrs Pavlichenko is in raptures over American food. At breakfast today she ate five helpings." Blatant lies! Where did they get it from? Did they question the waiters? Or examine the restaurant bill? Why are they obsessed with such nonsense? In your country I feel like the butt of jokes, the object of idle curiosity, something like a circus act. Like a bearded woman. But I'm an officer of the Red Army. I have fought and will go on fighting for the freedom and independence of my country.'

The beginning of my speech was, of course, too emotional, even angry. In my quest for the right words I crossed from English into Russian, and then, realizing, went back to English. I thought Mrs Roosevelt would take offence. But, having put her knife and fork aside, she was observing me with a tender smile. This was probably the way adults treat the antics of hooligan adolescents whom they nevertheless love. Eleanor did not interrupt me and merely nodded her head in agreement. I finished by saying that I was here exclusively on the orders of Comrade Stalin. It was within his power alone to prolong the stay of Junior Lieutenant Pavlichenko in the USA, or return her to the front, to a military unit fighting the German Fascist invaders.

'Everything is OK, my darling.' The wise Eleanor finally managed to insert a phrase in the middle of my disorderly outburst. 'Please, in the meanwhile, forget about Mr Jonson. Tomorrow we will fly to Los Angeles.'

Like all southern cities, Los Angeles, the 'City of Angels', in the state of California, was heavily populated, noisy and diverse. It stood on the shores of the Pacific Ocean, in a valley shielded by mountains on one side. Autumn, which had already come in the US Midwest, was barely noticeable here. In the morning the sun bathed its streets with bright light and by midday it became unbearably hot. In the evening the cool descended on the blocks of skyscrapers and small houses on the outskirts, and all the residents of the City of Angels enjoyed the amazing sight of the sun setting over the boundless ocean.

Of the multitude of obligatory meetings and addresses, I would not single out one that was truly memorable and interesting, except for the trip to the Los Angeles suburb of Beverly Hills. There stood the mansions of successful Hollywood personalities: actors, directors, cinematographers and producers. With no prior warning, the staff of the Soviet consulate took me straight to the home of Charles Spencer Chaplin, and thus I became acquainted with this genius, humanist and great friend of the Soviet Union.

Chaplin opened the door himself and took me into the sitting room, where his friends and colleagues had gathered. I recognized the actor Douglas Fairbanks, who had played the main role in my favourite film, *The Mark of Zorro*, and the slightly aged but still attractive actress Mary Pickford. The remaining guests, apparently no less renowned, looked at me with the same off-hand curiosity characteristic of ordinary mortals.

Offering me a seat on a sofa, Chaplin performed a circus trick: he stood on his hands and made his way over to a basket of winebottles and came back holding a bottle of champagne – in his teeth. The bottle was uncorked, the glasses filled, and, lowering himself to the floor by my feet, the great artist proposed a toast to the speedy opening of a second front in Europe.

The artistic company then moved from the sitting room to a small cinema. Chaplin showed everyone his new film *The Great Dictator*, in which he amusingly parodied Hitler. The screening was followed by supper. Seating me beside him, the great artist and director began to ask me for my views on the film. I said that I liked the film, but nevertheless Fascism at the moment was more fearsome than funny. It was just that the people in Europe and America did not yet know about all the bestial crimes committed by the Nazis.

Charlie Chaplin played a big role in the activity of the charitable society Russian War Relief and helped to collect significant sums for the population of our country, to provide the Red Army with equipment and armaments. Conversation with him was absorbing. He was up to date with events on the Soviet–German front and asked me to give him a detailed account of the defence of Odessa and Sevastopol and also about serving as a sniper. My meeting with him ended in a very unexpected way. Getting down on one knee, Chaplin said that he was ready to kiss every finger on my hand for those 309 Fritzes who remained lying in Russian soil. To my extreme embarrassment, he immediately carried out his intention. Naturally the correspondents were terribly pleased and began clicking their cameras. A photograph appeared in American newspapers with the caption: Charlie Chaplin kneeling before a Russian woman officer and kissing her hand.

On 19 October 1942, the members of the student delegation assembled again within the walls of the USSR embassy in Washington. Litvinov listened to the reports of our travel around the country. He made jokes, smiled and paid compliments. In his words, we had achieved the almost impossible. Public opinion in the USA had gradually shifted in favour of the Soviet Union. The wild inventions of the 'free press' about Soviet people and life in the USSR had collapsed under the impact of meetings with these brave, happy young people, and particularly with the appealing girl clad in a simple tunic.

We sat before the ambassador and listened in silence to his extensive speech. We were waiting for the main news: when and how we would be dispatched back to Moscow. But Litvinov avoided this topic, although he realized, of course, that the delegates to the international student assembly were fed up to the back teeth of life in the public glare. We had had more than enough of American hospitality, American cuisine – which had absolutely nothing in common with traditional food in Russia – and the endless and persistent American interrogations about things that were understood by any teenager in our own country.

Finally, Maxim Maximovich informed us of the latest directive sent to him from the Kremlin: we were to continue the trip, visit Canada and then fly to Great Britain. The mission to Washington was being smoothly converted into a mission to London. We rose and headed for the door in the gloomiest spirits. However, the ambassador had a private question for me, and he asked me to stay behind in his office.

'Did the trip with Eleanor Roosevelt go well?' Litvinov asked.

'Yes, very well.'

'What do you have to say about William Patrick Jonson?'

'How do you know about him?' I could not conceal my amazement.

'Read this.' The ambassador took a thick sheet of paper from his desk and held it out to me. Without doubt this application from Mr Jonson to the embassy of the Soviet Union in the USA looked impressive. Written on embossed paper, witnessed by a notary and registered in his office under a three-digit number, it proclaimed that the owner of the metallurgical company 'Jonson and Sons', a half-million-dollar account in the Bank of America, and other shares in both moveable and fixed assets in the states of Illinois and New York, widower William Patrick Jonson requested the government of the Soviet Union to give permission for his marriage to citizen of the USSR Lyudmila Mikhailovna Pavlichenko and to register this marriage in accordance with the laws operative in the USSR at the present time.

I do not think that Jonson realized what consequences this application to the embassy could have for me. I also presume that somebody (quite probably Eleanor Roosevelt herself) had advised him to apply directly to the government of the

Soviet Union. All this merely testified to the naivety of Americans, their boundless self-confidence and their absurd ideas about the world that lay beyond the bounds of their continent.

I put the application and the Russian translation attached to it on the ambassador's desk and calmly declared: 'Well, he's out of his mind.'

'Are you sure?' asked Litvinov sternly.

'Of course.'

'Then write a reply.'

'What sort? To whom?' I asked in surprise.

'Mr Jonson's letter arrived by post and was registered by the embassy chancellery. We must not only report back on this to the People's Commissariat for Foreign Affairs, but also make an official response to the petitioner, again on an embassy form, and then dispatch it to the address on the envelope. Compose your letter in Russian and our interpreter will translate it.'

'It's hard to think of something straight away. It's all very unexpected.'

'The simplest way –' Litvinov looked at me with great sympathy – 'is to say you have a fiancé, that you have a love of your own awaiting you in Russia.'

In the meantime, the departure of the Soviet delegation for Great Britain kept being deferred. As great fans of bureaucratic casuistry, the English fussed around, whether determining the status of the visit (diplomatic, military or public) or agreeing on the aircraft (a passenger plane or a bomber?) or waiting for suitable weather, which, by the end of October, was becoming changeable.

Mrs Roosevelt was up to date with these preparations. When a date was agreed upon (1 November 1942) she invited us for a last supper at the White House. There, the First Lady presented gifts to each of us. First and foremost was a large photograph of herself in a black evening dress with the president's portrait in the background and a dedication inscribed in the top right corner. Apart from the photograph, we received colourful albums containing pictures of Washington and New York, books and boxes of souvenirs of various kinds and sizes. I was given one additional box. Eleanor said with a smile that some American gentlemen, charmed by my looks, had decided to give me a set of jewellery. It did not occur to anyone to open the boxes right at the table laid for supper. The servants packed them in paper bags and took them out to the car.

It was only when I was back in my room that I looked at the gifts and, out of curiosity, I first opened the box covered with coloured fabric. Inside were diamond items set in gold, quite luxurious things: a necklace, two bracelets, a brooch and a ring. Appended was a docket for $8,000 from a jewellery shop, for all sorts of questions could arise during the customs inspection. Under the necklace I found a small photograph of William Jonson. On the back of it he had written: 'My darling, we will meet again. To Luidmila with great love from W.P. Jonson'.

But I saw no more of Mr Jonson. I took his remarkable gift back to Moscow and put it away. In our capital and in other cities of the world I subsequently had occasion to attend formal receptions and wear beautiful evening dresses, for which these diamond adornments would have been quite suitable. However, I never wore them, nor did I show them to anyone. They remained in my home as a memento of the trip to the USA, of the American gentleman who had cherished a strange, inexplicable feeling in his heart.

My relations with Eleanor Roosevelt developed quite differently. We saw each other again in November 1942, in England. She had flown in for the first international youth congress, where our student delegation was also present. Little time elapsed after the final victory over Fascist Germany before the 'Cold War' began – thanks to that vicious enemy of the Soviet Union, United Kingdom Prime Minister Winston Leonard Spencer-Churchill. Neither US President Franklin Delano Roosevelt, who died in April 1945, nor his wife were complicit in this. Eleanor lost her previous, extremely significant, influence on policy, but, being a person of democratic convictions, continued her wide-ranging public and charity work.

We corresponded, passing on our family news to each other, exchanging views on interesting literary items and discussing trips to international congresses dedicated to the struggle for peace. At my invitation, Mrs Roosevelt visited our country twice: in 1957 and 1958. We spent a lot of time in Moscow and travelled together to Leningrad, where we went to theatres and visited the Hermitage and Russian Museum, Peterhof, Gatchina and Tsarskoye Selo. Eleanor coordinated arrangements for a return visit by me to the USA, but the State Department (evidently recalling my fiery speeches at meetings in 1942) did not give permission. Here is one of Mrs Roosevelt's letters:

4 November 1957.

My dear Luidmila,

I was very glad to get your letter and I want to thank you warmly for the photographs. It was good of you to send me the photographs and I am happy to have them as a souvenir of our most pleasant reunion in Moscow.

Since my return I have spoken often of your warm welcome and the kindness you showed me. Trude and Joey Lash[5] were delighted to hear we had met and they join me in sending you many warm messages.

I hope you will be able to visit us here soon again.

With deep appreciation and my good wishes.

Very cordially yours, Eleanor Roosevelt.[6]

17

Island in the Ocean

From the USA our Soviet student delegation was taken to Canada, to the city of Montreal. We were not there for long. We had to go to the British air force base in Halifax. It was from there, in the evening of 3 November 1942, that we set off on our route across the Atlantic in a four-engine Boeing B-17 'Flying Fortress' bomber.[1] However, we did not get to see the ocean's blue expanses, because we were sitting on benches in the plane's bomb-bay.

Ten hours later, in the morning of 4 November, it safely touched down at another air base in the British Isles, not far from the city of Glasgow, Scotland. The airmen helped us out of the military aircraft. We strode along the concrete landing strip to a two-storey administrative building, over which fluttered the flag of the United Kingdom, sometimes called the 'Union Jack' – a dark-blue background with two crosses, red and white, superimposed one upon the other.

In the vestibule a pleasant fair-haired young woman of short stature and slim build emerged to greet us. She smiled cordially, shook our hands, introduced herself as Helen Chivers, and began speaking rapidly in English. We more or less understood her first sentences. Helen was a teacher, head of some youth organization and had come to Glasgow from London specially to greet us. But the rest was incomprehensible.[2]

Helen spoke the purest British English and, after two months in the USA, we had got used to American speech. It is, after all, a little different. Making use of my own modest knowledge, I explained this to our new acquaintance. She blushed in embarrassment and then started again, this time slowly, separating her words and using short, simple sentences. Immediately everything went well.

We spent two days in Glasgow. The weather was suitable for walking. It was quite warm and sunny. Mrs Chivers eagerly accepted the role of guide. From her we learned about the history of the city, which was founded in the sixth century and was now a major industrial centre. We also viewed its sights, in particular, the Cathedral of St Mungo and the Talbot clock tower, which were built in the Middle Ages.

However, we were much more interested in the modern day. Helen told us that the initiator of our invitation to Britain was the national council of students and its president, Mrs Margaret Gale. Therefore, it was envisaged that we would take part in an international youth congress which would be held in London from 24 to 25 November.

We had already attended a congress like this in Washington and had some idea as to how such a function would be organized. We knew how to behave, what to say, what to propose and argue for in discussion. We had come to campaign for the opening of a second front in Europe and to talk about the heroic struggle of the Soviet people against the Nazi German invasion. The ordinary people in US cities had fervently supported us. But the powers-that-be had adopted a cautious attitude and promised nothing. We would see how the British greeted us.

The train from Glasgow arrived in London in the early morning. The station was poorly illuminated. Helen explained that it was because of the black-out against German air attacks. We stepped onto the platform and inhaled the cool, damp air. Everything around was swimming in a thick fog through which the figures of passers-by seemed like phantoms.

We were greeted by activists from the National Students' Union, a cheery bunch of lads and lasses. We got into a car with them and went to the Royal Hotel, in central London. One could only marvel at the mastery of our driver. He deftly manoeuvred his way through the all-enveloping milky veil, avoiding collisions with the vehicles which would suddenly appear out of the fog. In other words, our great poet Alexander Pushkin was correct when he called this island in the ocean 'foggy Albion'.[3] It really was very misty.

At the hotel Vladimir Pchelintsev and Nikolai Krasavchenko were put up in a spacious three-room 'de-luxe' suite. I was given a more modest but comfortable one-room abode, with mirrors and easy chairs. We now had to get ourselves ready and change into our military uniforms. Awaiting us in the hotel's lobby were civil servants from the British Ministry of Information, leading officials of the National Students' Union, journalists and Soviet embassy staff.

Our first visit in London was to the Ministry of Information. We approached its massive building and were amazed. Standing stock-still on the asphalt square in front of us was a file of armed soldiers in parade uniforms. As we approached, a military band struck up the 'Hymn of the Soviet Union', the state flag of our country rose up the flagstaff and the soldiers presented arms. It looked terrific!

In carefree, totally 'civilian' America nobody had come up with this idea. But the British are devoted to their age-old traditions. They know all about grand ceremonies. The Red Army was now an ally of the armed forces of His Majesty George VI in a war against Hitler's Germany. Officers of Allied forces were to be greeted in a specific way, and the appropriate ettiquette was fulfilled to the letter.

After brief speeches had been exchanged, Pchelintsev and I were given the opportunity to 'inspect' the troops. The soldiers responded to our questions with a smile. At the request of photographers, I took a corporal's Lee-Enfield No. 4 Mark I rifle, which was very similar in construction to our own Mosin model. The reporters were delighted and flashbulbs popped. This photo appeared the following day in one of the English papers (maybe *The Times* or the *Daily Mail*, I don't remember precisely; all I have is an article with the heading 'Lieutenant Lyudmila inspects the Home Guard').

A meeting with the press now awaited us in the Ministry of Information conference hall. Our experience with the American press would not be in vain. We were on our guard and prepared ourselves to answer the most unexpected, strange and, at times, simply idiotic, questions.

The press conference began in the usual way and continued for around three hours. As for idiotic questions – there were none. We looked out in amazement at the auditorium. Sitting there were earnest gentlemen in jackets, shirts and ties, and ladies in formal English costumes. They held notepads and pens and spoke calmly and in turn, with no commotion. One felt that they had come to the press conference armed with some knowledge about the course of the military action at Leningrad, Odessa and Sevastopol, where Pchelintsev and I had taken part. I cannot deny that this commanded respect. Apart from that, they asked us about the continuing battle for Stalingrad, the operations of our defence industries and new models of Soviet tanks, ordnance and aircraft.

There was also a question about the atrocities committed by the German invaders on the territory they had seized and a request for clarification: was this true? 'It's true!' Nikolai Krasavchenko replied sharply and said that he was confident that sooner or later the war criminals would answer for their deeds before an international tribunal.

We liked the way the staff of the British newspapers, magazines and radio stations conducted themselves. We discussed it when we were travelling to our embassy after the press conference. We found the explanation was quite simple. In contrast to the Americans, the British already knew what modern warfare and German Fascism were like. They had encountered the Fritzes on the battlefield. Military action had gone particularly badly for them at Dunkirk in the summer of 1940. They had suffered defeat along with their French allies.

This topic was continued in conversation with the Soviet ambassador to Great Britain, Ivan Mikhailovich Maisky. An experienced diplomat with a superb command of English and a profound knowledge of the history and culture of 'misty Albion', he had already held this position for ten years. He was very familiar with the customs and manners of the local people.

Ivan Mikhailovich gave us a whole lecture on the events of the last two years. Dunkirk had been followed by the Battle of Britain – a major air engagement involving hundreds of aircraft, both British and German. The Nazis wanted to destroy the air force of the United Kingdom and made bombing raids on its cities, industrial centres and military sites. For instance, there were mass-scale strikes on London, Belfast, Portsmouth and Coventry, which was almost razed to the ground. But Hitler did not succeed in crushing the will of the British people to resist and he cancelled Operation Sea Lion, the invasion of the British Isles.

'Do not be surprised at the determination of the British,' Maisky told us. 'Although, of course, the Nazis are not up to mounting major military action in the Atlantic area. They are seriously bogged down at Stalingrad.'

'So, the Russians are sheltering good old England?' asked Krasavchenko jokingly.

'Well, there are still some Luftwaffe forces on the shores of the English Channel,' Maisky replied. 'In April this year they bombed Bath and Exeter. And quite recently, in October, they attacked Canterbury. According to the local press, there were about thirty enemy aircraft involved.'

'It would be nice to show our support for the Allies,' I said.

'You have a trip planned there.' Ivan Mikhailovich looked at me with a smile. 'And I have a programme drawn up for your whole stay. It's quite a tight schedule. For instance, tomorrow, 7 November, you have to be at Empress Hall in the morning for a meeting of progressive elements of the British community devoted to the twenty-fifth anniversary of the Great October Socialist Revolution and, in the evening, there will be a formal reception here at the embassy to mark the same occasion.'

It was an excellent asphalt road from London to the south-eastern part of the island and the county of Kent, which is also known as the 'garden of England' and this name is completely justified. The autumn sun lit up well-cared-for fields on either side of the road, apple orchards, meadows and copses. Now and then we caught sight of attractive small homesteads, the grey towers of castles and fortress walls beside them, villages of stone houses and, nearby, tidy country churches, which looked like toys from a distance.

We left the capital of the British Empire in the early morning of 8 November, in a convoy of two cars. One was provided by the Ministry of Information and carried its staff. These people were dressed in military uniform: Captain John Harker, forty years of age and amiable and smiling, and Lieutenant Robert Smith, a lean young man with quite a stern look about him. They had two cine-cameras, some lights, and cases containing some kind of equipment. Captain Harker explained to us that he had been charged with filming all our meetings with the residents of Kent and then making a full-length film about the tour of the Soviet student delegation around Britain. He asked for our help in this and we of course immediately agreed.

The second car belonged to our embassy. Embassy staff member Sergei Krainsky was to accompany us everywhere and act as interpreter. We were delighted at this. Sergei had already spent three years in the United Kingdom. He had a good knowledge not only of the language, but of the rules governing life here.

First, we called at Birkbeck College, where classes were in progress even on a Sunday. The young people greeted us cordially. We told them about events on the Soviet–German front and answered various questions. However, our programme was timed down to the hour, so then we hit the road again.

The cars turned off towards the fortifications of the southern defensive sector. We were to visit a tank brigade which would take part in the landing on the European continent with the opening of the second front. When that would happen was still unknown, but we were given a ceremonial welcome, with a guard of honour, a band, a short meeting, and a pleasant conversation with the major-general in charge of the brigade.

He had a typically English appearance: tall and lean, with reddish hair and blue eyes. His trench coat and breeches were ironed in exemplary fashion, but on his feet he wore boots with puttees, at which we were very surprised. In the Red Army military commanders of this rank did not wear puttees, but full-length black calfskin boots, often with a lacquer finish.

The general shook our hands with a smile and told us about his brigade. We learned that it consisted of three tank battalions, each comprised of around fifty-two tanks and other military hardware, and there were about 600 personnel in a battalion. The tanks were of two designs: Churchill Mark III and Churchill Mark IV. He then invited us to go to the training ground and view the instruction process in one of the battalions. We viewed it from on high, having ensconced ourselves in the turret of a Churchill Mark IV tank.[4]

At the defence of Odessa from August to October 1941 I had seen no Soviet tanks. However, I had had a good look at the Czech LTvz.35s, under cover of which the Romanians attacked our regimental positions. Our soldiers would toss Molotov cocktails at them, and they burnt quite well. At the defence of Sevastopol we had our own T-26 and BT-7 light tanks. On occasion they helped the infantry to repel the Nazi attacks.

Compared to them the Churchill Mark IV seemed a real Goliath! It was about 7.5 metres long, over 3 metres wide, and weighed 40 tonnes; its frontal armour was 101–192 mm thick, its weaponry comprised a cannon, three machine guns and a mortar gun, and it had a crew of five.[5]

Lined up beside their tank, the crew formally saluted us. We approached the brave lads, shook their hands and expressed our sincere admiration for such powerful products from the British military industry. They really liked what we had to say. It turned out they were incredibly fond of their mechanical monster because it was quite spacious inside, the armour plating was reliable, and most German weapons would be unable to penetrate it. To give us the complete picture, they even allowed us to sit in the seats of the driver/mechanic and the machine-gunner in the front of the vehicle, opening the double-lidded hatches right and left, and then helped us up to the turret.

The instruction was of a high technical standard. The tank crew showed us how they advanced in columns, spread their ranks for attack, negotiated ditches, ridges and water obstacles, and fired the cannons and machine guns. The dust on the training ground rose in a column, the engines of the armoured vehicles roared, and the caterpillar tracks rattled. The only thing that slightly surprised us was their speed: they did not exceed 25kph.

After the training session, the officers of the battalion invited us to dinner. A decent quantity of good wine was drunk to victory over our common enemy and to comradeship in arms.

'I hope we will meet on the battlefields of Europe when we rout the Nazi forces together,' I said on bidding farewell to the tank crews.

'Yes, of course,' replied the general. But there was something joyless about his smile.

Our journey through the wonderful county of Kent continued. The weather was excellent, warm and sunny. The roads were in the very best condition and the distances between villages were not great. Within half an hour both cars were facing the checkpoint of the 70th Infantry Regiment.[6]

Vladimir Pchelintsev and I both belonged to this glorious military class – the infantry. Therefore, we were greeted by the regiment in a simple, comradely fashion and then immediately invited to go to the firing range to demonstrate the standard of sniper training in the Red Army.

For us this was nothing new. In some parts of the USA efforts had also been made to test our shooting skills and to confirm – if possible, of course – the wild inventions of the 'free press' that we were not front-line soldiers, but merely agents of Communist propaganda. It sometimes happened that the weapons they gave us had some minor flaws. Our hospitable hosts would observe us closely and show obvious disappointment when we fairly quickly discovered these problems, eliminated them and opened accurate fire on the targets. The recurrence of this scenario forced us to adopt some protective measures. As the more senior in rank, Vladimir would inspect the weapon first and make two or three shots – 'testing the barrel', as snipers put it. In the meantime, I would relate some light-hearted tale to a crowd of reporters and cameramen. Then he would hand the rifle or submachine gun to me with a brief comment about it. Behind me the entire company were following me with particular eagerness, and why not – a woman with a firearm! So, I had to operate faultlessly and spectacularly.

The infantry regiment's firing range was quite ordinary in appearance: a solid brick wall and, on it, wooden boards bearing targets; the distance from there to the firing line was around 50 metres. I was handed a British Sten Mark I submachine gun, very similar to the German Erma-made MP. 38, which those of us in the army called a 'Schmeisser'. Both Vladimir and I were familiar with it. They had become frequent trophies following clashes with Nazi machine-gunners, sappers and signallers. But the British model looked a lot cruder, and its 32-cartridge box magazine was situated not under the barrel but on the left side.

Pchelintsev examined the weapon, switched it to single-shot firing, went up to the firing line and took several shots at the targets. He informed me that the submachine gun was in perfect order. I once again switched the Sten to automatic mode and then fired three short bursts. All the bullets reached their target and the photographers were satisfied. They then spent a long time photographing me, Vladimir and the British infantrymen cheerfully chatting with us by the bullet-holed boards.

As a souvenir of our excellent shooting from a British submachine gun, the 70th Infantry Regiment formally presented Vladimir and me with special metal badges and certificates making us honorary officers of their unit.[7]

The day, so rich in experiences, ended with a visit to the Bernhard Baron Settlement. There was a boarding school there for the children of those serving in the army of the United Kingdom.[8] The cadets, boys and girls aged from 10 to 15, surrounded our cars in a dense throng, and then out came the warden, Basil Henriques and his wife Rose. They showed us round the institution. The senior cadets demonstrated their mastery of shooting and unarmed combat, while the younger ones performed dances and folk songs. Supper was followed by a session of their young people's debating club, in which our student delegation also took part.

Canterbury is a small town situated in the south-east of Kent, 25km from the coast. It is one of Britain's most ancient towns. The Roman Emperor Claudius founded it in AD 43 on the site of a former Celtic settlement. In the sixth century it was the residence of King Ethelbert of Kent. It was then that a bishopric and abbey were established. Since then the town has been the residence of the archbishop of Canterbury, head of the Catholic and then, from the Act of Supremacy of 1534, of the Anglican Church. Canterbury Cathedral, built between the twelfth and fifteenth centuries, was a majestic and beautiful edifice, but now it was badly damaged.

'Why?' I asked, interrupting the interesting commentary from Sergei Krainsky, our escort from the embassy.

'It was bombed by the Germans,' he replied. 'They made several strikes on the town.'

'Is there some military site here?'

'No. Just light industry. The Nazis most likely wanted to intimidate the English by wiping out the symbols of their history.'

Our car stopped by Canterbury town hall. In the reception hall we were greeted by the mayor, Mr Frederick Lefevre, in his traditional costume: a long, colourful velvet gown with a massive gold chain on his chest. He was accompanied by his wife, who wore a similar symbol, but rather more modest. After exchanging greetings, we set off together with the mayor to view the town.

Its appearance brought back sad memories. We walked along a street which had been turned into a narrow pathway between the ruins of houses. The ancient English two-storey houses in the Tudor style, wooden framing filled with bricks, stones, clay and even straw, were easily destroyed. It was how Sevastopol, the city which had become so dear to me, had looked in June of that year, when the Nazis launched their third assault on it. With daily artillery attacks and bombing raids, they practically razed it to the ground. With an aching heart, I now viewed such scenes in a town far from my native land and reflected that the war unleashed by Germany had inflicted too many woes on all Europeans.

Soon the celebrated Canterbury Cathedral was standing before us. Almost the entire interior of the church was piled with rubble and there were gaping holes in the walls. But many of the magnificent medieval stained-glass windows had survived. Along a long, narrow aisle leading to the altar, a man of lean build with a crown of grey hair, and dressed in a black cassock, came out to meet us. It was Hewlett Johnson, dean of Canterbury, the so-called 'Red Dean'.

That was what Sergei Krainsky had called him, when he told us about Canterbury and its residents. The Reverend Johnson was a graduate of Oxford University and had served the Church since 1904. He had greeted the news of the Great October Socialist Revolution with enthusiasm, consistently campaigned for the establishment of diplomatic relations between the USSR and Great Britain, and had written several interesting books about our country. At the present time he was chairman of the Joint Committee for Soviet Aid.

The dean took us on an excursion around the church, showing us its special features, explaining the significance of the various sculptures and images, and mentioning the names of the saints, clergy and statesmen connected with Canterbury Cathedral. In subsequent conversation the Red Dean devoted more attention to me than to Krasavchenko and Pchelintsev. Judging by his behaviour, it was difficult for him to understand how a woman could take up a weapon and go off to war – that is, adopt a traditionally male occupation. He expressed himself in quite a flowery manner.

'But surely, my dear lady, you must feel oppressed by the burden of the enemies you have felled?'

'No, not at all,' I replied. 'Enemies are always enemies. It is in the nature of women not only to create new life, but also, if necessary, to defend their children, their family, their homeland. Our state has given me that opportunity.'

'Yes, yes, you are right!' The clergyman immediately retreated. 'I know, Russia is a special country. Your people always fight to a victorious conclusion. I admire your personal courage. A military uniform suits you just as well as an ordinary woman's dress. But I hope, after the war, to see you here in different, peacetime, garb.

'Of course! The war will end sometime.'

'That time will come,' said the dean encouragingly. 'The walls here will be built anew; the internal fittings will be restored. The church will be filled with parishioners. We will pray that there will be no more wars, that women shall never don military uniform, but rear their children. The Church would prefer to see woman as a Madonna with an infant in her arms, as in Raphael's canvases, rather than with a machine gun.'

'I completely agree with you,' I said. 'But before that time can come, we must first crush Fascism. That's why I am in a military uniform. We will start to rear children when peace comes to the entire world.'

The dean escorted us to our car and, in farewell, made the sign of the cross over us. As we drove away, he stood watching us for a long time. I remember his black-clad figure against the background of the huge and magnificent building which had been spared by the ages, but not by modern-day barbarians.

The final destination in our journey through Kent was Dover, a major port, industrial centre and Royal Navy base. Since the beginning of the war it had been a frontier town. The Germans had repeatedly shelled it, using large-calibre guns sited in northern France, only a few miles away on the other side of the English Channel, and subjected it to mass-scale bombing strikes. We were able to drive freely into Dover only because we had a special pass.

At last I saw the sea which surrounds this island nation. Under the rays of an autumn sun it kept changing colour – from sky-blue to aquamarine to azure. Our British hosts showed us how the picturesque shores of southern England had been turned into a fortified district with all its stark details: minefields, strands of barbed wire, winding trench lines, dugouts, machine-gun points and well-equipped artillery positions. The British had rigorously prepared for an enemy invasion of their land. Fortunately, it did not occur.

Upon our return to London we visited Maisky and presented him with a report on our trip. Our impressions were totally positive. We were now waiting for Ivan Mikhailovich to pronounce the long-desired words: 'You will depart for Moscow tomorrow . . . the day after tomorrow . . . in two days' time . . .' Alas, these words were not forthcoming. Instead of this declaration the ambassador gave us a pensive look and said: 'My Young Communist League comrades, the British winter is not far off. It is not as severe as in Russia, but there are occasional snowfalls. You need winter coats.'

'Where will we get them?' asked Pchelintsev in surprise.

'We'll have them sewn to order. Tomorrow various types of fabric will be brought to your hotel. Choose the material that best suits.'

This turned out to be no simple matter. The durable, thick, rather coarse, unteased cloth which serves for army overcoats in our own country was not produced here. We had to settle for ordinary coat fabric, which was very similar in colour and texture. Even greater difficulties arose with regard to the accessories: the brass buttons with stars on, the raspberry-coloured tabs, the lieutenants' metal 'cubes' of red enamel, the chevrons of gold galloon. The embassy ordered them one by one from a private workshop. The winter coats turned out to be not bad at all, and we appreciated the care Ivan Mikhailovich had taken when, on yet another trip, we found ourselves exposed to rain with a penetrating cold wind and hail.

We were now headed north-eastward, to Cambridge, a city 70km from London on the banks of the river Cam. We had been invited to a meeting by the students of Cambridge University, one of the oldest in England. Our visit began at Trinity College. As we drew close to the great gates, we saw in a niche over the gateway a statue of King Henry VIII, the founder of the college in 1546. Many illustrious people had graduated from it, including the present king of the British Empire, George VI, as well as students such as Isaac Newton, Francis Bacon and even Lord Byron, the poet.

Trinity College comprises several buildings, mainly three-storeyed and built three or four centuries ago. There is a vast courtyard with a carefully trimmed green lawn and a beautiful fountain in the centre. But what we liked best were the comfortable, thoroughly modern, lecture halls, the superbly equipped laboratories, the Fitzwilliam Museum with its huge collection of objets d'art and the Wren Library, which housed more than a thousand priceless medieval manuscripts and the first book to be printed in England by William Caxton.

In the evening of 11 November the students assembled for the meeting. It proved to be noisy and lively. We heard many kind words with regard to the Soviet Union. The president of the London branch of the students' union, Mrs Joy Reid, called it a historic meeting. Ernest Benians, master of St John's College, said that in our guise he was greeting the heroic Red Army. The chairman of the council of graduate courses for Cambridge University, Richard Taylor, told us a fair number of interesting things about student life and learning. In particular, we learned to our surprise that many Cambridge students were working a night shift at military factories, and that was their contribution to the common struggle against Nazism.

Our presentation was structured in the usual way: Krasavchenko spoke about the partisan movement in the rear of the Nazi forces, Pchelintsev about the sniper's profession, and I myself about the defence of Odessa and Sevastopol. In concluding my brief speech, I also mentioned Canterbury, comparing this battered English town with Sevastopol, which had been bombed by the Fritzes just as mercilessly.

The audience asked us numerous questions. I would describe their reaction as one of anxiety. It was apparent that they were familiar with events on the Soviet–German front and sincerely wished us victory over the enemy.

We returned to London in the afternoon of 12 November. Twilight was already descending on the capital. Counting on being able to relax in the hotel in the evening after an arduous two-day trip, we ordered supper in the de-luxe suite. But an hour later a car from the embassy arrived for us. It turned out that we were expected at a meeting organized by the society for friendship between British and Soviet youth. None of us was intending to speak; we were too tired. However, the atmosphere of the meeting, which was attended by about 300 people, was so cordial and emotional that we could not fail to respond. True, only Vladimir Pchelintsev spoke. The resolution adopted at this meeting was a highly pragmatic one: the youth organizations of Great Britain resolved to collect 25,000 parcels as gifts to the soldiers of the Red Army.

Londoners had had more than enough fear to cope with in the autumn of 1940, when Hitler's air force was bombing the city. They had spent nights in underground stations and days sorting through piles of rubble and destruction. It was gratifying to see that by the end of 1942 concerted efforts had been made to restore the appearance of the city. We saw that for ourselves when we went for a stroll on the morning of 13 November.

My favourite area was Piccadilly in the centre of London, in Westminster. I would walk around there, viewing the luxury shops (for instance Fortnum and Mason) with curiosity, the magnificent buildings (the Ritz Hotel, the Criterion Theatre, St James's Church) and the monument featuring the statue of Eros in Piccadilly Circus. The street led to the well-laid-out and still-green Hyde Park, where one could encounter ladies and gentlemen horse-riding along the paths.

It was not for nothing that Ivan Mikhailovich had allotted us time for relaxation. The Soviet student delegation needed to see the England of ordinary people, not from a car window, but up close, side by side with them. The ambassador also advised us to gather our thoughts and recall our responsible mission. There was a weighty reason. Among those desirous of meeting with us were none other than the prime minister of Great Britain, Sir Winston Churchill, and his wife Clementine.

On hearing this, we were at first bewildered. What had Soviet newspapers not written about Mr Churchill during the pre-war years! He was referred to as an inveterate enemy of the socialist order and the young workers and peasants' state. It was pointed out that he was the organizer of the intervention by British, French and US forces in our country during the years 1918–21. He was blamed for the so-called Munich Agreement with Hitler and Mussolini in 1938 (although it was not Churchill at all who signed it).

Seeing the look of surprise on our faces, Maisky merely laughed. 'My Young Communist League comrades, such is today's reality! Of late Winston Churchill has shown himself to be a far-sighted, wise politician. He immediately realized what danger Germany's attack on the Soviet Union presented for the entire world. As early as June 1941 Churchill's government concluded an agreement for joint action against Hitler with the USSR. And quite recently, in May of this year, an Anglo-Soviet treaty of alliance against Nazi Germany and post-war cooperation and mutual assistance was signed in London.'

The meeting with the prime minister took place at the Houses of Parliament. Efficient servants bowed as they opened the doors for us. We entered a small square hall with an enormous fireplace adorned with white marble. In the centre of the hall was a table and, around it, some easy chairs. Heading towards us from the fireplace was a man of rather short stature, very solid build, broad shoulders and a massive round head. He had a cigar in his mouth. His grey and slightly bulging eyes viewed us attentively. I would describe his glance as penetrating.

'Allow me, Mr Prime Minister, to introduce some guests of Great Britain, three young people from the Soviet Union,' said Maisky.

Churchill removed the cigar from his mouth, took a step towards me and offered his hand. It was broad and soft, but strong. The prime minister said with a slight smile: 'Madam Pavlichenko, how do you like Britain? Are our fogs getting you down?'

'No, the fogs do not bother us,' I replied. 'We are happy to visit a wartime ally. Fog is good camouflage. There is probably less trouble from enemy aircraft.'

Churchill then spoke with the head of our group, Nikolai Krasavchenko, and even asked in jest whether it was easy for him to have such a nice girl as Lieutenant Pavlichenko under his command. After this, Maisky introduced Vladimir Pchelintsev. At this point we were slightly surprised because the prime minister showed some knowledge of the system of decorations in our country. Viewing the golden star of Hero of the Soviet Union on Vladimir's chest, he asked for what feats he had been given this supreme award. Pchelintsev replied that it was for combat in defence of Leningrad, for the 100 Nazis he had wiped out there.

The chat continued for about twenty minutes. Then Churchill invited us to the fireside, where a weak flame was burning, and offered us a seat. A beautiful slim woman of about fifty-five, elegantly and meticulously dressed, appeared in the hall. Maisky immediately introduced her to us: 'Mrs Clementine Ogilvy Spencer-Churchill.' The prime minister's wife shook our hands with a smile and listened as the Soviet ambassador described each of us. We all sat down in the armchairs by the table. A side door opened and a servant wheeled in a table arranged for coffee, with a coffee pot, a milk jug, cups, and plates of sandwiches and biscuits.

Winston Churchill lit his cigar. He had sat down beside Ivan Mikhailovich and they continued a serious conversation about the future of the Anglo-Soviet treaty of alliance concluded in May. Our attention was occupied by Mrs Churchill. She talked enthusiastically about the activities of the British Red Cross Aid to Russia Fund which she had founded in September 1941. Clementine had made the first donation to it and then millions of British subscribers had joined in. They responded to her call and began to contribute a penny a week to the fund from their wages. The fund also organized charity events – in particular, football matches – proceeds from which went into its account. The fund did not have excessive means at its disposal, but it was able to acquire and send to our country medicines, hospital equipment, foodstuffs, clothing, blankets and even artificial limbs for invalids.

The prime minister's wife was interested in the way medical services were organized in the Red Army, and what assistance its soldiers and officers received on the battlefield and afterwards. I undertook to answer her on the basis of my own experience. When I was wounded at Odessa, I was given first aid by an orderly from the regimental medical company and then ended up in the divisional medical battalion, where a surgeon performed an operation to remove a piece of shrapnel. In the event of complications, I would have been dispatched to an army field hospital and then, if necessary, to a hospital in the rear for a full operation.

Mrs Churchill thought it was a very rational system. She asked me various questions in an effort to clarify details to do with the use of medicines, medical technology and care for the wounded. I willingly answered her. Our conversation became very animated. Pchelintsev and Krasavchenko did not contribute, as they had never been in a hospital.

The chimes of Big Ben sounded and our amiable hosts rose and gave us to understand that the audience was over. On parting we once again exchanged handshakes and friendly smiles. Clementine thanked me for my information, which would help her to define the directions of her work for the Aid to Russia Fund more precisely.

Incidentally, during its existence between 1941 and 1951 Clementine Churchill's fund collected more than £8 million[9] and equipped several hospitals in Stalingrad and Rostov-on-Don. In the spring of 1945 the prime minister's wife visited Russia. In acknowledgement of her significant contribution to assisting the Red Army, Stalin rewarded Clementine in the Kremlin with a gift of his own – a gold ring with diamonds, while the government of our country awarded her the Order of the Red Banner of Labour.

I could not help making comparisons between Clementine and Eleanor Roosevelt. They had a lot in common: age, education, social position and family situation. They both took an active part in public life. However, Eleanor was more straightforward in her bearing, more democratic, and she acted rather more in the role of a political functionary. She ran all her husband's election campaigns, travelled the country, checking upon the fulfilment of his commissions and reporting on them to the president, and attended cabinet sessions. Clementine still tended to remain a privileged lady from English high society. She was not attracted by essentially male pursuits. She confined her obligations to charity work, but was brilliantly successful at it.

Our travels through the island continued: Cardiff, Birmingham, Newcastle, Liverpool, Coventry – instrument-making, metallurgical and arms factories, shipyards (we attended the launch of a new warship), educational institutes and military units. Everywhere we were greeted cordially and often given presents such as ceremonial versions of sniper rifles.

The British became particularly enthusiastic at the end of November, with the news of the Soviet advance at Stalingrad, and then the encirclement of Field Marshal Paulus's army and the surrender of thousands and thousands of German soldiers. Our allies realized that this was a turning point in the Second World War, and that Hitler's Germany would not recover from a defeat like this. But now our thoughts were constantly on returning home.

18

'Comrade Stalin Has Ordered Us . . .'

In the evening twilight the four-engine Liberator B-24 bomber was like a huge fish hauled up onto the shore. Its fat belly seemed to be lying on the ground. It gave that impression on account of its triple undercarriage with struts that were too short. One was situated under the fuselage at the front and the other two under the wings, which were over 33 metres in wingspan. In spite of this, the glazed nose with its machine-gun barrels gave the plane a menacing appearance. There were machine guns on top as well, right behind the pilot's and navigator's cockpit.

The bomber was not preparing for a military flight this time. On the trolley that the aircraft mechanics wheeled up to the multi-tonne winged colossus lay not bombs, but suitcases, boxes and baskets. They were our belongings, mainly gifts from the Allies. No question, the amount had more than doubled. The soldiers deftly tossed the things into an open bomb hatch, and then the doors closed.

Dressed like aviators in fur flying suits, gloves, high fur boots and flying headgear, the members of the Soviet student delegation climbed up the aluminium gangway into the plane with the crew, but we were accommodated in the cargo section adjoining the combat compartment rather than in the cabin. No passenger comforts had been provided there. Instead of seats there were quite hard, narrow benches along the sides. They were uncomfortable to sit on and difficult to lie on. There were no portholes, only a few electric bulbs on the ceiling emitting a weak light.

We were faced with spending the next twelve hours over the night of 4–5 January 1943 in these gloomy, unheated premises. That was the time the Liberator usually took to fly from a British Royal Air Force air base near Glasgow to Vnukovo airport near Moscow. The bombers had been flying this route since October 1942. It went from the north of Scotland over the North Sea, the Skagerrak, the western part of Sweden, and the Baltic Sea with no touch-downs in between. The section over the front zone between Leningrad and Moscow presented a certain danger. However, the bomber flew at night, at a height of over 9,000 metres and at a speed of 300kph. The German fighters could not get up that high. This heavy craft, put together by designers from the American firm Consolidated before the Second World War and boasting a range of 4,560 km, had turned out to be a very successful and useful vehicle.

The crew started up the engines, one after another. Finally, all four engines were roaring. The aircraft shuddered and taxied forward. Its pace quickened and the engines became louder and louder. A fairly lengthy charge along the runway ended with a powerful jerk upwards. The Liberator rose over the aerodrome, gaining height, circled and set out on the course plotted by the navigator. Now we could hear only the even hum of the engines.

But the engine sound made it impossible to talk. We somehow managed to spread ourselves out on the benches, Krasavchenko and Pchelintsev on the right-hand side and me on the left. Gradually crystals of frost appeared on all the metallic parts of the fuselage plating. They grew hour by hour, turning the space into something resembling the Snow Queen's bedroom. The cold constricted our breathing. But the fur flying suits with special underwear, including an electrical element, preserved the heat – except that one's skin tingled slightly from the weak electrical current in the copper grid sewn into the undershirt and long johns.

Members of the bomber's crew would often come down the gangway from their cabin and ask how we were feeling. In the four months they had spent in the USA, Canada and Great Britain, Nikolai Krasavchenko and Vladimir Pchelintsev had picked up a couple of hundred everyday English words and were able to respond quite reasonably. With the dictionary and textbook I had advanced a lot further in my study of the language and spoke it fluently. On our last trips to British military units, where we viewed artillery ordnance, or aeroplanes, or ships, I had even dared to make short speeches, which the Allies liked very much.

Now we were returning to our homeland and, of course, thinking about the war. For me and for Pchelintsev the question was clear: what front, army, division and regiment would we now be sent to? At first we supposed that we would be off to Stalingrad. The American and British newspapers were writing about the feats of sniper Vasily Zaitsev, who had wiped out 225 Nazis in three months. However, by the end of December 1942 the Soviet forces had encircled the German 6th Army and routed the Romanian and Italian divisions which were besieging the fortress on the Volga, along with Hitler's troops. At Stalingrad events had moved towards a conclusion – the complete victory of the Red Army over the enemy.

However, the siege of Leningrad continued. Vladimir Pchelintsev, who had served on the Leningrad front since the first days of the war, told me a lot about it. The Fritzes' advance there had been brought to a halt in November 1941, but we did not have enough forces to drive the enemy back from the cradle of the Great October Socialist Revolution immediately. A positional war had begun, and big losses had to be inflicted on the enemy with meagre resources. Pchelintsev maintained that it was here, on the marshy plains of the Neva, Svir and Volkhov rivers, that the mass-scale development of sniping had begun, and that he was one of its pioneers, for which he had received the title Hero of the Soviet Union.

The aircraft's mechanic, Robert Brown, came down to see us from the cockpit. He brought a thermos flask of hot coffee, cups and a plate piled with cheese and ham sandwiches. He shared them out and informed us that Moscow was an hour and a half away; a radio message had been sent to Vnukovo and the plane would be met by our relatives.

And there it was – a huge snow-covered Russian field! It stretched as far as a ragged belt of forest looming blue in the distance. To the left were some buildings and from there people were running towards the bomber, which had stopped at the very edge of the runway. I could see Rita, Pchelintsev's wife, and my dear mother, Yelena Trofimovna. We embraced, kissed each other three times, and stood for a long time in a hug. Mother was weeping and saying: 'Thank God, thank God, my darling! Went away for a month and came back after four.'

The room in the family hostel of the People's Commissariat of Defence became crowded in no time. The suitcases had to be moved against the only free wall and things gradually taken out of them. The large and cumbersome raccoon-fur coat could at least be put away in a closet. On a nail banged into the closet I hung the smooth-bore Winchester M1897 trench gun given to me by workers at a Canadian arms factory in Toronto. The food from British officers' field rations, with which we had been provided at the military base in Glasgow, looked appetizing when served on the table on china plates, which were also gifts: cheese, ham, tinned fish, chocolate, biscuits. To this still-life picture I added a bottle of White Horse Scotch whisky. I no longer remember when and by whom I was presented with the half-litre glass bottle with its yellow label.

That day my mother and I talked nonstop. I described how cordially the Americans and British had greeted us, how they had applauded at meetings, donated money to the Red Army fund, how the international student assembly had accepted the anti-Fascist 'Slavic Memorandum', how the family of US President Franklin Delano Roosevelt had invited the Soviet student delegation to their ancestral estate, Hyde Park, how the renowned actor and director Charlie Chaplin had asked me to pass on greetings to the Soviet people. As a teacher of foreign languages, Mother was interested in the foreign newspapers which I had brought back. We discussed the differences between British and American English. She pointed out some words in the articles and asked me to translate them. All this turned out to be very useful for her, as Mother never travelled abroad.

Our trip was not considered complete until we had made a report on it. We were given a week to prepare it. To make sure I was not distracted and did not forget anything or mix it up, I did not even leave the building. In total I covered around thirty sheets of paper, much of which I crossed out, expanded or corrected. For the report we had to single out the most important events and to make it not only accurate but politically consistent.

The student delegation first presented their reports at a session of the Young Communist League central committee secretariat, then at the offices of the Red Army political authority, and again, on 20 January 1943, at a meeting of the youth committee of the Soviet Information Bureau. The minutes of this meeting served as the basis for a major radio broadcast, and so millions of USSR residents learned about the journey made to capitalist towns and cities by the three Young Communist League members campaigning for the speedy opening of a second front in Europe.

Several excerpts from my report went over the airwaves:

We were compelled to travel to the United States of America via Astrakhan, Baku, Tehran, Cairo and Brazil, and to meet along the route with peoples of various nationalities and different colours. Nobody knew at first that it was a Soviet delegation, but, when they found out that we were from the Soviet Union, attitudes changed at once, becoming cordial and simply wonderful . . .

From Miami we travelled by train to Washington and, from the station, set off for the White House, where we were received by the US president's wife, Eleanor Roosevelt. We had breakfast with her and then went to our first press conference at the Soviet embassy. It needs to be said straight away that Mrs Roosevelt paid us special attention. Following her example, other official persons in America were also pleasant and friendly towards us . . .

We often had to hold press conferences and to reply to all possible questions from the American press. Americans value information and love various kinds of news items. However, at the press conferences the journalists did not ask a lot about military developments. They tried to find out something about us personally, about living conditions at the front. They were surprised that our soldiers were living in trenches. All in all, they had no conception of modern war. America lives in peaceful conditions. Not a single bomb has exploded on its territory. The mayor of New York once declared a practice air-raid alarm, and the following day the press reported that five people had died from heart failure . . .

America itself is, on the one hand, a land of luxury and, on the other, a land of destitution. The negroes there live very badly. We had occasion to visit areas where basic living conditions were lacking. I was also surprised at the racial segregation: on the trains there are special carriages – for Whites only, and for Coloureds only . . .

We had no idea how radio listeners responded to our accounts. However, those in charge made their own evaluation of the delegation's activity abroad. Krasavchenko and Pchelintsev earned the ordinary plaudits of 'good'. I was told that they were particularly pleased with me and my work was rated as 'excellent'.

It was then announced to us that the delegation had been disbanded. Nikolai Krasavchenko returned to his work with the Moscow city committee of the Young Communist League. Vladimir Pchelintsev was soon off to the front, where he continued to fight bravely and wipe out enemy soldiers and officers with his sniper rifle and, by the end of the war, he had taken his tally to 456. I was also getting ready to leave Moscow, as the 32nd Guards Parachute Division, in which I was listed as commander of a sniper platoon, had been assigned to the south-west front.

But it all turned out differently. At the end of January I was invited to the operational section of the division, where a very courteous man in a tunic with the indigo tabs of a captain had a long conversation with me. His questions touched on the most varied details of my biography: knowledge of a foreign language, involvement in military action at Odessa and Sevastopol, trips to the USA, Canada and Great Britain, and meetings with Eleanor Roosevelt. As well as that, I filled in a five-page form. It required a variety of information, not only about myself, but about my parents, son, husband and other relatives (right down to the way they lived, what they did, and where they were buried). The captain said that I was being transferred from the 32nd Division and placed at the disposal of the Red Army High Command reserve; in other words, I would not be going to the front.

'But why, Comrade Captain?' I asked, raising my voice.

'We'll probably find you something else to do. It will be more in line with your exceptional capabilities.'

'I'm a sniper!'

'First and foremost, you are an officer and you swore on oath . . .'

He was right about the capabilities. By order of the central personnel authority of the USSR People's Commissariat of Defence (Order No. 0281, dated 3 June 1943), I was promoted to the next military rank of lieutenant. But instead of fastening two ruby-coloured squares to the raspberry-coloured tabs on my collar, I attached two stars to the epaulettes of my tunic. And from January 1943 the tunic itself changed its appearance: it had a stiff, turned-up collar instead of a turn-down one and slit rather than stitched breast pockets. I was unable to get the new style of uniform straight away, but the parade epaulettes with golden braiding were presented to me immediately.

Late in the evening one day my mother and I were whiling away the time listening to music from a radio set. I had brought it from the United States, and the sound quality was excellent. A concert was being broadcast which played the requests of the victors of the Stalingrad front, both soldiers and officers, who had in February completed the rout of the German army under Field Marshal Paulus. The concert included a little classical music, a few folk songs and some popular Soviet tunes. Suddenly, there was a knock on the door. Two young NKVD officers entered, greeted us and suggested that I get ready to go with them.

Poor Yelena Trofimovna, who was drying cups after our evening cup of tea, dropped one on the floor. Mother's hands began to tremble with fear. It was no secret how the 'organs' made arrests. Their staff would suddenly appear at the homes of those under suspicion, address them politely, and quickly take their victims away. I put on a tunic, donned my shoulder strap and fastened my officer's belt around my waist. On the right-hand side of it hung the dark brown leather holster for my TT pistol. If they ordered me to remove it, they would take away the pistol – and that would mean an arrest.

'Comrade Lieutenant, you are going to the Kremlin,' said one of the officers.

'To the Kremlin?' I strode over to the bookcase, picked out the Anglo-Russian dictionary, thrust it in my pocket, and put the English grammar textbook in the inside pocket of my overcoat, for these books belonged to the supreme commander-in-chief. If the occasion arose, they needed to be returned to him.

The distance from Stromyn Street to the centre of Moscow was about 10km. The embankment of the river Yauza, the ancient brick houses and some unsightly structures from the Soviet era like the Rusanov Club, of which the second floor resembled part of a huge cogwheel, receded into the distance behind us. Objects leapt out of the dark into the car headlights – the trees on the boulevard, the tram rails, the walls of multi-storey buildings. Trying to concentrate, I wondered whether some new particularly important mission would be given to me, or if Joseph Vissarionovich was interested in the details of our recent trip to the USA.

In the reception room the lieutenants gallantly helped me to remove my overcoat. Unbuttoning the pistol holster, I handed the weapon over to Stalin's secretary – a bald, rather stout man of short stature, Alexander Nikolayevich Poskrebyshev. He placed my TT in a desk drawer, said that I could collect it after the visit, and pointed to the door: 'Go through. Comrade Stalin is waiting for you.'

The dark-brown oak panels of the office, the two tables pushed together to form a letter T, the very large map covered by blinds – all this remained from August 1942, when our Young Communist League youth delegation was heading for America. Only now I was standing before the general secretary of the Communist Party central committee on my own. Joseph Vissarionovich took a step towards me, shook my hand, and smiled:

'Hello, Lyudmila Mikhailovna.'

'Greetings, Comrade Commander-in-Chief! Lieutenant Pavlichenko, reporting at your command! Here are your books, a dictionary and a textbook.' I put them on the edge of the long table and once again stood at attention.

'Did they come in handy?'

'Very much so! I actually managed to say things.'

'I heard you had a successful trip.'

'We tried to fulfil your orders, Comrade Stalin!' I continued to stand erect and, as the military code dictated, to look the senior authority in the eye.

'Do take a seat,' and Joseph Vissarionovich indicated a chair next to the table and sat down opposite me. 'I heard that, at the invitation of President Roosevelt and his wife, you spent a week on their estate Hyde Park.'

'That is correct, Comrade Stalin.'

'It is possible that this autumn I will also have to meet with this American.' The commander-in-chief raised his celebrated pipe to his mouth and took a deep puff on it. 'Tell me, what sort of people are they?'

I do not know why, but this time I was extremely nervous. It was one thing to ask for books, quite another to report to the head of state about the results of a complex trip. It turned out that we had not fulfilled its main objective – to promote in every way the opening of a second front – in as much as the Allies had not actually commenced any military operations in Europe. Our student delegation had succeeded in merely exerting a certain influence on the public mood in the USA, Canada and Great Britain, evoking sympathy from ordinary folk for the struggle of the Soviet people against Fascism. The leaders of these countries were playing their own game and had no particular sympathy for our country. However, President Roosevelt and his wife, as opposed to Mr Churchill, seemed to me to be people who were more sincere, honest and capable of appreciating another point of view.

My speech was muddled, with long pauses. Joseph Vissarionovich did not interrupt, but towards the end he tried to calm me and asked tenderly: 'Why are you nervous, Lyudmila Mikhailovna?'

'It's a responsible task – to report to you personally.'

'You did not get confused when you were out on sniper duty. If you had been as nervous as that at the front, you would have been long gone.'

'The two situations cannot be compared at all,' I replied softly.

'Well, let's compare them,' joked the supreme commander-in-chief. 'Talk about your service as a sniper. About training sharpshooters, their weapons, the tactics you employed in the steppes near Odessa and in the hills near Sevastopol. There must have been some differences between them.'

I did not expect that Stalin would be so interested in our military profession. He knew quite a lot about its special nature. His questions were to the point and very specific. In replying to them, I really calmed down, became emboldened and decided to make a request. I asked the supreme commander-in-chief about returning to the front.

'You have shell shock and wounds,' said Joseph Vissarionovich. 'Why do you want to go back to the front line again?'

'There have been very many casualties in this war,' I answered. 'But somebody has to fight. I want to go back to my comrades in arms. I have the knowledge and experience. So I have a greater chance of surviving.'

I saw that he liked my reply. But he did not speak at once. 'It's out of the question for you,' he suddenly concluded. 'Can you do arithmetic?'

Surprised by such a turn in the conversation, I nodded. Stalin took a pencil, pulled a large pad on the table towards himself and began to explain like a teacher in school: 'If you go back to the front, you will kill a hundred Fascists. However, they may also shoot you down. But if you train a hundred snipers, pass on to them your priceless knowledge, and each of them shoots even ten Nazis, how many will that be? A thousand. There's your answer. You are more needed here, Comrade Lieutenant.'

The words of the commander-in-chief made an impression on me. They had a serious basis. At the beginning of the war, according to the official schedule of the People's Commissariat of Defence, confirmed in April 1941 (Order No. 04/402), each rifle regiment had only eighteen sharpshooters; now, however, following changes in the army regulations in 1942, a regiment was required to have eighty-seven snipers, a company – nine, and a platoon – three. In the Red Army there were hundreds of regiments and, consequently, the number of 'super-sharpshooters' could already be measured not in single units, but in dozens, even hundreds. Somebody had to train them and to train them quickly, skilfully, and to a high standard.

The comprehensive development of snipers in the Red Army demanded qualified instructors in sharpshooting. That is why, in March 1942, a school for sniper instructors was established in the village of Veshnyaki near Moscow – later known as the Central School for Sniper Instructors. That proved insufficient. Soon three-month courses for sharpshooters were set up there, and from July the training period was extended to six months. In total, over the period of the Great War for the Fatherland, from 1941 to 1944, over 400,000 snipers were trained within the framework of Osoaviakhim and Vsevobuch (General Military Training without Disruption of Production), in schools for top-class riflemen-snipers run by military districts, and at army training centres.

The meeting of a group of front-line 'super-sharpshooters' with Stalin in the Kremlin on 28 July 1943 was an important step in promoting the development of snipers within the Soviet forces. Both Vladimir Pchelintsev and I took part. As well as that, another ten people with over 150 dead enemy soldiers and officers to their tally came to Moscow from various fronts. Unfortunately, I do not remember them all by name. But one who stood out noticeably among them was the Siberian Vasily

Zaitsev, Hero of the Soviet Union, who had distinguished himself at Stalingrad, where he wiped out 225 Nazis in three months.

The meeting was held in a business-like atmosphere. The supreme commander-in-chief asked us to speak openly and to the point about operational difficulties and submit our requests and wishes. We talked of the need for a unified command: the soldiers who had been taught the skills of super-sharpshooting should be under the command of a single person in a regiment rather than battalion, company or other commanders. No less important was a change in the list of registered specialized military fields: it was time to add the word 'sniper' to it. There were demands made of quartermasters: in many fighting units summer, autumn and winter camouflage clothing was not changed in time, and armoured shields, which helped snipers to avoid serious wounds and even death at times, were not being issued. Many spoke of the necessity of improving the Mosin rifle: in particular, the stiff trigger was a hindrance, especially for new troops.

At the beginning of August 1943, I was ordered to the Red Army high command reserve, and I became a student of the 'Red Banner' Vystrel tactical rifle course for the improvement of the infantry officer corps, in the faculty of battalion commanders. The course was held in the town of Solnechnogorsk, Moscow Region, not far from Lake Senyezh. There, officers with battle experience – often after hospital treatment – raised their skill levels. The programme was intense. The sessions ran for twelve hours and were held mainly in the field. We studied the tactics of modern combat in rifle battalions, the art of commanding them in conditions most closely approximating battle conditions, and – with particular thoroughness – manual firearm weaponry, which I, of course, pursued with particular enjoyment. After three months of intense practical sessions my fellow course-mates went off to the front: to command infantry battalions. After graduation from the faculty for battalion commanders, a course on which I was the only woman, I remained in this celebrated and completely unique military training establishment until May 1944, engaged in teaching work as a sniper instructor.

During the years of the Great War for the Fatherland around 20,000 officers underwent training on Vystrel courses and about 200 of them were awarded the title Hero of the Soviet Union for their outstanding feats in battles with German Nazi forces. My name also appeared in this roll of honour as, on 25 October 1943, I was awarded this exalted title by decree of the Presidium of the USSR Supreme Soviet.

19

I Am Sidelined!

The total defeat of Hitler's Germany was drawing near. After the liberation of Kiev, Ukraine's state university, which had been evacuated to Kazakhstan in 1942, returned to the capital. The Germans had inflicted severe damage on it: they had blown up the main block and plundered the laboratories and libraries of various faculties. But, thanks to the efforts of the professors, academics and teachers, the university resumed its activities in January 1944, opening classes for students on senior courses. I found out about this and went back to the city of my youth; I wanted to be reinstated in the history faculty, pass the state examinations and finish the diploma dissertation I had begun way back before the war. I put in an application to the senior command and I was released from the army for a year to complete my higher education.

In October 1944, having exchanged my tunic for a staple dress and put away my orders and medals in a box, I became a fifth-year student in the Kiev State University history faculty. Once again I had to pore over textbooks, to recall the axioms of Marxism–Leninism, the basics of archaeology, Greco-Roman history and the history of the USSR, and to sit tests and examinations in Russian, Ukrainian and Latin. It was not out of the question that I would fall flat on my face, for I had turned twenty-eight. True, among the students there were a fair number between the ages of twenty-five and thirty who had taken part in the war, but I was the oldest woman student on the course.

Having completed my dissertation with a grade of 'excellent', in May 1945 I returned to Moscow, where I had earlier been allotted an apartment and where my mother Yelena and my son Rostislav remained. My subsequent military service was in the ranks of the navy; I became a research assistant in its general staff, in the fleet history section. My wounds from the front and shell shock played up more and more as the years went by. In June 1953, while a major in the naval coast guard, I was compelled to retire for reasons of illness (as an invalid, second class) with the right to wear the uniform.

However, an officer's pension is no reason to sit home and do nothing. September 1956 saw the foundation in Moscow of the Soviet Committee for War Veterans, the ruling body of the Organization of Soviet War Veterans, which united thousands of combatants in various regions and districts of our country. Then came its first All-USSR conference, which elected a presidium, a committee chairman (Marshal of the Soviet Union, A.M. Vasilyevsky), an executive secretary (the pilot and Hero of the Soviet Union, A.P. Maresyev), and a presidium bureau, which directed the work of the permanent public commissions (organizational, international and those responsible for publicity, invalids' affairs, liaison with educational institutes and perpetuating the memory of soldiers who lost their lives). I played a very active role in preparing for and running this function and was elected to the presidium.

We embarked on regular activities to publicize the glorious military traditions of the Soviet Army, met frequently with young people in schools, technical colleges and higher educational institutes, and also made trips to visit military units. There, they eagerly informed us about the contemporary armed forces of the USSR, invited us to training sessions and demonstrated new weaponry.

It was sad to see how the sniper's art, which had blossomed to an unprecedented level in our country during the struggle against Fascism, was gradually fading away and declining to nothing. There had been changes in military doctrine. The Ministry of Defence now considered that the use of the atom bomb would spare land armies from clashes with the enemy on battlefields. After a thermonuclear explosion, which would leave a scorched desert behind it, sharpshooters would have no need to fire at anyone and the enemy would vanish like dust. Thus, in the mid-1950s many sniper schools and courses were closed down and experienced officers were demobilized. The traditions behind the training and instruction of snipers were lost. For instance, the new regulations provided for mobile rifle detachments, which included only a single super-sharpshooter! The new Military Regulations for Land Forces barely mentioned sniper operations in the course of general military combat. Apparently, its authors assumed that a sniper would not have any serious influence on the outcome of a battle.

Of course, there were special forces units which had to conduct military operations in forests, mountains and population centres – i.e. where the use of heavy weapons was simply impossible. These soon received appropriate development. In such conditions, hitting the target with the first shot sometime plays a truly defining role and determines the success of the entire operation.

Already by the end of the Second World War the Mosin magazine rifle, which had served us faithfully and reliably, seemed to many to be obsolete and in need of modernization. Attempts were made to replace it. In particular, in 1945 and 1947 the designer S.G. Simonov presented his versions of sniper rifles based on his SKS carbine, but both models had substantial shortcomings. In 1958 the central missile and artillery directorate issued terms of reference for the development of a new 7.62mm self-loading sniper rifle. Fulfilment of this commission was taken on by three groups of engineers (in order to create healthy competition and to achieve the best result).

The first group was headed by the renowned arms designer Sergei Gavrilovich Simonov, Hero of Socialist Labour and two-times state prize-winner. He had received these awards for designing an anti-tank weapon in 1941 and in 1945 for the self-loading SKS-45 carbine. He was also the creator of the self-loading AVS-36 rifle, which had been adopted by the Red Army in 1936; I had encountered this weapon in Sevastopol. The 14.5mm Simonov anti-tank rifle was particularly popular in the forces. It penetrated the armour plating of the average German tank. Our infantrymen halted a fair number of attacking Nazi armoured vehicles at Sevastopol using the PTRS, the Simonov anti-tank rifle with its characteristic long barrel.

Young engineers emerged as rivals to the sixty-five-year-old Simonov, who had long earned general recognition. This was a new generation of Russian small-arms inventors. They had been educated through army service and were beginning their working life in workers' positions at Soviet defence factories. The second group was headed by Alexander Semyonovich Konstantinov, an engineer from the city of Kovrov, who had worked in a design bureau under the leadership of Degtyarev, inventor of the legendary DP light machine-gun.

The third group embarked on the commission a little later and worked in Izhevsk at the Izhmash military factory under the direction of Yevgeny Fyodorovich Dragunov. He had been born and grown up in this city and, during the war, served as an armourer in a regimental workshop; he had a superb knowledge of manual firing weapons and subsequently returned to his old factory and became well known as the inventor of some interesting models of sporting rifles. Vladimir Pchelintsev, Vasily Zaitsev and I actually met him in Izhevsk, because the factory management invited us as former soldiers to take part in the project as consultants. We were incredibly pleased at this. Taking part in the invention of a new, modern sniper rifle is a great honour for practitioners of sharpshooting. We set to work enthusiastically.

Dragunov's first models were sporting rifles. He brought this sporting style to his design for a sniper rifle. We were surprised when we saw in the drawings a rifle butt of so-called 'skeleton' design (with a gap in the middle) as well as a pistol-style hand-grip. After all, an army weapon has to withstand a much greater load than a sporting model, to operate without fail in any climatic conditions and to be comfortable to handle not only on the firing line, but also on the march.

The requirements of the missile and artillery directorate contained a number of contradictions. For example, in the interests of improving firing accuracy, all parts of the mechanism had to fit together firmly. But, at the same time, large gaps between these parts were conducive to stable interaction in firing and loading.

Fulfilling these demands required long and considered work, which proceeded in several stages.

Thus, in the first stage, in 1959, Dragunov's team presented an initial version of the rifle which fulfilled the fairly strict demands for firing accuracy. The sniper rifle Simonov's group had come up with immediately dropped out of the competition. For some time two rifles – Dragunov's and Konstantinov's – demonstrated approximately the same results in comparative firing trials and in other tests. However, in 1962 the specialists of the missile and artillery directorate opted for Dragunov's model.

The talented inventor was able to fulfil practically all the objectives which the military personnel had set the design group. The team had overcome many difficulties. In particular, developing the fore-end assembly, simple at first sight, turned out to be the most complex. They worked for about a year improving the ten-cartridge box magazine. The technology for manufacturing the highly accurate barrel was the work of I.A. Samoilov. Also welcome here, incidentally, were new telescope sights much more complex than the PE, PEM and PU with which I was so familiar.

Developed by A.I. Ovchinnikov and L.A. Glyzov, the PSO-1 sight featured a reticle with a small chevron-like aiming mark flanked by lateral corrections of 10 mil on each side. Aim-points for 1,100, 1,200 and 1,300 metres lay vertically below the aiming chevron. All this made taking aim better and quicker. Apart from that, the rifle also had conventional open sights – though, owing to the height of the upper edge of the butt, the back sight was not particularly convenient to use.

In 1963 the SVD – the Dragunov sniper rifle – was accepted for use in the Soviet Army. I believed that our armed forces had received an excellent model, with a weight of 4.52kg, which was normal for infantry (including magazine and telescope sight), a length of 1,225mm, a firing speed of thirty shots per minute, and a direct firing range of 1,300 metres with telescope sight and 1,200 metres with open sights. The automatic action was based on the use of the powder gases produced from firing. Unlike the SVT, the breechblock frame was not combined with the gas cylinder. The piston and the tappet were installed as separate elements.

The directors of the Izhmash factory appreciated the contribution of veteran super-sharpshooters to the creation of the new sniper's weapon. At an official gathering Pchelintsev, Zaitsev and I were presented with honorary certificates and gifts; we each received a manually assembled combat pistol of unique design.

During these years I had occasion to travel not only to the east of our country, to the Udmurt Autonomous Socialist Republic, but also to the south, to the Crimea, and to Sevastopol, which had long been like a hometown for me. In 1961 the USSR marked the twentieth anniversary of the day when the Great War for the Fatherland began. The release of journal and newspaper issues on the topic, publication of memoirs by military figures, and conferences incorporating both theory and practice were timed to coincide with this date. For new generations of Soviet people the feat of our people in the struggle against Fascism remained a great and indisputable achievement.

From Sevastopol I was sent an invitation to attend a meeting organized by the scholarship council of the museum about the city's heroic defence and liberation, and to prepare and deliver an address there. It took place on 25 October 1961. The length of the address (twenty minutes) and its topic – Sevastopol snipers in combat with the German Nazi invaders – had been agreed earlier. The session's proceedings were to be published.

'It has become accepted among us to speak often and at length about sniper such-and-such killing an enemy soldier or officer,' I began my address. 'But what did this cost the sniper? Has there been any occasion of late to discuss in detail this serious and arduous front-line operation?'

First, I named the snipers who had not lived to see this glorious day – from the 7th Brigade of the naval infantry, Chief Petty Officer Noi Adamia, Hero of the Soviet Union; and from the 456th NKVD Regiment, Corporal Ivan Levkin and his regimental comrade Corporal Ivan Bogatyr, who had also been awarded the title Hero of the Soviet Union. There were those who lost their lives without having received any awards, but showed great ability in the sniper's art: for example, the youthful Sevastopol resident Yuri Fyodorenko.

The audience of the scholarship council was a select group: staff of the three city museums, historians and veterans of the city's second siege. There was no need to convince any of these people; they knew all about snipers as it was. But I had the published text of the proceedings in mind and therefore decided to talk about the tactics of super-sharpshooters on the battlefield, about their psychological training. Being a sniper is not just a profession: it is a way of life.

'On a day like today –' and I pointed to the window beyond which the southern October sun was shining – 'a sniper would get up at three o'clock in the morning and be at his post by four.'

A sniper usually settled in the neutral zone, in no man's land, with his own side's last military outpost behind him and the Nazis in front. You are aware that the strip of no man's land in the Sevastopol fortified district was narrow, as wide as 150 metres in some sections, but generally significantly narrower, and therefore the snipers were, of necessity, in close proximity to the Germans. In the course of a day it was possible to take five to ten shots. And they were not bad snipers at Sevastopol, were they? They were excellent snipers . . . The idea has somehow become accepted that we tricked one another with bits of foliage. It was not a matter of foliage. Imagine that you have come across an enemy sniper on your section of the front. You are informed that the sniper is getting in the way, disrupting mobility. Then an order is given to our sniper to take out the enemy, and you have to spend two or two and a half days trying to locate him. And all this time the sniper is operating alone; his lookout leaves him on his own because extra personnel can be extra victims and giveaways.

Many methods can be used to lure a sniper into taking a shot. Glass, tins, anything at hand were used; we had no special devices. But when you locate an enemy sniper, a so-called sniper duel begins. You see the sniper through your sights, his eyes, the colour of his hair, but he sees you as well. At this point, everything can be decided in a fraction of a second. A duel like this puts a sniper out of commission for several hours; he is so weary that it is difficult to wring anything out of him.

We had managed to ensure that the Nazis did not move around their positions during daytime. But now the Nazis had to be hunted down and wiped out. Each annihilated Wehrmacht soldier or officer had a psychological impact on the enemy. It meant that a new method of operating had to be found, and we found it – sniper hideouts. They were set up 500–800 metres into the enemy rear. You walk out at night, traversing the front line with apparent calmness, but the hairs on your skin stand on end. Only volunteers went out to these hideouts, because there was little chance – no more than 10 per cent – that you would come back alive.

You arrive at the hideout at three in the morning and you keep watch till eight o'clock. There are three to five snipers, observing the enemy. The command comes, and a sniper attack begins, followed by shouting. The Nazis are shouting that they have been attacked by partisans. They are in a panic. Then the Fritzes take possession of themselves, and dozens of mortars descend on us. There were many instances when my comrades were killed in hideouts. However, we never left their bodies in enemy hands, but carried them out ourselves.

Snipers played a big role in combat. When the order was given to our infantry to advance, the machine-gun emplacements had to be covered, and a sniper went out to deal with this. An hour or two before the advance a sniper would go out into no man's land, creep up on the enemy's forward line and keep his weapon trained on the emplacement, and that meant lying low directly in front of it. We also fulfilled tasks like this.

During the defence of Sevastopol the senior command placed a high value on the snipers, and we fully merited it.

To become a sniper, it is not only important to be able to shoot accurately. One other thing is important – a cold hatred for the enemy, so emotions are subordinated to calculation. Here the iron will of the soldier plays a role. Snipers did not take their eyes of the enemy by day or night, and information in reconnaissance log-books would often be verified through snipers' operations. A sniper had to know by heart every bump in the ground, every bush in front of his or her position.

The nervous tension characteristic of sniper operations both at Sevastopol and in other sectors of the Soviet–German front affected one's health. The ailment known as 'post-traumatic neurosis' was a normal occurrence for snipers, if they went a long time without suitable rest.

I remember the first rally of Sevastopol snipers, convened at the initiative of Major-General Petrov, commander of the coastal army. He was the first to pay attention to the arduous operating conditions for snipers and gave orders for additional dry rations for all of us on sniper watch – you could not deliver a hot dinner to us out there, and we usually ate late at night. Petrov also ordered that we be given one day off every week.

Sniper operations in the coastal army started at the river Prut, within the 25th Chapayev Division. Also in action during those days was Junior Lieutenant Vasily Koftun, who had graduated from sniper school before the war. When the first reinforcements arrived on the Prut, we sharpshooters assembled in his platoon. We looked at him with envy. He had a tally of fifty dead Nazis, while we had one or two each.

It should be mentioned that, when a sniper returned from an operation, he called at the first dugout he came across; sometimes he did not have the strength to reach his own, and every soldier and sailor regarded it as his duty to relinquish space and invite him to rest up. They would serve the sniper with hot tea, and the hot tea would be boiled with smokeless powder; everyone regarded it as his or her duty to make our snipers' lives easier.

When we got leave one day a week, we went into Sevastopol and, approaching the city, we would be greeted first by children. There were times when a sniper might hunt and hunt, without recording a single kill – the enemy would be hiding – and then arrive in Sevastopol on leave, to be greeted by children. Some little squirt of a kid, sometimes with no trousers and a runny nose, would ask with an air of importance: how many Fritzes have you killed? You may not have killed a single one. You could explain to your commander that there were no Fritzes around. But try explaining that to a child. If you replied to them that there were no Fritzes around, you got the answer: you're not defending me very well.

The children of Sevastopol knew that we were short of cartridges, of ammunition, and I once received a catapult as a present from some children from Matyushenko hill. I asked why, and I was told: a sniper needs to practise every day, but you haven't got many cartridges. Don't waste cartridges; practise with a catapult. It might appear amusing. But the incident testified that in the hero-city there was widespread understanding of our front-line situation, not only among adults, but also among children.

The population of Sevastopol strove to help the troops of the coastal army in every respect. There were problems in the city with water, which was rationed. I would arrive in the city knowing that the first woman I met regarded it as her duty to give me her water ration, to wash linen and clothing for me, to provide a place to rest, however modest it might have been. It was in this that the strength of our defence lay. Three forces – the people, the army and the navy – came together to form a single fist which smashed the Nazi German invaders for 250 days. Today we are very grateful to the people of Sevastopol, who do not forget those legendary days and preserve the memory of our military glory. Defenders come and go, but Sevastopol remains![1]

When visiting Sevastopol again and again (for example, in May 1964 for the twentieth anniversary of Sevastopol's liberation and in May 1965 for the jubilee of the Great Victory), I always felt a certain prevailing atmosphere. For its residents the veterans' tales of fierce resistance to the enemy were not just empty words. Destroyed and burnt by the enemy, the city had risen again to its former beauty, but its new buildings, streets and squares seemed to have preserved the memory of battles past. Our appearances at schools and technical colleges and at various kinds of enterprises always evoked an ardent response from audiences. We saw that both young people and those of more mature age knew quite a lot about the feats of Soviet soldiers and officers on the battle lines of Sevastopol during the years 1941 and 1942, that the passing of time had not veiled the essence of those events for them.

That is why meeting young sportsmen and women who enjoyed shooting was particularly pleasant. This occurred at the initiative of the manager of the Dynamo Sporting Society's city firing range, Filipp Fyodorovich Mozhayev. Senior coach of the Crimean section of this society, honoured coach of the Ukraine, and USSR Master of Sport in target shooting, he originally sent me a letter in which he informed me that he proposed to hold city shooting competitions for a prize named in honour of Hero of the Soviet Union Lyudmila Pavlichenko, and he wanted to ask my consent. 'Why not?' I thought, and replied in the affirmative. After all, shooting was an excellent pastime for young people. It was at rifle- or pistol-shooting clubs that the snipers of the future were able to demonstrate their prowess.

Mozhayev was an officer by education; in 1944 he had graduated with distinction from the Leningrad college for riflemen and mortar bombers, and during the years of the Great War for the Fatherland he had gained the Order of the Red Star and the medal 'For Military Services'. His subsequent service was in the Trans-Baikal military district, where Major Mozhayev trained army snipers. Upon retirement, Filipp Fyodorovich moved to Sevastopol. Being a man whose heart and soul were devoted to shooting, he organized a sports club here as well, or, to be more precise, a centre for rifle training; he designed a range for it and managed to get his design translated into reality.

The range was in the centre of the city – on Krasny Spusk, on the way to the railway station, not far from Pushkin Square and Ushakov Square. This sporting facility was of the highest standard. Apart from the range itself, with its firing line and targets placed at distances of 50, 25 and 10 metres (for air guns), it included two classrooms, a coaches' room, and a gun safe with an armour-plated door, where up to 100 rifles and about fifty pistols were stored, as well as boxes of cartridges. All the premises were divided by lockable metal grilles equipped with alarm buttons wired to the nearest militia station. At night there was a security guard on duty.

Funding, of course, plays a big role in any undertaking. But it is very important that it be headed by someone who is honest, knowledgeable, blessed with initiative and able to inspire others. Mozhayev reminded me in some respects of my first teacher, senior instructor Potapov of the Osoaviakhim school in Kiev. One of the key similarities was that he had the true sniper's character – calm and balanced – as well as outstanding capabilities as a teacher. He had a lot of students, and in a variety of categories: school children, students, workers and officers from the Black Sea Fleet. All in all, he coached around 100 USSR masters of sport, candidate masters of sport, and holders of the rank 'First-Class Sportsman'. His pupils competed successfully at international, USSR and republican competitions. Mozhayev's own children also attended the shooting range and pursued target shooting. They became USSR masters of sport – his elder daughter Yelena in rifle shooting and his younger daughter Irina in pistol shooting.

After consulting with each other, Filipp Fyodorovich and I decided to open the city competitions for the Hero of the Soviet Union Lyudmila Pavlichenko Prize with pistol shooting. I also wanted to take my place on the firing line, to have one or two shots to get things under way, so to speak. In recent years short-barrelled weapons had begun to appeal to me more. I no longer had the strength to handle a rifle well.

On the appointed day quite a lot of people gathered in a classroom at the shooting range: not just participants in the competitions, but other pupils of Mozhayev's. I spoke briefly about the saga of Sevastopol. The youngsters began to ask questions. They showed interest in very specialized topics: the types of sniper rifles used during the Great War for the Fatherland and their telescope sights, camouflage methods and combat with enemy snipers. These questions pointed to the superb theoretical grounding that the club members had received. Today, under the peaceful skies of Sevastopol, they are sportsmen, but tomorrow, if our country requires it, they will be front-line super-sharpshooters.

The participants then proceeded to the range. The competitions were superbly organized – no fuss, no haste, everything clear and according to plan. The best performance came from Mozhayev's younger daughter, Irina, a student in her fourth year at the Sevastopol institute of instrument-making. She used a Margolin pistol and performed the standard MP-5 and MP-8 exercises (firing at speed at circular targets from distances of 25 and 50 metres). To the applause of those in attendance, I presented her with an honorary certificate. Then we had a long talk and strolled around the city. Sevastopol in May 1970 was as beautiful as it had been in May 1942: bright sun, blue sky, blue sea and, on Marine Boulevard, many gardens with luxuriant flowers: chrysanthemums, roses, gladioli, tulips.

The following day I took part in a formal ceremony for the lighting of the eternal flame on Sapun Hill, the site of the building housing the three-dimensional model depicting the storming of Sapun Hill on 7 May 1944 which had opened over ten years earlier; there were also a memorial and an exhibition of Second World War military technology. A meeting took place in the morning on Malakhov Heights, attracting a large gathering. A brass band played, red banners fluttered in the sea breeze and there were speeches about the feats of the soldiers and officers of the Red Army, the tenacity, courage and boldness of those who defended the main naval base of the Black Sea Fleet from the assaults of the Nazi hordes, and those who subsequently, in the course of a rapid advance, routed the Nazis, driving them out of the fortress city.

From the eternal flame that burnt on the defensive tower of the Malakhov Heights I lit a torch and passed it to Hero of the Soviet Union F.I. Matveyev, who had taken part in the liberation of Sevastopol – as a sergeant in the 997th Guards Rifle Regiment which had stormed the German fortifications on Sapun Hill on 7 May 1944.

On an armoured transport and accompanied by an honorary escort, we carried the torch along the streets of Korabelnaya Storona and the city centre, and then along General Ostryakov Avenue, out onto the Yalta highway to Sapun Hill. Here, the torch was borne along the central path of the memorial complex, and Matveyev lit the eternal flame in a special niche at the foot of the Obelisk of Glory.

Before departing for Moscow, I made one more trip through the suburbs of Sevastopol. Small launches regularly departed from the wharves near the Graf Quay. They crossed the main bay and took passengers to the north side, to Inkerman and the Mikhailov ravelin, and other city population centres by the sea. On the north side I had to take a bus to the Fraternal Cemetery. It was not a long journey but, for me, a particularly significant one.

The main path of the cemetery led to the hill and Church of St Nicholas. Although there had been fighting by the memorial in June 1942, most of the beautiful stone tombs erected in the nineteenth century had not suffered. The church on the hill, which had the appearance of a fairly tall pyramid, was still closed and the top part, where a cross had once stood, was in ruins. I had to walk around the right side of the church and down the hill to the north-eastern wall of the cemetery, where the graves of those who had taken part in the defence of Sevastopol were located. Here everything was simple and modest, with no monuments of black and white marble, no vaults with cast-metal doors, no fluted columns or busts of heroes on top of them. I placed a bouquet of red carnations on the memorial and sat down on a wooden bench under the acacia tree which shaded the whole area from the rays of the bright sun.

An amazing majestic silence reigned over the Fraternal Cemetery. Just the cheeping of the birds fluttering between the cedars. Just the gusts of wind which occasionally blew in from the sea and rustled the thickets of wild rose. Just the crystal-clear vault of the heavens gleaming blue over the paths, trails and grave-stones of the soldiers' memorial separated from the world by a tall, solid wall. Nothing had changed here since the time when the troops and officers of the 54th Rifle Regiment buried Junior Lieutenant Alexei Kitsenko, a valiant officer and my husband.

He had fallen in a war unparalleled in its ferocity. We had been together on the line of fire, but I had survived to see the victory and he had not. Recalling those desperate days now, it occurred to me that what our generation had had to endure was not just a great ordeal but a great honour. We had succeeded in defending the country. It was as if we were all born, raised and had studied and worked just for that – to put our bodies on the line for our homeland in its hour of need.

Moscow – Sevastopol, 1967–72

Notes

Within the text of this English edition there are some insertions in square brackets from the original Russian editor, Alla Igorevna Begunova and from the English translator (marked TN). The endnotes are from Alla Begunova, John Walter, Martin Pegler and David Foreman.

1 Factory Walls

1 Pavlichenko gives few details of her relationship with the father of her son, though it was presumably not only short-lived but possibly also scandalous enough to persuade her parents to move away from Belaya Tserkov. She claimed on enlistment in the summer of 1941 to have had no contact with Alexsei Pavlichenko for three years, and is thereafter silent. He seems to have been one of countless Russian soldiers who simply disappeared during the war.

2 If There is War Tomorrow

1 Here Pavlichenko repeats the Party line. Although pro-Republican journalists reported thousands of deaths at the time, modern assessments suggest that no more than a few hundred died. Moreover, the German-commanded Nationalists *did* see the attack on Guernica as part of a broader strategic goal.

2 The milliradian, usually abbreviated to 'mil' or 'milrad', was created in the nineteenth century to overcome difficulties encountered with the conventional system of degrees, minutes and seconds, which often hindered rapid calculation. The idea was taken up by artillerists and ballisticians, who saw the ease with which adjustments could be made to allow for changes in range and deviations caused by wind or the lateral drift of a spinning projectile. The basis was the radian, half the diameter of a circle, subdivided into a thousand parts (the milliradian). The circumference of the circle was then divided into these mils, the imprecision of pi resulting in a total of approximately 6283. However, beginning with the French and including the NATO forces of today, most armies rounded-off the total to 6400. Though this is mathematically erroneous, the difference is too small to have any practical effect on the shooting of a

military rifle. The Russian system, however, was based on the subdivision of the six equilateral triangles contained within a circle, each divided into a 100 and then, after 15 September 1918, 1,000 units. Consequently, the 'mil' used by Pavlichenko was 1/6000th part of the circumference though, once again, the differences between this and the 1/6400th system were not significant at combat range. The adjusting drums of Soviet and many other telescope sights emitted an audible click as they turned through each tenth of a mil. A change of 'three clicks', therefore, would be 0.3 mils.

3 From the Prut to the Dnyestr

1 Here and below the statistical data are cited from N.M. Khlebnikov, P.S. Yevlampiev and Y.A. Volodikhin, *The Legendary Chapayevs* (Moscow, 1967).
2 Pavlichenko's reminiscences are misleading. Though the Fw. 189 had been air-tested, and Fw. 189A-0 had been issued to training Staffeln in the autumn of 1940, all of the Aufklärungsstaffeln (H) involved in the aftermath of the invasion of the USSR flew the conventional single-engined Henschel Hs. 126. The first Fw. 189A-1 and 189A-2 aircraft did not arrive on the Eastern Front until the Spring of 1942.
3 I.I. Azarov, *Odessa Under Siege* (Moscow, 1966), pp. 26–32.
4 This was UR-82.

4 Frontiers of Fire

1 *Engineering Forces in the Battle for the Soviet Homeland* (Moscow, 1970), p. 114.
2 Pavlichenko's letter to her elder sister Valentina is dated 27 August 1941. At the present time it is held in the Central Museum of the Russian Federation Armed Forces, File no. 4/18,680.
3 I.I. Azarov, *Odessa under Siege* (Moscow, 1966), p. 81.
4 A reference to the female companion of the original Chapayev.
5 From the collection of war memoirs *By the Black-Sea Fortresses* (Moscow, 1967), p. 205.
6 *By the Black-Sea Fortresses* (Moscow, 1967), p. 135.
7 The modern village of Krasnoselovka, Comintern District, Odessa Region.
8 I.I. Azarov, *Odessa under Siege* (Moscow, 1966), pp. 141, 143.

5 The Battle at Tartaka

1 The BM-13 designation of the Katyushas remained classified as a state secret until the end of the war.
2 The modern village of Prilimannoye, Ovidiopolye District, Odessa Region.
3 *By the Black Sea Fortresses* (Moscow, 1967), p. 137.

6 Across the Sea

1 *By the Black-Sea Fortresses* (Moscow, 1967), pp. 51–2.
2 This ship was named after the French socialist Jean Jaures. 'Zh' is the Russian language's closest rendering of 'J'.
3 According to modern research, the master and fifteen crew were lost; twenty passengers and crew were rescued.

7 Legendary Sevastopol

1 Pavlichenko qualifies the guns as Ausf. F, but this version of the Stu.G.III did not appear until March 1942.
2 L.N. Tolstoy *Sevastopol Sketches* (Moscow, 1969), pp. 20, 22.
3 Thus perished sniper Tatiana Baramzina, Hero of the Soviet Union (posthumous).
4 This TT model 1933, 1940 issue, serial no. PA945, as well as other pistols (Mauser, Colt, Luger-Parabellum, Browning) from Pavlichenko's personal collection are kept at the Central Museum of the Russian Federation Armed Forces, File no. 2/3776.
5 *By the Black Sea Fortresses* (Moscow, 1967), pp. 182–3.
6 *By the Black Sea Fortresses* (Moscow, 1967), p. 203.

8 Forest Trails

1 Now the village of Verkhnesadovoye, in the Nakhimov district of Sevastopol.
2 As becomes evident, this took place in November.
3 For the likely identification of von Steingel, see John Walter, *The Sniper Encyclopedia* (London, 2018).
4 *By the Black Sea Fortresses* (Moscow, 1967), pp. 219–20.

9 The Second Assault

1 A pipe, a tobacco pouch and two silver cigarette cases belonging to Pavlichenko are kept at the Central Museum of the Russian Federation Armed Forces, File no. 2/3776.
2 This is an excerpt from the pamphlet *Heroic Annals: The Defence of Sevastopol*, which Pavlichenko wrote in 1958, commissioned by the State Political Publishing House, pp. 23–5.

10 Duel

1 This excerpt from the newspaper *For the Motherland* was reproduced in the collection *Kievan Combat Stars* (Kiev, 1977), in the piece entitled 'Chapayev Sniper', p. 363.

11 On No-Name Height

    1 Now the village of Verkhneye-Chernorechenskoye, Balaklava district of Sevastopol.

12 The Spring of 1942

    1 Letter from Pavlichenko to her mother, E.T. Belova, dated 15 March 1942. The letter is held in the Central Museum of the Russia Federation Armed Forces, File no. 4/18681.

    2 A Stakhanovite was an exceptionally productive and industrious worker.

13 A Word from the Army Commander

    1 This is among the worst maritime disasters of all time, ranking with *Lancastria*. The death toll is unknown, possibly well in excess of 5,000, though there were in fact eight survivors.

    2 The document is kept in the central archives of the Ministry of Defence, Russian Federation, File no. 33, Op 682524, Item 613.

14 Moscow Stars

    1 This document was made available by the State Museum for the Heroic Defence and Liberation of Sevastopol.

15 Mission to Washington

    1 This is actually the Pulitzer Prize-winning journalist and author Joseph P. Lash (1909–87), born in the USA to Russian-Jewish parents and now best known for biographies of Franklin and Eleanor Roosevelt. A close friend of Eleanor Roosevelt, Lash had been conscripted by the time of the ISS conference. An attempt to join naval intelligence failed owing to his background, which included communist sympathies, so he enlisted in the US Army on 28 April 1942. Married to Nancy Bedford-Jones (1935), Lash became involved romantically with Gertrude 'Trude' Pratt (1908–2004). Gertrude divorced her husband in 1943 and a year later married Lash, who had divorced (or been divorced by) Nancy.

16 My Darling

    1 Although Pavlichenko is careful to give the spelling of the name in English, in the rarely encountered form 'Jonson', it is uncertain that this is the correct interpretation. William Johnston III, a research metallurgist listed in the 1935 New York census, is the most plausible candidate, as he would have been not only in the right age-bracket but also of the right profession.

2 The 'Tin Goose' was a three-engined transport made only in 1926–33. Pavlichenko is probably referring to the four-engine B-24 Liberator, made in Ford's Willow Run factory in 1942–5.

3 This award is presently held in the Central Museum of the Russian Federation Armed Forces, File no. 2/3776 .

4 These guns had an interesting history. They were purchased from Colt during the First World War, but the order was placed by the British, to be offset by credits secured against Russian gold. It has been reliably claimed that 51,100 M1911 pistols were accepted from Colt's commercial production, in the C23000–C89000 serial-number range, and shipped between 19 February 1916 and 8 January 1917. How many of these guns – which were marked АНГЛ. ЗАКАЗЪ (an abbreviation of 'English Order') on the left side of the slide – reached the Russian army before the October Revolution is an open question. It is assumed that many of the Colts were lost in the Civil War, and that this explains their rarity in the Red Army.

5 Gertrude 'Trude' Pratt and Joseph P. Lash, officers of the International Student Service.

6 The letter is held in the Central Museum of the Russian Federation Armed Forces, File no. 4/3761/15-38.

17 Island in the Ocean

1 The RAF used three types of B-17, known as Fortress I, II and III. Originally intended for high-altitude daylight bombing, they proved to be a failure and were relegated to long-range anti-submarine patrol work or reconnaissance with Coastal Command and as intercontinental transports with Ferry Command based at RAF Ayr (also known as RAF Heathfield). This is likely to have been one of the transports that Pavlichenko describes.

2 This is possibly Helen Louisa Chivers, born in 1916 and married to Arthur. She appears in London electoral rolls to 1939 and then in Glasgow after 1947.

3 In fact the phrase appears in a letter by Batyushkov written a year after his visit to Britain in 1814.

4 These tanks were supplied to the Soviet Union under Lend-Lease from July 1942. They were involved in combat in the Kursk bulge, in the lifting of the blockade on Leningrad, and in the liberation of Kiev.

5 The Churchill IV does not seem to have been introduced until 1943, so it is likely that Pavlichenko is describing the Churchill I, the only one to carry a 3-inch mortar, and a Churchill III, introduced to service late in 1942, which was basically the precursor of the Churchill IV but with a fabricated turret instead of the later one-piece casting. The dimensions are roughly the same as the ones given here but the Churchill III and IV had one 6pr gun and two 7.92mm Besa machine guns, not three, and neither carried the mortar.

6 The 70th Regiment of Foot had been incorporated in the East Surrey Regiment as a result of the British Army reforms of 1881.

7 At the present time these articles are kept in the Central Museum of the Russian Federation Armed Forces, File no. 2/3776.

8   The Settlement was financed by Russian-born tobacco magnate Bernhard Baron (1850–1929), who had invented one of the earliest cigarette-making machines and had extensive shareholdings in Carreras and Gallagher. Baron funded the construction of a huge purpose-built block in Stepney, East London, to house the Jewish children's clubs – including the Oxford and St George's Club for Boys – formed during the First World War by Basil and Rose Henriques.

9   Equivalent to about £200 million today. In the city hospital of Volgograd (Stalingrad) there is a bronze bas-relief depicting Baroness Clementine Ogilvy Spencer Churchill wearing the Order of the Red Banner of Labour on her breast. The accompanying text describes the activities of her fund during the Great War for the Fatherland.

19 I Am Sidelined!

1   The complete text of the address is held in the State Museum of the Heroic Defence and Liberation of Sevastopol.